CAMBRIDGE STUDIES IN ECONOMIC HISTORY
PUBLISHED WITH THE AID OF THE ELLEN McARTHUR FUND

GENERAL EDITOR
M. M. POSTAN
Professor of Economic History in the University of Cambridge

COMMERCIAL CRISIS
AND
CHANGE IN ENGLAND
1600–1642

COMMERCIAL CRISIS
AND
CHANGE IN ENGLAND
1600–1642

A STUDY IN THE INSTABILITY OF A
MERCANTILE ECONOMY

BY

B. E. SUPPLE

Assistant Professor
Graduate School of Business Administration
Harvard University

CAMBRIDGE
AT THE UNIVERSITY PRESS
1959

PUBLISHED BY
THE SYNDICS OF THE CAMBRIDGE UNIVERSITY PRESS

Bentley House, 200 Euston Road, London N.W.1
American Branch: 32 East 57th Street, New York 22, N.Y.

Printed in Great Britain
SPOTTISWOODE, BALLANTYNE & CO. LTD.
London and Colchester

*To
my Mother and
Father*

CONTENTS

Preface — page ix

List of Abbreviations — xi

INTRODUCTION — 1
  (i) Industry and trade — 2
  (ii) The nature of instability and crisis — 8
  (iii) Harvests and instability — 14
  (iv) Conclusion — 19

PART I. YEARS OF CRISIS

1 THE RECOVERY FROM STAGNATION, 1600–1614 — 23

2 THE COCKAYNE PROJECT, 1614–1617 — 33
  (i) The issues involved — 33
  (ii) The course of trade — 39
  (iii) Conclusion — 49

3 THE DEPRESSION YEARS, 1620–1624 — 52
  (i) Depression in the textile industry — 53
  (ii) Contemporary opinion — 58
  (iii) Official action — 64

4 CURRENCY MANIPULATION AND THE CRISIS OF THE EARLY 1620's — 73
  (i) Devaluation abroad—the decline in exports — 73
  (ii) The Eastland trade, 1618–1622: a case study — 81
  (iii) The balance of trade and the exchanges — 89
  (iv) Recovery — 96

5 PLAGUE AND POLITICS, 1625–1632 — 99
  (i) Plague and the old draperies, 1625 — 99
  (ii) East Anglia, southern Europe and the crisis in 1629 — 102
  (iii) Other trades and other areas, 1627–1631 — 112

6 THE DECLINING YEARS, 1632–1642 — 120
  (i) Stagnation — 120
  (ii) Insecurity and crisis, 1640–1642 — 125

PART II. YEARS OF CHANGE: REAL AND MONETARY FACTORS

7 A CHANGING ECONOMY: THE OLD AND THE NEW — 135
   (i) The decline of the old draperies — 136
   (ii) A quality product — 149
   (iii) New draperies and new horizons — 152

8 MONETARY INSTABILITY, 1600–1642 — 163
   (i) Bimetallic maladjustments and a scarcity of money — 164
   (ii) The official approach to monetary affairs — 178
   (iii) Conclusion — 192

PART III. THE APPROACH TO ECONOMICS

9 ECONOMIC THOUGHT — 197
   (i) The economics of crisis — 198
   (ii) The economics of diversification — 221

10 THE GOVERNMENT AND THE ECONOMY — 225
   (i) The assumptions of economic policy — 225
   (ii) The nature of economic policy — 233

APPENDIXES

A. Statistics of the cloth trade — 257
B. MSS. of the controversy on exchanges and the balance of trade, 1622–1623 — 268
C. Contemporary sources consulted — 271

Index — 277

PREFACE

The present study was to a considerable extent completed in 1955 as a dissertation for the Ph.D. degree at Cambridge University. It was subsequently awarded the Ellen McArthur Prize and revised for publication. Two chapters were eliminated and the arrangement of others altered, the chapter on 'the government and the economy' was added, the introduction was considerably augmented, and extensive stylistic revision was undertaken. The book as it stands is therefore the product of some years of work and has benefited from the help and advice of a considerable number of people.

The original intention was to compare the causes and consequences of commercial depressions in England in the forty years prior to the Civil War. Such a grandiose design might well have been impossible in the time available if the sources of information and statistical series had been as abundant as they are for later periods of English economic history. Even so, it will be apparent that the rich sources of information on local and regional history have largely been ignored. On the other hand, it was found necessary to take into account monetary as well as industrial and commercial questions. To some extent, also, it was inevitable that there should be consideration of economic thought and policy. For the influence of economic crises was widespread, and many aspects of the economic history of seventeenth-century England can be studied only against the background of intermittent commercial fluctuation. Obviously this also applies to England's place in an international economy, and the interrelationship between internal instability and long-term economic development is a crucial one. On these grounds it was necessary to broaden the scope of the book to include economic changes which took place over the whole period. The disadvantages of the selective treatment of such subjects will be only too obvious to the reader, but no such study can hope to satisfy every expectation.

In the main the information used has been derived from contemporary sources and from secondary authorities which are too well known to need constant identification. Most work was done in the British Museum, the Cambridge University Library, the Goldsmiths' Library of the University of London, and the Public Record Office. Two histories, above all others, have dealt at length with the central topic of this work: W. R. Scott, *The Constitution and Finance of English, Scottish, and Irish Joint-Stock Companies to 1720* (3 volumes, Cambridge, 1910–12), vol. I, chapters VII to XI; and Astrid Friis, *Alderman Cockayne's Project and the Cloth Trade* (1927). The latter has proved most useful as a source of statistical and documentary information—specifically for the period 1614–18—and has been so acknowledged in footnotes and in Appendix A. But from the present point of view the scope of both works was found to be limited and it was found impossible to rely on their necessarily selective use and interpretation of contemporary material. This last point explains and perhaps justifies the radical differences which emerge between the results of the present author's researches and those exemplified in the two books. The principal reason for this divergence is possibly the greater attention devoted in this volume to the implications of the seventeenth-century monetary system. Unfortunately, two important books appeared too late to be consulted in this work: R. H. Tawney, *Business and Politics under James I: Lionel Cranfield as Merchant and Minister*, and R. W. K. Hinton, *The Eastland Trade and the Common Weal in the Seventeenth Century*.

The publication of this book was made possible by a grant from the Ellen McArthur Prize Fund; my gratitude in this respect needs little emphasizing. In the course of my researches I benefited from the constant advice, assistance and criticism of my supervisor Mr C. H. Wilson, and my debt to him is the greatest of all. I should also like to thank Professor F. J. Fisher, who never stinted the time he was prepared to devote to answering questions on a subject of which his knowledge is so extensive. In addition, Professor M. M. Postan and Dr F. C. Spooner were most generous in their help during my residence at Cambridge, and at a critical time Professor Asa Briggs kindly read the first draft and proffered some pungent and invaluable suggestions. Any historical poverty in the following pages is, of course, the author's sole responsibility.

I am also extremely grateful to various people for allowing me to utilize the finished products of some of their own research. Professor Fisher kindly permitted me to study the proofs of his edition of Lionel Cranfield's commercial correspondence (compiled for the Historical Manuscripts Commission to form Volume II of the *Sackville MSS.*). Mrs A. M. Millard was similarly beneficent in suffering me to appropriate, with so little effort, some of the statistical results of years of painstaking investigation into London's import trade. Finally, Mr R. T. Spence was good enough to supply me with information on the export of unfinished cloth which he derived from a study of the Earl of Cumberland's licence for those commodities.

My thanks are also due to Mary Dagges, Hilma Holton, and Beverly Beatty, who so ably shared the tedious task of typing the various manuscript drafts.

My debt to my wife, Sonia, is much more than platitude could express.

Cambridge, Massachusetts BARRY E. SUPPLE
April 1958

LIST OF ABBREVIATIONS

Add. MSS.	Collection of Additional Manuscripts preserved in the British Museum.
A.P.C.	Published *Acts of the Privy Council of England*.
B.M.	Pamphlet material in the British Museum.
C. 107/20	Reference to Chancery Masters' Exhibits in the Public Record Office.
C.J.	*Journals of the House of Commons*.
Commons Debates, 1621	*The Commons Debates, 1621*, ed. W. Notestein, F. H. Relf and H. Simpson (7 volumes, New Haven, 1935).
Cotton MSS.	Collection of Cotton Manuscripts preserved in the British Museum.
C.S.P.D.	*Calendar of State Papers Domestic*.
C.S.P.V.	*Calendar of State Papers Venetian*.
Econ. Hist. Rev.	*The Economic History Review*.
Egerton MSS.	Collection of Egerton Manuscripts preserved in the British Museum.
Foedera	*Foedera, conventiones, literae, & cujuscumque gen. Acta Publica, inter Reges Angliae & alios, ab a. 1101 ad nostra usque tempora*, ed. Thomas Rymer (20 volumes, 1704–32).
Harleian MSS.	Collection of Harleian Manuscripts preserved in the British Museum.
Hargrave MSS.	Collection of Hargrave Manuscripts preserved in the British Museum.
H.M.C.	*Historical Manuscripts Commission, Reports*.
Lans. MSS.	Collection of Lansdowne Manuscripts preserved in the British Museum.
L.J.	*Journals of the House of Lords*.
P.C.	Registers of the Privy Council in the Public Record Office.
Remembrancia	*Analytical index to the series of records known as Remembrancia, 1579–1664*, ed. W. H. and H. C. Overall (1878).
Rushworth	*Historical Collections*, ed. John Rushworth (4 volumes, 1659–1701).

S.P.D.	State Papers Domestic in the Public Record Office.
Steele	*A Bibliography of Royal Proclamations of the Tudor and Stuart Sovereigns*, ed. R. Steele (2 volumes, 1910).
Stowe MSS.	Collection of Stowe Manuscripts preserved in the British Museum.
T.E.D.	*Tudor Economic Documents*, ed. R. H. Tawney and Eileen Power (3 volumes, 1924).
Trans. Roy. Hist. Soc.	*Transactions of the Royal Historical Society.*

INTRODUCTION

The decay of merchandizing or vent abroad of our home-bred wares must needs hinder the employment of the makers thereof and so consequently increase great numbers of the poor, and be the ruin of all the inland trades, for that they depend one upon another; and the decay of either is very prejudicious to this State.

WILLIAM SANDERSON, 'A Treatise of the State Merchant' (1629), in Cambridge University Library, MS. Gg. v. 8, fol. 227.

Perhaps more than any other field of study in the economic history of seventeenth-century England, that which concerns the development and changing fortunes of commerce lends itself to descriptive and analytical treatment. For one thing, it provides many convenient foci around which a story may be constructed. For another, its surviving records exemplify a dynamism which sets it apart from the history of agriculture. It is indeed difficult not to adopt the prejudices of the majority of contemporary observers—in whose eyes trade was the main prop of the economy, and from whose pens, consequently, there flowed an abundance of illuminating documentation. Yet it is not alone the conveniences of economic historiography nor the chance survival of one type of source material which justify a careful study of the commerce of the period. Even the existence of extreme naïvety in official circles would not have entirely explained the careful and detailed administrative attention devoted to trade and the classes dependent upon it. And no degree of misplaced enthusiasm for purely academic exercises could have produced a situation where the significant advances in economic thought were so much confined to matters of commerce and currency. Clearly, England's relationships with the economies of other lands had a crucial role to play in her own internal prosperity. Perhaps the most rewarding way to investigate the implications of this proposition is to concentrate largely upon periods of economic crisis. As long as we retain the knowledge that there were good times as well as bad, an economy suffering from extreme dislocation can tell us much concerning its own structure. When we have compared one crisis with another we can hope to know far more about the stability of the economy, and even its course of development.

The modern approach to the study of economic fluctuations and economic growth has been both facilitated and conditioned by a sharpening of the tools of statistical analysis and by the accumulation of statistical series whose abundance is chastening to the student of the early modern period. Techniques now used to study the nineteenth century have their disadvantages as well as their undoubted merits.[1] For the historian of the early seventeenth century, however, there can be no choice: such sophistication of analysis is beyond his reach, the quantitative data are much too sparse. Thrown back on to a reliance upon literary evidence, the historian is no less forced to define the sort of phenomenon which he admits as evidence of, in this case, trade fluctuation. It will become apparent that the present writer has primarily adopted the criterion of unemployment in the textile industry as the mark of a significant slump in the period under consideration. In addition he has looked to 'external' factors—to political and economic events abroad, to currency instabilities, to harvest fluctuations—to explain the more important dislocations in England's economic structure. The basis of these views lies, on the one hand, in an appreciation of the importance of the manufacture of textiles at home and of woollen exports in overseas sales as a whole, and, on the other, in the fact that the English economy of the time was not such as to generate the type of trade cycle so familiar in the nineteenth and twentieth centuries. These two subjects will be dealt with separately.

(i) INDUSTRY AND TRADE

At first sight the organization of England's economy might not seem to bear out the conclusion that there could be an intimate relationship between events overseas and prosperity at home. The nation was both small and poor. The bulk of the population, of about 5,000,000, lived in rural surroundings. London, it is true, was on the way to reaching the half-million mark which it achieved by the end of the century. But London was unique. Norwich, the second city of the kingdom, could boast only 15,000 inhabitants. In the main Englishmen inhabited the countryside or the large villages which passed for towns, and whose principal economic role lay not in manufacturing but in finishing and distributing, in marketing and arranging supplies of food and raw materials. Although, of course, there was still a relative abundance of land, the existing technology and the shortage of capital (to name only two of a host of interacting factors) kept standards of living at, or below, a level today associated with underdeveloped or backward economies. Most people would seem to have been employed in supplying the rudimentary wants of a poor society. With a primitive technology, most pursuits, outside those where large units of fixed capital were essential,

[1] F. J. Fisher, 'The Sixteenth and Seventeenth Centuries: The Dark Ages in English Economic History?', *Economica*, n.s. XXIV (1957), 2–3.

Introduction

were deprived of the economies of large-scale operation. Consequently the average unit of production was kept small and this, combined with a poor system of internal transport, meant that local areas frequently duplicated each other in providing limited and inelastic markets for a diversity of local tradesmen and craftsmen—retailers, butchers, bakers, carpenters, builders, blacksmiths, tailors, etc. Clearly, compared with the twentieth century, a greater proportion of the population was engaged in satisfying the basic needs of the community.[1] Occupied, as many of them were, with the struggle for daily existence, close to the land and its potentialities, frequently still deprived of the commercial activity which was felt by those agricultural communities in the happy position of providing London with its workaday necessities,[2] it might well be asked how local economies could feel any except the remotest repercussions of economic events in other areas of England, not to speak of a field so far removed from the resources of their own districts as that of overseas trade.

Yet, in fact, England was far from being a static agglomeration of self-sufficient communities. For one thing, factors were at work which had broken down the barriers (if, indeed, they had ever existed) between some regions and involved them, albeit to a limited extent, in a common economic destiny. We cannot yet speak of a national market for the factors of production or for most consumer goods. But regional specialization and trade were sufficiently far advanced to create an economic balance which could be alarmingly susceptible to commercial disturbance. In addition, important sections of the population relied for their daily income on the prosperity of the export market.

The growth of London was itself a potent factor stimulating regional specialization and hence interregional dependence.[3] Clearly, the principal effect of this was felt in agricultural production, but of no small significance was the demand of the capital for fuel, clothing, timber, metalware, etc. The growth of the London market exerted pressure on the resources of remote areas as well as those of the home counties. 'It is no good state', wrote Sir Thomas Roe, 'for a body to have a fat head, thin guts, and lean

---

[1] For this point and for the relatively small numbers engaged in agriculture, see A. J. and R. H. Tawney, 'An Occupational Census of the Seventeenth Century', *Econ. Hist. Rev.* v (1934), 38–43.

[2] See Add. MSS. 10113, fol. 64 (1611) where Edward Hayes noted that 'complaints have been frequent that in the country far from London markets have been dead, that corn and cattle sent to markets and fairs by poor farmers to pay their landlords could not be sold, because no money was there stirring'.

[3] For the development of London see F. J. Fisher, 'The Development of the London Food Market, 1540–1640', *Econ. Hist. Rev.* v (1935), 46–64; 'The Development of London as a Centre of Conspicuous Consumption in the Sixteenth and Seventeenth Centuries', *Trans. Roy. Hist. Soc.* 4th ser. xxx (1948), 37–50; 'The Sixteenth and Seventeenth Centuries: The Dark Ages in English Economic History?', 10.

members.'[1] This criticism of London's position in the economy veiled an apprehension which was, in the main, justified. The capital had come to condition many of the day-to-day workings of the community. Quite apart from the far-flung influence of its demand for consumer goods, London, as the fountain-head of privileges, the centre of government, the site of the principal law courts, the seat of the great trading companies, the crux of the land market, the main repository of trading capital, and the primary source of credit, was the inevitable controller of much economic activity in other parts of the land, and, as we shall see, the narrow bottleneck through which (to the chagrin of provincial merchants) textiles produced in the remotest areas passed for shipment abroad.

There were other places, too, where a concentration of population not only provided goods for a non-local market, but created a market for non-local sources of supply. Important amongst these were various of the agricultural counties; the textile-producing counties of East Anglia, the West Country and Yorkshire; the iron-mining and iron-working regions of the Weald and the Forest of Dean; the fast-developing Black Country; and the coal, glass and salt district along the Tyne and the Wear. One of the greatest gaps in our knowledge of the period is, indeed, the structure and development of internal trade which made these, and other, local divisions of labour possible. To judge from the complaints of urban craftsmen and the demand for improvements in transport, it was growing at a fast rate; to judge by the more moderate comments concerning that *bête noire* of social reformers, the middleman, it was becoming increasingly respectable.[2] But it is easier to intimate the importance of domestic commerce than to measure it. Surviving records of the coastal trade, for instance, tell us much, although by no means all, concerning the economic relationships between the various local economies which comprised the England of the time;[3] but they provide no measure of change in those relationships.

It would be out of place here to describe fully the economic geography of England in the early seventeenth century. In some respects the seeds of future industrialism were commencing their familiar growth. In other respects England remained nearer to the fifteenth-century mould than to the nineteenth. For instance, there was, as yet, no approximation to the nineteenth-century balance of economic power: the exploitation of agricultural and industrial resources was most advanced in the South and

---

[1] Sir Thomas Roe, *His Speech in Parliament: wherein he sheweth the cause of the Decay of Coin and Trade* (1640; published 1641), p. 11.
[2] Fisher, 'The Sixteenth and Seventeenth Centuries: The Dark Ages in English Economic History?', 11–12.
[3] T. S. Willan, *The English Coasting Trade, 1600–1750* (Manchester, 1938).

Introduction

East, where also lay the main centres of population; the North, and parts of the West, were still, by comparison, underpopulated, underdeveloped, and economically and commercially primitive. Nevertheless, it is essential to go into slightly more detail concerning the manufacture of woollen textiles, for they occupied a unique position in the structure of English industry and trade.

The actual production of cloth was widespread; the Privy Council, in 1622, anxious concerning the decay of the cloth trade and wishing to ascertain local opinions on it, wrote to twenty-five counties in which it was presumed that the textile industry flourished.[1] But significant manufacture for distant sale was somewhat more localized, and the resulting specialization means that it is possible, and sometimes necessary, to speak not of one 'textile industry' but of a variety of non-competing wool-manufacturing sectors.[2] Wiltshire, Gloucestershire, Somerset, Worcestershire and Oxfordshire produced the traditional, heavy, white broadcloth which was the staple item of the old draperies, and which gave to the West Country its unique industrial importance. In the same areas and in Dorset there was a growing manufacture of newer types of dyed cloths of a high quality: stammells, medleys, Spanish cloths, etc. In Devon, Dorset, western Somerset and parts of Wiltshire there were also regions specializing in narrower and cheaper cloths: kersies, dozens, straits, and some coarser varieties of broadcloth. In Wales and Lancashire goods made out of mixed fabrics sustained a not inconsiderable industry. Textiles endowed East Anglia with a busy industrial economy; there, in Suffolk, Essex and Norfolk, the old draperies, both white and coloured, jostled with the worsted industry, and with the new draperies, the bays, says, perpetuanoes, and a host of other types made from combed wool. To the north, the West Riding, with its dozens, kersies, plains, straits, and more substantial products was an important producing area, while expensive coloured cloths in Kent and Berkshire, and kersies in some areas of the South, were other examples of textiles manufactured for non-local sale.

It is impossible to obtain even approximately exact figures of the numbers employed in textiles as a whole. In Gloucestershire it is possible that some 15 per cent of the work force was so engaged in 1608,[3] and, acknowledging the probable wide margin of error, we may compare this with an even more tentative estimate, from the nineteenth century, of 101,000 for the total Gloucestershire population in 1600,[4] and with

[1] A.P.C. 1621–1623, p. 190.
[2] See, for example, Margaret Gay Davies, *The Enforcement of English Apprenticeship: A Study in Applied Mercantilism, 1563–1642* (Cambridge, Mass. 1956), pp. 109–11.
[3] Tawney, 'An Occupational Census', 36.
[4] W. H. B. Court, *The Rise of the Midland Industries, 1600–1838* (Oxford, 1938), p. 21.

contemporary guesses that 20,000 or 24,000 people were dependent on the county's textile industry.[1] In general, however, the statistical approach proves barren. Nevertheless, the weight of contemporary opinion, the repercussions of dislocation, the nature of governmental action, and a wealth of other qualitative evidence leaves no doubt that the manufacture of cloth was England's primary non-agricultural occupation. More than this, at least three areas—the West, East Anglia, and the West Riding—found that their daily well-being was tied to a considerable degree to the overseas sale of their products.

It was not only that the overseas market was of strategic importance to cloth production. England's exports, in their turn, were dominated by woollen textiles—cloth was unrivalled as a saleable product: 'if all were divided into 10 parts, wool and cloth make nine parts, but this must be understood of the cloth exported compared with the value of other commodities exported, for compare wool and corn, the value of the corn far exceeds the wool.'[2] With the former verdict modern research agrees; perhaps as much as 90 per cent and certainly over 75 per cent of England's exports were of articles made from wool. No wonder that to contemporaries it appeared that 'the cloth trade is ... the axis of the commonwealth, whereon all the other trades ... do seem to turn, and have their revolution',[3] or that it could be called 'the flower of the king's crown, the dowry of the kingdom, the chief revenue of the king ... the gold of our Ophir, the milk and honey of our Canaan, the Indies of England'.[4]

Since cloth made up the bulk of exports and since the industry was so highly concentrated, in all cases of an abrupt decline in overseas demand society was faced with the phenomenon of mass unemployment. For no economy, whatever the possibilities of by-employment or the availability of land, could hope to absorb the idle labour resulting from a cessation of activity in an industry which permeated entire localities. Again this gave a special character to the contemporary economic scene. Cloth production was sufficiently far advanced to have ceased, in the main, to be a by-employment for a predominantly agrarian population. Hence, for the government and for the community at large the existence of the textile industry meant the perennial threat of an outbreak of distress and disorder amongst a landless, and even propertyless, class. This situation had helped produce the Elizabethan Poor Law and made

---

[1] S.P.D. Jas. I, 128/49I (1622); S.P.D. Chas. I, 244/1IV (1633).
[2] Hargrave MSS. 321, pp. 40–1 (temp. James I). Cf. Sir Edward Coke in the 1621 Parliament: 'Divide our native commodities into 10 parts and 9 arise from the sheep's back.' *Commons Debates, 1621*, III, 318.
[3] E. Misselden, *The Circle of Commerce* (1623), pp. 63–4.
[4] E. Misselden, *Free Trade* (1622), p. 40.

Introduction

generations of statesmen wary of encouraging industrial growth. Lord Burghley had felt that 'the diminution of clothing in this realm were profitable to the same', in part because 'the people that depend upon making of cloth are of worse condition to be quietly governed than the husbandmen'.[1] Although, as will be seen, such extreme restrictionism no longer secured widespread support, the situation which gave it rise fifty years before was no less urgent a problem in the early seventeenth century.

The framework of overseas commerce into which the cloth trade fitted was a relatively simple one. The spectacular colonial ventures of the time and the search for treasure and exotic commodities in Asia, Africa and America should not be allowed to mask the fact that trade was primarily intra-European. From England woollens went largely to clothe eastern Europe, Germany and Holland—with smaller, although rapidly increasing, markets in southern Europe and the Mediterranean.[2] There was also some small export of minerals, foods and manufactured goods. In return, imports consisted of the linens and fustians of northern Europe; the silks of Italy, France and Spain; the dyestuffs, raw silk, hemp, flax, oils, yarn, metals, potash and timber used in home industries; the fruits of southern Europe; and (to a strictly limited extent) spices, sugar and tobacco from more distant areas. In years of bad harvest there would be an import of grains directly or indirectly from the Baltic and perhaps from France. Much of this importation in normal years was of luxury goods, and its variations would only indicate the fluctuations in the high prosperity of a tiny portion of the population. Much of the remainder was closely connected with the textile industry or with shipbuilding, and would tend to vary in amount with internal activity rather than affect it.

Thus a study of commercial fluctuations in general, the object of which is to accord primary importance to those factors which affected most people, is not unduly selective if it concentrates to a great extent on the export trade, and textile sales in particular. In the main London's exports will be used as an index of the nation's—a procedure justified by the capital's commercial predominance. And, since the major crises came in the trade to northern and eastern Europe (the principal areas for the sale of cloth), the old draperies and commercial dealings with the Continent will provide the main subject-matter of the following pages.

To contemporaries the claim that 'when trade flourisheth the king's revenue is augmented, lands and rent improved, navigation is increased, the poor employed . . . [but] if trade decay, all these decline'[3] was a

---
[1] T.E.D. II, 45.
[2] For the long-term changes in England's cloth markets, see chapter 7.
[3] Misselden, *Free Trade*, p. 5.

truism beyond argument. It suffices for the immediate purpose that England's most important manufacture was also her leading export-industry; that this industry was a spectacular exception to most occupations at the time; and that the economy was always susceptible to the dynamic impact of trade fluctuations, which affected its monetary and capital supplies, and the levels of production and employment in its predominant industrial activity.

However, before we see how these things worked themselves out in the decades before the Civil War, it is necessary to say something further concerning the types of economic instability with which we shall be dealing.

(ii) THE NATURE OF INSTABILITY AND CRISIS

Even were comprehensive statistical series to be discovered it is unlikely that anything like the modern trade cycle would be found operating in the early seventeenth-century economy. The extremes of commercial paralysis regularly alternating with periods of hectic expansion, which run through the economic history of the nineteenth century, seem to be associated with the growth of capital goods industries and the factory system. A marked feature of non-agricultural occupations in the period under discussion was, however, the relative unimportance of fixed capital. The principal items of durable capital goods were houses, ships, mills, mines and industrial tools such as looms and spinning wheels. Given the methods and organization of trade and industry, an extremely high proportion of the country's non-agricultural wealth consisted of circulating capital. And the effects of this situation were exaggerated since, firstly, some of the items of fixed capital, e.g. mills, were by no means specific in their uses, and, secondly, the arrangements of domestic production meant that employees frequently provided their own workplaces and the necessary, but inexpensive, tools and machines.

Since fixed capital played such a small part in the industrial structure it was impossible to experience the crippling crises of excess productive capacity so familiar after the Industrial Revolution. Equally absent were the intensifications of market fluctuations which derive from the presence of capital goods industries in an economy. Further, the lack of a highly developed and sensitive network of credit meant that a credit crisis, in its modern connotation, would rarely be a significant erosive of general prosperity. Except for the variations in purchasing power resulting from harvest fluctuations (which will be dealt with in the next section) the home market for industrial goods tended, on the whole, to be maintained at a stable and low level and to be conditioned by regional rather than national factors. It was, therefore, frequently overseas demand which was the strategic determinant of alterations in internal activity. As English exports largely consisted of woollen goods and as the cloth industry was the principal non-agricultural occupation, so trade inevitably came to play a dynamic role in the variations of internal prosperity.

It should, consequently, not be surprising that the economic booms and slumps of the early seventeenth century did not partake of any of the marked *rhythmical* character of the modern trade cycle. The pre-factory economy was not of a type calculated to produce regular and self-generating oscillations of economic activity. Instead, since increases and decreases in production and employment so often arose from alterations in exports, and since these latter derived, with indeterminate frequency, from extraneous developments abroad or arbitrary interference at home, variations in prosperity were random and discontinuous. Intermittent breakdowns in the English textile industry, and dislocations of a broader character, stemmed in the main from the intrusion of such factors as the growth of competitive manufacture in Europe, the outbreak of continental wars, the manifestations of semi-political difficulties (or economic jealousy) in stoppages of trade, the destruction of foreign purchasing power consequent upon a variety of factors, and the repercussions of the currency manipulations which were an ever-present result of Europe's monetary difficulties. Hence at any given point in time there would be much that was precarious about England's economic situation. Equilibrium, no matter at how high a level of prosperity, was always unstable. But, while the causes of these 'random perturbations' lay outside the economic structure, an understanding of their extremity and effects is dependent upon a realization of the nature of internal economic relationships.

Part of the volatile nature of the effects of commercial disruptions was undoubtedly caused by the ease of disinvestment consequent upon the nature of capital at the time. As already intimated, outside a few special trades, the individual entrepreneur had a preponderance of his investment in the form of circulating capital and could therefore withdraw from participation in his activity far more easily than his nineteenth-century counterpart—much of whose capital was immobilized in fixed items of investment. This importance of working capital was matched, given technological poverty, by the significance of labour, whose share as a cost of production was commensurately more significant. Hence, a sudden expansion in output would be secured less by a change in organization or techniques than by an increase in employment and a multiplication of units of production. Conversely, a fall in demand would quickly put pressure on wages and employment. In these circumstances, one marked feature of society—much as a government enamoured of the concept of a stable and ordered economic framework might dislike it—was a considerable horizontal and even vertical mobility of capital, entrepreneurial skill and labour.

Peers, gentry, yeomen and husbandmen participated in a variety of industries and trades only some of which depended on the exploitation of the resources of the land. Outside the landed classes there were wholesale cross-currents of economic interest: butchers became graziers, clothiers invested in trade and agricultural produce, mills were converted from one use to another. For the merchant, trade in one commodity or to one market would rarely comprehend the entire range of his commercial activities, while he did not necessarily confine himself to active trading. The mobility of mercantile capital showed itself in many ways: in the distribution of investment between a variety of trading areas and commodities, largely in order to diversify risks; in the expansion of an individual's field of activity consequent upon the accumulation of resources, expertise and contacts—which led cloth traders into the financing of industrial production, joint-stock investment, participation in the money market, custom-farming, projecting and large-scale land-owning.[1] This high mobility of mercantile assets implied that for the merchant a slump in exports might not necessarily be the disaster which it could be for those more directly employed in industry. With investments both diversified and in a circulating form, he might often, when particular markets, or dealings in a particular commodity, were depressed, contract his operations in one direction and expand them in another. Bankruptcies could, of course, occur but they are perhaps not as good an index of crises in overseas trade as some historians have imagined: if sufficiently comprehensive information were available, concerted movements of capital might prove more useful measures of trade fluctuations than abrupt losses. In a slump it was normally the clothier, not the merchant, who first besieged the Privy Council with complaints. These shifts of capital would occur less with the rich London merchants than with provincial traders. The latter did not always possess capital sufficient to enable them to hold stocks until markets were at their most favourable. While all would be concerned to secure a speedy turn-over,[2] the Londoners could afford to be more patient and to criticize provincial mer-

[1] For this aspect of the mobility of mercantile capital, see my unpublished Ph.D. dissertation, 'A Comparative Study of Commercial Fluctuations, 1600–1640' (Cambridge University, 1955), 436–59.
[2] Add. MSS. 10113, fol. 187: 'It is not gain altogether, but a necessity of speedy payments that causeth the merchant to bring in silver to keep his credit and to drive his trade.'

chants as 'young men and necessitated to sell away their cloth for the preservation of their credits, [and] not able to stand out'.[1] Outporters would therefore be more likely to be discouraged by commercial difficulties which lengthened the period of turn-over, and their capital would be more likely (unless entirely immobilized in unsold stocks) to be abstracted from overseas commerce in a depression. Thus the Exeter merchants, in 1621, found that the growth of the French textile industry, which prevented cash sales and forced them to sell 'for long time of payment . . ., causeth a great many to give over their trades, and seek other means to live'. Ipswich had similar difficulties and Exeter traders, some eighteen years later, complained that hindrances to imports were lengthening the period of return and reducing cloth sales.[2] However, in some crises not even the wealthy merchants of London would be able to 'stand out'. It is the argument here that only very rarely would they be unable to effect a withdrawal by channelling a preponderant part of their resources into uses other than the textile trade.

The textile industry itself was marked by considerable mobility of some factors of production. With no large units of specific capital to be constructed there were few hindrances to the violent expansion of output and to the sudden influx of money and labour.[3] The Tudor government feared (and enacted a framework of industrial regulation in an attempt to reduce) this responsiveness to economic trends. For the industry— over-expanded in response to a temporary boom—might suffer acutely when market conditions returned to normal, or when there was a slump. However, few efforts to limit the mobility of capital and labour were really successful. Besides the normal widespread use of capital in more than one field, a boom might see many men entering the cloth trade, while clothiers were accustomed to becoming middlemen, moneylenders, farmers, graziers, landowners, brewers, innkeepers, etc. In any case, the clothier might often be able to diversify his wealth and interests. It was certainly true that, manufacturing his cloth well in advance of the determination of its market, he ran a greater risk than the merchant that a freezing of his assets in unsaleable stocks would lead to bankruptcy. But in all except the most abrupt and severe slumps it seems unlikely that the larger entrepreneurs in the industry would incur catastrophic loss: either holdings of stocks were not large, or else they could be sold or pawned at not too great a loss, or they might even be held in expectation

---

[1] S.P.D. Chas. I, 398/22.
[2] Hargrave MSS. 321, pp. 87, 121; S.P.D. Chas. I, 418/67.
[3] For the mobility of labour in the sixteenth and seventeenth centuries, see M. G. Davies, p. 7; D. C. Coleman, 'Labour in the English Economy of the Seventeenth Century', *Econ. Hist. Rev.* 2nd ser. VIII (1956), 291.

that prices would rise. What is important is that in every case disinvestment and a stoppage of activity would commence automatically as no fresh capital was put into the productive process. In many cases it would take a more positive form as clothiers actually left the industry, like the Essex manufacturers on the eve of the Civil War who had previously 'employed many poor people . . . [and who] now deal little or nothing in the same, but betake themselves to other ways of livelihood, some turning innkeepers, . . . some farmers, graziers and the like, whereby rents of farms are increased by the multitude of tenants . . . and those poor men, artificers, as weavers, combers and the like, appertaining to the trade of clothworking, are brought (many of them) to beg their bread, and the rest to live upon the parish charge'.[1]

The last point deserves emphasis. There was, it seems, less opportunity for the employee (or for the very small independent 'manufacturer') so to diversify his interests as to provide effective insurance against the onslaught of bad times. In normal years and during trade expansions the mobility of labour was high—there were relatively few effective barriers to occupational change—but during a crisis in the textile industry the sheer numbers involved would render labour the most immobile of the factors of production. Some buffer against hardship might have been afforded by the fact that many of the workers were never far removed from some sort of agricultural pursuit. But, especially in the western counties and East Anglia, there were thousands who drew the preponderant part of their subsistence from earnings in the cloth industry.[2] Even the counter-attraction of the harvest period, whose urgent demand for labour served to reduce the output of textiles,[3] was a purely temporary phenomenon, and mainly affected spinners.[4] As already mentioned, the mass unemployment resulting from a slump could not be absorbed in one gulp: men redundant in one occupation produced a problem of re-employment radically different from that of capital redundant in one use. So it was that the employees themselves, especially in the western and eastern counties where both the reliance on textile earnings and the concentration of labour were at a maximum, were in most cases the unfortunate residuary legatees of a decline in cloth exports. The nature

---

[1] Mr. Grimstone, *His Speech in Parliament . . . upon the preferring of the Essex Petition* (19 January 1642), B.M. E. 200 (4).
[2] For East Anglia, see S.P.D. Jas. I, 162/68; S.P.D. Chas. I, 141/1. For the West, see S.P.D. Jas. I, 128/49I, 130/73; S.P.D. Chas. I, 177/53, 244/1IV, 380/87. Cf. E. Lipson, *The Economic History of England*, II, (5th ed., 1948), 66.
[3] H.M.C. Sackville, II, 176; S.P.D. Chas. I, 5/98, 80/13.
[4] Preamble to 14 Car. II, c. 5 (1662): 'The custom hath been retained time out of mind and found expedient that there should be a cessation of weaving every year, in the time of harvest, in regard the spinners of yarn . . . at that time [are] chiefly employed in harvest work.'

of the capital involved in trade and industry often protected it from the harmful effects of crisis. This mobility of capital and entrepreneurial skill distinguished the organization of commerce and manufacturing in the seventeenth century. No less was it distinguished by the speed with which, owing to the merchant's failure to buy and the clothier's willingness to let stocks run down, commercial dislocation rebounded upon the heads of the workers in the clothing industry.

The fact that the economy's sensitivity to disturbance was enhanced by the high mobility of its factors of production had considerable relevance, however, to normal times as well as to the effects of fluctuations in prosperity. With fixed capital relatively insignificant and with the underemployment of a poor labouring force, there was a need for continuous supplies of liquid capital merely to keep the economy going, to employ the labouring force. Equally, since credit techniques were still relatively undeveloped, the daily workings of the country were dependent to no small degree upon continuity in the circulation of ready money; in a very real sense it was true that 'plenty of money is the life of trade, scarcity is the maim of trade'.[1] Where the supply of working capital and cash was so significant England's relationship with other economies became doubly important: not only as the arbiter of employment in the principal industry, but as the source of the lubricant—liquid wealth—which was essential to the continued activity of society. It was partly this factor which gave trade its pre-eminence in contemporary eyes. On the one hand, from the quick turn-over and relative size of commercial transactions there derived abundant supplies of circulating capital. The strategic position of the merchant, largely unhampered by official regulation and in close touch with a wide variety of possible employments for capital, meant that his was regarded as the supreme occupation, that he became the outstanding type of entrepreneur, the provider of capital *par excellence*.[2] On the other hand, impairment of the supply of ready money was likely to lead to widespread dislocation. This was especially so since the flexibility of prices, and consequently the equilibrating potentiality, was necessarily limited at the time. A strong element of instability was in fact introduced by contemporary monetary arrangements. In the main, currency consisted of gold and silver coins—token money in England never being very important. With no buffer of paper money and with a limited use of negotiable credit instruments, the supply of money was

[1] Hargrave MSS. 321, p. 1.
[2] Henry Parker, *Of a Free Trade* (1648), p. 2: 'The merchant ... is often commander of great sums of ready money (greater than other men commonly though better landed, and estated, can raise upon sudden public exigencies).' Cf. *C.S.P.V.* *1607–1610*, p. 475; *C.S.P.V.* *1628–1629*, p. 59.

conditioned by factors which controlled the supply of gold and silver. Europe was plagued by a badly run bimetallic system in which violent movements of bullion and specie were provoked by normal market factors and by arbitrary manipulations of mint prices by local or central authorities. England, therefore, was perpetually threatened with a harmful reduction in its supplies of coins and bullion of one metal—and sometimes of both. Where, as was the case for most of the period, silver was being lost, considerable inconvenience was felt, which partly goes to explain the vehemence of contemporary complaints concerning a 'scarcity of money'. More than this, currency alterations abroad, which were initially attempts to alter European bullion flows, had alarming effects on the amounts and values of trade.[1] Indeed, the wave of European debasements and enhancements which accompanied the outbreak of the Thirty Years War provoked the period's most profound crisis and had a disastrous effect upon England's cloth exports, supply of money, internal prosperity and balance of payments.

It should now be apparent why overseas commerce was (rightly) seen as of such importance to the economy—an importance which cannot be measured solely by the amount of capital involved when compared, for example, with agriculture. Directly impacting on the prosperity of England's largest industry, sharply altering the demand for goods and the supply of capital and cash to an economy whose instability and sensitivity it is too easy to underestimate, overseas economic relationships deserve a large chapter in any story of England's economic development.

(iii) HARVESTS AND INSTABILITY

To a considerable extent the well-being of the average Englishman of the early seventeenth century—his daily subsistence, the amount of money he could spend on consumer goods, the level of economic activity which surrounded him—depended upon seasonal variations in agriculture as well as the random fluctuations in general commerce. Although this topic will not be discussed at any length in the following pages it merits some attention here. How correct was the opinion that 'In time of dearth of corn in England there is . . . want of money. In time of plenty of corn in England there is no want'?[2]

From the point of view of the present work there were three spheres in which harvest fluctuations had significant repercussions: the immediate impact on the standard of living of textile workers; the effects of changing grain prices on the effective demand for goods, especially textiles; and the

[1] For this point, and the whole question of currency, see chapters 4 and 8.
[2] Add. MSS. 10113, fol. 159.

Introduction

reaction for trade and bullion flows of the intermittent need for food imports.[1]

During the period under discussion variations in the price of foodstuffs had a far greater effect upon standards of living than in modern times. This was clearly so since the average standard of living in the early seventeenth century was low, the proportion of income spent on bread grains was high, and there was relatively little surplus to be channelled into food consumption in years of high prices—while an exceptionally good harvest, in liberating purchasing power, had a proportionately greater impact upon non-food consumption. More especially, a bad harvest coinciding with an independent increase in unemployment (from, say, a fall in exports) would accentuate local troubles and poverty. Such a coincidence was, in fact, the principal problem of poor-law administration,[2] and it was a particular misfortune of the early seventeenth century that during two of its major export slumps—1621-2 and 1629-31—the harvests were, indeed, extremely bad. Where local populations were said to 'suffer as much in the want of work as in the price of corn',[3] it was no wonder that widespread rioting accompanied food scarcity. Of course, with the unemployment of a class of people whose normal earnings rarely produced a sufficient surplus over expenditure to provide for a reasonable saving, there might be no chance of buying bread *whatever* its price. It was noticed, for instance, in 1623 that in the northern counties 'scarcity and famine be great . . . yet the prices of corn are . . . such . . . as have been in time of indifferent plenty, and this happeneth because of want of monies and want of employment and labour for the poor'.[4] In its most direct manifestation the problem of the harvest was the problem of poverty. Relatively few people lived far away from a bare margin of subsistence.

The question of the relationship between the price of grain and the effective demand for consumer goods—especially textiles—is a particularly thorny one. For one thing we know very little about the size of the

---

[1] There is no intention of dealing here with the interaction between high or low food prices and money wages (costs of production). There seem to be two possible, and contradictory, views: (*a*) that the increased demand for labour in good years forces wages up, while in bad years (of high food prices) there is less demand so that the price of labour falls; (*b*) that high prices for food (by increasing the cost of subsistence) tend to raise wages, while they might have a tendency to fall in years of good harvest. See Adam Smith, *The Wealth of Nations* (Everyman ed., 1910), I, 74–7; W. W. Rostow, *British Economy of the Nineteenth Century* (Oxford, 1948), p. 50; Fisher, 'The Sixteenth and Seventeenth Centuries: The Dark Ages in English Economic History?', 10. It is possible that long-term influence, for instance the higher price of food in the metropolitan area, had a greater, and more direct, effect on wages than short-term (harvest) fluctuations.

[2] E. M. Leonard, *The Early History of English Poor Relief* (Cambridge, 1900), *passim*.

[3] P.C. 2/40, p. 431 (1 April 1631).

[4] Add. MSS. 34324, fol. 179. Cf. S.P.D. Chas. I, 176/36.

domestic market for commercially produced cloth.[1] However, there can be no doubt that the home demand had some influence on the varying prosperity of the textile industry. How could harvest variations affect home demand?[2] The demand for agricultural goods, particularly bread grains, is notoriously inelastic—prices fluctuate sharply in response to alterations in supply. Also, as already intimated, bread grains absorbed a heavy proportion of the expenditure of the community. It can therefore be assumed that an abundant harvest, by sharply reducing bread prices, appreciably increased real earnings in the non-agricultural sections of the population, liberating a significant amount of purchasing power to be exerted for other goods, but reducing farming incomes. Conversely, a bad harvest tended to reduce expenditure by non-agriculturalists on items other than food, since purchasing power would be absorbed by rising bread prices, while it increased farmers' wealth. From another point of view these variations can be seen as shifts of real wealth: in the former case from the farming community to the consumer, and in the latter instance in the reverse direction. Clearly, the final effect of the above fluctuations depended largely on the proportion of the population which had to buy its own foodstuffs as against that which was producing for sale. Secondly, how this redistribution of wealth affected demand for goods would be determined by the relative tendencies to spend the increments to income on consumption.[3]

There is only one good statistical appraisal of occupational distribution: for Gloucestershire in 1608.[4] Admittedly it has data for only some 17,000 persons, but they can be used with some confidence. They show that although agriculture was the most prominent occupational category, it employed less than one-half (46·2 per cent) of the adult male population of the county. Even acknowledging the fact that Gloucestershire was a leading centre of textile manufacture, this is a surprisingly small estimate.[5] Nevertheless, the important factor is not the number 'employed' in

---

[1] One of the few contemporary estimates is in Hargrave MSS. 321, p. 267 (1618–19). This gives a total annual production of 360,000 (presumably notional shortcloths of 24 yards—see Appendix A), of which, it claims, 220,000 (or 61 per cent) were purchased in the realm. This seems very large, unless the author was including production by the family for itself.

[2] For obvious reasons there can be no detailed discussion of the inflationary or deflationary stimulus of accumulating stocks of corn or letting them run down. See R. C. O. Matthews, *A Study in Trade Cycle Theory; Economic Fluctuations in Great Britain, 1833–1842* (Cambridge, 1954), p. 28.

[3] There was a third class of people who produced sufficient food to satisfy their own needs, with no surplus for sale. They might possibly have been able to do this in both good and bad years, but it is very unlikely that a smallholder who was self-sufficing in normal times would not have to buy food in a bad harvest year.

[4] Tawney, 'An Occupational Census'.

[5] *Ibid.* 39–40. Cf. S.P.D. Interregnum, 16/139: 'Two-third parts of this nation do depend immediately upon the manufactures of it of one kind or another.'

agriculture, but the number who stood to gain or lose, as producers, from price fluctuations. Here it appears that 'in the group of yeomen and husbandmen the independent producers must, on almost any view, have outnumbered the wage workers by at least two to one, and probably by considerably more'.[1] However, in the context of the total community, this group of agriculturalists who tended to gain or lose directly with the movement of food prices, was much smaller than might have been expected, say some 31 per cent. In addition, other factors lead us to believe that over the whole country even more people depended on the market for their daily bread, and even less found a poor harvest beneficial to them. Firstly, the Gloucestershire survey dealt largely with men, and so exaggerated agricultural as against textile occupations—in which latter female labour was more important. Secondly, compared with south-east England, the western counties had a relative abundance of land which would have increased the proportion of independent food producers. Finally, some agricultural producers might not have benefited from high food prices—either because their output was so reduced as to force them to buy foodstuffs for their own consumption, or because they were in fact not producing those commodities in short supply.[2] In general, then, the mass of the population was susceptible to the influence of grain prices as consumers and not as producers: their real income was reduced in bad harvest years.

A generally recognized phenomenon is that an increase in farmers' incomes will be accompanied by a less than proportionate increase in current consumption. Conversely, in this period most consumers, having low levels of savings and standards of living, would disburse perhaps all the increments of real income on expenditure on consumer goods. In the language of the economists, the non-farmer's marginal propensity to consume exceeded that of the farmer.[3] Consequently, in bad harvest years the decreased purchase of goods other than food by the general public would, in its depressive effect upon industry, be augmented by the *retarded* increase in the effective demand of the newly rich farmers. On the other hand, good years would redistribute income to a section of the population more likely to expend all its income on current consumption. Some of these features of internal instability will be dealt with when we come to describe those years in which they operated most markedly. But

[1] Tawney, 'An Occupational Census', 49–53.
[2] See the complaint of one Welsh landowner in 1623 that his income had shrunk 'because his living consists of great tenements and mountain land without corn, and for the last two years neither cattle, wool, sheep, butter nor cheese carried any price'. Quoted in T. C. Mendenhall, *The Shrewsbury Drapers and The Welsh Wool Trade in the XVI and XVII Centuries* (1953), p. 23.
[3] Cf. Matthews, p. 28.

it is as well to indicate here that we know far too little about prices and incomes to speak with any certitude concerning the subject. For instance, it is theoretically possible that a good harvest could have a *depressive* effect owing to prevalent work habits. If employees used higher real income to buy leisure rather than goods, and this is quite likely,[1] then low food prices would in fact reduce the incentive to work with a consequent drop in productivity and production, there would be no increased purchase of other goods, and the reduction of farmers' incomes would take effect. Another possibility is that the inflationary or deflationary influences of harvest fluctuations would be ameliorated by a tendency to vary the bread grains eaten: using the extra purchasing power derived from good harvests to buy wheat rather than barley or oats, and compensating for bad times by an increased consumption of cheaper beans and peas.

Variations in the amounts of grain supplied by the English agricultural system did not, of course, go uncompensated by international trade. Most importantly, an abrupt and large increase in the import of foodstuffs unaccompanied by an augmentation of exports might have distinct deflationary results since specie would be exported to pay for them and internal purchasing power would be diverted from expenditure on native goods to demand for imported food. In point of fact England in normal times provided for its own subsistence, but in exceptional years it became dependent upon imports to make up a deficiency: 'Whenever wet seasons . . . do come, we have but little increase . . . which enforceth us of necessity to fetch and to buy our bread from the Hollanders, or from the East Country, which we pay for in ready money for the most part.'[2] In contrast to the Dutch, whose trade was a transit one of semi-permanent carriage and warehousing, the English only bought grain when there was need of it at home, in spite of the continual exhortations that they should enter into the profitable entrepôt trade. Contemporary opinion was unanimous that the demand for overseas corn, which formed no part of England's normal trade, most often entailed payment in specie. In general the international market for corn at this period seems to have been closely connected with movements of treasure and the Dutch certainly carried it to the Baltic to pay for grain.[3] Unless they exported vast quantities of English goods, and there is no evidence of this, then they must have expected to be paid in specie, or at least in bills which increased England's

---

[1] Fisher, 'The Sixteenth and Seventeenth Centuries: The Dark Ages in English Economic History?', 8-9; Coleman, 'Labour in the English Economy of the Seventeenth Century', 290-1.

[2] Sir Ralph Maddison, *Great Britain's Remembrancer* (1655 ed.), p. 37.

[3] A. E. Christensen, *Dutch Trade to the Baltic about 1600* (Copenhagen and The Hague, 1941), pp. 378, 399, and *passim*.

international indebtedness. For the Dutch were England's principal suppliers of grain (their permanent control of the trade ensured this),[1] they secured considerable benefit by demanding specie payments,[2] and the Baltic was the main origin of supplies of corn. Intermittent demands for grain merely served to stimulate the volatile specie flows associated with the Baltic trade, and the consequent instabilities could only have been lessened to a small extent by the increased purchasing power in Eastland countries which might have been exercised for English goods.

To the seventeenth-century Englishman few things were of more importance than the state of the English harvest—for many it might, quite literally, have been a matter of life and death. In addition, there must have been a considerable correlation between the price of bread and the level of general economic activity, while from time to time the need for the import of foodstuffs altered the balance of trade and helped augment those international movements of specie which were the bane of Europe at the time. From the present point of view, however, harvest fluctuations were only one factor among many which made for the extremely precarious state of the English economy at the time. It has, for instance, been impossible to find any major economic crisis which was solely, or indeed largely, caused by a poor harvest. The more spectacular developments in the English textile industry and the deeper economic crises owed far more to affairs of commerce and currency.

(iv) CONCLUSION

The foregoing sketch of some salient features of England's precarious economic position in the early seventeenth century has been primarily intended to introduce the role of commerce in the daily well-being of an economy highly vulnerable to dislocation. The fluctuations which provide the principal subject-matter of this book do not, of course, cover the entire story of English economic development. They took place against the background, and to some extent independently, of more fundamental long-term changes. These latter developments are no less important for an understanding of certain features in the economic history of the period.

On the whole it is possible that England's total exports of textiles

[1] V. Barbour, *Capitalism in Amsterdam in the Seventeenth Century* (Baltimore, 1950), pp. 88–9; Sanderson, fol. 253; S.P.D. Interregnum, 9/61. In 1638 alien merchants handled 98,501 and English merchants 56,795 quarters of London's grain imports (N. S. B. Gras, *The Evolution of the English Corn Market* (Cambridge, Mass. 1915), p. 102).

[2] Barbour, pp. 26–7; Henry Robinson, *Certain Proposals* (1652), p. 15; Maddison, p. 37. *Sir Walter Raleigh's Observations* (1653), pp. 16–17: 'Amsterdam is never without seven hundred thousand quarters of corn.... A dearth in England, France, Spain, Italy, Portugal and other places is truly observed to enrich Holland seven years after.' Lewes Roberts (*The Treasure of Traffic* (1641), p. 40) claimed that such a dearth enriched the Dutch by £2,000,000 in specie.

increased over the four decades prior to the Civil War. Certainly, there was a positive boom up to 1614. After that the old draperies, with rival industries speedily developing abroad, declined, and their decline was marked by a series of abrupt and painful short-term slumps. On the other hand, newer types of textiles were developed and these proceeded to capture (again with fluctuations in their prosperity) the markets of southern Europe and the Mediterranean. However much this last development tended to compensate for the breakdown of the traditional markets in northern and eastern Europe, England had to bear with extreme industrial disturbances in the western counties and, for instance, Suffolk, which stemmed from the fall in overseas demand for the classic English broadcloth.

The latter had been regarded as England's particular possession for generations. It was therefore only with difficulty that inherited ideas concerning 'cloth' were changed. Firstly, men had to accustom themselves to the idea of effective foreign competition, and therefore to the need for competitive prices; England no longer had any sort of monopoly of the overseas market and survival demanded a revolution in the modes of thinking about the textile trade. Secondly, as continental industries grew to alarming proportions, it became only too obvious that if the commercial well-being of the economy was to be maintained, the old reliance on textile exports would have to be reduced to some extent. The grounds for this equally revolutionary change were laid before 1640, although the full effects were not evident until after the Restoration. Asian, African and American trades were increasingly tapped; re-exports grew in importance; and the carrying trade commenced a long, and ultimately successful, rivalry with the Dutch for world supremacy. The narrow waters which divided Great Britain from Germany and the Low Countries had only a short time left before they were ousted as England's main economic frontiers. This island was on its way to becoming not only an industrial but also a properly commercial society.

Meanwhile, whatever the tendencies of secular trends, England still had to adjust itself to intermittent commercial depressions which served to condition the development and structure of the economy and the ways of thinking about economic matters. To these short-term factors we can now turn.

Part I

Years of Crisis

1. THE RECOVERY FROM STAGNATION, 1600-1614

The last years of Elizabeth's reign can no longer be considered as a prosperous era of economic expansion. The sixteenth century had seen violent swings in the course of the cloth trade together with price fluctuations and disruptions of internal economic affairs whose causes and consequences are still open to dispute.[1] A boom in textile exports in the first half of the century had been accompanied, especially in the 1540's, by widespread dislocation in agriculture, industry and internal trade. This had been followed by a protracted decline in overseas sales during the third quarter of the century. Thenceforth cloth exports remained at a low level, and the resulting problems were intermittently aggravated by poor harvests, privateering, closed markets and the burdens and dangers of the Spanish war. Measured by the statistics of the cloth trade the post-Armada economic difficulties can be viewed as fluctuations around a stable level.[2] On the other hand, qualitative evidence has led some historians to see a deeper and more general depression in the years after 1586, although it may well be that the war itself exerted a selective, inflationary influence on certain trades.[3] Certainly the mundane realities of trading conditions, cloth exports, plague, famine and unemployment are better indications of the economic history of the last years of the last of the Tudors than the romance of the Spanish Main, the glories of a matriarchal court, the conspicuous consumption of the nobility, or the inflationary gains of the land-owning yeomanry. An age which produced such remedial legislation as the Elizabethan Poor Law and the product of whose demographic introspection was a widely held theory of overpopulation, cannot claim sustained prosperity as its distinguishing feature.

During the sixteenth century woollen manufactures had finally established their predominance in England's exports, and London's trade, which overshadowed all other ports', had been largely captured by English merchants. The Merchant Adventurers had secured control of the cloth trade to Germany and the Low Countries and, since this trade bulked so large in London's total exports, they came to handle over half England's cloth sales. In the year ending Michaelmas 1598 the company exported

[1] F. J. Fisher, 'Commercial Trends and Policies in the Sixteenth Century', *Econ. Hist. Rev.* X (1940), 95-117; L. Stone, 'State Control in Sixteenth-Century England', *Econ. Hist. Rev.* XVII (1947), 103-20.
[2] Fisher, 'Commercial Trends', 117.
[3] Stone, 'State Control', 108; W. R. Scott, *The Constitution and Finance of English, Scottish, and Irish Joint-Stock Companies to 1720* (Cambridge, 1910-12), I, 93-104; Davies, pp. 132-7.

almost 63,000 out of some 100,500 shortcloths shipped by English merchants from the port of London. Altogether, counting both English and alien merchants, almost 74,500 cloths went to Germany and the United Provinces, almost 12,000 to the Baltic, over 6,500 to the Levant, some 6,250 to France, and smaller quantities of around 2,000 each to Italy, Barbary and Russia, for a grand total of 105,715 7/12, of which alien merchants handled some 5,000.[1] These statistics can be compared with those for 1606.[2] In that year English merchants exported about 125,000 cloths from London, of which 95,608 went to Germany and the Netherlands. Clearly, through their control of the trade across the narrow seas, the Merchant Adventurers were concerned with some three-quarters of London's cloth exports. Their trade is a useful starting point for any consideration of the course of English commerce.

In the opening years of the century the trade of the Merchant Adventurers was in some confusion. As a regulated company their principal aim had been to limit the shipping times and mart towns used by members so as to create a seller's market for English cloth. But after the ban on their operation as an official organization in the Empire in 1597 they had lost much of their power to control that branch of the trade which went to Germany. Both members and non-members proceeded to trade outside the mart town and at other times than the official shipping periods, adherence to which the company still attempted to enforce from England.[3] These interlopers were known to have exported over 8,000 cloths in the year ending Michaelmas 1598 and the real total must have been considerably higher. What was equally bad from the company's point of view was that interlopers even bought cloth at the German mart town for resale at inland fairs. The dealings of these 'Nuremburg traders', which had commenced some twenty years earlier,[4] were anathema to an organization whose avowed policy was the maintenance of prices by the reduction of competition between English merchants. A powerful group of Adventurers had in fact put pressure on the Privy Council to restrict the sale of cloth to Middelburg, the mart town in the Low Countries, and in August 1598 there was an attempt to forbid trade to the rivers Elbe and Ems. However, complaints from other members of the company, and from clothiers, clothworkers and Trinity House, helped force the

[1] S.P.D. Eliz., 268/101. Unless otherwise indicated, all cloth figures in this book will be given in terms of notional shortcloths. This convenient fiction was used by customs officials as a standard measure into which the many varieties of old draperies could be translated according to their length, breadth and quality.
[2] A. Friis, *Alderman Cockayne's Project and the Cloth Trade* (1927), pp. 61–2.
[3] G. Unwin, *Studies in Economic History* (1927), p. 165.
[4] J. Wheeler, *A Treatise of Commerce* (1601; ed. G. B. Hotchkiss, New York, 1931), p. 369; H.M.C. Sackville, I, 8.

council, in the interests of maintaining exports, to ease the ban on export to Germany.[1] A compromise was arrived at by which the government sanctioned exports only to marts stipulated by the company. From mid-1599 until early 1601 Emden was the unofficial 'residence' of the Adventurers and thenceforth the company, although still not recognized by the Imperial authorities, maintained its staple at Stade.[2] Meanwhile interlopers kept up their trade with Hamburg.[3] It was not until 1607 that official relations with Stade were resumed, and in 1611 the company moved to Hamburg, where it remained throughout the rest of its existence. As long as the company's precarious position continued, its powers of control over its own members were reduced and the 'straggling trade' which it most feared continued apace.[4] In view of this situation and the fact that anti-monopoly interests were increasingly being heard, it is no surprise that Wheeler, the Adventurers' Secretary at Middelburg, should have written, in 1601, *A Treatise of Commerce*—which was at once a defence of the company and an attack on the 'straggling trade'.[5]

Thus the last years of Elizabeth's reign were marked neither by security in the organization of trade nor by any degree of commercial progress.[6] And in 1603 there came a grim reminder of the vulnerability of commerce to extraneous interruptions of normal relationships. In that year London was visited by a catastrophic outbreak of the plague, whose results were severely aggravated by the concourse of people who flocked to the capital at the accession of James I. Over 30,000 people were killed by the disease[7] and, as was usual, measures were taken to reduce the normal (and abnormal) summer concentration of population—measures which served to interrupt social, legal and economic life: gentlemen were ordered to return to their country homes, the Law Terms were adjourned,

---

[1] *A.P.C. 1598–1599*, pp. 24–5, 112–13, 165–6, 176, 302–3, 619–20; S.P.D. Eliz., 270/128, 271/128; Lans. MSS. 152, fol. 146.

[2] Lipson, II, 210; *H.M.C. Sackville*, II, 6–7; Lans. MSS. 150, fol. 19.

[3] For the council's efforts to prevent this, in the summer of 1601, see Lans. MSS. 150, fols. 21, 24; *A.P.C. 1600–1601*, pp. 440–1, 451.

[4] For the normality of the use of interlopers' ships by Lionel Cranfield when he or his factor felt the market situation warranted it, see *H.M.C. Sackville*, II, 19, 74, 81, 103, 131–2, 143–4. For a bitter controversy provoked by the refusal of various members to conform to the company's orders of 1598–9, relating to the German trade, see Lans. MSS. 150, fol. 17b; Lans. MSS. 152, fols. 153–4, 156, 158, 160, 162, 170; *A.P.C. 1599–1600*, pp. 277, 361, 390–2, 401; *H.M.C. Sackville*, I, 31–4.

[5] The book came, in any case, at an anxious time for the Merchant Adventurers. In 1601 the Earl of Cumberland had been granted an unlimited licence to export unfinished cloth. It was not till the next year that the company secured, for a fee, the sole right to use this licence—without it their control of the trade would have been severely hampered. See Friis, pp. 72–3.

[6] Even the formation of the East India Company was as much an indication of difficulties in the Levant trade—whose merchants invested idle capital in the longer route to Asian commodities—as a mark of expansionism.

[7] C. Creighton, *A History of Epidemics in Britain* (Cambridge, 1891), I, 476.

and St James's, St Bartholomew and Stourbridge Fairs were postponed.[1] What was more important, trade was severely hampered by the wholesale flight from London: 'merchants and all others of any estate and accompt . . . departed into the country' and only started to return in December. London, wrote Thomas Dekker, 'stood . . . forsaken like a lover, forlorn like a widow, and disarmed of all comfort'.[2] Commercial activity, as a consequence, was brought almost to a standstill for six months. The East India Company could not muster a quorum of its governing body, royal finance suffered, and the money market was severely restricted.[3] Not for the first or the last time a plague, by disrupting activities in the bottleneck through which England's exports passed to the Continent, had repercussions on the cloth trade greater than might have been expected. As with another severe plague-year, 1625, there was a sharp drop in exports, but the decline was as temporary as the visitation of the plague:

Exports of shortcloths by English merchants from London [4]

1598–1600 (av.)	97,700	1603	86,600
1601	100,400	1604	112,800
1602	113,500		

If this abrupt slump in the cloth trade caused any immediate great distress in the textile-producing counties, the evidence has not come to us.[5] But there are indications that, in these early years, the Wiltshire industry at least was under prolonged pressure. In 1602 and 1603 some weavers of that county instituted suits against competitors who took apprentices and journeymen contrary to the provisions of the Statute of Artificers or who operated more looms than were allowed by the cloth statutes.[6] That this action reflected declining employment with a consequent unrest among the established industrialists, is substantiated by a plan which was propounded in Wiltshire in 1603, and which was obviously designed to curb both the development of 'capitalistic' production and the influx of labour to the textile industry.[7] The 'orders agreed upon for the occupation of weavers', which were drawn up by various clothiers and weavers for the consideration of local magistrates, involved

---

[1] Steele, I, nos. 951, 957, 964, 968, 970, 973.
[2] Sir G. Birdwood (ed.), *The First Letter Book of the East India Company, 1600–1619* (1893), p. 39; Thomas Dekker, *The Wonderful Year* (in *Three Elizabethan Pamphlets*, edited by G. R. Hibbard, 1951), p. 186.
[3] Birdwood, pp. 29, 30–2, 39; G. Malynes, *England's View in the Unmasking of Two Paradoxes* (1603), p. 194.
[4] Figures have been rounded to 100. Source: F. J. Fisher, 'London's Export Trade in the Early Seventeenth Century', *Econ. Hist. Rev.* 2nd ser. III (1950), 153.
[5] The records of the Privy Council for 1603–13 have been destroyed by fire.
[6] Davies, pp. 139, 202.
[7] *H.M.C. Various*, I, 74–5; Davies, pp. 224–5.

a limitation of the number of looms to be maintained by clothiers and weavers and a strict enforcement of apprenticeship regulations: all those who had become weavers within the last two years were to be expelled; unmarried journeymen who had not properly qualified were to 'return and serve their seven years out or else to be put from their occupations'; unapprenticed master weavers were not to take any apprentices, were to keep only one loom, and were to employ only journeymen; provision was made for the continuous enforcement and regulation of apprenticeship—which could not be terminated before the age of 24 'to avoid young marriages and the increase of poor people'; and town weavers' corporations were to have powers of control extending to a radius of three miles. The orders were never enforced, but they clearly demonstrate that the influx of capital and labour into the broadcloth industry exceeded, in some men's view, the level warranted by normal demand.

That there was possibly a real problem of underemployment producing a downward pressure on wages is shown by other, and more general, evidence. Malynes, writing in 1603, expressed the wish that 'labourers' and workmen's wages were augmented, although our cloth should cost so much the dearer ... and that with great regard the poor people were set on work, and ... their handiwork were vented'.[1] As if in answer to this wish came a statute commanding the assessment of minimum wages. 1 James I, c. 6 was obviously directed at the cloth industry; it claimed that wages 'have not been rated and proportioned according to the plenty, scarcity, necessity, and respect of the time', as intended by the statute of 1563. It ordered wages to be so assessed, provided for penalties to be imposed on clothiers who payed rates below the official ones, and tried to ensure that no J.P. who was a clothier should be concerned with the assessments. In Wiltshire, in 1605, forty-three clothiers were presented for not paying their weavers the assessed rates.[2]

It is most likely that these activities, and the general concern of the Commons with the cloth industry in 1604,[3] reflected much more than the slump in exports of a plague-year. They are more likely random indications of the long-term position of the traditional textile industry, whose coincidence is explained by the accidents attendant upon the survival of records. Cloth manufacture in general was marked by the relative ease of entry of capital and labour and the tendency of the labour force, in an economy close to the subsistence level, to hang on to poorly paid jobs. Sustained economic pressure, as has already been seen, was unlikely to be relieved by the availability of alternative employment, and

[1] Malynes, *England's View*, p. 88. [2] Davies, pp. 139, 202.
[3] See *C.J.* I, 154–5, 165, 167, 183, 184, 198, 202, 226, 237, 241, 246, 252.

the resulting instability of employment and earning power was not the least cause of official anxiety in these years. The natural response, both of governments and men long-established in the industry, was to set up artificial restrictions on mobility—limitations on the number of looms to be owned or managed by individual entrepreneurs, apprenticeship requirements, general industrial control—in the hope of making the influx of factors of production more difficult. This had clearly happened in the 1550's, with the Cloth Acts, and in 1563, with the Statute of Artificers, after a period of boom and slump.[1] There is little doubt that the attempted regulatory measures in the early years of the seventeenth century were a response to structural difficulties which the broadcloth industry was experiencing as a consequence of a prolonged period of low overseas demand, even though this attitude was to change in subsequent years.

Inauspicious as the last years of Elizabeth may have been, they were followed by a decade of expansion and prosperity in the cloth trade which probably more than compensated for the previous difficulties—although, since prosperity seems to make men hold their tongues and put away their pens, we know less about the cloth industry in the first ten years of James's reign than in any other decade in the period. The overall trade reached, in 1614, the highest recorded level of the early seventeenth century:

Exports of shortcloths by English merchants from London [2]

| 1601 | 100,400 | 1606 | 126,000 |
| 1604 | 112,800 | 1614 | 127,200 |

There is no means of obtaining exact figures for exports in the years (1605, 1607–13) for which the Port Books no longer exist; but it is possible, by statistical juggling, to arrive at some tentative estimates of cloth exports for these years, which show no catastrophic fall:[3]

1605	99,900	1609	113,800
1607	115,800	1610	95,000
1608	119,800	1611	96,000

Historians have agreed in viewing the years immediately before the Cockayne project as a time of long-run prosperity for trade in general,

---

[1] Fisher, 'Commercial Trends', 110–14; Davies, pp. 2–5.
[2] Fisher, 'London's Export Trade', 153. Figures rounded to 100.
[3] H.M.C. Sackville, I, 289 contains figures, for 1605–11, of the customs derived from cloth exports, as deduced from the accounts of the Great Farm of the customs. The problem of translation into shortcloths is a difficult one—principally because of the unknown amount handled by aliens, who paid 14s. 6d. duty instead of 6s. 8d. The procedure adopted here has been to compare the *total* cloth customs in London for 1606 (£46,920) with the Port Book figures of exports by *English* merchants of that year (126,000). The resulting multiplier of 2·685 has then been applied to the other customs figures, to arrive at an extremely tentative series for cloth exports by Englishmen. The assumption is the doubtful one that aliens exported a constant (high) percentage of total exports. It is possible that the estimates in the text are in fact too low.

The Recovery from Stagnation, 1600–1614

for cloth exports, and for the Merchant Adventurers in particular.[1] In 1606 the annual stint allowed to the members of the company was increased, which presumably reflected the high level of exports in that year[2] and in 1607 there were even signs that Blackwell Hall, the London repository of cloths to be exported, was becoming overcrowded.[3] Altogether, the cloth industry enjoyed a transitory Indian summer.

The major explanation of this changed environment after the economic gloom of the 1590's is to be found in the cessation of war largely consequent upon the Anglo-Spanish treaty of 1604 and the Spanish-Dutch truce of 1609. A period of at least partial pacification in the bellicose confusions of sixteenth- and seventeenth-century Europe demonstrated, although the lesson was not taken to heart, that nothing really advanced commercial development as much as peace. For England the opening of the markets of Spain and Flanders, the easing of the sea routes to the Levant, and the elimination of most of the heavy risks of trade occasioned by marauding privateers, all provided a better environment for commerce. The truce between the United Netherlands and Spain, while it may have increased Dutch shipping competition, must also have stimulated English exports through the increased purchasing power which north-eastern Europe derived from its profitable dealings with the forceful Hollanders—especially in the sale of grain: 'It is generally seen and holds for most parts that, when corn is well sold at Danzig, then all sorts of cloth and kersies sell away roundly in Poland, for by that means both the gentlemen and the clowns have money to pay their debts and take new credit.'[4]

Peace, which had eliminated many of the difficulties and dangers of commerce, concomitantly freed much capital which had previously found its profitable uses curtailed by war, or else had been attracted to investment in privateering, with its specious promise of dazzling profit. Mercantile capital now turned to peaceful outlets. This particularly applied to the outports of the South-west, Plymouth, Exeter and Bristol, whose merchants had previously been engrossed in warlike adventures or hampered in their trade by the dangers of the routes to south-west Europe, and who now turned to colonial ventures and to dealings with the newly opened markets in Spain and Portugal.[5]

[1] Scott, I, 130–1, 141; Friis, chapter ii; Fisher, 'London's Export Trade', 154.
[2] Anon, *Discourse . . . for . . . Enlargement . . . of Trade* (1645), p. 30. In the previous year there had been a restriction of individual dealings (*Discourse*, p. 31).
[3] *Remembrancia*, II, 285.   [4] *H.M.C. Sackville*, II, 189.
[5] For the benefit of this trade there was issued in 1607 the fourth edition of a book originally published in 1589: J[ohn] B[rowne], *The Merchants Avizo*, which was a guide to mercantile practice for apprentices and factors of merchants trading to the Iberian peninsula. It had been written in Bristol and dedicated to the Bristol Company of Merchants.

The campaign for free trade which broke out in the 1604 Parliament is best seen against this background of capital—and specifically provincial capital—seeking employment in peaceful commerce. The movement to free commerce from company regulation was, indeed, part of the general hostility of outport merchants to the control exercised by London and its companies over lines of trade. To these merchants the insuperable difficulty of the regulated company was that, in attempting to restrict competition between sellers by appointed times and places for sale, it gave a decided advantage to the wealthier traders, who could afford to bear with the relatively longer turnover of capital. It is much more likely that the agitation for the bills for free trade, which coincided with the Spanish peace, expressed the pressure of provincial, and perhaps London, mercantile capital at the prospect of trade expansion[1] than any long-term discontent with company organization provoked by the economic dislocations of the 1590's.[2] In Sandys' famous 'Instructions Touching the Bill for Free Trade'[3] there is hardly a mention of depression, or of free trade as a remedy for a slump. Nearly all the arguments are directly or indirectly concerned with the limitations imposed by companies on potential expansion: 'Under our gracious Salamon, a Prince of wisdom and peace, we are like to be in league or amity with all nations; whereby, as there will be greater freedom abroad to trade to all places, so fit to have greater at home for all persons to trade. This alteration of times may make that fit now, which in times of hostility might have seemed unfit.' And in answer to the objection that if their trade were thrown open the Merchant Adventurers would cease trading and leave stocks of cloth unsold (as they had done in 1588), Sandys claimed that 'the times being well altered from war to peace, this mischief would be but short, and other merchants soon grow to take their places, if they should, as (being rich) they may, forsake them'.

The bill, of course, never passed into law. But two years later Parliament summarily rejected plans to establish a company trading to Spain. In 1604 the original charter for a Spanish company (1577) had been confirmed, but fear of opposition prevented enforcement while Parliament was sitting and in 1605 a new charter was issued.[4] This had named 308 outport merchants (286 from the south-west ports) as opposed to 287 Londoners;[5] it also provided for a low entrance fee of £10. Nevertheless,

[1] Scott, I, 123–4; Friis, pp. 149–50; Fisher, 'Commercial Trends', 117.
[2] For this view, see Stone, 117.
[3] Reprinted in A. E. Bland, P. A. Brown and R. H. Tawney (eds.), *English Economic History, Select Documents* (1914), pp. 443–53.
[4] Friis, p. 156; a draft is in S.P.D. Jas. I, 14/21.
[5] The names of the London merchants show the broad-based nature of the company: important Levant and Eastland merchants, and Merchant Adventurers were included. This

the 1606 Parliament passed a bill stipulating freedom of trade to Spain, Portugal and France;[1] the outporters were clearly opposed, in all circumstances, to company organization which involved both London membership and privileged trading areas. Fear of London's commanding position was too strong—even during a boom such as that which the cloth trade experienced after the accession of James I.

The years under discussion were not free from intermittent official anxiety concerning other aspects of trade—and more particularly a supposed loss of coin.[2] In the main this resulted from bimetallic disturbances producing first an outflow of gold, up to 1611 when that metal was enhanced, and then a drain of silver. The bad harvest of 1608, it is true, drove wheat prices up to their second highest level of the period 1600-40 and necessitated heavy imports of grain,[3] which induced the sudden export of ready money: 'The dearth of corn in England of late ... hath been a great cause of transportation of our coin beyond the seas, for the provision thereof.'[4] But it seems unlikely that there was any chronic balance-of-payments problem, even though contemporaries, as was usual, sometimes confused a bimetallic or gross movement of treasure with the net losses of an unfavourable balance.[5] In the absence of a marked decline in overseas demand for English cloth neither the high prices for grain, nor any export of money there might have been, were significant enough to affect profoundly the prosperity of the economy.

Thus in the short run English exports were reasonably well maintained, and the cloth industry with them. But in the longer view the years between 1604 and 1614, for the old draperies, were merely the calm before the storm—the assumption of a position which could not be maintained. Two documents from 1610 bear witness that some men at the time fully realized the dangers inherent in a growing foreign manufacture of woollen textiles served by continental supplies of raw material, of which England no longer had a quasi-monopoly. They argued that wool and cloth prices

was partly common form—the leading London merchants often being non-trading members of some few companies—but in part it may have reflected the pressure to trade to the new market.

[1] 3 Jac. I, c. 6. In 1607 it was stipulated that the 1606 statute should in no way impeach the rights of the long-established Company of Merchant Adventurers of Exeter trading to France (4 Jac. I, c. 9).
[2] Below, pp. 165-7, 179-82.
[3] J. E. Thorold Rogers, *A History of Agriculture and Prices* (Oxford, 1866-87), v, 270. Grain imports to London by aliens alone in 1609 were over 40,000 quarters (E. 190/14/5); Mrs A. M. Millard kindly supplied me with this information. For government attempts to limit and control grain consumption see Steele, I, nos. 1058, 1062, 1068; Leonard, p. 144.
[4] Add. MSS. 10113, fol. 206. Cf. fol. 222 which claimed that in the three years prior to 1611 'there was ... imported in corn to the loss of £200,000'.
[5] Add. MSS. 10113, fols. 122, 198. In 1615 Sir Lionel Cranfield, working with customs figures, found that the balance of trade for 1605-11 was, on the average, favourable (Lans. MSS. 152, fol. 175).

were too high in view of the fact that 'now of late times the countries of the Netherlands, Lower Germany, France, Spain and Italy do all make great store of cloths, and practise daily more and more by wools of Spain, and of the East Country and other, which of force must impair the vent of our cloths'.[1] To the superficial observer, however, there seemed little cause for anxiety; 1614 was the crest of a prosperous wave for trade in general[2] and the Adventurers in particular. Complacency about England's situation might well have tipped the scales in the decision on whether to interfere with the structure of industry and trade. But it was only when the abortive Cockayne project precipitated events that the textile industry was left facing the reality of competition and a future which was far from rosy.

[1] Lans. MSS. 152, fol. 229. This document was probably by Richard Gore, who also composed Lans. MSS. 152, fol. 221. Gore was an active and important Merchant Adventurer, a Deputy in 1601 and 1614. See Lans. MSS. 150, fols. 21, 24; Hargrave MSS. 321, pp. 144-5; C.J. I, 229, 252, 432; Add. MSS. 14027, fols. 287ff.; A.P.C. 1613-1614, p. 389.

[2] Average annual customs for the five-year period 1611/12-1615/16 exceeded by 35 per cent those for 1599-1603 (Scott, I, 130).

2. THE COCKAYNE PROJECT, 1614-1617

From 1614 to 1617 the development of the textile industry was conditioned by the Cockayne project. In later years pamphleteers were to look back at the disastrous experiment in dyeing and dressing cloth exports and attribute to its influence the stagnation of the cloth industry in the following three decades. It may be that Alderman Cockayne's project did no more than precipitate an inevitable course of events, but there can be no doubt as to the immediate violent effects it produced both in the manufacturing areas and in the organization of the textile trade. It enables us to date with some certainty the beginning of the real decline in what had formerly been England's one staple product—the old draperies.

The story of the project has already been told in voluminous detail.[1] Nevertheless the salient features of the developments in these years are worth emphasizing and, in the process, it may be possible to distinguish some hitherto neglected aspects of the project.

(i) THE ISSUES INVOLVED

In 1606 and 1614 well over a half of London's total cloth exports, and a much greater proportion of the Merchant Adventurers' shipments, consisted of 'white' cloths deriving from the western counties,[2] and these went overwhelmingly to Germany and the Low Countries where they were dyed and dressed by local workmen. It was only natural that it should occur to men at the time that the value of, and the employment derived from, textile exports could be greatly increased if they were in the form of fully-manufactured (dyed and dressed) cloths. It was estimated in 1614 that dyeing and dressing woollen textiles would add anything from 50 to 100 per cent to the value of exports, while in sixteenth-century Leyden dyeing accounted for 47 per cent of the final manufacturing cost of cloth.[3] In an age whose economic policy frequently revolved around the twin aims of maximizing exports and the employment of the poor, the export of only semi-manufactured textiles could not but seem a shameful waste, and schemes to produce the desired metamorphosis—to redirect the emphasis of the English cloth manufacture and by-pass the Dutch finishing industry—had a history stretching back into the sixteenth

[1] Friis, chapters iv, v.
[2] See Appendix A, Tables 4 and 9.
[3] Add. MSS. 14027, fols. 265-6, reprinted in Friis, pp. 461-3; J. F. Niermeyer, *De Wording van onze Volkshuishouding* (The Hague, 1946), p. 76.

century. Indeed, the practice of licensing the export of white cloths had arisen in the sixteenth century to circumvent the legislation forbidding the export of cloth, above a certain value, which was not 'barbed, rowed and shorn'.[1] In 1601 the Earl of Cumberland secured a licence for the unlimited export of undressed cloth, and in 1602 the Merchant Adventurers acquired the sole right to use it on payment of 2s. 2d. per cloth.

In 1606 there had been an unsuccessful movement, backed by the London Company of Clothworkers and Alderman Cockayne, an Eastland merchant, to enforce the dressing of coloured cloths—principally Somerset and Essex fabrics.[2] But in 1613 Cockayne's far more grandiose plan, to dye and dress every cloth exported, was being discussed.[3] Negotiations proceeded into 1614. In July a proclamation forbade the export of white cloths (this in any case applied only to the Merchant Adventurers) after 2 November, while giving the right to export fully-manufactured textiles to all those who, before 20 September, underwrote specific amounts to be exported in the next three years. In December the Adventurers' charter was suspended and the projectors, led by Cockayne, were left in control of the trade to Germany and the Low Countries.[4]

Events had taken a startling turn. The hesitancy of generations of privy councillors had finally been overcome, the organization of 'the most famous company of merchants in Christendom' had been overthrown, and in a very real sense England's prosperity had become the object of a gigantic gamble, at least on the part of the government, as to whether England was capable of producing, and Holland willing to buy, a new type of product. And, for once, wholesale governmental interference in the course of trade could not attempt to justify itself by pointing to a pressing national emergency or some violent economic dislocation. For the traditional cloth trade 1614 was the *annus mirabilis*, whose level of exports (127,200) exceeded all past figures and was never again equalled in the period. The Adventurers alone shipped almost 100,000 cloths.[5] 'There is no complaint', it was said, 'for want of vent of their cloth in the six western counties' of Wiltshire, Somerset, Gloucestershire, Worcestershire, Oxfordshire and Herefordshire; and the company saw

[1] For an outline of the regulations applied to undressed cloth and licensing under the Tudors, see S.P.D. Eliz., 270/128.
[2] Suffolk, Kent and Reading cloths were by then exported dressed. For the 1606 plan see *C.J.* I, 288, 291; S.P.D. Jas. I, 20/9, fols. 29-30, 20/9*, fol. 27. For a similar scheme in 1599 see S.P.D. Eliz., 271/3.
[3] Friis, pp. 239-70.
[4] Steele, I, nos. 1148, 1154. The charter was finally relinquished in February 1615 (S.P.D. Jas. I, 80/38).
[5] The projectors later accused the company of having purposefully exported more than usual in order to over-stock the market and sabotage the project (*A.P.C. 1615-1616*, p. 30).

The Cockayne Project, 1614–1617

no reason to tamper with the organization of trade as 'we are now sure of . . . a certain and ample vent of the commodities of this kingdom'.[1] Clearly, those who pressed for interference must have had strong motives for so doing.

On the side of the government there was undoubted sincerity; although bribes were in fact distributed this was no more than standard procedure. Besides the increase in the value of exports and the possibility of extra employment, the government hoped to augment revenue by £40,000: £20,000 for customs on dyestuffs and 5s. per dyed and dressed cloth on 80,000 exported.[2] Clearly, the Privy Council, although its doubts were strong and James himself, proud and obstinate, had to push through the final decision, was seeking what was, by the standards of an age un-illuminated by the doctrine of comparative costs, the further good to be derived from the substitution of a fully- for a semi-manufactured export. On the other hand it is impossible not to question the integrity of the projectors under Cockayne. They had secured their privileges on the basis of an original confident promise to handle 50,000 dyed and dressed cloths,[3] which in any case presupposed that they would inherit the Adventurers' principal licence for 30,000 white cloths. But they could hardly have shown less enthusiasm for carrying this promise into effect. In spite of the proclamation of July 1614 which banned the export of unfinished cloths after 2 November, the new company, once in possession of its powers, early in 1615 secured liberty 'to carry [cloths] out undyed and undressed till they can provide sufficient store of workmen and materials, which', the writer continued, 'will be God knows when, which is thought hard that the ancient possessors should be turned out to make place for newcomers and strangers upon the same conditions'.[4] Nothing had been done by May—'There hath not been a cloth dyed nor dressed since Xmas more than usual'[5]—and only the government's insistence produced a contract to export, as from midsummer 1615, 6,000, 12,000, and 18,000 finished cloths in successive 'years'—a far cry from the optimism of 1614. The price of this promise was a charter and increased supervisory powers over trade.[6] Significantly, the charter guaranteed to the King's Merchant Adventurers (as they now were) the old company's licence for the export of 30,000 'unrowed, unbarbed and unshorn' cloths together with the exclusive use of Cumberland's licence for white exports in excess of this

[1] S.P.D. Jas. I, 72/70; Lans. MSS. 152, fols. 285, 291.
[2] A.P.C. 1613–1614, p. 303; Lans. MSS. 152, fols. 263–4, 291; Friis, p. 240.
[3] Add. MSS. 14027, fols. 261–2, 263–4, 265–6. See Friis, pp. 458–60, 461–3.
[4] S.P.D. Jas. I, 80/38.
[5] S.P.D. Jas. I, 80/108. See the export figures for the first three months of 1614 and of 1615 (S.P.D. Jas. I, 80/58).
[6] A.P.C. 1615–1616, pp. 176, 190, 217–22.

figure. The project had begun to take on the appearance of a change in the personnel rather than the products of the English cloth trade.

In later discussions it materialized that the King's Merchant Adventurers were guilty of some duplicity even in their meagre attempts to fulfil their obligations, since they often only dyed cloths slightly (thus allowing a final finishing abroad), or counted in their totals cloths dyed in the wool and inferior sorts of textiles.[1] The project has been viewed, in large part, as the response of Cockayne and other Eastland merchants to the competition of English cloth finished in Holland: as an attempt, in conjunction with merchants trading to the Levant and Russia, to secure the direct export of English cloth to their respective privileged areas, whether it was finished or not.[2] But these merchants did not normally trade to the principal final markets for English textiles, which in fact lay in the hinterlands of the marts used by the old Merchant Adventurers. If we assume that the projectors' only intent was to maintain their *own trades* with the textiles formerly handled by the old company, then it certainly could not be true that 'direct exportation to the countries where the cloth was used was Cockayne's real object'.[3] It is readily apparent that they had no strong desire to carry into effect the comprehensive plans for dyeing and dressing, but this was not because the question was immaterial to Cockayne and the projectors: on the contrary, they must have realized that it was important *not* to do so. In fact it seems that the plan was a calculated attempt to capture a portion of the profitable trade in white cloths to Germany and the Low Countries, while utilizing such dyed and dressed woollens as *were* produced to provide exports to the regions in which they had pre-existing privileges. Hence the significance in the new company of members of other trading groups: the Eastland company provided the Governor, Deputy, Treasurer and seven assistants, and the Levant and Italy merchants five.[4] These were the merchants with 'a double benefit over others'; the Eastland and Turkey traders, it was claimed, intended to dress and dye only two or four cloths in twenty for their own markets and export white cloths to Hamburg and Middelburg, while the ex-Adventurers who joined were promised continued facilities for the export of unfinished cloth to Germany and the Low Countries.[5] English merchants trading to the Baltic had, in 1602, petitioned in vain for the right to export undressed cloth, and twelve

---

[1] S.P.D. Jas. I, 80/125; Add. MSS. 14027, fols. 281–2 (Friis, pp. 463–6); Lans. MSS. 152, fols. 267–8 (Friis, pp. 472–3).
[2] Friis, pp. 224 ff., especially pp. 238–9.
[3] Friis, p. 239.
[4] Friis, pp. 281–4.
[5] S.P.D. Jas. I, 80/125–6.

years later it was said that 'the very same men of the Eastland company were they that followed it then, which now do follow this new project'.¹ Certainly, in the course of the experiment, the new company were insistent that they be allowed to ship finished cloths (as some of them did at the very beginning) to other areas in which they were privileged, rather than to Germany and the Low Countries as the government desired; and in October 1616 this right was granted.² But, far more importantly, the new men used the project in an attempt to prise open the rich trade in undressed cloths, to secure a share in it by initially promising to finish all textiles exports and then persuading the former Adventurers to participate in a new division of the old trade. The members of the old company, it was hoped, would be starved into submission, forced to join the projectors in order to employ their capital, and throughout the years 1614 to 1616 they were continuously offered membership of the King's Merchant Adventurers on favourable terms. In the event the old company played their hand carefully and successfully. From the beginning, on being called on to relinquish their charter, they made clear their assumption that the project was solely concerned with dyeing and dressing and that if this aspect should fail then the project would fall to the ground and the old company naturally be restored.³ Throughout subsequent years they never acknowledged any right of the new company to trade in undressed cloths. In the event, very few of the wealthiest Adventurers entered the new company, although a sizeable group of the old traders did participate—forced in by necessity.⁴ Instead the most important elements abstained from the cloth trade and a significant number channelled their capital into alternative uses, notably the capital market and the East India Company.⁵ This was probably the principal reason for the ultimate failure of Cockayne's company to handle even the trade in undressed cloth.

Whatever their real motives, the projectors had to act publicly as if they were convinced of the feasibility of the plan. On its side the Privy Council, in the preliminary negotiations, demanded satisfaction on a

¹ S.P.D. Jas. I, 72/70. The 1602 petition, which coincided with the negotiations which finally gave the Adventurers exclusive use of Cumberland's licence, is in *H.M.C. Sackville*, I, 35–8.
² See Friis, pp. 464–8, where contemporary documents are reproduced. Also *A.P.C. 1615–1616*, pp. 456–7, *A.P.C. 1616–1617*, pp. 53–4.
³ Friis, pp. 268–9.
⁴ S.P.D. Jas. I, 80/125, 127; *A.P.C. 1615–1616*, pp. 10–11, 30; Friis, pp. 281–2, 304. Some of these traders were forced to join the projectors because the bulk of their capital was overseas and this was the only way in which the government allowed them to utilize it.
⁵ For the influx of capital to the East India trade, and the money market, see Add. MSS. 34324, fol. 203; G. Malynes, *The Maintenance of Free Trade* (1622), p. 51; Cotton MSS. Galba, E. 1. fol. 363. The East India Company secured subscriptions of £1,400,000 in 1617: S.P.D. Jas. I, 90/53.

number of points. Firstly, with regard to the ability of English industry to handle an enormous increase in the output of fully-dressed cloth: while the Merchant Adventurers claimed that workmanship was poor, materials hard to obtain, and the prospect of increasing facilities highly dubious, the projectors managed to convince the council that English technical ability was sufficiently high and that men and materials would be readily available for the development of a new branch of the textile industry.[1] Secondly, from the commencement of the discussions it was appreciated that there was a danger that foreign countries might retaliate by banning the import of English cloth and stimulating the further development of their own textile industries. The projectors assured the council that this was impossible without English raw material, and that if this were effectively retained at home 'they cannot live without our cloth, albeit dyed and dressed in England'. Although the Merchant Adventurers vehemently confuted this thesis, indicating the ready availability of supplies of wool from Spain, Germany, France, Turkey, and elsewhere, and warned that manufacture had commenced overseas even in anticipation of the project, the government seems to have minimized this danger.[2] As the project got under way there were renewed attempts to ban the export of wool, fuller's earth and yarn.[3] The projectors were, consciously or unconsciously, misleading the council on this point, or perhaps they were merely confirming an erroneous view of European wool supplies which not even the disasters of the next decade were fully able to dispel from the minds of some Englishmen. England, the painful lesson was to teach, did not possess a monopoly of wool nor of facilities for cloth manufacture. And the myth that she did, which took so long to dissipate, must bear a large part of the responsibility for the disastrous long-term repercussion of the Cockayne project in providing a hot-house for the growth of continental textile production.

A further matter for keen investigation before the project was sanctioned was the capital or 'stock' available to Cockayne and his group to be used in the cloth trade. It was estimated that some £700,000 was needed annually to buy up the cloth that came to London for export. Unless this were forthcoming the government would be faced with unrest among unemployed weavers and spinners even though the European markets might be clamouring for English cloth. The projectors claimed that they had over one million pounds underwritten,[4] and this served to reassure the government that there would be no difficulties from

[1] See the documents reproduced in Friis, pp. 460–3; also S.P.D. Jas. I, 72/70.
[2] For these discussions see the documents in Friis, pp. 458–63.
[3] *A.P.C. 1613–1614*, pp. 546, 561; Steele, I, no. 1150; *A.P.C. 1615–1616*, pp. 68–9.
[4] See the documents in Friis, pp. 460–3.

lack of means. But in the event the promises were not fulfilled. Many original subscribers, who in the first flush of optimism had underwritten specific amounts of cloth, failed to perform their 'stints' and the most significant anxiety of the projectors became the lack of capital.[1] This shortage of funds can mainly be attributed to the determination of the leading members of the old company not to join the new—in spite of the successive efforts of the latter, who obviously realized their central weakness and had relied on co-operation to enable them to finance the great trade across the narrow seas. By the proclamation of July 1614, merchants were to be accepted into the new company up to 20 September. In October, however, the old Merchant Adventurers were informed that they could still come in if they wished. The charter of the King's Merchant Adventurers, in mid-1615, extended the period of grace yet once more— until September. In the autumn of 1616, when things were going very badly for them, the projectors even invited the old traders to join their company without paying any fees.[2]

But these efforts failed, and the projectors were stalemated: whatever their real aims they had to satisfy the council that they were concerned to carry out the dyeing and dressing part of the bargain. With more power than they ever anticipated and less scope for manœuvre and less capital than they had originally hoped, Cockayne and his fellows were left to stumble on into three years of miserable experiment, which produced the first of the series of convulsions which shook the broadcloth industry in the years before the Civil War.

(ii) THE COURSE OF TRADE

Early in 1615 John Chamberlain wrote to Sir Dudley Carleton in Holland: 'the new company have all at their will; yet they are already puzzled for that the clothiers begin to complain and make petitions for want of utterance of their cloth.' The company had run into difficulties as soon as it assumed its full powers. In spite of the fact that, as yet, it had no obligation to export dyed and dressed cloth, and had secured the power to ship whites alone, it was failing to buy up the cloths which came to London.[3] Compared with the same period in the previous year, the first three months of 1615 saw a fall in undressed exports of over 8,500 shortcloths and almost 4,500 longcloths, which in each case was a decline of well over 50 per cent.[4] By May 'the great project of dyeing and dressing

[1] Below, pp. 40–1, 46–9.
[2] Lans. MSS. 152, fols. 252, 278.
[3] S.P.D. Jas. I, 80/38.
[4] S.P.D. Jas. I, 80/58. Shipments of Suffolk shortcloths (which *were* dyed) fell from 1,929½ to 922½.

cloth is now at a stand, and they know not well how to go forward nor backward, for the clothiers do generally complain that their cloth lies on their hand, and the clothworkers and dyers weary the King and council with petitions wherein they complain that they are in worse case than before'. By midsummer the price of cloth had fallen £10 per pack.[1]

This dangerous decline in the normally important spring purchases of undressed cloths by exporters can, perhaps, be partly attributed to the abundance of textiles already in the Low Countries consequent upon the 1614 boom. Indeed, the old Adventurers in July 1614 had warned the council against going ahead with the project just when the Dutch had purchased a year's supply of cloth.[2] Certainly, the famous Dutch edict banning the import of dyed and dressed cloth, which had already been promulgated,[3] could have had little influence at this juncture since there were no English restrictions on the export of undressed cloth. Either the market demand was not there or, if it was, the projectors were unable to satisfy it. The latter seems much more likely. The projectors were already experiencing the shortage of capital which was to bedevil them throughout their short period of power.

The market for white cloth was one which had to be sustained by constant supplies of liquid capital. If merchants' means were such that they could not buy all the cloth coming up to London at the busy times of the year without having to wait for the 'returns' from the earlier shipments, then the repercussions could be widespread and dangerous. It had been estimated that under 50 per cent of the £700,000 worth of cloth exports were on credit, 'the rest in money';[4] and the Merchant Adventurers had earlier warned that

> the market for white cloth is so quick as that without money hardly find you your turns served. For the clothier he giveth no time nor carryeth his cloth from house to house to seek his merchants as the coloured clothiers do, but goeth home with his money in his purse, that he may pay his workmen, and follow his trade ... so his light and often returns maintain a living and give the poor people work.[5]

This need not have been a question of actually possessing liquid assets in England, but at the least merchants had to have sufficient credit to be able

---

[1] S.P.D. Jas. I, 80/108, 126.
[2] Document in Friis, pp. 461–3. See *A.P.C. 1615–1616*, p. 30 for the allegation of the new company that the Adventurers had exported an abnormal amount in 1614 in order 'industriously ... to clog the trade, and to take away, as much as in them did lie, all possibility either of sale or return from the said new company'.
[3] *A.P.C. 1615–1616*, p. 220; Friis, p. 277.
[4] Document in Friis, p. 460.
[5] Lans. MSS. 152, fol. 284.

to take up money by bills of exchange. As Misselden wrote: 'The English merchants which trade into Germany and the Low Countries do buy their cloth with ready money, *when other merchants that have not the benefit of the exchange, are fain to take time of the clothiers, to pay them at the return of their estates in wares.*'[1] Thus either the merchant had to have the money on hand or he had to be of sufficient standing to borrow it. It seems clear that this was the main stumbling-block for the Cockayne group, who, even in normal times, simply could not match the resources or the credit of the old company. 'Trust', in the words of an Italian anecdote, 'is the merchant's treasure and the more trust a merchant inspireth the richer he is.'[2] In this and in the real sense the projectors were poor. Deserted by the Adventurers, they could not muster sufficient 'stock' to maintain the cloth market—their assets, being small, too easily became frozen.[3] Hence pressure was brought to bear on the old company to pool its resources: 'our late dissolved Merchant Adventurers think they are hardly dealt with, to be barred from bringing their goods that are abroad, or carrying out any hence, unless they will join with the new company, which having undertaken that they are not able to perform, make all means to drive them to it by compulsion.' But no agreement could be reached with the main body.[4] The projectors had to continue virtually alone, although the small-scale traders who were forced to join them might have given some temporary aid. The £1,100,000 promised was clearly of little practical importance—there was no real substitute for the capital and entrepreneurial skill which had been withdrawn from the cloth trade.

Since original expectations were so high the government, in the troubles of mid-1615, was still primarily concerned with the failure to dye and dress cloths. Negotiations with the Merchant Adventurers proving useless, the new company was held to its original course, although it was now realized that the introduction of the changes in manufacture would have to be more gradual and that, in the face of a falling market, the projectors would have to be strengthened. In the summer of 1615 they contracted to export, in successive years starting on 1 June, 6,000, 12,000 and 18,000 fully-manufactured cloths. In return they obtained, as already noted, a charter with full rights to export undressed textiles, extended powers of commercial regulation, a promise of government aid in dealing

[1] Misselden, *The Circle of Commerce*, p. 109. My italics.
[2] J. W. Thompson, *Economic and Social History of Europe in the Later Middle Ages* (New York, 1931), p. 436.
[3] To judge from the decline in the export of Suffolk shortcloths (S.P.D. Jas. I, 80/58), which were the staple of the Eastland trade, the Eastland element in the new company was finding its resources stretched too far to allow it to maintain even its own trade.
[4] S.P.D. Jas. I, 80/71, 108, 110; *A.P.C. 1615–1616*, pp. 10–11, 30, 167–8.

with the Dutch ban on dressed imports and in finding—if necessary—a new residence, and a further prohibition on the export of wool.[1] Nevertheless, nothing had been done which promised to expand the resources of the King's Merchant Adventurers.

Early in 1616 trouble again arose over the general condition of the cloth trade and the particular failings of the new merchants. 1615 had seen a considerable decline in the export of the staple white broadcloths, and production had fallen by perhaps as much as 16,000 shortcloths.[2] The export of white cloths for the period 30 October 1614 to 1 November 1615 was over 20 per cent below that for the same period two years earlier,[3] the sale of Suffolk shortcloths continued to suffer,[4] and in many respects the King's Merchant Adventurers were not fulfilling their obligations with regard to the fully-manufactured textiles which they *did* export. From the subsequent discussions a confused picture emerged of the 'want of stock', of the hindrances imposed by foreign governments on the trade in English cloth, of state-subsidized production abroad, and of increased supplies of European wool.[5] At this juncture the council's patience with the projectors came very near breaking point as they demanded that they be awarded new and increased powers and rights in order to encourage the export of dyed and dressed cloth, and especially that they might ship the latter to areas other than Germany and Holland. It even seemed possible that the old company might be restored. But once again James insisted that his pet 'project be carried forward against the better judgement of his councillors: 'After much canvassing and debating at the council table', wrote Chamberlain, 'Alderman Cockayne and his new company have carried away the bucklers from the Merchant Adventurers, contrary to the opinion of the major part, but the king overruled the case; I pray God it may prove well for him and the realm.'[6] The projectors were allowed to continue on condition that finished cloths should be sent to the mart towns (Middelburg and Hamburg) for three months in the first instance—and only if they then remained unsold could they be re-exported elsewhere. Further, it was stipulated that after the first three years the King's Merchant Adventurers should continue to ship

---

[1] *A.P.C. 1615–1616*, pp. 176, 190, 217–22. The charter recognized the need for more capital by extending the period in which the old traders could join the new company. The grant of incorporation was made on 29 August 1615 (*C.S.P.D. 1611–1618*, p. 305); the charter is reproduced in Bland, Brown and Tawney, pp. 454–60.
[2] Document in Friis, p. 465.
[3] I owe this reference to the kindness of Mr R. T. Spence, who derived it from an analysis of the accounts of the Earl of Cumberland's licence.
[4] 1615 probably saw a fall of 3,000 in their export (document in Friis, p. 467).
[5] Documents in Friis, pp. 463–6.
[6] S.P.D. Jas. I, 86/111 (27 March 1616). Also see *A.P.C. 1615–1616*, pp. 374–5, 376, 386–7, 410–12, 416–17; S.P.D. Jas. I, 86/40, 48, 55; documents in Friis, pp. 466–8.

The Cockayne Project, 1614–1617

at least 18,000 dyed and dressed cloths yearly. On the other hand the council, at the company's request, put its weight behind the policy of confining the export trade in undressed cloth to London and backed the company in its attempt to rate the export of finished textiles according to the amounts of other cloth and goods shipped by individual merchants.[1]

Things were going very badly for the projectors. While their inability to handle the white cloth became increasingly apparent, they had to tackle the hopeless task of forcing finished cloth into European markets which either did not want them or were restricted by a governmental prohibition of such English textiles. It was true that by July 1616 the company had achieved the required stint for the first year and managed to export 6,000 fully-manufactured cloths,[2] but this, small as the amount was, had obviously been done only with the greatest difficulty: the company had had to tie the sale of dyed to that of white cloths, and some of its members were forced 'to lose upon the dyed cloths, and gain upon the white'.[3] Meanwhile, as the English export-trade floundered along incompetently, competitive manufacture abroad increased. The future did not augur well and the producing areas at home began their protests at commercial stagnation.

In August the council had to consider complaints by the Gloucestershire clothiers 'debarred from their usual sale of their cloth'. The new company protested that the cloths were badly made, that they themselves had unsold stocks of £400,000 as against the clothiers' £5,000 or £6,000, and that they were handicapped since some of the original underwriters were failing to purchase their stints. Although the council remonstrated with the reluctant underwriters and commanded the company to buy up the clothiers' stocks, nothing had been achieved in this direction by September.[4] It quickly became apparent that the government had a serious textile depression on its hands. Unemployment was rife, cloth had fallen in price, the cloth customs had declined by more than 25 per cent, and, it was claimed, 'in Gloucestershire, Worcestershire and Wiltshire either one half or a third part of the looms are abated'. White cloth, for the first time in months, could 'be sold alone without dyed and dressed coupled with them, yet will . . . not so away'.[5] Stocks of western cloth accumulated in London and to the King's Merchant Adventurers it seemed a 'hard time which hath no precedent', the merchant being 'so many ways already

[1] A.P.C. 1615–1616, pp. 456–60, 524–5; S.P.D. Jas. I, 86/112.
[2] A.P.C. 1615–1616, pp. 658–9.
[3] Document in Friis, p. 463.
[4] S.P.D. Jas. I, 88/40, 45; A.P.C. 1616–1617, pp. 1–4, 7–9.
[5] See Lans. MSS. 152, fols. 271–8.

engaged, toiled, entangled'.[1] Significantly, the slump was hitting western counties, where white broadcloth was the staple product, most severely. Amid widespread complaints the council wrote to Gloucestershire, Somerset, Wiltshire and Worcestershire—the leading textile counties in the West—requesting full details of the fall in their sales, and discovered a sorry state of affairs.[2] In London Sir Lionel Cranfield (who ceased active trade before the project and whose various government positions were to lead to the Lord High Treasurership in 1621) claimed that 'in the old Merchant Adventurers' time there never was any stand of cloth before and at the shipping as now it is', and that, in any case, it was most unlikely that the projectors would be able to achieve their second stint of 12,000 dressed cloths. Meanwhile the new Adventurers pleaded that, with £400,000 worth of cloth unsold at Middelburg, they 'must have vent there or help here'.[3] Compared with 1614, exports to the Low Countries and Germany in 1616 had diminished by more than one-third, and total shipments of shortcloths from London fell from 127,000 to 88,200.[4]

In the autumn of 1616 a fresh round of discussions and investigations followed the realization that not only was the project itself failing to produce the desired result, but dislocation was extending to the normal lines of industry and trade. These negotiations demonstrated the embarrassment of the Cockayne group which had led to the depression and also provided some insight into the more general difficulties which were beginning to eat away at the prosperity of the English textile industry.

Some spokesmen claimed that the Dutch restrictions on the import of dyed and dressed cloth 'is supposed to be the principal cause of the stand of cloth at home'.[5] While this clearly limited the possible achievements of the experiment, it also reduced sales of white cloths as long as the new company invested in dyed and dressed textiles and coupled them with undressed for sale abroad. In the council's view this problem could best be solved by counter-pressure, and it offered official help against the Netherlands, even to the point of agreeing to a removal of the mart from Middelburg. Plans were in fact advanced for the shift (possibly to Flanders), but naturally the projectors were reluctant to leave the rich, established trade in white cloth and objected on the grounds that they had obligations, and debts due, in Middelburg, that the cost of moving would prove prohibitive, and that the relevant textiles were suitable only for the market in the Low Countries. Nevertheless they had to give at least paper

[1] S.P.D. Jas. I, 88/83; *A.P.C. 1616–1617*, pp. 17–18.
[2] S.P.D. Jas. I, 88/89; *A.P.C. 1616–1617*, pp. 20–2; Lans. MSS. 152, fols. 249–51.
[3] Lans. MSS. 152, fols. 267–8.
[4] Friis, p. 326; Fisher, 'London's Export Trade', 153.
[5] *A.P.C. 1616–1617*, p. 8. Cf. p. 2.

The Cockayne Project, 1614–1617 45

acquiescence to the preparations for economic warfare entailed in the projected ban on trade with the Low Countries. But the prohibition was never put into effect: negotiations with the States and vacillations continued right up to the end of the project.[1] More in line with the projectors' early aims to capture the white trade and use finished cloth for their pre-existing trade, were their plans to solve the problems posed by the Netherlands' prohibition by allowing the export of dyed and dressed cloths to areas, other than the Low Countries and Germany, in which they were already privileged. They claimed this had been the arrangement at the commencement of the experiment—without which some of their members would not have participated.[2] The council, at first opposed to this step, ultimately, in October, agreed (after consultation with the Eastland, Turkey, Russian and French merchants) in a desperate and belated attempt to save the project.[3]

To a considerable extent, however, these problems were only on the periphery of the basic and immediate issue. This was the general decline in the prosperity of *all* types of old drapery. Quite apart from the effects of artificial restrictions on the trade in dyed and dressed fabrics there were other factors at work which hindered commercial dealings in white broadcloth.

Some anxiety was provoked by the relatively high price of wool which, combined with the pressure on the price of cloth, seemed to be forcing many clothiers out of business. If, through the growth of foreign manufacture and dislocations in the textile trade, there was a declining market for cloth why was this not reflected in falling prices for raw materials? The answer given by contemporaries was that wool remained in relatively scarce supply, as far as the traditional manufacture was concerned, because of the demands of the new draperies, or even of export: 'In Wiltshire, within two years last past a great number of looms laid down, but wools better sold and more dear than ever heretofore, which argumenteth a transportation of wool over sea, or an increase of new drapery here.' In September 1616 it was claimed that the price of cloth had fallen 10 per cent and that of wool had increased by the same proportion, that the new 'drapery consumes a third part at least of the wools of England and

---

[1] For all this, see *A.P.C. 1616–1617*, pp. 9, 11–12, 26–7, 55; Lans. MSS. 152, fols. 247, 249–50, 253–4, 255–6, 259, 260–1, 263–4, 265–6; S.P.D. Jas. I, 89/39, 55, 90/24; S.P.D. Chas. I, 180/77 (wrongly calendared); John Maclean (ed.), *Letters from George, Lord Carew to Sir Thomas Roe* (1860), p. 71.

[2] Lans. MSS. 152, fols. 247, 260–1, 265–6, 278; *A.P.C. 1616–1617*, pp. 24–5. Sir Julius Caesar, in a speech to the council, acknowledged that either some of the contract would have to be remitted, or the merchants would have to be allowed to send finished cloths to other areas 'where they may find best vent' (document in Friis, p. 471).

[3] *A.P.C. 1616–1617*, pp. 19, 53–4; Lans. MSS. 152, fols. 245–6.

Wales', and that the shipment of raw materials abroad seriously aggravated the situation; and the King's Merchant Adventurers particularly emphasized the need for cheaper wool in order to lower cloth prices and defeat foreign competition.[1] There were, in fact, attempts to reduce the price of raw materials based in part on the traditional assumption that middlemen served an inflationary rather than a useful function: their activities were restricted and additional controls were imposed on trade in order to prevent the export of wool.[2] This latter policy was also the means adopted to try to curb the development of European textile manufacture. In many ways it was the latter which was the most dangerous manifestation of the prevailing economic troubles. The Low Countries provided financial incentives to their own manufacturers and, in any case, production and competition grew apace: 'The Dutch undersell us in our coarser sorts, which is a great part of our trade, and our finer sorts which they cannot make, being unproportionably dear, they will rather make shift with their own meaner cloth than wear our finer at such excessive rates.'[3] It was in this sense that the Cockayne project marked the beginning of a new and uncomfortable age for English cloth, in which the successful expansion of the new draperies was matched by the painful decline of the traditional industry in the face of competition abroad and rigid costs at home.

Yet in September 1616 the cloth trade was facing a short-term crisis. Besides competition abroad or high costs at home the new company also blamed the slump on the false methods of manufacture used by English clothiers.[4] But the underlying cause of the slump could not have been any of these factors—it resided principally in the shortage of capital which, as already noted, dogged the King's Merchant Adventurers.

In 1621 the re-established Merchant Adventurers were to contrast 'the skilful and substantial merchants that usually bear a remainder of 20 or 30 thousand cloths upon their hands ... and nevertheless continue their

[1] Documents in Friis, pp. 468, 470–2, 477; cf. Lans. MSS. 152, fols. 273–8.
[2] A.P.C. 1616–1617, pp. 19, 24, 26, 35; Lans. MSS. 152, fols. 265–6. In 1615 and 1616 there had already been an extended survey of the mechanism of the home trade in wool, culminating in a council order (A.P.C. 1615–1616, pp. 624–6, 23 June 1616) which gave clothiers the sole right of purchase from May to Michaelmas. The new draperies were excepted from this policy, since their small-scale manufacturers needed the independent provision of wool by middlemen throughout all the year.
[3] See Lans. MSS. 152, fols. 273–8; A.P.C. 1616–1617, pp. 19, 28–9; documents in Friis, pp. 473–4, 477.
[4] This was a usual complaint by merchants at times of depression. In August 1616 the charge was levelled against the Gloucestershire clothiers (A.P.C. 1616–1617, pp. 1–3), while in September the merchants attacked 'the ill-dealings of the querulous clothier', for 'the clothiers are themselves the chief cause of the stop of trade whereof they so much complain' (Lans. MSS. 152, fols. 273–8). The new company requested extended powers to control false manufacture (Lans. MSS. 152, fols. 265–6). For a discussion of this question in general during the period, see below, pp. 142–6.

buying in Blackwell Hall', with the influx, during the years 1614–16, of 'ignorant weak newcomers . . . [who] with all the spurs that were almost weekly put into them by the complaints of the clothiers at the council . . . and by their orders enforcing the particular brethren to buy up the cloth, assessing certain quantities, . . . yet were not able to buy up the cloth or maintain the markets in any good measure'.[1] This opinion, prejudiced as the old company undoubtedly was, could not have been so far from the truth. It has already been seen how dependent the cloth market was on supplies of liquid capital; how the projectors, without help from the leading members of the old company, were in a weak position for handling the necessarily large output of textiles; and how, in August, with their stocks valued at £400,000 they were most reluctant to buy up Gloucestershire cloth. By September their true weakness was fully bared: some of their assets were frozen, or temporarily immobilized, in stocks of dyed and dressed cloth whose sale was going badly;[2] and in general the hindrances even to the sale of white cloths had slowed capital turnover, given the limited reserves of the new men, sufficiently to reduce drastically their purchases at Blackwell Hall. Unlike the old company, the projectors could not withstand any except the slightest delay in the normal proceedings of the cloth trade.[3] If this situation were to continue then the restoration of the old company would become inevitable.

In August the new company had complained of the shortage of capital caused by recalcitrant underwriters. The council brought pressure to bear on these men, but no satisfactory conclusion seems to have resulted since complaints by the projectors and exhortations and threats on the part of the government continued throughout the remaining months of the project.[4] There were repeated attempts to attract more capital—and especially that of the old company.[5] In any case, over half the exports in the first six months of 1616 had been shipped by the members of the original organization who had, perforce, joined the King's Merchant Adventurers.[6] While the rest held back it seemed impossible that any remedy for the 'stand' of cloth could be found. It was this stagnation of

[1] Hargrave MSS. 321, pp. 186–7.
[2] The company's real attempts to fulfil its promised quota entailed investment in products not finding a market. The movement to allow the export of this cloth directly to areas other than the Low Countries and Germany can thus be viewed as an attempt to liberate frozen capital. Sir Julius Caesar even advocated that some of the quota be remitted, 'which will exceedingly ease and encourage them'. See Lans. MSS. 152, fols. 257–8.
[3] For instances when the restored Adventurers were able to give support to the cloth market even though their own sales were not going well, see below, pp. 113–14.
[4] S.P.D. Jas. I, 88/45; A.P.C. 1616–1617, pp. 4, 11–12, 19, 23–4; Lans. MSS. 152, fols. 273–8; documents in Friis, pp. 470, 481.
[5] Lans. MSS. 152, fols. 252–4, 278; A.P.C. 1616–1617, p. 55.
[6] Friis, p. 304.

the market for textiles—and not the dyeing and dressing project—which now became the main concern of the government. With great difficulty the new company was finally persuaded, much against its will, to guarantee the purchase of the 15,000 cloths expected in London before Christmas; and its request that a weekly 'remainder' of 1,000 western cloths should not be considered a 'stand' was sharply refused by the council.[1] Even so there had to be a mandatory scheme by which individual merchants were allotted stints, for whose performance the council demanded bonds. The shortage of capital also stimulated plans for the provision of capital by the king, the council, the nobility and wealthy citizens in the hope of relieving the clogged market.[2] On the other hand suggestions were made (although they were not carried into effect) to expand the home market for textiles by making obligatory the wearing of broadcloth in outer garments and at funerals; and the threat of a proclamation to this effect served to produce a chronic decline in the prosperity of haberdashery businesses.[3]

But all this was to no avail. The situation deteriorated through the autumn and the new company became obdurate as to its inability to extend its guarantee to buy up cloths beyond Christmas unless it were assured of overseas sales or an increased market at home for fine cloths.[4] Again, and equally unsuccessfully, the old company was urged to participate in the trade on the basis of dyeing and dressing,[5] 'which course', wrote Chamberlain early in November, 'need not be taken if the thing were feasible, or that any gain were to be had by it, but as they say clothing decays apace and hath already received a great blow by this project so I pray God that these . . . conclusions do not ruin or bring down our merchants'.[6] The tide of official opinion now turned sharply against Alderman Cockayne and among the public 'some few curse [him] only and hope his hanging will be the catastrophe of all'.[7] The government's patience was exhausted, for its principal anxiety centred on the saturation of the market which the Alderman and his friends, in spite of their original promises, were patently unable to relieve. It is possible that if sales had been reasonably maintained, even though few cloths were dyed and dressed, the projectors might have continued in power. But the unsold textiles at Blackwell Hall and the council's overwhelming desire

[1] Lans. MSS. 152, fols. 262, 269–70, 271–2; *A.P.C. 1616–1617*, pp. 13, 17, 18–20, 25.
[2] S.P.D. Jas. I, 88/89; Lans. MSS. 152, fols. 255–6, 257–8.
[3] Lans. MSS. 152, fols. 243–4, 249–50, 253–4, 257–8; *A.P.C. 1616–1617*, p. 27; S.P.D. Jas. I, 89/55; Steele, I, no. 1189.
[4] *A.P.C. 1616–1617*, p. 60; documents in Friis, pp. 472–3, 477–81.
[5] *A.P.C. 1616–1617*, pp. 56–7, 61, 63, 67–8.
[6] S.P.D. Jas. I, 89/17.
[7] S.P.D. Jas. I, 89/35, 55.

to get merchants to purchase cloth led, late in December, to the inevitable re-establishment of the original company of Merchant Adventurers.[1]

Thus the deciding factor in the collapse of the Cockayne project was a fall in demand, on the part not so much of European consumers as of those merchants who had secured control of the cloth trade. The projectors, in fact, had played out their hand; they could go no further[2] and it was obviously with relief that they handed over to the old company. The latter now reaped the benefit of its long-standing refusal to co-operate with the new group—although at a direct cost of perhaps £80,000 in payments to the king and in other bribes,[3] as a consequence of which it imposed a tax on cloth exports which was severely criticized in the early 1620's. Ostensibly the terms of the restoration merely transferred responsibility for the dyeing and dressing project, but it was abundantly clear that the immediate reason for the recall was the desperate need to buy up cloth, specifically in the coming Twelfth Day market.[4] In the event the Adventurers were quickly relieved of their assumed obligations (to dye and dress a certain proportion of cloths) until midsummer 1617, and it was soon apparent that the terms of the renewal would never be enforced. When, in October 1617, the council investigated a dissension between the clothworkers and the Adventurers, it admonished the former to rest satisfied with the small amount of relief work afforded them by the company, 'it being now his Majesty's pleasure and resolution not to disturb the trade of whites with any further essay, but to leave the same to the train and course of trade now in practice and according to the use before the late alteration'.[5]

The notorious Cockayne project was finally dead.[6] Issues of economic strategy and economic nationalism had to be subordinated to the urgent needs of a textile crisis provoked by a too-eager experiment and inexperienced merchants.

(iii) CONCLUSION

The two eventful years 1615 and 1616 achieved no favourable results and taught some harsh lessons. They demonstrated, for instance, that the

[1] For a detailed description of the change-over, see Friis, pp. 351–61.
[2] In December the Eastland merchants suffered a severe blow through the bankruptcy, in Elbing, of a merchant holding £80,000 worth of goods belonging to Englishmen. Cockayne lost some £1,000 in the crash. This (and a similar bankruptcy in Hamburg) must have done considerable harm to some of the projectors' capital resources (Maclean, pp. 63–4).
[3] S.P.D. Jas. I, 95/21; S.P.D. Chas. I, 285/46.
[4] A.P.C. 1616–1617, pp. 108–10, 112–13.
[5] A.P.C. 1616–1617, pp. 114, 353–5.
[6] However, it was not until October 1618, after serious dislocation in the producing area, that the export of Somerset blues undressed was allowed: A.P.C. 1618–1619, pp. 194–5, 202, 273; S.P.D. Jas. I, 97/97, 98/53.

international division of labour by which the Dutch dyed and dressed England's semi-manufactured textiles was not an arbitrary phenomenon sustained by artificial survivals of company regulation. On the contrary, by the early seventeenth century it reflected economic realities against which England might tilt only at her peril. It was now uneconomic for the English industry to attempt to add another process to the manufacture of the old draperies. The achievements in this direction were pitifully inadequate and as late as 1632 some 75 per cent of the shipments to the Low Countries and Germany were still of unfinished cloth.[1]

These years also provided further proof that, contrary to widely accepted views, England did not have a quasi-monopoly of textile manufacture: that to attempt to force the Low Countries to accept textiles in a form which they disliked or which was not suited to the structure of English industry only provoked retaliatory action and a stimulation to European industry which soon reduced even the obstinate king to acquiescence in semi-manufactured exports. Nearly all the warnings given by the old company in 1614 proved painfully correct and, as later commentators were quick to point out, the brief period of the experiment must bear a large part of the responsibility for at least the speed with which competition developed to hasten the long-term decline of the old draperies for the rest of the period. It was true that Holland suffered to some extent as her finishing industry was deprived of some of the accustomed imports of white cloth,[2] but even this was probably due more to the ineptitude and lack of capital of the new company than to any other factor. In any case it was poor consolation for the concomitant damage done to English industry. In all respects the projectors' original assurances had proved fallacious.

While the experiment was an abject failure, the projectors themselves came nowhere near achieving their ultimate aim of sharing a prosperous trade with the old company. They were, of course, severely hampered by the difficulties encountered in the export of even that small amount of finished goods for which they were obliged to contract. However, even towards the end, when trade to Holland was freed from dependence on the sale of dyed and dressed cloth, a more obvious weakness was the scarcity of capital and their own lack of credit-worthiness which prevented them taking advantage of their powerful position astride England's richest trade. It was for this reason that a severe depression settled on the western clothing counties (the centre of white manufacture) in 1616: with the leading ex-Adventurers refusing to be enticed into the trade and many

[1] Calculated from E. 190/36/5.
[2] S.P.D. Jas. I, 89/55, 90/24; Maclean, p. 71.

The Cockayne Project, 1614–1617

of the original guarantors having second thoughts on the pickings to be obtained, the new company was unable to maintain the London cloth market without a much quicker turnover of capital than could reasonably be expected at a time of trade-disturbance. They failed because, in the last resort, they had come to the limit of their resources. At bottom theirs was a failure, by seventeenth-century racketeers, to gain, by conspiracy and misrepresentation, a share in a profitable monopolistic trade.[1] The members of the older company proved the stronger, and to some extent established the truth of their frequently reiterated claims to be essential to England's well-being.

These lessons and experiences had been dearly bought. The traditional textile industry had only suffered harm from the experiment: short-term unemployment and a competitive weakness which was the first step on a sorry path of economic stagnation. While the memory of all this was still green, dislocations in the European markets were to hurl the industry into yet another—and this time a much greater—crisis.

[1] In spite of James's reiterated threats when the project was doing badly, Cockayne escaped lightly from the collapse of his schemes. In 1623 he still had £10,000 to lose in a domestic fire, and the next year was able to give £10,000 for his daughter's dowry (*C.S.P.D. 1623–1624*, pp. 110, 312). For his prosperity after 1617, see Friis, pp. 358 ff.

3. THE DEPRESSION YEARS, 1620–1624

Within five years of the restoration of the Merchant Adventurers there occurred perhaps the most acute breakdown of the English economy of the first half of the seventeenth century. Certainly if we measure an economic depression by the depth and extent of the reaction to it, then this one was unrivalled.

However, the storm did not break until 1620. With the miserable failure of the Cockayne project the Merchant Adventurers concentrated, with some success, on re-establishing their previous position. A bribe to the king secured them their legal tenure again; they obtained protection against interlopers and against any further attempts to enforce the finishing of cloth for export; and a settlement of the problem of licences for unfinished exports was arranged, by which shipments up to 60,000 cloths were to be shared equally between their own licence and that of the Earl of Cumberland.[1] Cloth exports never again reached the level of 1614—the advance of foreign manufacture, partly under the enforced stimulus of the events of 1614–16, and the competition of the newer fabrics for factors of production at home, ensured a permanent restriction of the overseas market for old draperies. Nevertheless, 1618 saw a distinct recovery from the slump in 1616: London exports rose from 88,000 to 102,000 shortcloths (a figure not to be exceeded for ten years) while the Adventurers' shipments increased appreciably to some 68,000.[2] In the course of 1618 there was considerable anxiety about the supply of money and there was some danger that James would push through a plan to enhance the silver coinage; but business on the whole seems to have been lively and a committee of merchants reported in December 'that there was no want at all of money within the kingdom' since all credit dealings had increased and prospered.[3] The economy—even that part of it most closely connected with the textile industry—was reasonably steady. Yet the signs of recovery were misleading, for in fact the resulting equilibrium was unstable and there was little scope for industrial or commercial manœuvre. English cloth was merely holding its own in Europe, the industry at home had taken severe punishment, and the Merchant Adventurers had clearly been weakened by the payment to the king and by the efflux of capital during and after the experiment—for some of the

[1] *C.S.P.D. 1639*, p. 539.
[2] Below, Appendix A, Table 1; Friis, p. 382.
[3] S.P.D. Jas. I, 104/29; for the monetary discussions see below, pp. 183–4.

The Depression Years, 1620–1624   53

money taken out, and invested in the money market or the East India trade, had not returned to the cloth trade.[1] If an extraneous disturbance should arise the cloth trade would be at its mercy.

(i) DEPRESSION IN THE TEXTILE INDUSTRY

By 1620 such a dislocation had appeared. For almost four years England was enveloped in the gloom of a depression which paralysed the cloth industry and spread over many other branches of economic activity until men could find only one parallel for their plight: 'When was it seen a land so distressed without war?'[2]

Early in 1620, the European currency manipulations which were to retard economic prosperity for some years to come were already provoking a deepening anxiety concerning the export of silver.[3] In May, a normal time for large shipments of cloth, more sinister signs of malaise appeared. From Wiltshire there came complaints of growing unemployment: clothiers were unable to find a market for their cloth and in one locality alone over 2,500 people lacked work. A temporary sub-committee of the Privy Council was appointed to interview leading Merchant Adventurers and the Wiltshire representatives then in London; but it soon became necessary to convert it into a standing body to overlook a rapidly weakening cloth industry. The Merchant Adventurers were subsequently questioned and an investigation was made, by circuit judges, of 'the low price of wools and the great decay of trade in that kind'.[4] In spite of assurances to Wiltshire justices of the peace that the merchants would buy up the unsold cloth,[5] nothing positive was achieved, and the export figures for 1620 show the extent of the fall since 1618, with the German market suffering most:[6]

Cloth exports from London by Englishmen

	1618	1620
Total	102,332	85,741
By Merchant Adventurers	67,853	58,051
To Germany	c. 35,000	22,336
To the Baltic	7,843	2,848

It is significant that concomitantly with the decline in the German market, at least in these early years of the slump, the manufacture of coarse cloth

---

[1] Malynes, *The Maintenance of Free Trade*, p. 51; Cotton MSS. Galba, E.1, fol. 363; Add. MSS. 34324, fol. 203.
[2] Add. MSS. 34324, fol. 179.   [3] Below, pp. 184–5.
[4] S.P.D. Jas. I, 115/20, 58, 116/23, 180/75; A.P.C. *1619–1621*, pp. 192–3, 197–8, 200–1, 288–9, 293–4; Add. MSS. 34324, fol. 191.
[5] A.P.C. *1619–1621*, pp. 205–6.
[6] See Appendix A, Tables 1, and 3. For the decline in the German market also see S.P.D. Jas. I, 89/54 (wrongly calendared), 116/23; *Calendar of Wynn Papers* (Aberystwyth, 1926), no. 922.

was severely hit, and its price fell by more than that of finer textiles. For the cheap cloth found its best market in eastern Europe[1] and where English textiles increasingly met the competition of native industries, working on coarse wool, it was only to be expected that, at least initially, the cheaper goods would suffer most.[2]

There was no alleviation of England's economic ills in 1621. Parliament met in that year and its preoccupation with the depression gave a sombre and distressing tone to its proceedings: 'Trade like the moon is on the wane, . . . the countries [counties] that suffer are several, the sufferings several, . . . trade runs high in importation . . . low in exportation. . . . The kingdom is hindered even within the kingdom by a decay of the trade of cloth.' 'Ports are decayed, and looms decrease,' cried another M.P., 'I had rather be a ploughman than a merchant.' In February it was intimated that some clothiers had a year's unsold stock on their hands and parliamentary discussion broadened to include the 'want of money', the balance of trade and the general impoverishment. The Great Committee for the Decay of Money underwent a metamorphosis into one for the Decay of Trade. Very early in its life the Commons called the clothiers of Kent, Worcestershire, Suffolk, Essex, Somerset and Gloucestershire to voice their complaints in committee, and representatives of all the principal trading companies, and even the interlopers, were heard in April in an attempt to get to the root of the disorder.[3] It was now evident that nearly all trades (to Germany, Holland, France, Spain, Russia, the Baltic) were hit to some extent by the slump; clothiers were being offered disastrously uneconomic prices since 'the price of English cloths [is] near one fourth part abated';[4] and the picture is one of an economy reduced to destitution: 'the trading and commerce among his [the king's] subjects is much decayed, and his people by the means aforesaid so impoverished, that the greater part have not wherewithal left to pay and those that have money will not disburse it upon land or any other commodity whatsoever.'[5]

As if registering the national character of the emergency, the Privy Council, in September, wrote to the twenty leading outports for their opinions on the decay of trade and the scarcity of money.[6] The fourteen

[1] S.P.D. Chas. I, 180/77; S.P.D. Eliz., 283A/51; Lans. MSS. 152, fol. 162; H.M.C. Sackville, II, 33-4.
[2] Friis, pp. 401-2; Sir Thomas Culpepper, A Tract Against Usury (1621), p. 32; S.P.D. Jas. I, 130/143.
[3] Commons Debates, 1621, II, 75; III, 45, 370, 379; IV, 95.
[4] Hargrave MSS. 321, p. 243. Also see S.P.D. Jas. I, 120/121 and the statement of the Shrewsbury Drapers that 'even northern cloth which is at least ten per cent cheaper than ours is at a stand' (quoted in Mendenhall, p. 191).
[5] Commons Debates, 1621, VII, 581.
[6] A.P.C. 1621-1623, pp. 40, 71. Cf. ibid. pp. 79-80, 208.

The Depression Years, 1620-1624

surviving reports demonstrate the extent of the commercial despondency which had settled over England: theirs was a tale of shrinking markets, unfavourable trading conditions, credit tightness and widening poverty.[1] The economy, as it entered 1622, seemed doomed to a never-ending descent along a spiral of unemployment, idle capital, economic stagnancy and an unfavourable balance of trade.[2] And in autumn the weather took a hand in the slump. After two excellent harvests, which had reduced many farmers to the verge of bankruptcy, the yield of 1621 was atrocious. Grain prices shot up and served to help absorb what little purchasing power there was amid widespread unemployment.[3] The Wiltshire spinners and weavers in 1623 begged for fair wage-assessments 'now especially in this great dearth of corn, that the poor artificers . . . may not perish for want of food, whiles they are painful in their calling'.[4]

Indeed, from the point of view of recorded exports, 1622 was the worst year of all, and it was now the turn of shipments to the Low Countries to shrink drastically:[5]

Cloth exports from London by Englishmen

	1620	1622
Total	85,741	76,624
By Merchant Adventurers	58,051	50,187
To the Low Countries	35,716	26,518

Faced with a decline in their markets, thirty-seven of the Merchant Adventurers trading in 1620 had, by 1622, ceased exporting cloth— although this exodus was matched by an influx of thirty-six new traders. The overall decline in overseas sales in the two years after 1620 was more than accounted for by the reduction in the export of the standard undressed cloth (from 48,235 to 38,689) and Suffolk shortcloths (from 11,494 to 9,910). The former were almost entirely produced in Wiltshire, Gloucestershire, Somerset, Worcestershire and Oxfordshire. Hence it was only to be expected that most of the extreme destitution of 1622 was centred in the West Country and in Suffolk.

With the heavy stocks of unsold textiles still on hand, and with total exports (the lowest of the period) some 40 per cent below the level of

---
[1] Reports or summaries survive for Bridgwater, Bristol, Chester, Exeter, Hull, Ipswich, Lynn, Milton, Newcastle, Plymouth, Poole, Sandwich, Southampton and Yarmouth. Hargrave MSS. 321, pp. 1-6, 66-9, 80-94, 103-7, 119-22, 133-7. The full report from Hull is reprinted in G. Hadley, *A History of Kingston-upon-Hull* (Kingston-upon-Hull, 1788), pp. 113 ff.
[2] For the balance of trade, see below, pp. 89-94.
[3] For a fuller description of the impact of harvests in these years see Supple, 'A Comparative Study', pp. 479-80, 493-9.
[4] *H.M.C. Various*, I, 94.
[5] Figures from E. 190/23/3, E. 190/25/1. For a discussion of the differential decline from 1618 to 1622 in the German and Low Countries market, see below, pp. 97-8.

1614, 1622 was the bottom of the economic trough: England seemed to be on the verge of ruin. In February the council reassured the ten principal textile counties that increased mercantile purchases were imminent and ordered the J.P.s to see that clothiers kept their workfolk employed. But the situation was obviously very serious and already 'they are much discouraged in the clothing counties for want of money, the trade of clothing is so much decayed for want of vent . . . that many poor people are ready to mutiny for want of work' and attacks on food supplies had already started.[1]

From February onwards, usually a period of heavy purchase for the spring shipment to the Low Countries and Germany, intimations of economic distress poured into Westminster from local centres of erstwhile production. The common theme was of clothiers finding mounting stocks of cloth they could not sell and, with their liquid capital tied up, ceasing to employ carders, spinners and weavers—even the Wiltshire House of Correction made a loss on its carding and spinning. The textile workers, unemployed and faced with famine prices, presented the government with an urgent problem of widespread rioting. Wiltshire, perhaps the hardest hit, was the first to experience such trouble, but Gloucestershire soon had its own share of tumult.[2] The Suffolk magistrates reported that almost £40,000 worth of cloth lay unsold in twenty towns—some for as long as two years—and that 'the . . . clothiers are so decayed in their estates . . . by reason of the great losses they have received . . . by merchants that have bankrupted, the sale of their cloths at underprices, [and] the great quantity of cloth that doth lie dead upon their hands, for want of utterance and sale of them, that a great number . . . that formerly have been men of great ability, and did set multitudes of people on work, are . . . so disabled in their estates, that they are not able to do anything . . . in their said trade, but live themselves in great . . . misery'.[3]

Early in March, Oxfordshire clothiers joined with those of Gloucestershire in complaining that 'they cannot continue their trade without vent of cloths and return of their stock'—meanwhile they were obliged to pawn their products and borrow money. In Gloucestershire the clothiers said that they could only continue production for fourteen days and, so far had the depression spread, the J.P.s warned that 'our whole country [is] greatly impoverished and stored with other poor than those that have

---

[1] S.P.D. Jas. I, 127/8, 16; A.P.C. 1621–1623, pp. 131–3. The government had ordered the Adventurers to buy up stipulated amounts of cloth (S.P.D. Jas. I, 129/12), but the order had little effect on the crisis.

[2] W. Yonge, Diary (Camden Society, 1847), p. 52; H.M.C. Various, I, 93–4; S.P.D. Jas. I, 128/49.

[3] S.P.D. Jas. I, 128/67.

their dependence upon clothing'. Exeter had 300 unemployed weavers and, in April, Wiltshire reported over 8,000 out of work, clamouring for bread and attacking horses taking food to market. In May an attempt was made to seize malt barges on the Severn, while rioting now broke out in the cloth villages of Somerset.[1] In April the government had been moved to appoint a twelve-man committee of investigation into the depression and had invited the twenty-five leading textile counties to send representatives to give evidence on the subject.[2] Nevertheless, in May, the council was forced to write urgent letters to the justices of Wiltshire, Gloucestershire, Oxfordshire, Somerset, Devon, Dorset, Berkshire, Northamptonshire and Hampshire ordering them to control 'tumultuous assemblies' and enforce the poor-law.[3]

Although 'poverty' was the usual plea in the face of increased taxes even in normal times, it is significant that in the early summer of 1622 protestations were received against heavy contributions to the Palatinate from ports and cloth centres. In London, the clothworkers were hard-hit by poverty and some of them forced to emigrate.[4] With the autumn another bad harvest only increased the government's anxiety—wheat prices for the harvest year 1622 (commencing with Michaelmas) stood at 51s. 1d. compared with 25s. 5d. in 1620, 40s. 9d. in 1621 and 37s. 8d. in 1623.[5] By December the slump had paralysed parts of Essex as unsold stocks of new and old draperies froze industrial assets, threw many people out of work, and caused unrest and dislocation.[6]

On the eve of 1623, after almost three years of depression, it was yet the case that 'things [in England] are but in ill terms by reason of the decay of trade and scarcity of corn, especially in the country, where the poorer sort of people do suffer much in those counties that do consist of clothing, and in some places they . . . gather to-gether in companies'. Throughout 1623 there seems to have been relatively little improvement in the situation. In Somerset and Wiltshire the early months of the year saw food shortages, unemployment and severe pressure on wages. The growing bands of migrant unemployed spilled into London and in June it was still possible to write that 'the cloud [of depression] that erewhile rose up like a man's hand is spread abroad, and hath overspread all our

[1] S.P.D. Jas. I, 128/20, 49–51; 129/79; 130/73, 81; 131/4, 4I; Yonge, p. 53.
[2] A.P.C. 1621–1623, pp. 190, 201–2. For the clothiers' evidence: Stowe MSS. 354, fols. 63, 65; S.P.D. Jas. I, 130/28, 143. For the committee's final report (which will be considered below): S.P.D. Jas. I, 131/55.
[3] A.P.C. 1621–1623, pp. 214–15, 224–5.
[4] Communities complaining of distress were: Barnstaple, Bath, Bridgwater, Chichester, Exeter, Ipswich, Northampton, Poole, Suffolk, Taunton, Wells and Worcester (S.P.D. Jas. I, 130/42, 44, 49, 51–2, 61, 63, 79, 109, 111, 122; 131/63). For the clothworkers: S.P.D. Jas. I, 133/3.
[5] Rogers, v, 270–1.   [6] A.P.C. 1621–1623, pp. 371–2, 392; S.P.D. Jas. I, 137/13.

horizon', while in October it was held that the German trade 'is so poor that it is not worth following'.[1] But by then the worst was passing. Although in spring 1624 the Commons claimed that the slump 'hath occasioned the turning of many clothiers out of their occupations, and as many people depending on them out of their work',[2] nevertheless, as will be seen, that year saw distinct progress and by early 1625 the historian may speak of a 'recovery'.

(ii) CONTEMPORARY OPINION

The four years after 1619 had proved a severe testing time for the English cloth industry and trade. The contraction in overseas sales had spread, disastrously, to activity in the producing areas; the West, East Anglia and the North had alike suffered—as had the City and the outports: 'the fire that even now was spied in a sparkle, hath enflamed the whole city, all the kingdom'.[3] So far we have only dealt with the appearance of textile unemployment. The catastrophic economic decline during the early 1620's was bound to stimulate endless discussion of its causes; but, in the main, contemporary commentators failed to establish the correct causal link between the collapse of England's cloth exports and the monetary anarchy on the Continent which accompanied the outbreak of the Thirty Years War. This critical question will form the subject-matter of the following chapter. It suffices to say here that exports plummeted and the balance of trade turned against England primarily because monetary manipulations in Europe amounted to a virtual devaluation of foreign currencies and induced highly unfavourable terms of trade for English goods.

The prolific response to the slump left a profusion of manuscripts and pamphlets which defy detailed enumeration. A host of individuals, corporate bodies and vested interests voiced their opinions on the causes of and remedies for the crisis. Some concentrated largely on the symptoms of the crisis and were consequently led to blame England's trouble on a 'shortage of money'; others put forward more sophisticated arguments concerning currency and the exchanges. However, in the field of the reduced sales of English cloth, contemporaries seeking an explanation of the depression concentrated on the following points: the poor quality of home textiles, the growth of manufacture abroad facilitated by the export of English wool and stimulated by the Cockayne project, the impositions

[1] S.P.D. Jas. I, 134/99, 138/54, 74, 144/24, 145/3; *H.M.C. Various*, I, 94; Journals of the Common Council (Record Office of the Corporation of London), 32, fols. 146b, 148; Misselden, *The Circle of Commerce*, p. 1; *Wynn Papers*, no. 1154.
[2] Harleian MSS. 2224, fol. 1.
[3] Misselden, *The Circle of Commerce*, p. 1.

The Depression Years, 1620–1624   59

on cloth at home and abroad, the wars in Germany which disrupted trade and destroyed purchasing power, the lack of home demand, the absence of good commodity-returns, and the monopolistic character of the trading companies.[1]

The probable role of most of these factors in the crisis has already been well summarized in a recent article.[2] It is there seen that they all have serious deficiencies as explanations of a short-run depression; for, in fact, even where they might have applied to reducing sales they were not causally coincident with the slump: the timing of their appearance and the timing of the crash do not agree. Nevertheless, a brief study of contemporary opinions is essential. Without it we could not understand the inherent economic weaknesses which placed the textile industry at the mercy of currency manipulations and explained the depth and persistence of the depression; nor could we grasp the course of administrative action in these years or the outlook of the men most immediately involved in the disaster.

Led by the Merchant Adventurers, nearly every vocal interest (except, obviously, the clothiers) claimed that overseas sales had in part diminished owing to the deceits practised by domestic manufacturers. Official memoranda, merchants' analyses, evidence from the London drapers, parliamentary debates, published works, the outports: all complained of the same phenomenon.[3] And this opinion was endorsed by the committee of investigation, which reported in July 1622 that one cause of the slump was 'the false and deceitful making, dyeing and dressing of our cloth and stuff which disgraceth and discrediteth it in foreign parts'.[4] The Adventurers particularly complained of the difficulties caused them in the Low Countries by the 'Tare'—the system of abatements for cloths not up to stipulated standards—which was exacted there. However, as will be seen,[5] low-quality manufacture was far more likely to be an effect, rather than a cause, of a fall in exports. Such complaints occurred regularly at times of poor sales—the King's Merchant Adventurers had hurled this accusation at the Gloucestershire clothiers in 1616 and few years passed in the early seventeenth century without merchants bemoaning the corrupt manufacture of the old draperies. With the technological possibilities of

[1] Contemporary opinion on all these points is concisely summarized in the report of the committee of investigation of 1622 (S.P.D. Jas. I, 131/55, 22 June 1622).
[2] J. D. Gould, 'The Trade Depression of the Early 1620's', Econ. Hist. Rev. 2nd ser. VII (1954), 81–8.
[3] S.P.D. Jas. I, 120/95, 121, 130/28, 140–1; Add. MSS. 34324, fol. 181; Hargrave MSS. 321, pp. 87, 107; Cotton MSS. Galba, E.1, fol. 363; Commons Debates, 1621, III, 45, 119; Misselden, Free Trade, passim. Misselden was particularly keen on this point and advocated decentralization of control of standards and quality.
[4] S.P.D. Jas. I, 131/55.
[5] Below, pp. 144–6.

cost-reduction severely limited, debasement of quality might be the only feasible way in which clothiers could sell their cloth, or employees their labour, at the lower prices which resulted from economic stress. The protests therefore indicate how unprepared the textile industry was when it had to face currency and commercial dislocation. A prosperous industry might well have sustained the extra cost of 'true' manufacture; a depressed industry only worsened its own position, under market pressure, by having to force some outlet at the cost-point of least resistance.

The development of competitive industries in Europe was also by no means a new complaint, and neither did it cease for the rest of the period. In these years it received added strength from the memory of the events of 1614–16, although even they would not have explained the abrupt decline starting in 1620. The Merchant Adventurers, for obvious reasons, took the lead in blaming the project, others soon followed them, and the general fear of competition was widespread.[1] The 1622 committee's verdict was that 'the making of cloth and other draperies in foreign parts in more abundance than in former times ... we conceive to be the chief cause that less quantity of ours are vented there'. In nearly every case, also, it was claimed that the export of British raw materials (wool, fells, fuller's earth) significantly aided this production. In the circumstances of falling wool prices at home it is not surprising that some wool should have been attracted (illegally) abroad. But on the whole British supplies were not as indispensable to foreign industry as some contemporaries, more nationalistic than well-informed, might have believed.[2] Nevertheless, although competition alone could not have produced the crisis, the undoubted development of the European industry presented England with increased competition at a moment when she was least able to bear it. It was the narrow scope for price-variation allowed English cloth by this manufacture which helped deepen the depression when other disturbances arose and which enhanced the anxiety which Englishmen felt about foreign textile production.

There is little one can add to what has already been written concerning impositions.[3] The duties in Flanders and the United Provinces, the pretermitted customs imposed in 1618, and the Adventurers' impositions (established in 1617 ostensibly to repay the loan taken up to purchase their restoration from James) were universally condemned. Once again

---

[1] S.P.D. Jas. I, 128/49I, 130/28, 141, 143, 133/55; Hargrave MSS. 321, pp. 83–4, 87, 107, 120, 136–7; Stowe MSS. 354, fol. 65; Misselden, *Free Trade*, pp. 41–2; Culpepper, p. 32; Malynes, *The Maintenance of Free Trade*, pp. 46–7; Hadley, p. 113; *Commons Debates, 1621*, II, 75.
[2] See below, pp. 141–2.
[3] Gould, 'The Trade Depression of the Early 1620's', 84–5.

The Depression Years, 1620–1624

the chronology fails to substantiate the claim that the taxes 'caused' the slump. Yet they were sufficiently heavy—at times augmenting the price of shortcloths by as much as £2—to impose a significant burden on English sales.[1] Once again we are dealing with a factor which contemporary critics held to be operating because cloth was at the margin of competition; but it is one powerless to explain an abrupt decline.

The outbreak of the Thirty Years War was similarly widely discussed as a possible cause of the decay of trade. The destruction of purchasing power, the monetary disturbances, and the insecurities of communications, currency and contracts meant that the war was a constant threat to commerce. The Adventurers especially blamed the hostilities for the decline of their German trade, and Staplers, outporters and pamphleteers all agreed that war (including the French troubles) was, in the main, a potent hindrance to textile exports.[2] The investigating committee was somewhat undecided as to the real meaning of the wars for English prosperity. While they were listed as a cause of the slump, the committee claimed that destruction and disturbance 'are probable means to open the way for our better vent, when it shall please God to send peace'.[3] Yet this argument begged the question. There can be no doubt that war in the areas of final consumption, as always, greatly weakened the cloth markets. Earlier in the century, for instance, it is possible to trace, through mercantile correspondence, distinct oscillations in the trade in northern kersies dependent upon the threat or manifestation of war in Hungary.[4] In the early 1620's nothing but harm could have come from the great European conflict; for, besides the immediate and direct repercussions, the resulting instability in eastern Europe directly conduced to the wave of debasements which, at one remove, so drastically reduced the export of English textiles.

The question of the lack of returns belongs elsewhere, since where merchants were seriously embarrassed in their export trade by difficulties with imports the problem was intimately bound up with currency instabilities and largely confined to the Baltic trade.[5] The Merchant Adventurers, it is true, claimed in 1620 that one reason for their failure to buy up Wiltshire cloths was that they were 'straitened' in their returns

[1] For estimates of the various impositions, see Stowe MSS. 354, fol. 65; S.P.D. Jas. I, 130/28, 133/35.
[2] S.P.D. Jas. I, 116/23, 130/28; Hargrave MSS. 321, pp. 83, 104; Cotton MSS. Galba, E.1, fol. 362; *Wynn Papers*, no. 922; *Commons Debates, 1621*, II, 416; III, 45; VII, 225; *A.P.C. 1621–1623*, pp. 75–6; Misselden, *Free Trade*, pp. 17–18, 52–3, 132; Malynes, *The Maintenance of Free Trade*, pp. 46, 56.
[3] The permanent trade commission appointed in the autumn of 1622, when it came to consider this question, copied the original report almost *verbatim* (Add. MSS. 34324, fol. 197).
[4] H.M.C. *Sackville*, II, *passim*.
[5] Below, pp. 81–9.

because they were not allowed to import goods of Levantine origin from the Low Countries and Germany. But their petition for liberty in this respect was met by the council with a refusal to relax the Levant Company's privileges of direct importing which had been granted in 1615. The Adventurers' analysis—in any circumstances not a significant part of their case—far from indicating a major cause of commercial decline, seems to have been an attempt to use the prevailing economic atmosphere to extend their own privileges. They had already tried, unsuccessfully, to secure the same end in 1617 and were to continue their efforts in subsequent years.[1] As for home demand: contemporaries intermittently bemoaned its low level and advocated the enforced wearing of English woollens, but, even if this might have provided some slight relief, it is clear that the lack of work in the textile industry arose primarily from the drastic fall in exports, not from any dip in domestic sales.

Finally we come to the factor which produced the most drastic change in official policy: the attack on the trading companies and on the metropolitan control of trade. The Merchant Adventurers—whose overseas sales, and therefore London purchases, underwent the maximum decline—naturally had to bear the brunt of the attack, for they handled some three-quarters of total London shipments. The crescendo of criticism rose from the normal continuous murmur of the excluded interloper and the capital-deficient outport trader to include the protests of M.P.s, woolgrowers and clothiers. The clothiers were especially bitter since their immediate experience of the crisis was a lack of purchasers for cloth and their natural and immediate response was a desire to increase the number of potential buyers. The discussion centred on the ability of the Adventurers to purchase all the supplies of cloth coming to London, and on their willingness to give 'reasonable' prices for these textiles. The common accusation was made that they used their potentially monopolistic position to beat down the prices offered to clothiers. Adverse opinion was crystallized by the slump in the 1621 Parliament and elsewhere.[2] Vested interests, including the Staplers, excluded from normal trade were quick to seize the opportunity afforded by the depression to press for a liberalization; the outports (constantly enraged by the London merchants' competition) put forward a strong case; and the clothiers were obdurate in their demand that the trade be thrown open. Typical of the feelings of manu-

[1] Steele, I, no. 1160; S.P.D. Jas. I, 180/75; A.P.C. 1616–1617, pp. 393–4, 406–7, 412–14; A.P.C. 1619–1621, pp. 200–1, 283; A.P.C. 1621–1623, p. 4; A.P.C. 1623–1625, pp. 111–12, 114, 424, 436–7.
[2] See Commons Debates, 1621, II, 214 ff., 364–5, 422; III, 45 ff., 188 ff., 245, 442 ff.; IV, 95 ff., 175, 411; VII, 225, 593. Add. MSS. 34324, fol. 203; Hargrave MSS. 321, pp. 80–1, 88, 103; Cotton MSS. Galba, E.1, fols. 362–5; Stowe MSS. 354, fols. 63, 65; S.P.D. Jas. I, 128/49I, 50, 130/28, 143.

facturers was the statement of the Suffolk clothiers:[1] 'the merchants being incorporated and settled into companies, do by constitutions among themselves so cross the ancient and accustomed course of their trade concerning the free selling and buying of their cloth (limiting it to certain times, persons, numbers and at what prices the members shall buy and sell again, as well here as beyond the seas) that they hold it to be one chief cause [of the depression].' Even the 1622 committee blamed, in part, 'the policies of the Merchant Adventurers, which draw upon them suspicion of combination in trading; and the smallness of their number which do now usually buy and vent cloth'. It recommended that good 'government' be continued but that 'combination' be eradicated and membership extended.

The Adventurers' response to these charges was to give their own reasons for the commercial decline,[2] to argue that company organization maintained 'reputation' and increased the value of exports, and to plead the uselessness of augmenting the number of participants in a declining trade: 'we could carry thrice more [cloths] if they would vent, *ergo* no need of more merchants'; 'what needs that [the addition of more merchants] when there are already ten times as many Merchant Adventurers as the quantity of the trade will employ?'[3]

The long clamorous controversy, bitter and sincere though it was, produced no real evidence that the decline in exports was due to the operations of merchants acting collusively. Thus, there was no indication that merchants maintained an excessive profit margin between the (admittedly falling) price paid to clothiers and that obtained abroad. Informed opinion almost unanimously held that the price of English cloth overseas was under pressure and yet could not be further reduced without destroying net profits. The narrow profit margins on which exporters were forced to operate during the slump meant that they could not sustain even a small rise in the exchanges without paying the clothier less for his cloth;[4] and as late as 1625 the Commons complained to the king about the Adventurers' impositions of 5s. 0d. and 7s. 6d. on short and long cloths 'which is more than at this day the merchant doth clearly gain by this trade of cloth'.[5] While they remained in the cloth trade it

---

[1] S.P.D. Jas. I, 128/67.
[2] The company, at various times, attributed the slump to difficulties with returns, impositions overseas and customs at home, currency disturbances, foreign manufacture, wars, false manufacture at home, and (returning the attack) the activities of interlopers (Add. MSS. 34324, fol. 191; S.P.D. Jas. I, 116/23; A.P.C. 1619–1621, p. 283; *Commons Debates, 1621*, III, 45; IV, 150, 175; VII, 225).
[3] *Commons Debates, 1621*, III, 442; VII, 225.
[4] Add. MSS. 34324, fols. 155–7, 171; Misselden, *The Circle of Commerce*, pp. 107–10.
[5] Harleian MSS. 2244, fol. 1.

was the Merchant Adventurers' depression as much as anybody's and their opponents would have found it impossible to adduce the only proof which would have established their case: that more merchants, by increasing sales abroad, presumably through *lower* sales prices, would have been able to take more cloth off the clothiers' hands by offering them *better* prices. It is difficult not to agree that, in the context of the time, 'to add more persons to be Merchant Adventurers, is to put more sheep into one and the same pasture, which is to starve them all'.[1]

Contemporary opinion thus failed to seize upon the effective cause of the crisis. Nevertheless, it establishes a framework which demonstrates the inability of the economy to withstand a sudden shock. For it is well to remember that the full impact of the depression can only be explained by reference to the harm derived from the Cockayne project, the growth of rival industries, the financial burdens on English cloth, the disturbances provoked by continental warfare, and the widespread pre-existing difficulties for English merchants. These meant that the economy, once any untoward event took place, would experience yet another of those periods of extreme economic decline which are perpetual historical rivals for the appellation 'the Great Depression'.

(iii) OFFICIAL ACTION

In considering the reaction of a seventeenth-century government to a depression such as that of the early 1620's, there is no need to presuppose a coherent 'mercantilist' philosophy. Presiding over a poorly policed island which was greatly dependent for its prosperity upon the vagaries of commerce and for its power on a mercantile marine, the government, in such circumstances, concentrated on twin needs: to alleviate local destitution, in order to prevent riots and tumults, and to revive commerce, in order to maintain economic stability and power.[2]

Clearly the Poor Law, comprehensive in aim though it was, could not possibly alleviate all the distress which resulted from the cessation of economic activity. Therefore, although the council attempted to stir J.P.s into enforcing the law—and especially that part which provided for the raising of funds to 'set the poor on work'—the justices were adamant that their powers alone were useless, in view of the numbers of the unemployed, and that relief could only come to the workless within their own trades, by a revival of manufacture.[3]

[1] Add. MSS. 34324, fol. 195.
[2] For government economic policy during the period, see ch. 10.
[3] *A.P.C. 1619–1621*, pp. 205–6; *A.P.C. 1621–1623*, pp. 131–3, 214–5, 224–5; S.P.D. Jas. I, 128/50, 129/79, 130/81, 131/4, 137/13.

The Depression Years, 1620–1624

Spurred by the discontent which erupted into sporadic violence, the Privy Council's immediate response was always to put pressure on business interests to keep the manufacturing process going. It was, for instance, ready to protect clothiers against arrest by their creditors.[1] In the more general field there were constant exhortations to clothiers to continue production and to merchants to maintain their purchases. In May 1620 the J.P.s of Wiltshire were commanded to see that the clothiers re-employed their workers on pain of appearing before the Privy Council. In February 1622 the same demand, tempered by an assurance that current stocks would be purchased, was made of clothiers in the ten principal textile counties, and the rule was propounded that, with respect to merchants, clothiers and woolgrowers, 'whosoever had a part of the gain in profitable times since his Majesty's happy reign must now in the decay of trade (till that may be remedied) bear a part of the public loss as may best conduce to the good of the public and the maintenance of the general trade'.[2] But the principle that owners of capital should continue to operate their enterprises at a loss was, even with the best will in the world, obviously limited in its application to the clothiers' case. For their difficulty was the freezing of capital which resulted from the merchant's failure to buy. They might 'have wrought out some all, others the greater part of their estates and stock into cloth which lieth upon their hand, so they cannot continue their trades, to set the poor people on work . . . except the said cloths at reasonable prices be taken off their hands, by the merchants or some other means'.[3] In these circumstances the council turned to the merchants—primarily to the Merchant Adventurers.

Early in 1620 the company was approached and evidently gave some assurance that purchases at Blackwell Hall would be maintained, although this did little to alleviate the depression. Two years later the council obtained a similar 'promise' backed by an enforced stint allocated to individual merchants: 'merchants are enjoined to buy a quantity of cloth weekly at Blackwell Hall . . . or otherwise they shall be disenfranchised of their liberties'. This was in February 1622. A month later the council, wishing to adopt the same course, was met by the threat from the Adventurers that having already obeyed the last month and 'the traders being already so wearied and discouraged by . . . restless complaints . . . , if there be no other course to content the clothiers . . . but by buying up the cloth by assessment so long as they complain, we shall be contented . . . to leave all and to be utterly excluded from returning to the trade in

---
[1] S.P.D. Jas. I, 130/97, 131/95, 134/94; A.P.C. 1621–1623, pp. 278, 313–14, 381–2.
[2] A.P.C. 1621–1623, pp. 131–3. For Wiltshire in 1620: A.P.C. 1619–1621, pp. 205–6. This attitude was of long standing (Lipson, III, 304).
[3] S.P.D. Jas. I, 128/67. Cf. 128/49.

... better times'.[1] This categorical and threatening refusal brought deadlock—and it was perhaps to break it that the famous committee of investigation was formed a fortnight later. The government could not expect nor, in the long run, force the merchants to continue trading at a loss to serve a social philosophy no matter how philanthropic. Primary consideration had to be given to the causes of the crisis and to possible means of increasing overseas sales.

Although, in fact, it was Parliament which produced the two measures of trade liberalization which were the outstanding official response to the depression, the Privy Council, as usual, was the centre of complaint, investigations and controversy. In 1620 and 1621 sub-committees of inquiry into the 'decay of clothing', the collapse of the exchanges, and the balance of trade met and heard evidence.[2] One notable feature of governmental policy in these years was the eagerness with which local opinion and advice was sought, and a special sub-committee was appointed to analyse the reports of the twenty outports which, in September 1621, had been approached by the council to help discover 'the true causes of the decay of trade and scarcity of coin within this kingdom and to advise of some fit course for the removing of so great inconveniences'.[3]

Yet by the spring of 1622 the council, in spite of its hectic activity, must have been concerned at the lack of progress. With rioting in the West Country and the Adventurers refusing to enforce compulsory purchase, the situation seemed more urgent than ever. It was decided to appoint an expert committee of investigation. On 10 April the twenty-five textile counties were invited to confer with the committee and with the Adventurers on the causes 'of this great decay and abatement of trade in the vent of cloth'. The commission was issued two weeks later and for two months the committee took evidence from merchants, gentry, manufacturers, customs officers, drapers and dyers. It reported on 22 June and, as might be expected, its report was a *résumé* of contemporary opinion. The causes it adduced for the decay of trade were: foreign manufacture, corrupt manufacture at home, heavy impositions on cloth, the activities of middlemen trading in wool, the wars in Germany, the activities of trading companies, the scarcity of coin, the lack of returns (especially from the Baltic), and the limited domestic demand for English

---

[1] *A.P.C. 1619–1621*, pp. 205–6; Yonge, p. 52; *A.P.C. 1621–1623*, pp. 131–3; S.P.D. Jas. I, 129/12, 133/35. It is possible that the Adventurers did temporarily stop trading (Add. MSS. 34324, fol. 203).
[2] *A.P.C. 1619–1621*, pp. 192–3, 197–8, 200–1, 205–6, 288–9, 293–4; *A.P.C. 1621–1623*, pp. 79–80, 208; Add. MSS. 34324, fol. 191; S.P.D. Jas. I, 116/23.
[3] *A.P.C. 1621–1623*, pp. 40, 71.

The Depression Years, 1620–1624

cloth.¹ After advocating certain remedies, none of which was startlingly new, the committee concluded by recommending that a permanent commission be set up to overlook trade in general and textiles in particular.

Arrangements were soon in progress to form such a commission, although the Privy Seal was not issued until 21 October and its meetings did not commence until November.² There were over fifty commissioners, with a very broad representation of economic interests and geographical areas. Their terms of reference were the widest possible, covering most facets of contemporary economic trouble,³ and from one point of view the appointment of this body, which was really a precursor of the Board of Trade, was the principal administrative move to counteract depression. The commission's importance was such that, for the future, most executive matters concerning trade, cloth, and economic life in general fell initially into its field of operations rather than into the hands of the Privy Council. Consequently, a continuous record of its proceedings would prove invaluable for a full understanding of commercial developments in the period. Unfortunately this is not available and we can only catch frustrating glimpses of what was obviously a hardworking body of men.⁴ To judge from other evidence, however, the appointment of the commission, while of great institutional significance, did not lead to any radical departures in terms of policy.

How was government policy shaped in the depression with respect to the causes adduced by contemporary opinion? Except for the attitude to company organization the official reactions were standard. There were attempts to enforce the laws relating to the quality of textiles and even to extend the methods of control of standards.⁵ There was a general effort

---

¹ For the committee, see *A.P.C. 1621–1623*, pp. 190, 201–2; Stowe MSS. 354, fols. 63, 65; S.P.D. Jas. I, 130/28, 140–1, 143; Cotton MSS. Galba, E.1, fols. 362–7. The members were: Thomas Coventry, Abraham Dawes, Heneage Finch, Robert Heath, Thomas Mun, George Paul, Paul Pindar, William Richardson, L. Stafford, John Suckling, Richard Sutton and William Turner. Their report is in S.P.D. Jas. I, 131/55.

² Add. MSS. 34324, fols. 193 ff.

³ *Foedera*, XVII, 410–15. The commission was charged with investigating the causes of the low wool prices, the best means of preventing the export of raw materials, the best means of codifying the laws regulating cloth standards, the true influence (for good or bad) of company trading, the remedies for monetary scarcity, the state of the balance of trade, the problem of commodity returns, the ways of aiding navigation, the Eastland trade, the East India trade, the home demand for cloth, etc.

⁴ For the period 1622–4 the following records mention the commission. They do not include those resulting from the hearings of the exchange controversy in 1622–3 (see below, pp. 268–270). S.P.D. Jas. I, 140/82, 148/92, 162/68, 168/80; S.P.D. Chas. I, 44/25, 155/52; Add. MSS. 34324, fols. 193, 195, 197, 203, 209; Add. MSS. 12496, fol. 113; Hargrave MSS. 321, pp. 115–19, 178–9, 196–9; *C.S.P.D. 1623–1625*, pp. 93, 97, 105, 124, 140; *A.P.C. 1623–1625*, pp. 34, 40–1, 53–4, 105, 115–16, 245; *Remembrancia*, VI, 16 and 17; *Discourse...for Enlargement... of Trade* (1645), pp. 17–18.

⁵ *A.P.C. 1618–1619*, pp. 25–6, 27, 42, 52–3, 316; *A.P.C. 1621–1623*, pp. 156, 265–6, 486–8; *A.P.C. 1623–1625*, pp. 40–1, 53–4, 248; Steele, I, no. 1223; S.P.D. Jas. I, 96/39–40, 184/44; Add. MSS. 34324, fol. 201.

to tighten the administration of laws designed to prevent the export of raw materials.[1] The Adventurers' impositions (the only part of the financial burden on cloth exports which the government could or would attack) were under constant pressure until their reduction in 1624. Moves were made towards increasing domestic demand for cloth by drawing up a proclamation to enforce its wearing.[2] And the council, in 1622, acquiesced in the demands of the Eastland Company that imports of Baltic produce be confined to English ships or vessels of the country of origin.[3]

The one significant innovation in government policy during these years was in the direction of loosening the Merchant Adventurers' grip on the trade to the Low Countries and Germany. The council itself had never been reluctant to interfere, to some extent, with the vested interests of capital organization if it felt that this might increase employment. But in the early 1620's it was the House of Commons which took the initiative in experimenting with the organization of trade in the hope of reviving commerce and industry.

All the interests desiring an extension of the privilege of trading to the Low Countries and Germany had some voice in the 1621 Parliament. In February a free trade bill directed against the Adventurers' monopoly was introduced and a strong attack on the company was launched. The consideration of this bill—to open the trade to the Staplers—continued with vehement discussions, and a second opportunity of attacking the Adventurers was afforded by the protests of the outports (led by the Cinque Ports) that their livelihood was being destroyed by London companies. 'The more buyers', ran a very common feeling, 'the better for the commonwealth', and Sir Dudley Digges argued that the outport merchants, since they would avoid both the expense of bringing textiles to London and the cost of the company's impositions, would be able to defeat foreign competition by sale at lower prices. The Adventurers, of course, defended themselves with spirit, but the tide, in such a hostile ocean of criticism, had obviously set against them. The Commons, representative of interests and areas much wider than the metropolitan cartels and faced with a crisis of national scope which they could not help but interpret in terms of regional economic jealousy, were in no mood to respect the sanctity of chartered organizations. Even so the final resolution before the summer recess was milder than it might have been in

[1] A.P.C. 1618–1619, pp. 17–18; A.P.C. 1621–1623, p. 391; A.P.C. 1623–1625, pp. 34, 115–16, 285, 366, 389; Steele, I, no. 1334.
[2] S.P.D. Jas. I, 89/54 (wrongly calendared), 127/16, 131/55, 135/53; Add. MSS. 34324, fol. 197; A.P.C. 1621–1623, pp. 132, 153; Steele, I, no. 1334.
[3] Below, pp. 87–9.

view of the militant debates of the foregoing months. On 4 June Sir Dudley Digges was appointed to deliver a message to the Lords recommending for special attention the proposal 'for the increase of trade, that the outports may be freed from the restraint of exportation of all new woollen manufactures'.[1] This suggestion was taken up by the Privy Council.

The Merchant Adventurers had only included the new draperies in their privileges after the Cockayne project, and the request that this portion be annulled fitted well into the prevailing climate of opinion, especially since it concerned that branch of textiles on which men were pinning their hopes of prosperous expansion. The proposal was immediately propounded to the company and, with surprisingly little protest, they agreed that the outports might ship the new draperies to privileged areas on condition that they kept to the mart towns and obeyed the Adventurers' general regulations, while the company asked for reconfirmation of its control of the old draperies and further protection against the inroads of interlopers. On these terms a council order was issued on 11 June, which was given proclamatory force a month later.[2] The depression had produced its first significant move towards commercial liberty: while the traditional manufacture was left in the hands of the traditional trading organization, men looked for expansion of the new product outside the framework of company regulation.

The worst of the slump, however, was still to come, and criticism of the Merchant Adventurers did not abate. In spring 1622 the council became desperate in its anxiety to clear the clothiers' stocks of cloth. It commanded the company to suspend its impositions, to buy up cloth by assessing its members, and to allow interlopers to trade temporarily. The Adventurers' answers were firm: its impositions were essential to repay the debt incurred in 1617 and without them it would have to cease trading; the interlopers might come in under protest if they were confined to dealing in new draperies; but in no circumstances would individual members be forced to buy up cloths.[3] This protest produced a virtual stalemate and the matter was handed over to the investigating committee. While the council had gone far in altering traditional ideas on company trading, the lessons of the past taught it that it could not afford to force the Merchant Adventurers beyond the point at which the company would withdraw from active commerce. Any feasible liberalization of

---

[1] *Commons Debates, 1621*, IV, 411; for the proceedings on this question see II, 75 ff., 317, 364–5; III, 188 ff., 442 ff.; IV, 175; VII, 225 ff., 593. Also Hargrave MSS. 321, pp. 175–6, 180–96.
[2] S.P.D. Jas. I, 121/144; *A.P.C. 1619–1621*, pp. 391–2.
[3] S.P.D. Jas. I, 129/12.

trade had to be acceptable, however reluctantly, to the men who still were able to handle over half of London's exports. It was perhaps the same considerations which prevented the council carrying out its drastic threat in May that 'if the Eastland merchants did not forthwith buy off their cloths the clothiers [of Suffolk and Essex] themselves should have free liberty ... to ship forth their cloths into foreign parts'.[1]

Once more, action had to await parliamentary initiative and not until 1624 did commercial institutions receive another 'dose of freedom'. When the Commons met that year they quickly settled down to discuss the decay of trade, although by that time the worst was over. The Adventurers' charter was sent for and in April and May their affairs were discussed in relation to the decline of the textile industry. This time there were more positive discussions and decisions. After reports from the Committee for Trade the Commons concluded that there were two main grievances demanding redress: 'restraining of the trade ... in Germany and the Low Countries (the principal places of vent) to one company only of the Merchant Adventurers' and 'too much burdening with charges and duties'. The latter, it was recommended, should be reduced as much as possible while, for the former, trade in the new draperies, kersies, dozens and all coloured cloth should 'be left free for all merchants to all places'.[2]

As in 1622, the recommendations of Parliament were accepted with little hesitation, although this time there was some slight alteration of their terms. The company, for long years on the defensive, made the best of a bad job and agreed that, to preserve the London body, they would allow all merchants to join them while 'leaving the ... outports in their full liberty to ship their own commodities whither they please'. It was now the turn of the commission for trade—the principal executive organ for such matters—to consider the problem. Fortunately its report has survived. On 3 July it informed the council of its conclusion: all merchants might join the company; all outport traders could freely handle coloured cloths (i.e. in addition to the new draperies); all merchants could freely trade in kersies, dozens and new draperies, 'trade who will, when and whither they will'; pressure was to be brought to bear on foreign impositions; the council was to reconsider the English customs on cloth; and the Merchant Adventurers' impositions were to be reduced by one-third and confined to imports and the export of white cloth. The report was

[1] *A.P.C. 1621–1623*, pp. 223–4; S.P.D. Jas. I, 131/40; E. 134/5 Chas. I/Easter I (April 1629), deposition of Thomas Chapman.
[2] *C.J.*, I, 672, 681, 689, 695, 698, 706, 752 ff., 780 ff.; Harleian MSS. 2244, fol. 1; S.P.D. Jas. I, 160/70; Hargrave MSS. 321, pp. 113–15; *C.S.P.D. 1623–1625*, pp. 206, 239, 246, 254, 259; *Discourse ... for Enlargement ... of Trade*, pp. 42–3.

read and approved by the Privy Council on 10 July.[1] The result of all this was that it was now legal for any outport merchant to trade in all cloths except the undressed, and for all merchants, even the erstwhile interlopers, to trade in new draperies and the cheaper varieties of the old draperies. The depression, by bringing together the varied interests hostile to the great London companies, had made a large inroad into the traditional organization of the most important branch of the English cloth trade. A ten-year experiment in relative freedom was under way.[2]

It is easy to see how the liberal measures of 1621 and 1624 were derived from the slump which spanned those years. Yet, conversely, it is no less easy to detect the connexion between the depression of the early 1550's and the *restrictive* nature of the government response in that period.[3] What is the explanation of this radically different approach to two similar phenomena? Undoubtedly one major reason lay in the heightened significance and power which an independent Parliament had achieved in the body politic by the early seventeenth century. Such a legislative organ—vociferously representative of the outports and the lesser gentry, highly suspicious of central monopolies, jealous of the Crown's authority and the power of rich City merchants, and eager for a relaxation of economic control—took every opportunity of tilting against an exclusive metropolitan monopoly. An institution so representative of interests which normally felt themselves desperately underprivileged would be difficult to restrain during an economic crisis when all its grievances were intensified and articulated. It is significant that in 1634, during a time of commercial dislocation, there was no Parliament, and then the Privy Council renewed the monopolistic powers of the Merchant Adventurers.[4]

However, there is need to consider other factors besides the growing power and representativeness of the House of Commons—if only because in the early 1620's there was no obvious cleavage of opinion between the Privy Council and Parliament. It may have been that, in the 1620's, as far as the organization of trade was concerned, the only experiment possible was in the direction of relaxation while, in the 1550's, after a period of relative freedom, increased regulation was the only feasible large-scale change: and in both crises a strong current of opinion

[1] Hargrave MSS. 321, pp. 115–19, 178–9; A.P.C. 1623–1625, pp. 268–9.
[2] The erosion of the Adventurers' privileges was not, of course, the only liberal measure of the Commons in these years. Besides the famous Statute of Monopolies (1624), a statute was finally passed in 1624, after lengthy debate in 1621, which, in an effort to raise the price of wool, repealed the act of 1552 against wool middlemen (21 Jac. I, c. 28). In addition, 21 Jac. I, c. 4 confined all informations on penal statutes to the lower courts in the county of the supposed offence; a response to troublesome activities of informers, in the depression years, in their attempts to enforce the economic legislation (Davies, pp. 71–3).
[3] Fisher, 'Commercial Trends and Policies', 103 ff.
[4] Below, pp. 121–2.

demanded some experiment. But perhaps of more importance was the growth of a new attitude of mind. Slowly, men in the seventeenth century were forced to acknowledge that they were living in a changing competitive world and that England held a position within it that depended upon the sale of goods and a thriving commerce. They had to come to terms, in a way which Tudor statesmen refused to do, with a large textile industry and could no longer fall back on an economic philosophy which was suspicious of industrial expansion because of the perpetual change and insecurity involved. The seventeenth-century statesman wanted to lift the economy out of crisis and develop the textile industry in order to maintain employment; his sixteenth-century counterpart wished for the type of stability which could only be obtained when the textile industry was regulated and restrained to a low level of activity. In other words, the emphasis which in the 1550's had been placed on *production*, and the possibilities of its control, had shifted by the 1620's to *demand*, and the possibilities of its expansion. Only in later years would the potentialities of forms of expansionism other than the sale of cloth come to be fully recognized.[1]

[1] Below, pp. 160-2, 223-4, 247-9.

4. CURRENCY MANIPULATION AND THE CRISIS OF THE EARLY 1620's

(i) DEVALUATION ABROAD—THE DECLINE IN EXPORTS

We have already seen the confusion which resulted from contemporary investigations into the causes of the slump which undermined English textiles in the early 1620's. No possible explanation of the decline went uncanvassed and this is understandable, since the depth of the depression was to some extent a function of the overall weakness of the English cloth industry within the European economy. Yet the abrupt nature of the crisis and the particular form which it took lead one to believe that there must have been a single factor which, above all others, precipitated the catastrophe which made these years among the bleakest of the century. It will be the argument here that for an explanation of the slump one must turn to the short-term impact of European currency manipulations on prices and incomes abroad.

Prices and incomes in the early seventeenth century were quoted in terms of 'imaginary' or 'ghost' monies, which frequently had no physical existence, but actual transactions were satisfied by a variety of real (metallic or token) coins. In the economist's phrase, the circulating medium did not necessarily coincide with the money of account. The coins actually in circulation were, however, rated either directly or indirectly in terms of the imaginary money and this meant that currency manipulation was facilitated: besides being able to debase the fineness by a recoinage, mint authorities, with the stroke of a pen, could change the valuation put on the circulating media by 'calling down' or, more usually, 'calling up' (enhancing) the relevant rating. It was the latter case which was more important and its result was to depreciate the money of account. Enhancement and debasement had immediate and direct effects on the flows of bullion, and these will be dealt with in chapter 8. The significant thing here is that an enhancement or a debasement of the silver coinage each resulted in less silver being represented by any given unit of the money of account, either because the coin (and its silver content) remained the same while its rating was raised or because the rating remained constant while the weight of fine silver in the coin was reduced. Unless the prices, in terms of the 'imaginary' money of account, of goods and labour rose at least commensurately with the enhancement or debasement, then silver prices—the amount of metal paid for goods or services

—would be bound to fall; this was the most frequent consequence of such manipulation. Of course, enhancement and debasement both increased the quantity of money by making the existing circulating stocks of silver go further in terms of the money of account, and the tendency, therefore, *was* for prices to rise to some extent: 'the measure being altered ... there went more number to make up the tale, and of necessity other things went and were named more accordingly in price.'[1] And this tendency would be emphasized if the public lost confidence in the currency and refused to hold it, so increasing the velocity of circulation: 'when monies are enhanced they never are carried to the mints for to be converted into other coin. But they remain current, between man and man running like a post-horse, every man fearing to receive a loss by the fall.'[2] But, historically, such inflations were rarely proportionate to the manipulation. In a debasement, as Ricardo pointed out, although the silver-value of each reissued coin fell by the full extent of the debasing, there might not be sufficient reissue to increase prices as far as expected: 'By a limitation of its quantity, a debased coin would circulate at the value it should bear, if it were of the legal weight and fineness, and not at the value of the quantity of metal which it actually contained. In the history of the British coinage, we find, accordingly, that the currency was never depreciated in the same proportion that it was debased; the reason of which was, that it never was increased in quantity, in proportion to its diminished intrinsic value.'[3] And in both debasements and enhancements the extent of the price rise might lag behind that of the manipulation because of the conventional nature of prices, institutional stickiness, ignorance, and confusion—which all served to slow down the inflationary operations of the increased quantity of the money of account. Meanwhile the par of exchange moved directly with the fluctuation in currency. Since exchange rates were quoted, of course, in monies of account (so many Flemish shillings or Polish groschen for 20s. sterling) and were based on the silver coinage, the par would be determined by the silver represented by the standard unit of the money of account. As the amount of silver represented by, say, one groschen decreased in proportion to the degree of enhancement or debasement, so, therefore, the par of exchange moved proportionately to such an alteration, in a direction 'unfavourable' to the currency concerned. Thus, if the tampering took place in the Low Countries more Flemish

[1] Malynes, *England's Interest*, pp. 7–8.
[2] Malynes, *The Maintenance of Free Trade*, p. 31. A loss of confidence would be especially likely during a violent and unprincipled debasement.
[3] *The Works and Correspondence of David Ricardo*, ed. Piero Sraffa, I (Cambridge, 1951), 353. This reference was noted in Fisher, 'Commercial Trends and Policy'. Men at the time also noticed that the value of debased currency could be maintained (Richard Eburne, *Plain Pathway to Plantations* (1624), p. 51).

shillings would be needed to 'buy' (i.e. balance) the amount of silver represented by 20s. sterling.

The effects of this situation on commerce were marked, for the fall in silver prices consequent on a lagging inflation, or, what is the same thing, the divergence between the internal and external valuations of the manipulated currency, immediately altered the terms of trade. Importers to that market found that, selling their goods at prevailing nominal prices brought them less silver than normally; and this might be brought to their notice since, although they were receiving more of the (depreciated) units of currency than formerly, they got less for them when they returned home the proceeds by exchange. To make trade as profitable as previously it was, that is, to secure sufficient silver from sales to cover costs and profits, they would have to increase their prices in the depreciated currency to a level too high for the lagging price system: 'If the money rise in denomination above its true worth in valuation and the exchange also rise accordingly: *if this merchant do not raise the price of his commodity in due proportion answerable thereunto*, he shall be sure to come home by weeping cross, however he make his return, whether by exchange, or in money, bullion, or wares.'[1] The converse applied to exporters from the relevant region: they could buy goods in that market cheaper (i.e. with less silver) than before. Together, imports to the area, becoming dearer, would fall and exports from it, becoming cheaper, would increase. The situation had all the attributes of a modern devaluation—with the additional feature that its impact was immediately brought home to the public through the changed *internal* valuation of the currency.

Historically, there have been many such retardations of inflation following interference with the currency. In Tudor England one had occurred during the Great Debasement and provoked a disturbing boom in cloth exports.[2] At the end of the second decade of the seventeenth century a wave of enhancement and debasement started in northern and eastern Europe which, as silver prices fell, soon priced English cloth out of those markets.

The disruption in England's export trade is indicated by the following figures:[3]

Exports of shortcloths by English merchants from London

	Total	To Hamburg	To the Dutch Mart	To the Baltic
1618	102,300	35,000	31,500	7,843
1620	85,700	22,300	35,700	2,848
1622	75,600	23,700	26,500	4,054

[1] Misselden, *The Circle of Commerce*, pp. 16–17; my italics.
[2] Fisher, 'Commercial Trends and Policies', 99.
[3] See Appendix A, Tables 2 and 3.

Thus the fall of some 16,600 from 1618 to 1620 was wholly explained by the decline of exports to Hamburg and the Baltic. By 1622 there were signs of recovery in these two 'markets'[1] but depression had hit the Dutch outlet. We shall deal with this difference in timing later in this chapter,[2] but there can be no doubt that the initial onslaught of depression came primarily in the trade to the German and east European markets.

Germany and Poland in the years after 1617 were the victims of an unparalleled outburst of monetary confusion and currency manipulation. This *Kipper- und Wipper-zeit* was largely the result of the efforts of local magnates and mint-controllers who, as debtors or owners of stocks of coin and bullion, stood to reap short-term profits from such alterations to the coinage. Germany, it has been said, besides its religious and political difficulties, was 'doubly cursed with a mint and monetary system such as has no equal in history for its appalling confusion and perniciousness'.[3] It was the scene of almost constant tampering with the coinage by an innumerable body of local mints, of which the Saxon dynasty controlled forty-five, the Dukes of Brandenburg forty, Silesia had eighteen, and the Lower Rhenish Circle sixty-seven.[4] Poland's monetary situation was no less anarchic, with mints leased to speculators who worked them for private gain and with a fine disregard for the benefits of a stable currency.[5] In Germany it was the outbreak of the Thirty Years War which set in motion an unrestrainable process of debasement and enhancement, while in Poland feverish manipulation had commenced in 1616–17. In Holland there was, in the long run, considerably less interference with the currency because the mints were kept on a tighter rein; but in northern and eastern Europe, major markets for English cloth, the depreciation reduced silver prices to such a degree that English exporters were unable to sell cloth at competitive prices and at the same time show a profit when the proceeds were remitted ('by exchange, or in money, bullion, or wares') to England to be realized in the home currency.

In Danzig the fine silver content of the groschen, which stood at 0·557 grammes in 1617, declined steadily to 0·313 grammes in 1622,[6] and other Polish towns suffered from similar depreciations, which are demonstrated in the following table and represented graphically in Fig. 1.

[1] Of course the port of destination was not necessarily in the land of final consumption; although it was more likely to be there in the case of Hamburg and Elbing than in the case of the Dutch marts.
[2] Below, pp. 97–8.
[3] W. A. Shaw, 'The Monetary Movements of 1600–1621 in Holland and Germany', *Trans. Roy. Hist. Soc.* n.s. IX (1895).
[4] C. V. Wedgewood, *The Thirty Years War* (1938), p. 47.
[5] See, for example, S.P.D. Jas. I, 118/139.
[6] J. Pelc, *Ceny w Gdansku w XVI i XVII Wieku* (Lwów, 1937), pp. 4–5.

Currency Manipulation

Silver content of groschen in Polish towns [1]
(in grammes)

	1617	1618	1619	1620	1621	1622	1623	1624	1625
Danzig	0·557	0·544	0·495	0·414	0·324	0·313	0·316	0·324	0·322
Cracow	0·579	0·517	0·486	0·405	0·324	0·304	0·324	0·324	0·314
Lwów	0·504	0·487	0·472	0·324	0·296	0·202	0·270	0·304	0·286
Lublin	0·436	0·390	0·354	0·324	0·295	0·270	0·270	0·324	0·295
Warsaw	0·532	0·486	0·486	0·405	0·306	0·318	0·330	0·324	0·314

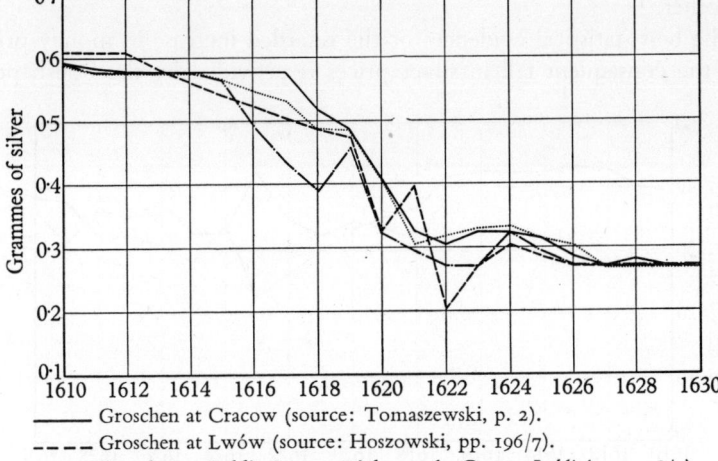

——— Groschen at Cracow (source: Tomaszewski, p. 2).
– – – Groschen at Lwów (source: Hoszowski, pp. 196/7).
–·–·– Groschen at Lublin (source: Adamczyk, *Ceny w Lublinie*, pp. 58/9).
············ Groschen at Warsaw (source: Adamczyk, *Ceny w Warszawie*, p. 3).

FIG. 1. Fine silver content (in grammes) of Polish groschen at Cracow, Lwów, Lublin and Warsaw, 1610–30.

In Hamburg the declining silver content of the reichsdaller can be traced by the figures of its enhancement in terms of local shillings:[2]

mid-1618	42s. 6d.	February 1621	53s. 0d.
September 1619	46s. 6d.	March 1621	54s. 6d.
October 1619	48s. 0d.	May 1621	54s. 0d.
August 1620	52s. 0d.	May 1622	48s. 0d.

In Speyer the fine silver content of one (local) pound fell from 14·85 grammes in 1617 to 11·00 in 1620; similar events took place at Frankfort and elsewhere in Germany;[3] and contemporary writings during the period refer again and again to the wholesale manipulations of European

[1] Sources: Pelc, pp. 4–5; E. Tomaszewski, *Ceny w Krakowie w Latach 1601–1795* (Lwów, 1934), p. 2; S. Hoszowski, *Ceny w Lwowie w XVI i XVII Wieku* (Lwów, 1928), pp. 196–7; W. Adamczyk, *Ceny w Lublinie od XVI do Konca XVIII Wieku* (Lwów, 1935), pp. 58–9, and *Ceny w Warszawie w XVI i XVII Wieku* (Lwów, 1938), p. 3.
[2] W. A. Shaw, *A History of Currency* (1895), p. 105. Cf. p. 103.
[3] M. J. Elsas, *Umriss einer Geschichte der Preise und Löhne in Deutschland* (Leiden, 1936), I, 117; II A, 8, 14, 16; Shaw, 'Monetary Movements', *passim*.

currency. Exchange rates shot up as an immediate consequence, for, as Malynes pointed out, 'if you enhance the coin the exchange doth control it and rise accordingly ... to the end that the value thereof should be answered by the public measure of exchange'. In 1623 it was noted that 'As the money hath been raised in Germany and the Low Countries, so likewise hath the exchange there risen since that time accordingly; which being opposed to the raising of the money, maketh the one equivalent to the other.'[1]

The best statistical evidence for the retarded increase in money prices and the consequent fall in silver prices is provided by the Polish price

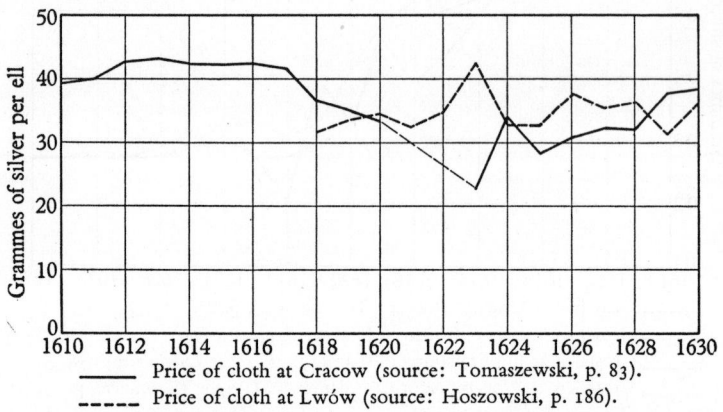

——— Price of cloth at Cracow (source: Tomaszewski, p. 83).
- - - - Price of cloth at Lwów (source: Hoszowski, p. 186).

FIG. 2. Prices (in grammes of silver per ell) of 'falendysz' cloth in Cracow and Lwów, 1610–30.

histories, which, however inexact they are, demonstrate that the general tendencies point in the expected direction. Fig. 2 shows the decline in the amount of silver needed to buy one ell of cloth at Cracow and Lwów. To a certain extent, therefore, it measures the sort of textile competition which English merchants met: the reduced amount of precious metal they would have had to accept if they did not wish to raise prices above the prevailing levels. Fig. 3 shows the same thing for other selected items in the price-income structure. On the whole it seems undeniable that in Poland there was a considerable divergence between the depreciation of the money of account and the movement of prices and incomes.[2] This phenomenon was noted elsewhere, for instance in Holland[3] and also in

[1] Malynes, *The Maintenance of Free Trade*, pp. 14–15; Misselden, *The Circle of Commerce*, p. 102. Cf. T. Mun, *England's Treasure by Foreign Trade* (reprinted 1933), p. 30. It is doubtful whether continuous exchange transactions occurred in Poland—see below, pp. 84–5.
[2] The Polish case is dealt with at greater length below, Section (ii).
[3] Misselden, *The Circle of Commerce*, p. 25.

Silesia, Moravia, Austria, etc., where 'It hath been observed for a great indiscretion in the . . . country people . . . to take the reichsdaller at so excessive an high rate [i.e. in terms of the money of account] in payment for their linens, and not to raise the price thereof answerable thereunto.'[1] But 'indiscretion' or not such a situation could only destroy the local market for English cloth as 'the sudden enhancement of monies in Germany and the Low Countries made our merchants to enhance [i.e.

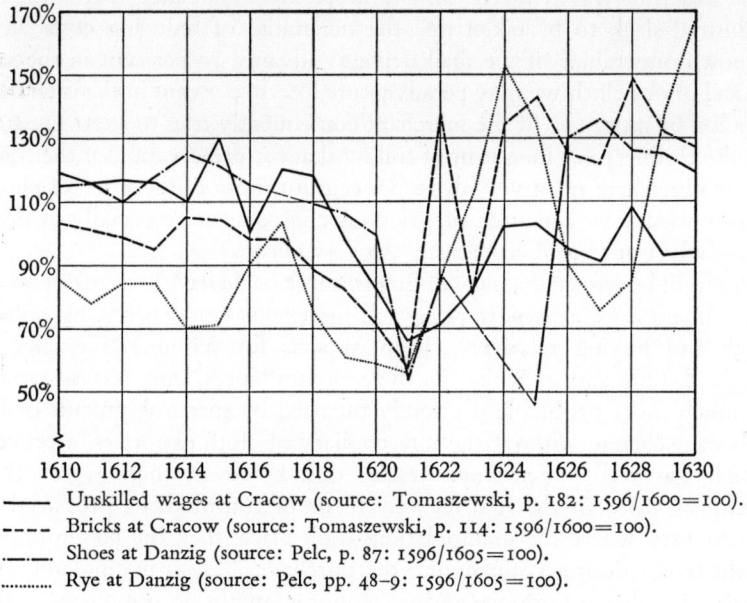

——— Unskilled wages at Cracow (source: Tomaszewski, p. 182: 1596/1600=100).
- - - - Bricks at Cracow (source: Tomaszewski, p. 114: 1596/1600=100).
.—.—. Shoes at Danzig (source: Pelc, p. 87: 1596/1605=100).
.... Rye at Danzig (source: Pelc, pp. 48–9: 1596/1605=100).

FIG. 3. Selected indices of Polish silver prices, 1610–30.

raise the prices of] their cloths, whereby they [the inhabitants] undersold us in their cloths which they did not enhance'.[2] The native consumer simply found imported textiles too dear. Further, the severity of the currency fluctuations threatened English traders who were creditors and whose future receipts, contracted in money of account, would now vary arbitrarily in terms of real silver; since the wars in Germany, it was said, 'the monies [have] become so variable, that when a merchant hath sold his cloth, and hopeth to have gained something thereby, by that time that the term for payment is expired, he receiveth less in value than the cloths cost, by the raising and rising of the monies'.[3] Hull traders also

[1] *Ibid.*, p. 39.   [2] Add. MSS. 34324, fol. 195.
[3] Misselden, *Free Trade*, p. 52. Cf. similar statements: *Commons Debates, 1621*, III, 45 ff.; VII, 225 ff.; Add. MSS. 34324, fol. 191; S.P.D. Jas. I, 180/75.

found that reigning prices in the Baltic market were too low to cover their total costs, 'by which we lose, and cannot be able to help it, by not being able to raise the price there, by reason of the extraordinary rising of their money and other store of clothing in the country, so that either overcheap pennyworths must cause our cloth to vent there, or else they will not vent at all; the decay thereof will appear in his Majesty's Customs House books; and we find that this trade grows daily worse and worse'.[1] The situation was rendered all the more inflexible since there was no industrial slack to be taken up—the difficulties of reducing costs were almost insuperable: 'if we shall strive to advance 10 per cent in the sale [price] of our cloth we may peradventure lose 40 per cent in the utterance of a less quantity . . . [if the merchant consequently tries to exert pressure on the clothier] . . . then it must follow that for preservation of the trade the clothier here must yet fall 10 per centum more in the price of cloth, which would be a matter of grievous consequence, especially at these times when our wools are already so very cheap.'[2]

It might be argued that sales of English cloth could have been maintained, since in measure as export prices fell merchants could profit by selling cloth and buying relatively cheap imports for remunerative sales in England. One answer is that, in these circumstances, importation would be much more profitable if directly financed by specie shipments or by bills of exchange without the intermediary of cloth exporters, a process which was well under way. Besides this, however, there were other factors at work. If the returns were to be of commodities produced in the country where the manipulations took place, then the penumbra of credit transactions accompanying the purchase of cloth in England, sale abroad, purchase of imports and sale at home, might possibly increase the period of capital turnover to an uneconomic extent, so that the merchant was unable to finance the next shipment of textiles. And this would particularly apply during a slump. If, on the other hand, the imports were bought in the disturbed market but produced elsewhere—e.g. in Italy, as many imported goods were—then their prices would be relatively unaffected by the currency manipulations, so that they would not be significantly cheaper.

It therefore seems reasonably clear that the effective and immediate cause of the depression in the cloth industry during the early 1620's was a series of currency manipulations in some of the principal European markets for English textiles, which priced the cloth out of those markets. However, it was not the case that an otherwise prosperous and economic-

[1] Hadley, p. 114.
[2] Add. MSS. 34324, fols. 171-2. For the rigidity of costs, see below, pp. 144, 148, 153.

ally strong export industry was brought down solely by the repercussions of enhancement and debasement. Continental devaluation could only operate as disastrously as it did given the existing conditions of manufacture at home and abroad. Wartime insecurity and a growing continental industry which had secured competitive cost advantages before 1618 had already created an unfavourable environment before monetary fluctuations threw English costs completely out of line. At home the industry was still suffering from the after-effects of Cockayne's scheme. The fact that the possibility of reducing real costs was limited was also very important: had the structure of the old draperies been less rigid, had the industry been able to reduce prices in the face of overt competition, then the impact of foreign enhancement would have been correspondingly less and England would have been able to meet what was, in the long run, as much a growth of foreign manufacture as a glutting of the market. Further, it was the pressure on prices produced by depreciation which brought into the open the financial burdens imposed on cloth at home and abroad.

For these reasons contemporary references to the situation with regard to currency manipulations are rare and, where they do occur, mostly oblique. In any case the merchant, who was the person most likely to know and understand the connexion between silver prices and exports, hardly ever spontaneously approached the council or public opinion concerning the fall in overseas sales, and when called on to explain it was rarely given to elaborate disquisitions. In general, the commentators did not phrase their analyses of the crisis in terminology familiar to modern readers, and, with some confusion, the contingency often showed itself, in their documents, under a variety of guises. Above all they emphasized those uncompetitive features which were exposed by the currency alterations: taxes, foreign manufacture, war, the general difficulties of merchants. Other aspects of the commercial scene to which much attention was devoted—exchange rates, the augmentation of imports, the drain of bullion which resulted from the unfavourable balance of trade—will be dealt with in section (iii) of this chapter. Before this, however, it will be useful to study a case which involved critical difficulties in returns and which both consolidates the arguments put forward here and demonstrates some of their weaknesses.

(ii) THE EASTLAND TRADE, 1618–1622: A CASE STUDY

The English trade to the Baltic was, unlike that of the Dutch, a supply and not a transit trade: exports were almost invariably of home goods and returns were mostly made to England. In these years the trade is of particular interest. Firstly, because the Eastland Company was virtually the only mercantile group spontaneously to complain of worsening conditions of trade; secondly, because of the nature of their complaints and the extent to which the suggested remedial measures were actually taken. The explanation of both these stems from the unique position of the company when faced with enhancement and a general fall in silver prices in its markets.

The company's shipments, relatively considered, fell by more than those of the Merchant Adventurers. London's exports to the Baltic declined from 8,713 shortcloths in 1616 to 7,843 in 1618 and 2,848 in 1620. The outport merchants suffered equally and Ipswich traders late in 1621 claimed that their exports to the Baltic had fallen from 3,000 or 4,000 to 1,000 cloths.[1] Since the staple export to the Baltic was of dyed and dressed cloth from Suffolk, the result of this fall-off was a concentration of depression in a highly distressed area. The immediate cause of the decline was the operation of the currency disturbances: the Polish coinage was the worst affected of all and, as already described, silver prices soon collapsed. The complaints of the Hull merchants, quoted above, were matched by those of the London traders to the Baltic:[2]

Although the monies of late are excessively risen in the eastern parts and Germany, yet *the cloth and other native commodities of those countries rise not proportionably to the monies*. By reason whereof monies being risen upward of 50 per cent within less than two years last past in these countries, *the English are enforced to endeavour the sale of their cloth rateable to the true value of their monies* which, far exceeding the rates of former times (before the rising of the monies) and the price of cloth now made in those countries, there is by this means far less quantities of English cloth vented than otherwise there would be.

But this was not all. The merchants went on to attribute the decline in exports to the economic difficulties they experienced in their commodity returns. If these hindrances did exist then they explain why the company was so much more vociferous than other groups in these years; for whereas most other merchants, as we shall see, were still able to continue profitable dealings other than in cloth exports, the Baltic merchants now found that, in all directions, their activities were circumscribed.

The factor to which the company devoted most attention was the

[1] The figures for 1616 and 1618 are in Friis, p. 382; that for 1620 is derived from E. 190/25/1. For the outports see Hargrave MSS. 321, pp. 119–22 (Ipswich); Hadley, pp. 113 ff. (Hull); B. Hall, 'The Trade of Newcastle and the North-East Coast, 1600–1640' (unpublished M.Sc. (Econ.) thesis, University of London, 1933), pp. 63, 145, 153–4. For the early appearance of decay in the Eastland trade, see S.P.D. Jas. I, 105/42, 115/109.
[2] S.P.D. Jas. I, 118/138; my italics.

effectiveness of Dutch competition in the Baltic trade. The Hollanders, it was said in June 1620, 'with their ready money . . . buy 30 in the 100 better cheap than the English because the English carry cloth and other native commodities . . . and besides they have a great advantage in the . . . prices of their freights [so that they can import Baltic produce] better cheap than the English can'. These twin themes of the Dutch use of ready money and their inherent efficiencies in freighting recur again and again in the documents dealing with the Baltic trade during these years. Such commercial advantages, it was said, 'enforce our nation to endeavour to sell their cloth proportionable to their estimation of their monies and so to raise their charge of maintenance . . . by the sales of cloth, for that by returns in foreign commodities the exporters of our native commodities are not able to keep market with the strangers merchandizing with ready money'. Consequently 'the English merchant exporting the manufactory of the land is already in part, and likely to be in short time wholly, discouraged and driven out of trade'.[1]

It was certainly true that the Dutch had a semi-permanent advantage in freight rates and shipping costs. This was principally derived from their specialization in fishing and in the bulky transit trade between southern Europe and the Baltic, which produced a commercial organization and a type of ship eminently superior to those of England.[2] In addition, as contemporaries were quick to point out, Dutch merchants, since they normally exported bullion and specie to the Baltic, were able to secure the lower prices and quicker turnover which came from trading with ready money in an area of currency enhancement. The Eastland merchants therefore claimed that their import trade suffered from this Dutch competition as much dislocation as their trade in cloth outwards suffered from currency disturbances; and they claimed, further, that there was a direct causal relationship here: that one important additional reason why their textile exports were too low was to be found in the difficulties they met in returning the proceeds to England.

The company concentrated on the hindrances to commodity returns; but in theory there were two other ways in which assets could be brought home: by shipments of specie or by bill of exchange. Bullion or specie shipments were, at that time, out of the question; for one thing, the currency confusion made it profitable to send money to the Baltic rather than bring it out; for another, merchants were already receiving too little silver for their cloth at Elbing or Danzig to hope to profit by

[1] S.P.D. Jas. I, 115/109, 118/138.
[2] Christensen, *Dutch Trade to the Baltic*; V. Barbour, 'Dutch and English Merchant Shipping in the Seventeenth Century', *Econ. Hist. Rev.* II (1930), 261–90; Charles Wilson, *Profit and Power: a Study of England and the Dutch Wars* (1957), pp. 2–3, 33–4, 41–2.

shipping it home: 'it is come to such extremity with the Eastland Company, that they cannot vent their cloth in other wares to make return, and by money their loss would be incredible'.[1] The problem of the exchanges needs to be dealt with at greater length.

Although there is some evidence of exchange dealings, from the Continent, with the Baltic,[2] most contemporaries were of the opinion that this was far from a permanent occurrence where England was concerned. It was not merely that, economically, the Eastland was a primitive area where there was no organized and regular money market and where even cash transactions were not necessarily normal—although this was certainly true.[3] Seventeenth-century exchange dealings were not a matter of pre-existing 'institutional' arrangements. Instead, they depended on the presence, in this instance, of merchants in the Baltic who had money there and wished to transfer it to England, and of other merchants who would find that giving bills of exchange, at the rates likely to rule, would be their best way of obtaining money in the Baltic market. Basically, the exchange rate had to be such that neither party could find a better (more profitable) way of transferring or obtaining funds. For most of the early seventeenth century, and most certainly from 1618 to 1622, this situation simply never obtained in the Baltic. From a reading of the contemporary sources and on the evidence of the Sound Toll Accounts, it appears that England and Holland both had a chronic deficit in their balances of payment with that area. This merely means that had there been exchange transactions then the rate would soon have moved beyond the specie import point for the Eastland, which was specie export point for England. That is, owners of silver coin in the Baltic would not be able to find 'takers', since people who needed money there would find it cheaper to import directly (or earn it by commodity imports) than to take it up by exchange at a very low rate of groschen per pound sterling; equally, in England potential deliverers would find the exchange too expensive a way of getting money to Danzig or Elbing. There were no exchange operations simply because, in each case, one necessary party to them found a more remunerative way of securing his desired object. Therefore even when the exchange was temporarily in use—as it might be if one party to the contract were forced by events to accept highly unfavourable terms—it soon, with the return of normal times, dropped into *désuétude*. This point was exemplified by Sir Ralph Maddison: 'This

[1] Malynes, *The Maintenance of Free Trade*, p. 53.
[2] N. W. Posthumus, *Inquiry into the History of Prices in Holland* (Leiden, 1946), I, 590 ff.; H.M.C. Sackville, II, 215–16; A.P.C. 1618–1619, pp. 290–1.
[3] For the prevalence of barter see S.P.D. Jas. I, 118/139; G. Malynes, *A Treatise of the Canker of England's Commonwealth* (1602), p. 65; Malynes, *The Maintenance of Free Trade*, p. 53.

Currency Manipulation

year the want of corn in England did enforce a great price of the exchange [i.e. the price of groschen in terms of pound sterling rose] in the Eastland from whence it was brought because there was much employment for monies and less than was used to be had there, that is the commodities of that country did exceed the wares exported, which enforced the exportation of our monies in specie.'[1] However, even where exchange could take place, that is, where the rate of exchange was within the specie export point for the Baltic, the merchant in the Baltic could get by exchange operations no more silver in English coin than he had silver in groschen. In this case there could be no help to exporters of cloth to a market where sales were contracting because silver prices were falling. For then merchants would have to give, for 20 shillings in England, an equivalent or greater amount of silver in the Baltic. And this would have perpetuated or increased their original losses on sales. For falling exports, therefore, even the *possibility* of exchange dealings was no help: for it would only have taken place at rates which could not have relieved the situation. As long as the commercial setting made it highly profitable to ship silver to the Baltic there was no chance of returning money at a rate sufficiently low to help the cloth exporter because, by then, exchange operations had ceased. And this was a feature of most of the early seventeenth century: Dutch ships to a large extent entered the Sound in ballast and carrying specie; Mun presumed that the Eastland trade, like the East Indian, needed specie;[2] and in general, for everyday commerce, there seems to have been no exchange between England and the Baltic.[3] The conclusion must be that even in the abnormal situation of regular exchange operations, these would not have helped English exporters; and that generally, and specifically during a slump, a chronic payments deficit with the Baltic market placed the existence of such a system entirely out of the question.[4]

[1] Add. MSS. 34324, fol. 179 (July 1623).
[2] *England's Treasure*, p. 15.
[3] S.P.D. Jas. I, 118/140; P.C. 2/44, pp. 482–4; C.S.P.D. *1640–1641*, p. 368; Malynes, *A Treatise of the Canker*, p. 70. For the direct attraction of specie to the Baltic see L. Roberts, *The Merchant's Map of Commerce* (1638), p. 176; T. Violet, *An Humble Declaration* (1643), p. 21; Barbour, *Capitalism in Amsterdam*, p. 52 n.
[4] Of interest here is the controversy, as to the need for treasure in the Baltic trade, between Charles Wilson and E. F. Heckscher (Charles Wilson, 'Treasure and Trade Balances: The Mercantilist Problem', *Econ. Hist. Rev.* 2nd ser. II (1949), 152–61; E. F. Heckscher, 'Multilateralism, Baltic Trade, and the Mercantilists', *Econ. Hist. Rev.* 2nd ser. III (1950), 219–28; Charles Wilson, 'Treasure and Trade Balances: Further Evidence', *Econ. Hist. Rev.* 2nd ser. IV (1951), 231–42). A detailed discussion of the issues involved would be out of place here and in any case the controversy is concerned with a period later than that under present consideration. However, my conclusions would definitely seem to favour the views of Mr Wilson, at least for England and the early seventeenth century. There is no evidence that Mun's discussion of multilateral bill transactions (Heckscher, 'Multilateralism', 222) applied in any significant degree to the commercial connexions between England and the Baltic. Merchants gave no sign that they were aware of any method of returning assets from the Eastland except directly to England's shores; and most often not only was there no way of

It is now clear why, in the absence of an exchange and while the flow of bullion was towards the Baltic, merchants envisaged a direct link between imports from Elbing or Danzig and textile exports from England. Even if the link were broken by shipments of specie to buy imports, cloth sales would suffer to an exactly commensurate degree. Since the export of money or treasure was illegal, the Eastland Company could not officially assess its chances of meeting Dutch competition directly and it was forced to discuss imports in terms of exports. Yet, on the whole, the emphasis that the company placed on the import situation in explaining the decline in cloth sales is not entirely unjustifiable. Dutch merchants were utilizing their undoubted cost advantages to beat the English out of the import trade; they were re-exporting Baltic materials to England after processing in the Low Countries;[1] and they were profiting by their ability to export ready money to an area where enhancement was rife and cash was at a premium. The Ipswich merchants complained that they sold little enough cloth in the Baltic and that 'neither do they know wherein to make return of that little they now send when it is sold. For money they cannot bring and the Hollanders and they that trade in money do ... fill this land with all Eastland commodities, making three returns in one year.'[2] The special problem of the Eastland merchants lay in the fact that they could not profit by the lower silver prices for imports because Dutch competition kept down the price of Baltic goods in England. Unlike other traders they could not turn to their own advantage the swing in the terms of trade which followed the currency manipulation.[3]

The claim that foreign competition in the import market directly transferring funds by exchange to other places, but there was no chance of dealing by exchange directly with England! In a precise sense, therefore, *English* trade with the Baltic was insulated from other routes and other transactions; and England seemed to be running a semi-permanent deficit with that area which came to be paid for in specie—either illegally by English or Scottish merchants or (also illegally) indirectly through Holland. The Eastland case was much nearer to that of India than Professor Heckscher was prepared to allow. Finally, as to the preference for bullion rather than instruments of credit in the Baltic, we may study (as well as the other references in the previous note) what Lewes Roberts had to say (*The Merchant's Map of Commerce*, p. 176): 'The Eastland population are noted to have so little gold and silver, as despising all in respect of it [sic], they sell their rich commodities ... at a low rate, especially those which are for daily food.'

[1] S.P.D. Jas. I, 135/60.
[2] Hargrave MSS. 321, p. 121.
[3] I think it is this situation which answers the problem raised by Mr J. D. Gould ('The Trade Depression of the Early 1620's', 88). Detecting the complaints of an inability to return goods he interprets them as signs of an over-abundance of exports (i.e. a favourable balance of trade, contrasting with accepted ideas). In the first case such complaints would not preclude an unfavourable balance since imports could be handled mainly by aliens. Secondly, as we have seen, the concomitant of such complaints was a fall in exports and a decrease in the profitability of *all* trading, because the Dutch took over a larger share of imports through their ability to take advantage of enhancements and their proficiency in commercial techniques. There is, in fact, no problem.

reduced cloth exports through the Sound was to be repeated in the 1630's.¹ In the early 1620's it was a particularly forceful case to offer to the government: in measure as the difficulties (or competitors) in the import trade were not removed, the disastrous depression in the textile industry could only get worse. In large part, of course, this argument was not strictly true. The primary factor in the collapse of the cloth market was the monetary confusion in Poland. Nevertheless, the Eastland Company undoubtedly suffered much more than they otherwise would have through the frictions in their returns, and, for instance, the 1621 Parliament was anxious lest a proposed limitation on corn imports hinder the cloth market.²

The company had a ready-made and obvious solution for their problems. It was one to which all the arguments rehearsed by merchants and non-merchants alike pointed: it was to meet Dutch competition by confirming the company's quasi-monopolistic privilege of handling Baltic imports; in other words, to eliminate the Dutch merchants by legal edict. In addition, while the home prices of grain were low in the early years of the crisis, the merchants requested that they be encouraged by having the right freely to re-export corn from England. A committee which considered these problems in 1620 produced a report which was in absolute agreement with the company's analysis of the decline in cloth exports, the currency enhancements in eastern Europe, the profitability of exporting money which enabled the Dutch to purchase goods quickly and at large discounts, and the need to ban the import of goods from the Baltic in any ships except those belonging to Englishmen or natives of the Eastland.³ There was, of course, a considerable illegal export of bullion and specie to the Baltic in this period,⁴ but this was no answer either to the textile slump or to the virile Dutch competition in returns, and the campaign to secure legal protection for the company's imports was intensified. The argument was in fact presented to the 1622 committee on the decay of trade who, in their report, gave full approval to the merchants' request.⁵

¹ P.C. 2/44, pp. 482–4 (March 1635): 'From those parts they have no exchange nor, by reason of the excessive raising of the monies, can make any return in coin or bullion; so that in what proportion other merchants bring in their returns, in the same measure they hinder the export of dyed and dressed cloth.' Cf. S.P.D. Chas. I, 279/70; C.S.P.D. 1637, p. 513.
² *Commons Debates, 1621*, II, 177 ff.; III, 280 ff.
³ S.P.D. Jas. I, 115/111, 118/139. The members of the committee were: Nicholas Leate, William Russell, Sir Thomas Smith, Thomas Stiles and John Wolstenholme. All had extended commercial interests, and Leate and Stiles were active exporters of cloth to the Baltic in 1620 (E. 190/23/3). The company's case was reiterated before Parliament in 1621 (*Commons Debates, 1621*, III, 45).
⁴ Hargrave MSS. 321, p. 4; S.P.D. Jas. I, 104/29, 130/28; Hadley, p. 114; *A.P.C. 1619–1621*, pp. 190–2; *Commons Debates, 1621*, II, 212.
⁵ S.P.D. Jas. I, 127/90, 130/28, 131/55; *A.P.C. 1621–1623*, p. 134.

88   Crisis and Change in England, 1600–1642

Government approval was not long in coming. In spite of a real danger in May that the failure to ship cloths would provoke the government into throwing open the Eastland trade to the East Anglian clothiers, the council acquiesced in the policy of protection for Baltic imports by Englishmen.[1] On 21 July 1622 a proclamation was published confining to members of the company the sole import of Eastland commodities (except corn) in English ships or ships of the countries of origin.[2] The action of the government is of particular significance since it came at a time when the prevailing tendency was to meet the depression by, in part, freeing trade from the supposed restrictions of company organization.[3] The measure was a distinct precursor of the Navigation Laws, and it presumably stemmed from a consideration of the particular importance of the Baltic trade, with its supplies of naval stores, potash, saltpetre and grain—although the importance was perhaps more qualitative than quantitative. Presumably the company also convinced the council of the direct connexion between its imports and its textile exports.

There is yet another factor to be considered. The company's problem of returns was affected to a great extent during the years of depression by the course of England's harvests. During the early years of the crisis commercial difficulties were aggravated by the run of abundant harvests which militated against the profitable importation of grain:

Grain prices in harvest years [4]

	1618	1619	1620	1621	1622	1623
Wheat	32s. 7½d.	25s. 10½d.	25s. 5d.	40s. 9d.	51s. 1d.	37s. 8d.
Barley	16s. 1¼d.	14s. 11½d.	11s. 4½d.	21s. 2¾d.	27s. 2¼d.	19s. 9¾d.

In normal times the company may have relied heavily on grain imports to bring home the proceeds of cloth sales, and the depth of the slump in exports to the Baltic from 1618 to 1620 may have been partly explained by the fact that the domestic market for corn was saturated by domestic production.[5] Some confirmation for this view is afforded by the events of the subsequent years.

Between 1620 and 1622 cloth shipments to the Baltic rose from 2,848 to 4,054, an increase of over 30 per cent. In 1621–2 the price of grain rose steeply and there was serious danger of famine. It is likely that this situation in part explains the rise in textile exports, since the English

[1] *A.P.C. 1621–1623*, pp. 223–4, 286–7; S.P.D. Jas. I, 131/40. Freedom to re-export corn was actually considered (*A.P.C. 1621–1623*, p. 282; S.P.D. Jas. I, 132/32), but it was never granted —presumably because of the bad harvest of 1622.
[2] M. Sellers, *Acts and Ordinances of the Eastland Company* (1906), p. 151; Steele, I, no. 1333.
[3] Above, pp. 68–71.   [4] Rogers, v, 270.
[5] The 1621 Port Book for English merchants' imports to London shows only negligible evidence of grain imports. I am indebted to Mrs A. M. Millard for this information.

merchant now had a better opportunity of 'making home' the proceeds in a marketable commodity. On the other hand, alien merchants still handled much of England's corn import and a considerable amount was paid for with bullion rather than cloth. Other factors were present too. The proclamation of 1622, although Dutch competition in imports was by no means destroyed,[1] may well have aided English merchants: in 1622 some 50·3 per cent of textile exports to the Baltic were shipped after June (when the proclamation was published) in contrast with only 29·6 per cent in 1620.[2] In any case, as shown in Fig.3 above, silver prices in Poland had started to turn in 1621 and cloth thus became a slightly more profitable export, while the council's threat to throw open the trade in May 1622 may have produced some effect. Nevertheless, in the Baltic market the grain trade was by no means an insignificant factor in the fluctuations of textile exports.

Thus in the case of the Eastland trade enhancements did not by themselves alone produce a decline in cloth sales. It is possible to envisage a situation where, in the event of their being unable to send bullion to (or receive it in) the Baltic, the Eastland merchants might have *partly* maintained cloth sales at a loss, *if they had had an effective monopoly of importation*, in order to profit on returns. This, however, they did not do, and could not do because of the currency enhancements and Dutch competition. For the trade as a whole adjustment may have been hampered by uncompetitive trading methods and abundant English harvests; the final impact of currency manipulation may have been cushioned by a sudden reversal of the clemency of the weather. Yet the dynamic element, the factor which brought the Eastland merchants to the testing point, found them wanting, and would in any case have reduced exports, was still the sudden swing in the terms of trade which followed the monetary anarchy of these years.

(iii) THE BALANCE OF TRADE AND THE EXCHANGES

It has already been pointed out that enhancements and debasements, by lowering silver prices in the relevant markets, not only discouraged imports into those areas but stimulated exports. This development was particularly active in 1618–23 and its effect on English commerce was such as to substantiate the almost unanimously held contemporary theory that for at least part of the period England had an unfavourable balance of trade with a consequent outflow of bullion.

[1] S.P.D. Jas. I, 135/60; S.P.D. Chas. I, 44/20 (1622); Sellers, pp. 59–60.
[2] E. 190/23/3; E. 190/25/1. April was the most important month in 1620 (68·2 per cent) and July in 1622 (50·0 per cent).

The repercussions on cloth exports in any case, of course, tended to act adversely on the balance of trade. But in addition there was a two-fold stimulus to import more goods. Firstly, imports would obviously be encouraged since, where they were produced in areas suffering from currency manipulations, they became cheaper in terms of silver, so that money would go by exchange and in specie to make profits on returns. In general, too, the effect of enhancement overseas was to make silver or gold coins worth more abroad so that it would be profitable to export money—which might necessitate increased imports. Profit on both net and bimetallic specie outflows would be secured by returns: 'I will not send my twenty shillings into France because it is called six and twenty shillings there, but because I can buy commodities for England which will make me a profit.'[1] In the second case, with a reduced silver income for whatever exports were still being handled, merchants were increasingly driven to return the proceeds in commodities rather than by exchange or bullion, for on the goods (even those produced outside the areas of devaluation) they might be able to raise prices and secure the profits denied to them by export sales; it was for this reason that, in a depressed market, cloth was frequently *bartered* against goods for import.[2] Alternatively, merchants who had previously specialized in exporting would now turn to dealings in the more profitable import trade. Thus one result of the currency manipulations was that the most profitable way of bringing home assets from the Continent was by commodity-import, and a commonplace of economic opinion was that 'high rates of money there ... causeth our merchants to buy their commodities because they can neither bring money nor exchange without loss'. Contemporaries had a nostalgic tendency to contrast this importation with 'former times' when the Merchant Adventurers had brought back specie from Europe. Whatever the truth of this, the Southampton merchants were not alone in claiming that 'by the Merchant Adventurers were wont to be imported many dollars which were coined into sterling money, but now is chiefly returned in silks and the like'.[3] The Adventurers themselves pointed out that events conspired to prevent returns in specie or by exchange.[4]

The import of 'silks and the like'—fine textiles principally manufactured in Italy and France—was one important way in which the Merchant Adventurers compensated for falling profits on their cloth sales.

---

[1] S.P.D. Chas. I, 23/75. Cf. Rice Vaughan, *A Discourse of Coin and Coinage* (reprinted in J. R. McCulloch, *Old and Scarce Tracts on Money* (1933)), pp. 76-7.
[2] H.M.C. *Sackville*, II, *passim*; Malynes, *The Maintenance of Free Trade*, p. 57.
[3] S.P.D. Jas. I, 131/108; Hargrave MSS. 321, p. 85. Cf. Malynes, *The Maintenance of Free Trade*, pp. 57, 76. The 'dollars' referred to are reichsdallers.
[4] S.P.D. Jas. I, 180/75.

Currency Manipulation

Their mart towns in Germany and the Low Countries served, on a smaller scale, the same function as sixteenth-century Antwerp. These ports were the meeting places of European trade routes and, since they centralized commercial transactions, they obviated the need for a complex system of multilateral payments. Thus cloth exports to northern Europe could be made to 'finance' (by barter or the setting-over of bills of debt) the import of luxury cloths from Italy, France and Spain, which were originally sent not directly to the lands of final consumption but to the fairs at Nuremburg and Frankfort and to the staple ports of Stade, Hamburg, Middelburg, Delft and Amsterdam. The Adventurers, in fact, always tried to ensure that their current marts were large-scale sources of commodity returns, including goods produced in southern Europe, and the statistics of silk imports, for instance, bear witness to their success in this respect.[1] In these circumstances the company was able to find a solution to its export problems which was denied to the Eastland merchants: 'The ancient fountains of the coin of England were Germany for dollars, France for quarter crowns, Spain for reals of eight. All these monies our merchants now bestow in silks with the Italians and return none in specie because the silks yield them more profit in their returns.'[2] Not only did merchants buy luxury textiles with the proceeds of exports, but they must have increasingly turned to importing as an independent, profit-making activity. But this activity, as far as the products of southern Europe were concerned, could not continue indefinitely. Although it was sustained at an active level considering the slump—and this indicates that some sections of the population were isolated from the effects of depression—the home market for these goods was limited because their prices were stable.

However, some imports proved appreciably cheaper to buy. This especially applied to the linens and fustians manufactured in those areas of northern Europe suffering from currency manipulation and experiencing a lag in silver prices. Thus, wrote Misselden in 1623, 'the cause that the linens of Germany have these two or three years last past come thence so cheap, notwithstanding the wars . . . , [is that] they have been bought with money given out at so high a rate, and the commodities not raised'.[3] Consequently imports from those areas boomed and linens and fustians

---

[1] See E. 190/24/4. Cf. Mun, *England's Treasure*, pp. 54–5; Wheeler, pp. 337–8; *H.M.C. Sackville*, II; Hargrave MSS. 321, p. 238. For the efforts of the Privy Council to ensure that the mart in the Low Countries was supplied with 'such variety and store of commodities, as the merchants may find means of ample and ready returns', see *A.P.C. 1613–1614*, pp. 20–2. Cf. *A.P.C. 1618–1619*, pp. 75–7; Lans. MSS. 160, fols. 136, 138, 140, 142–3.
[2] Hargrave MSS. 321, p. 1; also pp. 66–7, 142: 'All merchants agree that their hope of gain is upon the commodities they return and not by the commodities they export.'
[3] *The Circle of Commerce*, p. 39.

from Germany and the Netherlands poured into England. Some enhancement both of their own and English coins had been carried out by the Dutch, yet since much of the cloth shipped from the Low Countries had only been finished there and was German in origin it is clear that the great majority of cheap goods came from the areas of greatest currency depreciation:

Imports by English merchants to London, 1621 [1]
(Rateable values, rounded to the nearest pound)

	Linens and canvas £	Mixed fabrics (mainly fustians) £
From Germany	47,511	53,329
From France	44,095	6,830
From the Low Countries	39,313	10,192

One result of this boom was the development, or rather intensification, of a deep hostility to excessive textile imports. The 1622 committee, for instance, saw the cause of monetary scarcity in an unfavourable trade balance stimulated by 'the vanity and superfluity of our importation' of lawns, cambrics, hollands, Silesian and other types of linens.[2]

In addition, considerable anxiety was expressed concerning the Spanish trade: 'all the monies we take in Spain are now bestowed in foreign commodities.' To contemporary pamphleteers and politicians nothing seemed more obvious than that every commodity-import from Spain was a direct substitute for the return of silver. Hence the reiterated attacks on the import of a luxury such as tobacco. Even though the principal monetary confusions were in northern Europe it was clear that bullion earned in Spain would most likely be diverted to other areas, presumably to purchase imports, rather than brought back home: with three ships loaded in Spain with gold, silver and goods, it was claimed, 'The gold shall go for France, the silver for Holland, the commodities for England.'[3] Indeed, most people viewed the problem of the balance of trade as bilateral; i.e. where previously specie had been imported from a particular area, now goods had been substituted. This may have been merely a simple way of looking at things, but it reflected the situation which resulted from monetary disturbances: 'The importation of monies being hindered (by the enhancing of the coin beyond the seas) com-

[1] I am indebted to Mrs A. M. Millard for these figures which she abstracted from E. 190/24/4. For French linens see Hargrave MSS. 321, p. 2.
[2] S.P.D. Jas. I, 131/55; cf. Malynes, *The Maintenance of Free Trade*, p. 22.
[3] For the tobacco trade, see S.P.D. Jas. I, 120/121, 135/55; Malynes, *The Maintenance of Free Trade*, p. 26; *Commons Debates, 1621*, IV, 112, 175. The quotations in the text are from Hargrave MSS. 321, p. 3 and S.P.D. Jas. I, 118/131.

pelleth our merchants to make the greater employment upon foreign commodities.'[1]

There seems, therefore, abundant indication that for most of the period from 1618 to 1623 England's balance of payments was unfavourable as exports declined and imports grew; and the latter were augmented by the need for foreign grain after the harvests of 1621 and 1622. Hence one of the principal preoccupations at the time was with the balance of trade: the Privy Council and Parliament both devoted considerable attention to the topic, as did the temporary and permanent trade commissions in 1622.[2] In the field of economic literature the question was the main concern of Misselden's *The Circle of Commerce* (1623) where he concluded that 'until the kingdom come to an overbalance of trade, the causes of the decay of trade cannot be taken away: for the decay of trade and the overbalance of trade cannot stand to-gether'.[3] Thomas Mun was moved to give evidence to the trade commission of 1622 on 'the excess of the kingdom which spends beyond its means especially in these times when it hath lately lost so many hundred thousand pounds of yearly revenue in cloth'. Indeed, for Mun these years were crucial for the development of his own theories.[4] In the context of a large trade gap it is easier to understand the contemporary approach to some commercial problems of the day. Thus, merchants forced back on importing for a livelihood would naturally incur more opprobrium than was usually directed against the making of profits on returns—a process normally suspect since men believed it made for unfavourable terms of trade. An increased tendency to bring in foreign goods would be calculated to strengthen the normal complaints about the consumption of 'vain, superfluous, unnecessary things', of silks, cambrics, tobacco, wine and 'French baubles', and about the excessive consumption of luxuries: men living 'beyond their callings', 'pride, monstrous fashions, and riot . . . a people . . . vicious and excessive . . . improvident and careless . . . following our pleasures and of late years besotting ourselves with pipe and pot, in a beastly manner, sucking smoke and drinking healths until death stares many in the face'.[5] Finally, the almost neurotic expressions of fear of a loss of treasure and a scarcity of money are the more explicable against the background of an

---

[1] Malynes, *The Maintenance of Free Trade*, pp. 24–5. Cf. Add. MSS. 34324, fol. 167.

[2] A.P.C. *1618–1619*, pp. 306–7; A.P.C. *1621–1623*, pp. 79–80, 208; Add. MSS. 34324, fols. 181, 191 (cf. A.P.C. *1615–1616*, pp. 479–81), 197; S.P.D. Jas. I, 131/55, 135/53; *Commons Debates, 1621*, II, 89; III, 370.

[3] P. 31. Cf. pp. 132, 142. Misselden printed an estimated balance for 1622 showing a deficit of some £298,878 (pp. 127–9). He was fully aware of all the possible discrepancies involved (pp. 124–6).

[4] Add. MSS. 34324, fol. 175; below, pp. 211–16.

[5] The quotations are from S.P.D. Jas. I, 120/121; Add. MSS. 34324, fol. 191; Mun, *England's Treasure*, p. 72. Cf. Misselden, *Free Trade*, p. 12.

international payments deficit. For it is certain that, whatever the nature of bimetallic bullion flows, the balance of trade moved sufficiently against England to impose a serious drain upon bullion and specie reserves, although this movement was tempered to some extent by the accumulation of foreign-owned capital in England.[1]

The mechanism which transmuted an unfavourable balance of trade into an outflow of bullion was, of course, the rate of exchange. A heavier demand for foreign currency would drive the rate down until, if it continued long enough, it became cheaper to export specie than to buy a bill of exchange. No continuous record of exchange rates exists before 1624, and the complicated contemporary discussions of the subject, because of their own confusion, throw little factual light on the course of events. Yet the weight of evidence suggests that for extended periods the rate of exchange conduced to the export of money.

The situation, however, was made the more complicated since bills of exchange were not only means of transferring funds but were also important credit instruments: time was needed before a bill fell due for payment and the deliverer would want some compensation for his forbearance, while the time involved enabled the taker[2] to make use of what was essentially borrowed money. Merchants, therefore, used the exchanges to borrow capital for trade. Superficially, the fact that the state of the money market might play some part in the determination of exchange rates would seem to introduce an extraneous element into any analysis of the latter conducted mainly from the point of view of the fluctuations in exports and imports. Thomas Mun, for instance, pointed out that besides the supply of and demand for currencies deriving from the balance of trade the other most important reasons for a deviation of the exchange from par were 'the venture of the debt and the time of forbearance'.[3] However, by the early seventeenth century it was most likely that nearly all credit operations which utilized the exchanges were closely connected with actual commerce. There was sufficient legal scope for the use of other means of credit to confine the practice of borrowing and lending by bills

[1] There is some evidence of considerable holdings of funds by aliens which were possibly, in part, a result of the unfavourable balance. They seem, in the main, to have been used for operations in the short-term money market, including exchange transactions, and were often abstracted and sent abroad after a short interval. In any case, capital would normally have been attracted by the relatively high rates of interest in England. See Culpepper, p. 35; Add. MSS. 34324, fol. 173; Lans. MSS. 768, fol. 19. For similar arrangements in the early 1640's, see Henry Robinson, *England's Safety in Trade's Increase* (1641), pp. 6-7, 53; S.P.D. Interregnum, 9/61.

[2] The deliverer transferred liquid funds to the taker who, in return, drew a bill on his agent in another country requiring, ultimately, the payment (to the deliverer's agent) of a sum of foreign money equivalent, at a predetermined rate of exchange, to the original amount involved.

[3] *England's Treasure*, p. 39. Cf. G. Malynes, *Consuetudo, Vel, Lex Mercatoria* (1622), p. 261.

Currency Manipulation

of exchange to those who needed the money to buy goods for shipment, or who wished to transfer funds overseas in connexion with importing.[1] The currency manipulations after 1618 had introduced considerable uncertainty into exchange dealings and also increased the par of exchange for England since rates were normally quoted as variable amounts of foreign currencies for 20 shillings sterling.[2] But the unfavourable balance of trade soon drove the actual rate below par, less foreign currency was given, by exchange, for 20 shillings sterling than would have been needed to prove of equal intrinsic worth, and ultimately it became worth while to ship specie rather than to deliver by exchange. But such a decline of the exchange rate below specie export point involved a lengthier process of fluctuation than did a similar fall in, say, the late nineteenth century. This follows from the fact that the distance between par and the specie points was given by the cost of transferring specie internationally. In the sixteenth and early seventeenth centuries this cost was considerably greater than in later years, since, besides the normal freight charges, the risks at sea were very high and such shipments, out of England at least, were illegal. Consequently exchange rates could fluctuate widely before bullion or coin was shipped and in the sixteenth and seventeenth centuries trade balances were more likely to be adjusted by such extreme oscillations (which altered international prices) than by bullion flows: the distance between the specie points was relatively great.[3] The extent of the fall in the rate of exchange explains the persistence of the continual complaints after 1618 that sterling was catastrophically 'undervalued in exchange' and that, as a consequence, currency was being exported. Some men—notably Malynes—had always claimed that English currency was undervalued by a conspiracy of foreign bankers, but this protest rose to an alarming crescendo in the years 1620–3.[4] It was this situation which led the council to consider the possibilities of exchange control and then instigate an official investigation and a public controversy which, starting

[1] Also see Mun's analysis of the use of the exchanges: Add. MSS. 34324, fol. 169; *England's Treasure*, pp. 43–4.
[2] In contemporary terminology, England had the 'head of exchange'.
[3] For an instance of a significant deviation of the rate of exchange from parity without the movement of specie, see Robinson, *England's Safety*, pp. 54, 59. Two points have been ignored in the above analysis. Firstly, bimetallic trends left England with a badly mutilated, underweight silver coinage (below, pp. 167–8). Hence, with full-weight coins abroad the effective par would be below nominal par because, in fact, the circulating coins would be worth intrinsically less than their putative value in silver. However, foreign coins were by no means full-weight either and in any case the same relative arguments apply. Secondly, as the bimetallic trend was to lose silver for gold, and as exchanges were made according to the silver currency, the rate of exchange might in any case have been driven down by the bimetallic flow outwards.
[4] See, for example, S.P.D. Jas. I, 121/21, 131/108; Hargrave MSS. 321, p. 41; Malynes, *The Maintenance of Free Trade*, and *The Centre of the Circle*. For Malynes's long-term analysis, see below, pp. 201–11.

in the spring of 1622, continued before the permanent trade commissioners into 1623.[1] Both sides to the lengthy and detailed argument admitted that the exchange was below par and that specie was flowing abroad. But the proponents of an 'independent' undervaluation, who included Malynes, suggested exchange control as a means of stopping the efflux, while their adversaries, led by Mun, claimed that the exchange rates would rise if only the unfavourable balance of trade were rendered favourable and that any attempt to raise or increase them artificially could only serve to reduce cloth exports even further. The controversy seems to have ended, with no positive action resulting from it, in the summer of 1623 when there was some recovery in the rate of exchange—presumably the result of the stabilization of currency and silver prices and the recovery of exports in 1623–4.[2] To some men, of course, the exchange mechanism was no mystery. Coin is exported, one commentator wrote, 'when our commodities exported are overbalanced in value by foreign wares imported (which is the only cause of the undervaluing of our monies in exchange)'.[3] For Thomas Mun the acute discussions served to crystallize his logical analysis of the connexion between trade balances and exchange rates. He came to see most clearly that the exchanges, being primarily determined by trading-demands for currency, moved with the values of imports and exports: that an undervalued exchange was normally merely an indication of an unfavourable balance. The undervaluation, he wrote in 1623, 'which these men call the abuse of the exchange, ... is in truth nothing else but the declination of our trade which vents not half so many cloths and yet spends twice as much lawns, cambrics and the like as in times past'.[4]

(iv) RECOVERY

The theory that the decline in cloth exports and the unfavourable balance of trade after 1618 had as their principal cause the breakdown of the continental currency systems finds reasonable support when the recovery from the slump is considered. By 1624–5 trade conditions had almost

[1] *A.P.C. 1619–1621*, p. 393. For the controversy, see below, pp.186–9, 068–70.
[2] For the cessation of the controversy, see below, pp. 189, 268. Malynes himself confirmed the rise in the exchange rate, in autumn 1623, although he claimed that at 35*s*. 0*d*. (with the Low Countries) it was still inadequate. Nevertheless, this was only a 6 per cent undervaluation; see *The Centre of the Circle*, pp. 26 ff. In 1629 par with Amsterdam was 35*s*. 10*d*. (R. de Roover, *Gresham on Foreign Exchange* (Cambridge, Massachusetts, 1949), p. 136) and in 1623 35*s*. 0*d*. was probably above specie export point. Misselden in 1623 also gave the current rate as 35*s*. 0*d*.: *The Circle of Commerce*, p. 105.
[3] S.P.D. Jas. I, 121/22; cf. 131/107.
[4] Add. MSS. 34324, fol. 175. Cf. fols. 169, 171–2; *England's Treasure*, pp. 40–1, 48–9, 51, etc. Mun's book (published posthumously in 1664) was to a significant extent directly based on his memoranda of 1623; see B. E. Supple, 'Thomas Mun and the Commercial Crisis, 1623', *Bulletin of the Institute of Historical Research*, XXVII (1954), 91–4; below, pp. 211–12, 270.

returned to normal,¹ although the old draperies were never to recover their former prosperity. After 1622 we do not have figures of total exports until 1626, when London merchants shipped some 91,000 shortcloths, but quite apart from qualitative evidence it seems clear that, for instance, the Merchant Adventurers in 1624 achieved a high level of exports. In that year they shipped about 59,000 unfinished shortcloths, as against some 48,000 in 1620 and 38,000 in 1622.² Underlying this undoubted recovery was, it seems, the series of stabilizations and reforms of continental currencies during and after 1623, which date marked the end of the *Kipperzeit*.³ Further, we should expect that, given time, silver prices would rise, that the movement in nominal prices would tend to approximate to the depreciation, and that English cloth would secure a higher price. Silver prices certainly did turn in Poland⁴ and the presumption must be that the same thing happened in Germany. The chronology of currency manipulation and trade fluctuation appears, therefore, to be what we should anticipate from a theory which explains the latter as an effect of the former. Two points only remain for clarification.

The first is the increase in shortcloth exports to Hamburg from 22,300 in 1620 to 23,600 in 1622, during the worst part of the slump when a further fall might have been expected. One likelihood is that other things did not remain equal: in 1622 it was reported that 'The dearth of wool in high Germany hath been a cause why our merchants have of late undersold the Germans in their cloths, and so uttered great quantities.'⁵ Thus a temporary bottleneck in German industrial production might well have given some small stimulus to English textile exports. An additional possibility is that by 1620 the extent of the decline from the 35,000 exported cloths of 1618 was more than sufficient to reduce supply to a contracted market, and that the 1620 level was, within two years, too low to satisfy effective demand in Germany. It would not be surprising if merchants, especially given the confused trading conditions at the time, had easily over- or underestimated demand. Finally, it is significant that the reichsdaller at Hamburg was called down in value, to some extent, as early as spring 1622.⁶

The second problem is somewhat more difficult to solve: why did exports to the Dutch mart *increase* by some 4,200 from 1618 to 1620, and then decline by 9,200 in the subsequent two years? If Holland shared with

¹ Below, p. 9.
² Mr R. T. Spence kindly gave me the information for 1624, which he derived from the accounts of the Earl of Cumberland's licence. The 1620 and 1622 figures were derived by the author from E. 190/23/3 and E. 190/25/1.
³ Elsas, I, 117, II A, 9, 14; for Poland, Fig. 1, p. 77, above, indicates the currency stabilizations.
⁴ Above, Figs. 2 and 3, pp. 78 and 79.   ⁵ Add. MSS. 34324, fol. 195.   ⁶ Above, p. 77.

eastern Europe the decline in effective demand why did shipments increase up to 1620? If, on the other hand, she was free from those influences what explains the great fall in exports from 1620 to 1622? It is difficult to answer these questions without knowing more about how much of these shipments to the Low Countries was actually consumed there, and how much was finished and re-exported to Germany and eastern Europe. If, as seems likely, a considerable proportion *was* dressed and dyed and then shipped on, a possible explanation of the trend emerges. For in these circumstances the decline in the east European demand for English cloth may have taken time to reach the intermediate demand at the Dutch mart town, because of the turnover involved in the finishing processes. In other words, Dutch purchases of textiles may have been maintained or even increased because initially they were only purchases of semi-manufactured goods for final processing. It would only be at the second stage, when the finished goods encountered a depressed market, that a fall in demand at the Dutch port would take place. And this would be aggravated by the difficulties in communication arising from war, and if the 1620 purchases (which were very high) were unduly optimistic so that some stocks remained unsold even into 1622. If this theory is to hold good then the total export figures should be reflected in the trend in the statistics of the shipment of undressed cloth alone. This is, in fact, the case:

Exports of shortcloths by Merchant Adventurers [1]

	To Holland		To Germany	
	1620	1622	1620	1622
Total	35,700	26,500	22,300	23,700
Undressed cloths	29,000	20,600	18,900	19,400

Clearly the major fall in exports to Holland came in those unfinished textiles which would not meet their final market until some time after shipment. If the exports of 1620 found fewer sales than anticipated, then the resulting stocks would have pushed sales in 1622 even lower.

In spite of these complications it does not appear that there is any major breach in the hypothesis that European enhancements and debasements were primary causes of the slump in cloth exports. Many factors have been ignored in this analysis—specifically the long-term position of the textile industry. In another economic environment the monetary changes might well have been of less significance. Nevertheless, in the short run they played a role which it is difficult to exaggerate. There was some recovery from the depths of the depression, but in a precise sense the English textile industry never really recovered from the disastrous years immediately after 1618.

[1] Computed from E. 190/23/3 and E. 190/25/1. Figures are rounded to 100.

5. PLAGUE AND POLITICS, 1625–1632

(i) PLAGUE AND THE OLD DRAPERIES, 1625

Early in 1625 James I informed the trade commissioners that since their original appointment the customs had increased, wool prices had risen, and cloth sales had been much greater.[1] In July the Solicitor-General was able to report on the satisfactory state of the cloth trade; after years of gloom and depression the traditional textile industry was enjoying a modicum of prosperity: 'the trade in cloth is now so quickened as that cloth cannot be so fast made as it is sold and vented ... [in addition] there hath been no complaint all this time either by clothiers or workmen in the new manufactures for lack of work ... [and] ... the dyed and dressed cloths [are] now better vented than they were.' In addition, wool had risen in price and various grievances had been alleviated.[2] We know too that the Merchant Adventurers' exports of unfinished cloths under licence in 1624 exceeded those of 1622 by 21,000,[3] which must have been a great stimulus to the western counties. Certainly there was a partial return to relative prosperity, but in the summer of 1625 internal events ruffled what calm there was.

The accession of the first two Stuarts each coincided with a severe outbreak of bubonic plague. In 1603 the resulting social dislocations had caused a temporary slump in textile exports. In 1625 the worst attack of plague in the early seventeenth century produced a deeper crisis and demonstrated even more conclusively that the arrangements by which London had come to control the cloth trade had become, dangerous as this development was, indispensable to the prosperity of the textile industry. From May to November 1625, 35,417 people died of plague in London. By mid-June the sickness had spread to all parts of the City, the Trinity Term was adjourned, and mercantile communications were disrupted when, on the petition of Bristol merchants, the Privy Council forbade London traders 'with their goods and merchandizes' to go to the Bristol Fair in July. Late in July deaths stood at over 2,000 per week and Parliament was adjourned to Oxford. August (the worst month, with 4,000 weekly mortalities) saw a direct blow to the cloth trade with the closing of Stourbridge and Bartholomew Fairs.[4]

[1] Document in W. Cunningham, *The Growth of English Industry and Commerce* (3rd ed., 1903), III, 900–1.
[2] S.P.D. Jas. I, 180/78; S. R. Gardiner (ed.), *House of Commons Debates in 1625* (1873), pp. 39–40.
[3] Some 59,000 as against 38,000. Mr R. T. Spence kindly gave me the former figure.
[4] Creighton, I, 508; C.S.P.D. *1625–1626*, pp. 44, 51; Steele, I, nos. 1434, 1438, 1439, 1442; A.P.C. *1625–1626*, p. 109.

So far official ordinances had served to disturb trade; but this was not the most important factor. By August it was the disruption of everyday life in London and the flight of its citizens from the plague which were threatening continuous sales of the standard broadcloth of Gloucestershire, Berkshire, Wiltshire and Somerset. The council, which was itself prevented from attending to important business by reason of the plague, was so perturbed by the effects that, in a letter to these western areas and to the Merchant Adventurers, it warned that 'by reason of the . . . plague in and about the City of London, it is thought fit to remove the market . . . of cloth from thence to some other and more convenient place'. The Adventurers had been so scattered by the plague, which, as was usual, forced wealthy men away from the City, that it took over two weeks for a reply to materialize and even then it was a written answer rather than a personal appearance as requested by the council. William Towerson was the company's spokesman. On 29 August he wrote to the Privy Council: he disagreed that any shift of market was necessary, mainly on the grounds that the current harvest, by absorbing labour, had reduced textile production and that by the time output increased he trusted that 'God will have so abated the sickness that the merchants will return in competent numbers and buy up the cloth as heretofore'. More than this, he presumed, or threatened, that at such a dangerous time the merchants would not resort to a new staple town, having, in any case, 'better means to continue their trade and buying in London, even in this grievous visitation, than in any other place in the land'. The inconveniences, he concluded, would only be aggravated by transferring the market, and it would be better 'to bear God's hand and await his Mercy'.[1] To the clothier whose assets were frozen in unsold textiles Towerson's pious expectations could have been little comfort. The fact remained that it was a disruption in the bottleneck of the cloth trade, and not any disturbances in final markets or inefficiencies in centres of production or dangers in the alternative trade routes, which had provoked a large-scale decline in overseas sales.

By early September the government viewed the situation with increasing alarm. The Adventurers, it intimated, were so dispersed as to make it almost impossible to contact them; the clothiers of Gloucestershire, Berkshire, Wiltshire and Somerset had, both in their homes and at London, great stocks of unsold cloths; neither clothiers nor merchants would come to the metropolis; overseas sales were now beginning to be hampered because the plague caused English ships 'in many places to be rejected'; and if the situation were not soon relieved the manufacturers

[1] A.P.C. *1625–1626*, pp. 122, 135, 138; S.P.D. Chas. I, 5/98.

would cease production, 'which might breed great tumult and other inconveniences in the commonwealth'. In the event, however, the merchants' views prevailed: a shift of market place could not be effective without their co-operation and this was not forthcoming. The staple stayed in London, even though the disturbances continued and the Adventurers' trade was itself hampered by 'the great visitation of sickness in which time little monies could be received'.[1]

It was not the Merchant Adventurers' trade alone which was depressed in 1625, nor was the plague the only cause of economic dislocation. The Levant Company, for instance, was unable to muster a deputation for a council meeting, and the total effect on London was devastating: 'The want and misery is the greatest here that any man living knew; no trading at all, the rich all gone; housekeepers and apprentices of manual trades begging in the streets.' In October all visitors and carriers were prohibited from coming to London and in the counties around the City economic life slowed almost to a standstill as the plague prevented the sale or even pawning of agricultural and industrial goods, and as the money market tightened 'by reason of London's poverty and departure of the chief citizens thence'. In London itself the problem of the poor became acute, for they 'are increased in many parts of the City by reason of the stand of trade and death and decay of many tradesmen who were wont heretofore to set them on work'.[2] Even though the worst of the sickness in the capital was over by December and the restraints on the holding of Bartholomew and Stourbridge Fairs were removed, other areas suffered from the epidemic to a considerable degree. Exeter, for instance, experienced in January 1626 a wholesale flight of its tradesmen and a consequent increase in unemployment and a reduction of the income from poor-rates.[3] To all these problems in 1625 there was added the misery of a poor harvest. In June grain exports had been prohibited, by the end of the year the council was urging justices of the peace to ameliorative action, and in February 1626, in the textile counties of the West, the local magistrates were ordered to regulate closely the use of barley, 'which is for the most part the usual bread corn of the poorer sort of people, as being the cheapest'.[4] Another factor in the commercial and industrial difficulties of 1625 was the Anglo-Spanish War. The insecurity and loss consequent upon the war which Charles had inherited, together with the Crown, in

[1] A.P.C. 1625–1626, pp. 161–2; S.P.D. Chas. I, 20/4.
[2] A.P.C. 1625–1626, pp. 180–1; Creighton, I, 514; Steele, I, no. 1453; S.P.D. Chas. I, 8/34, 38; A.P.C. 1625–1626, pp. 251–2.
[3] A.P.C. 1625–1626, pp. 312–14.
[4] Rogers, V, 270 gives wheat and barley prices for the harvest year 1625 as 48s. 3¾d. and 25s. 2d., compared with 43s. 0½d. and 18s. 10½d. for 1624, and 33s. 0d. and 16s. 1½d. for 1626. See A.P.C. 1625–1626, pp. 100, 295–6, 348.

March 1625, had their greatest effect upon the trade in the new draperies and will therefore be dealt with in the next section. But to some extent all trades were affected, while the outports particularly suffered from the depredations of marauding privateers.

The commercial decline which England experienced in 1625 was, no doubt, by no means as serious as the crisis from which the textile economy had so recently emerged. Yet the outbreak of plague in London and the exodus of its leading merchants had exposed the serious weakness of a textile industry largely dependent upon a single outlet to its overseas customers. Hence the cloth trade suffered because institutional arrangements were too rigid to provide any reasonable alternative sales organization. In this sense the plague may well have altered the supply of coin and bullion, since there is a distinct possibility that the fall in cloth exports when combined with the urgent demand for imported grain after the bad harvest, turned the balance of payments against England in 1626.[1] This must have accentuated the bimetallic loss of silver and the combination of events would explain the controversy, in autumn 1626, as to whether the coinage should be debased in order to reverse the outflow of precious metal.[2] Once the plague was over, conditions for the old draperies returned more to 'normal' and, in 1626, 91,000 shortcloths were exported, which, after the depressed years of the early 1620's was a relatively high level.[3] Yet even in 1626 there was a danger that the Spanish military threat to Denmark would cause the collapse of the German market and 'hinder all trade and traffic of the greatest staple commodities of the kingdom, cloth and wool'.[4] The insecurity which had descended on commerce so disastrously with sickness and war was to haunt English trade and industry for many years.

(ii) EAST ANGLIA, SOUTHERN EUROPE AND THE CRISIS IN 1629

Essex, Suffolk, Norfolk and Cambridgeshire comprised, in the early seventeenth century, the main centre of production for the new draperies, the bays, says and perpetuanoes, manufactured from combed wool, lighter in texture than the old draperies, and supplying the textile needs of the warm areas of southern Europe. But East Anglia also produced important traditional fabrics, Suffolk shortcloths, which were expensive goods, dyed in the wool, and which, by the early 1620's, found their most important markets in the Mediterranean, the Baltic and Russia.

[1] See the contemporary discussions reprinted in McCulloch, *Old and Scarce Tracts on Money*, pp. 131, 136.
[2] Below, p. 190.   [3] Below, Appendix A, Table 1.   [4] *A.P.C. 1626*, p. 283.

Exports of Suffolk shortcloths from London by Englishmen [1]

	1606	1620	1622	1628	1632	1640
Total	14,507	11,494	9,910	5,089	16,347	14,315
To Baltic	6,885	2,297	3,247	1,562	2,142	4,391
To Levant and Italy	2,276	5,558	3,624	661	?	?
To Russia	2,103	1,111	1,079	1,667	2,084	1,367
To Barbary	1,112	153	284	450	?	?
To Spain	1,015	633	238	0	?	?
To Germany	424	1,068	675	488	33	0

For most of the 1620's, according to the evidence of a lawsuit in 1629, this manufacture seems to have experienced chronic stagnation.[2] In 1622, Suffolk had been amongst the hardest hit of the textile counties; seven years later Robert Alefounder, a clothier, deposed that 'the markets for Suffolk and Essex cloth have been at all times for the space of these four or five years past and now are much clogged with cloth'. Many other witnesses confirmed this relative cessation of activity and the story is a repetitive one of idle stocks and lack of sales. As shown in the preceding table the export of Suffolk shortcloths in 1628 reached the lowest recorded level of the period and by 1631 the London shipments (9,108) showed no advance over those of 1622—although there was a short-lived boom in 1632. This product clearly participated in the more general slump in East Anglian textile production in 1629–31 and the instability and depression of the late 1620's must have been partly due to the vagaries of the southern European trade at the time: the 1628 figures show a spectacular fall in exports to the Mediterranean. This would also explain the abrupt recovery in 1632.[3] Nevertheless, before the 'boom' the stagnation in those areas of Suffolk which manufactured old draperies, and especially the saturated market for them in 1629,[4] could only have worsened the general situation described below. And if this was a long-term position, then local contrast was spectacularly provided by the crisis which shook East Anglia in 1629.

While the Suffolk clothiers were making their gloomy depositions in 1629, there were abundant indications of a deep slump in the manufacture of bays and says in Essex. In April, the unemployed textile workers of Braintree and Bocking, two of the most important centres of production for the new draperies, besieged the Quarter Sessions 'complaining of extreme necessity and disability to maintain themselves and their families

[1] See below, Appendix A, Table 11 and 12.
[2] See the depositions in the Court of Exchequer, E. 134/5 Charles I/Easter 1 (April 1629). The Eastland Company was prosecuting some Suffolk clothiers for exporting cloths to its privileged areas. For the Suffolk depression in 1626, see S.P.D. Chas. I, 22/63.
[3] For the trade to southern Europe, see below, pp. 104–5, 110.
[4] S.P.D. Chas. I, 146/57, 57I.

... for want of work by those clothiers which were used to employ them', since they could no longer find a sale for the products. The Essex justices of the peace wrote to the council confirming the poor condition of the industry which threatened, so it was said, the livelihood of 30,000 spinners and weavers, and the government's answer was speedy and solicitous—rioting had broken out by the end of the month.¹ The government, as we shall see, took great pains to ensure increased purchases of bays and says in order to alleviate the unemployment. From all the evidence it will be apparent that the depth and persistence of the slump in East Anglia hardly find parallels, apart from the events of 1620–3, in the period. An investigation of the causes, however, necessitates a digression into the happenings of the years before 1629.

Spain and France were both leading markets for the new draperies, as was the Mediterranean area in general, and trade with all these regions was severely hampered by the wars of this period against Spain (1625–30) and France (1627–9). The Anglo-Spanish hostilities had, in fact, been a constant source of disturbance for English commerce since 1625. The menace of the Dunkirk privateers, for example, had occasioned a desperate outburst of protest, mainly from the ports of the south and east coasts, from the commencement of the war.² Newcastle colliers, Yarmouth fishing vessels, ships trading to Russia and the Baltic: all were threatened. The Eastland merchants (of both London and Hull) could not sail without convoy, and protection had to be provided for the Merchant Adventurers' trade to Germany and the Low Countries and for the fishermen and cloth fleets of the north-east coast. Hull, Bristol, Ipswich and Yarmouth were given financial relief on the grounds of 'the decay of trade and their many losses by sea', and the Levant Company had to form a special convoy 'in these times of hostility', for which the council provided economic protection by prohibiting trade by single ships or 'forestallers'.³ All merchants and all ports seem to have experienced some insecurity from the depredations during these years, with the French, Spanish, Flemish, Dutch and German trades suffering especial harm in 1629–30; in February 1630 it was reported that London 'has received more hurt in the last six months than for many years in the past'.⁴ By disrupting the essential lines of commercial communication the war succeeded in reducing some trades to near-paralysis. But the debilitating effects of the

---

¹ A. C. Edwards (ed.), *English History from Essex Sources* (Chelmsford, 1953), pp. 44–5; S.P.D. Chas. I, 141/1, 16; P.C. 2/39, pp. 197–8; C.S.P.V. *1629–1632*, pp. 44, 67–8.
² C.S.P.D. *1625–1626*, pp. 17, 22, 24, 30, 31, 86, 221, 251, 285, 306, 307, 309, 314, 328, 452; A.P.C. *1625–1626*, pp. 386–7, 403; S.P.D. Chas. I, 22/62, 25/75, 27/5, 98, 184/65.
³ A.P.C. *1626*, pp. 108, 109, 141, 150; A.P.C. *1627*, pp. 477–8.
⁴ C.S.P.V. *1629–1632*, pp. 206, 213, 276, 290, 291.

Dunkirk privateers were far more evident in the case of the outports or in trades, such as those handling the new draperies, which were managed by weak companies or no companies at all. For where a heavy trade from London was regulated by a strong organization, and where the value of the commodity was relatively high in relation to its bulk (for example, the old draperies), the convoying of compact fleets, which were in any case a normal method of arranging transport, was a relatively easy task. For this reason, England's staple export of old draperies to northern Europe, which was overseen by the Merchant Adventurers in its shipments across the narrow seas, was much less susceptible to disturbance than the looser trade in the new, lighter fabrics whose markets were far more scattered: the cloth fleet which was awaiting convoy to Hamburg early in 1626 carried some 15,000 cloths—or one-sixth of London's total shipments for the year[1] and the Adventurers' ships generally carried so much cloth that not more than half-a-dozen would be needed for any one of their four or six shipments. On the other hand, when hostilities at sea were fiercest, trade into the Mediterranean might be almost throttled.

In a more specific sense the Spanish struggle also restricted trade in the new draperies by creating great insecurity in the Spanish market. Only rarely in seventeenth-century wars were the belligerents' markets *completely* closed to each other. Nevertheless, ban and counter-ban, even when circumvention was tacitly allowed, produced a precarious trading environment. Trade with Spain and Flanders, except for an unsuccessful period of relative official freedom from April 1626 to the summer of 1627, was ostensibly prohibited by the English government in December 1625 and August 1627.[2] In January 1626 it was noted at a meeting of the trade commission, which was considering the potentialities of economic warfare, that 'the new draperies [are] vented nowhere but in Spain. But the use of them [is] now forbidden in Spain; yet of grace it hath since been tolerated, but the king keepeth power ... to confiscate them all.'[3] Clearly, normal commerce was impossible in such circumstances and in 1628 the war-time hindrances were blamed for harming the sales of the new textiles.[4] The severe disturbances in commercial dealings with the Iberian peninsula, and the repercussions for maritime transport of the enmity of Spain's Flemish subjects, must have produced significant dislocations in the textile areas of East Anglia for some years up to 1629.

The war with France, which had been precipitated by the Anglo-Spanish sea warfare, was similarly a serious blow to commercial dealings.

[1] S.P.D. Chas. I, 22/62.
[2] Steele, 1, no. 1458; *A.P.C. 1625–1626*, pp. 271, 408; *A.P.C. 1627*, p. 495.
[3] S.P.D. Chas. I, 18/81.
[4] S.P.D. Chas. I, 126/52.

Seizures and embargoes preceded the official outbreak of hostilities, and the war of economic attrition rapidly reduced the trade with France to stagnation. The import of goods in French ships was prohibited, letters of marque were issued, and English merchants, with the connivance of the home government, had to adopt circuitous routes and fictitious designations in order to bring their assets back from France.[1] However, disturbing as these events were, the stoppage of trade was never absolute. In 1628, for instance, in response to complaints from the farmers of the wine duties, the import of wine was allowed, and a year later, according to a Venetian diplomat, the mutual economic blockade broke down on an even larger scale: 'in one day thirty ships came into this river [Thames], freighted with wines and merchandise from France. This has not happened at any time during the last two years. His Majesty also continues to give permits for the exportation of fish, etc., so I think that the mutual interests of the two kingdoms are gently compelling them to reunite.'[2] But it is doubtful if such haphazard compromises (which in any case principally applied to essential goods) were much compensation to the unemployed spinners and weavers of Essex, looking for a steady market and conditions favourable to confident mercantile investment. While the war against France continued it was a severe handicap to the trade in bays, and the council, in the actions it took in spring 1629 in response to the local complaints of depression, demonstrated that it was well aware of this.

In April the council wrote to the Essex magistrates who had originally warned it about industrial unrest. The wars, it was acknowledged, had hindered the sale of bays and says 'for some years last past' but the government was confident 'that the ancient vent of those commodities will be in short time opened'. Meanwhile, for immediate relief, a promise was made to call 'the merchants formerly trading therein and some of the chief workmasters and . . . settle a course with them for the putting of the trade . . . into the ancient way'.[3] Superficially at least, the council's confidence was well founded: peace had been signed with France four days before the letter was sent and it was generally anticipated that commerce would soon be thriving as merchants flocked to a trade 'for which they have so long sighed'.[4] In the event the optimism proved premature: the sea warfare with the Spanish subjects still continued, and the French privateers did not allow the end of official hostilities to interfere with their disruptive and profitable activities, and by October the English merchants trading to France were in despair; in addition the

[1] Steele, I, nos. 1510, 1511; C.S.P.D. 1628–1629, pp. 189, 198, 316, 337.
[2] C.S.P.V. 1628–1629, pp. 11, 493.
[3] P.C. 2/39, pp. 197–8.
[4] C.S.P.V. 1629–1632, pp. 19, 68–9.

arrests, seizures and lawsuits, which traditionally plagued the life of English merchants in France, were to continue into the future.[1] But in April 1629 the Privy Council was not aware that the political hindrances to trade would continue for long; at the time it seemed merely that there was a short-term stoppage to be alleviated and this task the council approached with determination. Merchants were called to give their reasons for 'the great stand of trading in bays and says, being the manufacture of ... Essex'. They claimed that they were unable to purchase clothiers' stocks because their capital was tied up in wine imports which they could not sell, and the government immediately attempted to unfreeze these assets by ordering the Vintners' Company to buy up wine from certain merchants at current prices, and other means were used to improve the market for wine. In addition, other traders were brought before the council and exhorted 'to buy such considerable quantities [of bays] as now doth lie upon the hands of the clothiers' of Braintree, Bocking, Coggeshall, etc. The government was keen to the point of desperation and when, late in May, unsold textiles continued to accumulate both English and alien merchants were ordered to sign bonds to buy up specified quantities of woollen goods. But the results of the campaign were disappointing.[2]

Thus the peace with France, even accompanied by the opening of direct trade, and quite apart from the continuance of the Anglo-Spanish war, did not ease the industrial situation. Indeed, it coincided with the worst period of the slump in the new draperies. One strong possibility is that the East Anglian industry, weakened by years of insecurity, was sharply hit by the over-confidence which accompanied the signing of the peace treaty—the results of which were that too much wine was imported, with a consequent immobilization of mercantile capital, and that too many cloths were manufactured, 'which come from the country in such plenty that now there is no market and sale for them as formerly'.[3] Such an optimistic anticipation of a sale which never materialized was not extraordinary since production was carried on by small entrepreneurs at two or three removes from the final market. But besides this glut there came political disturbance from another direction entirely.

English export industries did not emerge unscathed from the constitutional controversy over the payment of customs duties in 1628 and 1629. The refusal of some merchants to pay tunnage and poundage unsanctioned by Parliament will be described at greater length in the next section in

[1] C.S.P.V. 1629–1632, p. 206; P.C. 2/39, p. 250; P.C. 2/40, p. 550; P.C. 2/41, pp. 534–5.
[2] P.C. 2/39, pp. 215, 237, 245, 250; C.S.P.V. 1629–1632, pp. 67–8.
[3] C.S.P.V. 1629–1632, pp. 67–8.

connexion with the trade in the old draperies. But the newer textile industry suffered more direct harm. First, because the refusals came initially in the wine trade and so indirectly affected exports from East Anglia to France; second, because erstwhile exporters of the new draperies were less able than the wealthier Merchant Adventurers to accumulate stocks of textiles even though they were not yet shipping them abroad. As early as March 1629 it was claimed that the slackness of trade which followed the controversy was producing unemployment and by the beginning of April it was seen as the cause of the fact that 'at present all the [cloth] carts go back to the country full, as no one buys'.[1] The spirit of obstinacy, it was said, 'lies not only in the merchant's breast, but moves in every small vein throughout the kingdom. Insomuch that last week the clothiers of Essex were up, but more in report than in deed.'[2] The Venetian ambassador reported that 'Internal affairs fluctuate owing to the unwillingness of the merchants to trade, to avoid paying the duties'; but he anticipated that the opening of the French trade, consequent upon the peace which had already been signed, would prove an irresistible temptation to the merchants to return to active commerce.[3] In fact by May this particular issue had been settled: the traders found that they could not, in the long run, afford the luxury of acting as the guardian of Parliament's conscience.

Thus a good case can be made out for the argument that the chronic unemployment in the East Anglian bay-producing areas during the spring of 1629 was largely due to an assortment of political factors. The insecurity accompanying open warfare and prohibitions on trade had served to weaken the industry over a period of years; in 1629 a sudden crisis was provoked by over-confidence and the freezing of capital which coincided with the apparent return to peace-time conditions; and the situation was aggravated by the sharp, though temporary, reaction of the merchant class to Charles's claim that his prerogative extended to the taxation of the articles of international commerce.

The government, faced with the problem of widespread unemployment, was forced to attempt to ameliorate it directly by poor-law enforcement, as well as indirectly by pressure on the merchants to buy up stocks of textiles off clothiers' hands. A measure of the problem's severity in 1629 is the urgency with which the Privy Council approached the former task.

On 29 April, since 'those parishes which complained and where the

[1] C.S.P.V. 1628–1629, p. 599; C.S.P.V. 1629–1632, p. 7.
[2] S.P.D. Chas. I, 141/16 (20 April 1629).
[3] C.S.P.V. 1629–1632, p. 19.

said cloth is wrought are much more charged with poor than other parts' of Essex, the justices of the peace were ordered to see that contributions to poor relief were exacted from neighbouring parishes. A week later the magistrates of Suffolk and Essex were commanded to provide alternative employment for the textile workers '(if not in their own trades) in some good and honest labour fit for them, until they may again be employed in . . . their own vocation'. If no work could be found for them, then direct financial aid was to be given. Thus the government was fully aware of the intractable problems of the seventeenth-century version of a 'depressed area', and this highly realistic approach was rounded out by an intimation that where a particular locality was unable to provide for its own poor, money could and must be obtained from adjacent areas. Within a week of the promulgation of this policy to the local officials, the Earl of Warwick was sent into Essex to see that the officers 'do take all possible care to keep the county in peace and quietness'.[1] Clearly, as in other years during the period, the dangers to the social order from unemployed textile workers deprived of any possibility of earning a living was, for the government, the central and critical aspect of a depression.

The depth of the unemployment was demonstrated by the council's vehement insistence on the legal right and absolute necessity of extending the area of financial responsibility for the destitute employees of the cloth industry. On 17 May the principle was enshrined in a proclamation 'commanding the due execution of the laws made for setting the poor on work'. This was obviously a crisis measure. It commanded the strict enforcement of the statutes for the relief of the indigent, the binding of pauper apprentices, the official provision of stocks of raw materials for the unemployed, and, in general, for the employment of the poor. If the parish was unable to provide the money then 'the whole Hundred, Lathe or Wapentake', or in the last resort, if they failed 'by reason of the multitude of the poor or want of ability in the inhabitants, . . . the whole county is bound to contribute thereunto'. The mandate, as shown by its provision for special conferences to deal with extraordinary outbreaks of unemployment, clearly had reference to conditions in East Anglia; and in answer to local vacillation, the council wrote to Essex and Suffolk, enclosing the proclamation and making the position perfectly clear: 'it is the resolution of all the judges that by the law you have sufficient power.'[2] These measures were whole-hearted and charitable, but it is impossible that they could have alleviated any but a small portion of the distress of

[1] P.C. 2/39, pp. 220, 237, 242.
[2] *Foedera*, XIX, 71–2 (cf. 72–3); P.C. 2/39, p. 263.

such an industrial crisis. Nevertheless, in the council's efforts of 1629, and even more in the subsequent campaign of 1630–1, can be seen the beginnings of meticulous attention to problems of poverty which was to blossom into a virtual 'Stuart paternalism'.

The emergency measures just described, the merchants' acquiescence in the payment of customs duties, and the official opening of the trade to France, did not prevent the continuance of industrial depression, which, on available evidence, certainly lasted into the summer of 1629 and was clearly present in East Anglia in autumn 1630 and spring 1631.

In fact few of the long-term depressive factors had changed. Difficulties in the French market continued, and for most of 1630 England was still at war with Spain. The English, it was said in 1630, considered the opening of the Spanish trade 'essential in order to relieve their present necessities', and Spain put considerable pressure on English merchants to press for peace by giving them the benefit of intermittent trade and allocating 'passports' (against the Privy Council's wishes) for safe sea passage. But, on the other hand, privateers continued their attacks, which were blamed for the high prices of butter and cheese brought by sea to London from Norfolk and Suffolk in 1630, and right up to the end of the war the Dunkirkers persisted in 'their depredations, showing extraordinary and insupportable contempt, as with odious distinction, upon ships and even small boats, they seek out the goods of the English and carry them off'.[1] The war had severely disturbed commerce, but even after the cessation of hostilities in November 1630, which came about, it was said, solely in order to facilitate trade,[2] the London merchants were still dissatisfied, 'for want of settled government in their trading and the manufactures they trade in', with the state of their commerce to Spain. Exports of new draperies were depressed in 1631 and in March 1632 it was reported that the trade to the Spanish market was still 'poor and miserable'.[3] These factors must have been largely responsible for the persistent manifestation of depression in East Anglian textile districts.

The second round of industrial depression which came to the eastern counties in the winter of 1630–1 coincided with a run of bad harvests which inflated grain prices to the highest level reached before the disastrous failure of 1648. In the harvest year 1630 wheat and barley stood at 64s. 6d. and 38s. 1¼d. respectively.[4] As during the conjunction of

[1] *C.S.P.V. 1628–1629*, p. 527; *C.S.P.V. 1629–1632*, pp. 267, 275, 280, 290, 436; Journals of the Common Council, 35, fol. 235.
[2] *C.S.P.V. 1629–1632*, p. 493.
[3] S.P.D. Chas. I, 204/22, 214/48; J. Pilgrim, 'The Cloth Industry in Essex and Suffolk, 1558–1640' (unpublished M.A. thesis, University of London, 1938), p. 204.
[4] Rogers, V, 270–1.

famine prices and unemployment in 1622–3, the prevailing misery could only have been accentuated by the scarcity of food, and it is distinctly possible that effective demand for consumer goods was sufficiently reduced to aggravate the slump. And the government's remedial efforts, which included a ban on grain exports and meticulous surveillance of local officials, could have done little to alleviate the situation.

Conditions remained abysmal for the workers in the new draperies. The slump had produced pressure on wages—the most pliable cost of production—in 1629 and the government then tried to prevent manufacturers increasing the size of the product without raising wages. In September 1630 the Privy Council was most anxious concerning the reduction of wages in Suffolk, Essex, Cambridgeshire and Norfolk, and the local magistrates were ordered to assess them properly, since 'these hard and necessitous times do require some better care to be had in that behalf'. Before the year's end Norwich officials wrote of the heavy burden of 'the scarcity and dearth of corn ... upon the poor ... whose number, by reason thereof and of the want of trade and consequently of means to set them on work, doth so increase' that the poor-rate had to be trebled. Subsequently the council was forced to take action in an attempt to maintain the 'due and accustomed wages' of the weavers, combers and spinners of the say-making industry in the Sudbury district around the Essex-Suffolk border—action which, at the request of local manufacturers (who claimed that 'all of that trade in other parts of the kingdom' were reducing wages) was directed at the whole industry in order not to put one area at a competitive disadvantage with respect to labour costs.[1]

The attempts to economize on the cost of labour, which reached such serious proportions in 1630 and 1631, were indicative of the severity of the crisis in East Anglia. Exactly two years after the first manifestations of depression, the justices of the peace in Essex, during the spring of 1631, intimated that 'although the poor do suffer much in respect of the high prices of corn, yet they are in far greater misery in the most populous parts of the county, whose trades consist in the making of bays', because the clothiers, with unsold stocks on their hands, no longer gave employment, so that the hardships of the poverty-stricken weavers occasioned, as it had done in 1629, 'a more than ordinary resort of them unto us at our present Quarter Sessions'. The industrial dislocation was both widespread and serious: in Middlesex, Essex, Surrey, Kent and Hertfordshire 'the poor suffer as much in the want of work as in the price of corn', and

[1] S.P.D. Chas. I, 147/43, 177/55, 189/40–40I; P.C. 2/39, p. 399; P.C. 2/40, pp. 114, 350 ff.; P.C. 2/41, pp. 440–1, 443.

in April the local justices were ordered to attack both problems. By May the new draperies in Suffolk were experiencing difficulties, with, it was claimed, unsold stocks creating a threat of wholesale unemployment unless the merchants bought them up and enabled the clothiers to finance the next round of production.[1]

The sufferings of the East Anglian textile industry were not the only signs of industrial unrest in these years. In 1630 and 1631 the old draperies and the western counties were no less depressed. To round out the picture of these years it will be necessary to consider how trade in the traditional manufactures fared in the troubled period after 1626.

(iii) OTHER TRADES AND OTHER AREAS, 1627–1631

The trade of the Merchant Adventurers to northern Europe in 1627 and 1628 was to some extent handicapped by an intensification of the perennial controversy with the Dutch as to the quality of English old draperies. More specifically their commercial dealings were disrupted and brought to a standstill by a complicated dispute over the abatements which were made in the price of cloths, sold in the Low Countries, which were not up to specified standards: there was disagreement as to the amount due and the Dutch wished the tare, as it was called, to be imposed at the centres of final sale and not, as desired by the English company, at the port of entry. The English government was, naturally enough, on the side of the Adventurers, although in 1627 it had to restrain the mercantile hostility towards the United Provinces and order the company not to carry out its real threat to cease trading: in the last resort the council had to represent the interests of textile producers against the desires of the company.[2] The general insecurity of trade to the Netherlands was further aggravated by the recriminations consequent upon the strife between the Dutch and English East India Companies, and at one point the government warned the Dutch that the uncertainty was forcing English merchants to seek alternative outlets for their cloth.[3] All these difficulties, together with the dangers of war-time trade which have already been described, explain the low level of London's exports of old draperies in 1627: 88,000 shortcloths. In fact the events amounted to a virtual stoppage of trade, and so uneasy were the Adventurers under political and moral pressure that, after some months, it was only in May 1628 that they could see their way clear to shipping 'the great weight and burden of cloth (being a whole year's gathering) . . . for Delft in

[1] S.P.D. Chas. I, 188/92, 190/54, 192/26; P.C. 2/40, p. 431; Pilgrim, p. 72.
[2] S.P.D. Chas. I, 82/26, 83/54; A.P.C. 1627–1628, pp. 90–1.
[3] C.S.P.V. 1628–1629, p. 86.

Holland'—although even at this juncture it was as much the pressure of frozen capital as the easing of tension which explained the opening of trade.[1]

That there are no signs of repercussions of the commercial difficulties of 1627 and 1628 in the manufacturing areas was partly due to the fact that the resources of Merchant Adventurers, and the potential long-run soundness of overseas markets, enabled them to continue their purchases although they were postponing export. However, as they indicated in May 1628, any undue prolongation of the stoppage would be bound to have harmful effects. In any event 1628 was a boom year for total London exports, some 108,000 shortcloths being shipped. On the other hand, as the company itself confirmed, much of this was surplus stock from 1627; and it is little wonder if the 'boom' of 1628, like the 'slump' of 1627, was not reflected in the textile-producing counties. The buffer of stocks of textiles, largely financed by London merchants, had insulated the clothing areas to a great extent against the effects of fluctuations in overseas trade. Such stoppages were to have more serious effects some two years later, but before this story is told it will be informative to glance at the impact on the Merchant Adventurers' trade of the constitutional controversy of 1628–9.

The Merchant Adventurers participated in the general refusal to pay customs duties, which so interfered with the production of new draperies. Naturally enough, the government brought to bear what pressure it could in an attempt to maintain trade and the income from customs, and as early as March 1629 the possibility of dissolving the obdurate trading companies was being canvassed. At the end of this month the Adventurers were haled before the Privy Council, only to admit their fear of the wrath of the House of Commons, and at the resulting company Court no one voted for a re-opening of trade. When the council, in desperation, turned to the Dutch merchants it was met with a tart negative: 'we shall be degenerate if we go about to betray the liberties of the English nation.'[2] But the government did not really need to adopt any positive policy—in the long run the Adventurers had either to resume trading or to transfer their capital into non-mercantile uses, and the latter step became increasingly unlikely as they accumulated unsold textiles. In the spring of 1629 matters came to a head. An anonymous author, while blaming the stop of trade on to constitutional factors, showed that the Merchant Adventurers held considerable stocks of cloth and it does seem as if company

---
[1] S.P.D. Chas. I, 104/40.
[2] *C.S.P.V. 1628–1629*, p. 599; S. R. Gardiner, *A History of England, 1603–1642* (1883–4), VII, 82–3, quoting Tanner MSS. 71, fol. 1.

members, although little active trade was done, continued to purchase goods from clothiers. An acute observer, writing early in April, pointed to 'underhand' purchases by the richer merchants, who dissuaded others from buying at Blackwell Hall and themselves bought up old draperies privately and in large amounts. 'Most of the chief traders', he claimed, 'have a great quantity of cloths in their hands, and the meaner merchants having twice the value of their estates in cloth, likewise not being able to forbear shipping and selling . . . so that [if] they be left alone for a week or two, they will of themselves come to their wonted manner of merchandising.' Events were to prove him right, and although plans to dissolve the company were still propounded, the Venetian ambassador's forecast that if the king remained firm the merchants would 'decide to pay rather than lose their profits' was the most realistic appraisal of the situation.[1]

While there was a limit to the Merchant Adventurers' ability to accumulate cloths, their capacity for such stock-piling certainly exceeded that of the merchants trading to France. Hence, while there had been immediate unemployment in the Essex bay-making industry, there were no complaints from the western centres of traditional manufacture. In the long run, however, notwithstanding the principles of individual merchants and the threats uttered by the House of Commons at its dissolution against traders who dared to pay the duties, the leading mercantile company would not allow such a question to interfere with its trade. By the middle of April there was reasonable hope that the Adventurers would set an example in acquiescence to the rest of the merchant community, and by early May the problem was obviously well on its way to a settlement. On 16 May it was reported that 'the Merchant Adventurers have agreed to ship their cloths. The resolution was gained by two hands.' Although it took some two weeks to make final arrangements, which included the organization of a convoy for the cloth fleet, this phase of the intrusion of constitutional affairs into economic matters was over.[2] 'I have ever said', wrote one observer, 'that the merchants would be weary of this new habit of statesmen they had put on, and turn merchants again by that time they heard from their factors that their storehouses began to grow empty. God send those men more wit who, living in a Monarchy rely on a Democracy.'[3] Whatever the motives which had perpetuated the stoppage, the merchants had averted a slump in the old draperies even while they would not or could not ship textiles. Ultimately, however, as

[1] S.P.D. Chas. I (Addenda), 530/47; S.P.D. Chas. I, 140/24; Gardiner, VII, 83; *C.S.P.V. 1629–1632*, p. 19.
[2] S.P.D. Chas. I, 141/16; *C.S.P.V. 1629–1632*, pp. 56, 75; *C.S.P.D. 1628–1629*, p. 550.
[3] Quoted in Gardiner, VII, 84.

the dead-weight of stock accumulated, they were forced to return to active trade, bringing in profit to defeat principle.

Even after textile exports were resumed in 1629, trade in the old draperies did not for long enjoy the commercial security essential for industrial prosperity. In 1630 the old dispute between the Merchant Adventurers and the Dutch, over the payment of tare, flared up again. In March the Privy Council had to order the company to revoke an order restricting trading to Delft, although it promised official help in the grievance before the next shipping. The company had been trying, in effect, to put pressure on the Low Countries by confining exports of all textiles, and not alone of white cloths (which, since 1624, were the only types of which it had a monopoly), to one staple port. By autumn the situation had reached an *impasse*. The Adventurers petitioned that, in self-defence, they had been forced to limit sales at Delft solely to transactions which included a covenant that the cloth would not be tared after it had left that mart. This had produced a rival combination of Amsterdam merchants who had seized the 'covenanted' cloths and secured an extension of the tare to cover coloured cloths and kersies. The latter had been handled by interlopers since 1624, and the company claimed, with some reason, that the independent traders would quickly acquiesce in the payment of the new tax, and consequently make it almost impossible for official members of the company to hold out in their efforts to defeat the new policy. It therefore requested that the trade in these goods be again confined to the mart towns so that the English merchants could close ranks and increase their bargaining power. The government instructed the English ambassador to help regain the confiscated cloths and, on 10 October, after noting with approval the Adventurers' intention to exert ultimate pressure by moving their mart to Emden in East Friesland, it complied with their principal desire and warned all merchants that exports to the Low Countries and Germany must be confined to the company's designated port towns.[1]

The immediate result of this last measure was a complaint from the manufacturers of coloured cloth in the Reading and Newbury areas. The clothiers petitioned that the restriction had decreased the sales of their cloths so that the poor were 'in a miserable condition', and prayed to have liberty to export to ports other than the officially designated ones. The Adventurers claimed that the Berkshire slump was caused by the intrusion of interlopers into the trade, in 1624, and the false manufacture of cloths. By December the Privy Council arrived at a compromise solution: coloured cloths still had to be shipped to the mart towns, but

[1] P.C. 2/39, p. 383; P.C. 2/40, pp. 98–100, 101, 132.

merchants not free of the company could export them whenever they wished, not keeping to the Adventurers' stipulated shipping times.[1] Nevertheless, the general difficulties with trade to the Low Countries continued and even though the Adventurers did not transfer their mart—either to Emden or the Spanish Netherlands, which was also considered—the net result was a virtual stoppage of trade with Holland. To aggravate this situation another controversy arose, this time with Flanders over the payment of 'licence money'. Licence money was the payment made for the right to sell English cloth which, since the sixteenth century, had been ostensibly prohibited in the Spanish Netherlands. The tax had been increased over the years and the protests of English merchants led to the cessation of textile exports in 1630. In any case, of course, trade to Europe in general was hampered up to late 1630 by the operations of the Dunkirk privateers.[2]

For the whole period of the interruption to normal commerce, in the second half of 1630 and the first half of 1631, there were constant intimations of unemployment in the clothing counties, combined with the distress consequent upon the high price of food.[3] In November 1630, in the area around Godalming, according to the clothiers, 'who have not so much vent for their cloth as heretofore', there were 'hundreds of poor ... ready to perish for want of means to buy food, especially in this present dearth and scarcity'. A month later, in the same area, there were further complaints of unemployment and of clothiers reduced to a 'miserable and distressed estate' by the burden of unsold stocks and ruinous debts. The western textile counties were also depressed. In Somerset the poor were 'likely to perish with their families for want of work ... [and] ... wanting work they have no money to buy [corn, for] the only means our poor have to subsist is the work from the clothier, which trade is now wholly falling by reason their cloths lie upon their hands, the merchants refusing to buy'. In Gloucestershire the clothiers begged the Privy Council 'to take some course with the merchants that their cloths may be taken off their hands more speedily, whereby they may have money to pay their poor workfolks'.[4]

By early 1631 the situation had only worsened. Hampshire still suffered from reduced production, unsold stocks, falling prices, unemployment and a rising poor-rate. In February Wiltshire was feeling the effects of the

[1] S.P.D. Chas. I, 177/52, 60, 180/72; P.C. 2/40, pp. 259–60, 268–70.
[2] P.C. 2/40, p. 286; C.S.P.V. 1629–1632, pp. 472, 499; S.P.D. Chas. I, 130/60; C.S.P.D. 1627–1628, pp. 107–8, 156; C.S.P.D. (Addenda) 1625–1649, pp. 232, 393; C.S.P.V. 1629–1632, pp. 75, 206, 213, 276, 290, 291, 436.
[3] Above, pp. 110–11.
[4] P.C. 2/40, p. 196; S.P.D. Chas. I, 176/36, 177/53, 56, 57I.

stoppage as 'now at this present . . . the said trade of clothing doth stand ill with the clothier in regard of the Hollanders' and our merchants' differences'. The Privy Council's solicitude concerning the depression extended to the home counties, and in May it appeared that the compromise of December 1630, intended to help the Berkshire coloured cloth industry, had been nullified by the general industrial decline so that, in that area, 'thousands of . . . poor . . . live in much want'. A Wiltshire clothier, Christopher Potticary, who in February had intimated that without the help of two wealthy Merchant Adventurers 'I should ere this time have been at a stand', claimed, in May, on his own and other clothiers' behalf, that 'the merchants finding a stop of trade in those parts [Flanders]', had ceased their purchases from the manufacturers: whatever reserves had previously enabled the exporters to maintain at least part of local production, were now dissipated by the continued disruption of the Flemish trade. And the Merchant Adventurers themselves bemoaned their unsold stocks, Holland having been closed for almost a year and Flanders being still *incommunicado*.[1]

The governmental anxiety provoked by these industrial events was deepened by the famine prices of the harvest years 1629 and 1630. Where unemployment coincided with scarcity, as frequently happened,[2] the council was driven to adopt a familiar two-fold plan: 'to have a provision . . . [of grain] . . . at easier rates' and to ensure 'that there be a course taken in the parishes to set the poor on work'.[3] The problem of famine was tackled with the Book of Orders, a body of administrative regulations designed to stabilize and control the grain market. The Book was amended and issued in September 1630 and in January of the next year it was issued permanently, while the provisions for general poor-relief were more strictly controlled. Among the hundreds of reports by justices of the peace on local situations, which were direct responses to the Privy Council's surveillance and hounding of the local bureaucracy, there survive some 300 relating to the corn situation alone, from 1631 to 1633. The campaign to control prices was reasonably successful: where, as was not infrequently the case, local prices were high because grain supplies were uncoordinated, or because there was an excessive non-food use of barley, the measures often served to reduce them significantly. On the other hand, nothing could be done about an absolute scarcity and often even where increased supplies lowered food prices in a depressed textile area,

---

[1] S.P.D. Chas. I, 182/45, 184/65, 76, 186/23, 188/55, 191/40II, 41, 192/47; P.C. 2/40, p. 431.
[2] P.C. 2/40, pp. 114, 196; S.P.D. Chas. I, 177/55, 191/40II, 192/26.
[3] P.C. 2/40, p. 431. For the whole problem of poor-relief in these years, see Leonard, pp. 151, 156–60, 172 ff., 249–50, 256–7, etc.

the magistrates still found that, owing to the lack of work, consumers were unable to buy even the cheapest grain.[1]

In 1629 the government had made a large-scale attempt to enforce the poor-law provisions in Essex. With the geographical extension of the slump, in the winter of 1630-1, to districts producing old draperies, and its aggravation by the harvest failure, there came a fresh and more broadly based relief campaign. In London the Court of Aldermen was engrossed, during the winter and spring, in providing corn, money, employment and housing for the poor. In the country at large there was an unparalleled outburst of central and local administrative activity—the latter spurred on by constant pressure from the former, and by the appointment of a general commission for poor-law enforcement in January 1631. Naturally enough, special attention was devoted to providing work for the able-bodied unemployed, which was the immediate reaction in Surrey, Middlesex, Essex, Kent and Hertfordshire. Local efforts were frequently enthusiastic and sometimes successful. By April 1631 parts of Hertfordshire, Essex, Richmond, Bedford and Beverley had raised stocks of raw materials, by fresh taxes, for this purpose; and in ten days during April, of twenty-eight reports from local magistrates, seventeen indicate that the poor were employed by the authorities, mainly in the working of flax and hemp, with more success attending efforts in the south and east than in the north and west.[2] Yet it is doubtful whether such measures were very significant in most areas of chronic textile depression. Praiseworthy in intention, but without the backing of strong administrative powers or the taxable potential of a modern community, they could not provide any real solution for the economic and social problems of the slump. Nevertheless, they did, in many areas, at least alleviate some of the harsher aspects of economic life. In any appraisal of whatever benefits were derived from the measures for social welfare under the personal government some consideration must inevitably be given to the important, if unwelcome, part played by the crises in the textile industry in 1629 and 1630-1.

Economic affairs must ultimately have been improved, and industry lifted from the doldrums, by a return to normal trading conditions. After considerable negotiations a working arrangement with the Dutch in regard to the tare was arrived at in the summer of 1631. The council, on 22 June, although some points still remained for clarification, was able to 'assent [that] in the meantime the trade . . . be opened again'.[3] The open-

[1] S.P.D. Chas. I, 176/6, 188/92.
[2] Repertories of the Court of Aldermen, 45, fols. 36, 42b, 51b, 71b, 164b, 184b, 234b-5; P.C. 2/40, pp. 196, 431; Leonard, pp. 255-6.
[3] S.P.D. Chas. I, 192/55; C.S.P.V. 1629-1632, p. 511; P.C. 2/41, pp. 53-6, 57.

ing of the trade to Holland marks the end of recorded complaint from the cloth-producing areas, and the sparse statistics available suggest a distinct upturn. For the old draperies 1631 was, on the whole, a bad year: London's exports stood at 84,300 shortcloths, the second lowest recorded figure of the period. But in 1632 there was a recovery to 99,000 cloths, and within this a breakdown demonstrates that the Dutch marts took some 36,400 compared with 26,500 for 1622 and 24,400 for 1640.[1] How far the exports of 1632 were sustained by drawing on unsold stocks of the previous year's production is not clear, although it is certain that the textile industry was in a better position in 1632 than it had been for some time.

The period after 1625 had been one in which economic warfare, political pressure, and mercantile friction conduced to a debilitated commerce and a permanently vulnerable textile industry. At times the financial reserves of individual Merchant Adventurers shielded the clothiers who supplied them from the effects of dislocation, while the merchants trading to southern Europe, who were important customers for the manufacturers of the new draperies, do not seem to have provided similar stock-piling aid to the East Anglia clothiers. But at times of almost complete trade-stoppages, for instance in the winter of 1630–1, both branches of the cloth industry were likely to experience sudden and disastrous outbreaks of unemployment. The course of food prices only worsened the situation, but the central government, in attempting to alleviate the resulting distress, constructed a system of relief which, within the political limitations of the age, was as efficient and charitable as it could possibly have been. Yet it was now clear that the traditional manufacture would never again be able to boast the long-term boom it had enjoyed before 1614. It was in the middle of an extended history of decline, painful adaptation, and widespread redundancy.

[1] Appendix A, Tables 1 and 3.

6. THE DECLINING YEARS, 1632–1642

(i) STAGNATION

In the last decade of the period the long-term contraction in the traditional markets for English broadcloth was most apparent.[1] The repercussions of this development, of the government's attempts to resist the cost-reducing debasements of the quality of textiles, and of the difficulties experienced by the Merchant Adventurers, produced an unhappy atmosphere in the textile areas of the West during the troubled 1630's. There were few signs of even temporary prosperity in the districts which specialized in the production of the staple old draperies. Some real adaptation was in progress as the manufacture of newer types of dyed and dressed cloths started to replace that of white broadcloth, but even here the resulting pressures on the factors of production provoked tensions and friction since the organization of the older industry proved to be relatively inflexible.[2] This inflexibility was also apparent in the response of the western counties to the official efforts to enforce standards and methods of textile production which went against the grain of the established industrial structure: the attempt in 1633 to ban the use of gig mills in the finishing processes and the plan, of the same year, to restrict the operations of market spinners (large-scale independent organizers of yarn production) were either drastically modified or discarded.[3]

In any case, 1633 was a bad year for cloth exports, only some 80,800 shortcloths being shipped from London. In April a proclamation for the reform of abuses in manufacture was published; but attempts to enforce it produced a real threat of unemployment among employees of the manufacturers of coloured cloth who wished to continue the use of gig mills, while the general requirements of the proclamation were distasteful to clothiers producing white cloths, who were especially affected, finding that 'by reason of the deadness of the times for sale of cloth, and loss of part of the principal stock sustained by the sale of them for the space of two years last past, their estates are decayed . . . and also that ready money for their cloths is hardly to be had'. In Gloucestershire, therefore, the Justices of Assize found that 'the clothiers did begin to cast off their workmen', and during the stormy year of 1634 in Wiltshire 'some of the

[1] For this decline, see below, pp. 136–48.
[2] Below, p. 147.
[3] Below, p. 146.

sufficientest clothiers ... have ... given over the making of cloth and ... divers others intend to do the like to the impoverishing of many poor people depending thereupon'. In December 1634 there was, 'for want of buyers', much cloth in pawn and unsold in London storehouses, while a month later the clothiers of Essex and Suffolk put the value of such frozen assets at some £100,000.[1]

Meanwhile the Merchant Adventurers, whose markets in Germany and Holland were contracting most of all, were themselves experiencing commercial difficulties. The settlement of the question of the payment of tare in 1631, which had eased trade in that year, did not prove permanent, and in 1634 'there was such a contention betwixt them and the Dutch ... that the company kept their warehouses shut about seven or eight months'. The Adventurers, faced in any case with a long-term decline in demand, reported that their trade 'is become less by the one half' while many members 'are entered into other trades of more charge but withal of more gain'.[2] It must have been this situation which once again turned the company's attention to the possibilities of restrictionism, and produced a campaign to protect its shrinking markets against interlopers and a 'straggling trade'. In 1621 and 1624, under the pressure of depression and a hostile House of Commons, the Adventurers' control over exports to northern Europe had been considerably weakened: they were left with exclusive rights only with regard to the trade in white cloths, and outport merchants and non-members from London secured extensive rights to trade in other types of textiles.[3] In May 1634, however, the company requested that, since its trading position was so weak, its monopoly be re-extended to 'all that trade in woollen draperies', the use of staple towns be enforced, interlopers be suppressed, and permission be granted for it to change the official residence in the Low Countries from Delft to Rotterdam. Within two months the council gave its assent to the latter move and decided, in view 'of the great decay of their trade' and its weakening by dispersion, that the Adventurers 'shall henceforth enjoy the sole trading in the Low Countries and Germany not only in all white cloths, but also in all coloured cloths [including Spanish cloths and kersies]'. Favourable audience was also promised to the company's request for a monopoly of the export of the new draperies to their mart towns 'for their further relief and comfort in their decaying trade'.[4] Nevertheless, discussions continued for some time, the Staplers appearing and receiving permission to join the company upon payment of a

[1] Steele, I, no. 1657; S.P.D. Chas. I, 244/1, 278/107, 282/130; P.C. 2/44, p. 156.
[2] *Discourse ... for the Enlargement ... of Trade*, pp. 46–7; S.P.D. Chas. I (Addenda), 535/32.
[3] Above, pp. 68–71.
[4] P.C. 2/44, pp. 89–90.

reasonable fine. Ultimately, a proclamation was published on 3 December 1634, by which the Adventurers secured the widest possible reassumption of their original privileges: both old and new draperies were once again given over to the sole control of the company and, consequently, confined to the official residences; all traders were enjoined to become members; and it was subsequently claimed that interlopers hurriedly left Amsterdam for Delft, where they could join the official organization.[1] In the early 1620's a crisis had been considered primarily from the point of view of the producing areas and the outports, by a Parliament essentially hostile to the Merchant Adventurers. Ten years later there was no Parliament in session and, we may assume, the interests of the outports were relatively poorly represented in London. The Privy Council, left to its own resources, returned to the main stream of traditional ideas on the benefits of regulated commerce. Trading difficulties were seen largely in terms of the unfavourable repercussions on London merchants, and, while the council established relatively low entrance fees to facilitate an expansion of company membership, a regulated monopoly was re-established over the most important branch of English commerce.

Within three years the Merchant Adventurers were involved in an effort to revive the declining fortunes of the Essex bay-making industry; although, since the markets for bays lay principally in southern Europe, the government's pressure on them must have been somewhat unfair. Late in 1636, according to the Chief Justice of the King's Bench, the local magistrates, and the bay makers of Bocking and Coggeshall, there was 'a great stop in the trade of bays and cloth in ... Essex' and the council was forced to suspend and then revoke the proclamation of the previous July which had increased the wages of spinners in that industry: it was feared that the depression would only grow worse unless labour costs were reduced, but the government urged strongly that the poor be kept in employment and be paid 'fit and competent wages'.[2] The slump continued into spring 1637 and the council, worried by 'the present stop and stay of clothing and of the vent of cloth, bays, and other manufactures of wool' in Essex, consulted with the Merchant Adventurers and the merchants trading to Spain and France. The former were warned that if no satisfactory conclusion was reached in their discussions with industrial representatives then the trade would be thrown open. Wages had already been adversely affected by the fall in sales, stocks of textiles were accumulating in London and Essex, and the position of some clothiers

[1] *Foedera*, XIX, 583–4; C.S.P.D. *1635–1636*, p. 36. For a controversy, in 1635, as to Colchester's rights to export locally produced bays and says, see S.P.D. Chas. I, 289/67, 290/11; P.C. 2/45, p. 15.
[2] *Foedera*, XX, 41–5, 94; P.C. 2/46, p. 423; P.C. 2/47, pp. 10–11, 30–1.

The Declining Years, 1632–1642 123

was considerably worsened by the freezing of their assets in bad debts due from various merchants. The bay manufacturers of Coggeshall, Bocking and Braintree reported that many employers had found their businesses so unprofitable that they had become, where possible, wage labourers, and that many of the remaining clothiers 'have been encouraged to engage their credits far beyond their stocks in borrowing money ... to keep the poor at work'.[1]

But by 12 May the council, in writing to the Essex authorities, was able to report some progress in its efforts to alleviate the depression. The principal complaints of the merchant groups had been of poor sales abroad, of the false manufacture of bays, and of the unsuitability of the fabrics for the market. The council secured an agreement by which the merchants, in return for a promise that bays would be well made and 'merchantable', consented to buy up the full output. On the other hand, however, the justices of the peace were enjoined to 'take order that by degrees fewer bays be made since that commodity is not now so vendible'.[2]

It is the last statement which is, perhaps, the most interesting comment to emerge from the discussions. It is difficult to see the particular cause of the slump in Essex in 1636–7. But there is a distinct possibility that the county, over the long run, was simply manufacturing more bays than overseas demand could readily absorb. The mobility of the factors of production in the bay industry was probably higher than in most other branches of the textile industry: the process of manufacture did not demand a heavy investment, there were no stringent apprenticeship requirements, and, as a consequence, men moved in and out of the industry, and from employed to employing and back again, with considerable ease.[3] With an over-supply of labour and no initial hindrances to a productive expansion the frequent intimations of over-production should come as no surprise. The weavers of Braintree and Bocking had complained in 1629 that employment had been lacking for six years, and the ease with which, in that year, output increased to glut the market was by no means a healthy sign; in 1632 there was another deep depression in Essex which resembled a crisis of over-production; in 1637 the local magistrates had noted that one fault lay with 'the taking of too many apprentices contrary to the law', although it is doubtful if the industry did, in fact, come under either

---

[1] Essex County Council, *Guide to the Essex Record Office*, Part I (Chelmsford, 1946), p. 103; P.C. 2/47, pp. 46–7, 336, 389, 422, 438, 459; S.P.D. Chas. I, 354/92, 355/144; *C.S.P.D. 1636–1637*, pp. 368, 409; *C.S.P.D. 1637*, pp. 44, 52, 64, 70, 80, 135; *C.S.P.D. 1639–1640*, p. 243. Most of the unsold stocks held in Essex in May were intended for the Spanish market, so that the threats against the Adventurers in April appear to have been unwarranted.

[2] P.C. 2/47, pp. 401–2. For the falsity of Colchester bays, see *C.S.P.D. 1635*, pp. 266–7; *C.S.P.D. 1635–1636*, p. 337; P.C. 2/45, pp. 37–8, 435–6.

[3] *Mr Grimstone, his Speech in Parliament* (1642), B.M.E. 200 (4).

the cloth statutes or the Statute of Arificers; finally, the county had by no means seen the last of chronic industrial dislocation.[1]

It was not alone in East Anglia that a fundamentally unsound situation existed in the textile industry. By the late 1630's it was apparent to all commentators that the old draperies—centred on the West of England—were in a depressed state.[2] A commission was appointed in 1638 to investigate the poor quality of English cloth, whose 'ancient reputation in foreign parts hath of late times been much impaired to the decay of trade and vent there and to the impoverishing of many thousands of our poor people'. Its final report, in 1640, was also concerned with the general reasons for the decay of the cloth trade and, although it was in large part a repetition of the report of the 1622 committee, it paints a striking picture of stagnation at home and powerful competition abroad.[3] The commission's anxiety concerning the excessively low wages being paid in textiles, and its desire to increase them were matched by William Goffe, who, in a pamphlet dated 1641, advocated industrial diversification because in cloth manufacture 'the price is beat down to so low a rate that the slow workmen cannot maintain themselves'.[4] These fears reflected the situation which gave rise to the re-issue, in May 1640, of the proclamation, which had originally been promulgated to meet the crisis of 1629, 'commanding the due execution of the laws made for setting the poor on work'.[5] And similar analyses, tempered by a realization of the potentialities of economic adaptation, emerge from the writings of Sir Thomas Roe and Henry Robinson.[6] By the end of the period men admitted that the possibilities of reviving the ancient textile trade had been exhausted. Their minds turned in other directions.[7] In any case, by 1640 constitutional questions began to intrude upon economic affairs. It was for this reason that no serious official consideration was given to the commission's report, and one of the last attempts on the part of the government to deal with commercial matters in isolation from all others had come in 1639, when a 'deadness of trade in London' had coincided with yet another effort to strengthen the monopoly of the Merchant Adventurers—by an

[1] S.P.D. Jas. I, 137/13; Edwards, pp. 44–5; *Guide to the Essex Record Office*, Part 1, p. 103. For 1629 and 1631, see above, pp. 103–4, 111. For the depression in Essex in 1641–2, see below, pp. 130.
[2] Below, p. 136ff.
[3] S.P.D. Chas. I, 398/118; G. D. Ramsay, 'The Report of the Royal Commission on the Clothing Industry, 1640', *English Historical Review*, LVII (1942), 485–93.
[4] W. Goffe, *How to Advance the Trade of the Nation and Employ the Poor* (1641), Harleian Miscellany (1808–13), IV, 385.
[5] *Foedera*, XX, 407; above, p. 109.
[6] Sir Thomas Roe, *Speech... wherein he sheweth the Cause of the Decay of Coin and Trade in this Land* (1641); H. Robinson, *England's Safety in Trade's Increase* (1641). See below, pp. 222–224.
[7] Below, pp. 221–4.

enforcement of the 1634 proclamation.¹ The troubled years which followed only served to emphasize the economic confusion which pervaded the textile industry, and turned the government's attention away from matters of purely economic interest. Nevertheless, the political anxieties which accompanied the preparations for Civil War themselves had serious repercussions for the economy, and we may suitably terminate our description of commercial disturbances in the whole period by delineating the economic crises of 1640-2.

(ii) INSECURITY AND CRISIS, 1640-1642

The crisis of mercantile confidence which, in these years, produced widespread dislocation in the already weakened economy, was largely due to the direct interference of the Crown under the stress of its financial needs, and to the sweeping public resistance to its political and religious policies.

In 1640 the government's financial difficulties seemed insurmountable. The First Bishops' War had reduced it almost to bankruptcy, the City persistently refused to advance any money, the Customs Farmers were at the limit of their resources, and efforts to negotiate loans abroad failed miserably.² In these circumstances Charles decided on a policy which amounted to the exaction of a forced loan. Since 1630, under the terms of the Cottington Treaty, large quantities of silver shipped from Spain and destined for Flanders had been given protection by England. Part of these shipments had come to be taken by Englishmen, in return for bills of exchange on Antwerp, and coined into native money at the Mint. Originally, this arrangement applied to the bullion owned by the Spanish government and used to pay its armies in Flanders; but the scheme worked so well that it was increasingly utilized by private merchants—in the main, Genoese operating from Madrid.³ At the end of June 1640 there was about £130,000 worth of this treasure deposited for minting. Charles I ordered that this sum be 'stopped'—that there was to be no issue of coins to its owners—and the owners were referred to the Treasurer, at whose hands they were to receive security for the principal and for the payment of 8 per cent interest. However, after much protest and bargaining, it was decided that, as a compromise, two-thirds of the bullion should be freed and the remaining £40,000 advanced to the Crown for six months at 8 per cent.⁴

¹ S.P.D. Chas. I, 407/98, 418/67; P.C. 2/50, pp. 170-1; *Foedera*, XX, 342-3.
² Gardiner, IX, 130, 132, 157; R. Ashton, 'Government Borrowing under the First Two Stuarts (1603-1642)' (unpublished Ph.D. thesis, University of London, 1953), p. 559.
³ A. E. Feavearyear, *The Pound Sterling* (Oxford, 1932), pp. 82-3.
⁴ S.P.D. Chas. I, 459/36; C.S.P.V. 1640-1642, pp. 58-9; Gardiner, IX, 170.

Whatever the arbitrary nature of the stoppage, and however much confusion arose in London and foreign monetary circles, these steps simply amounted to a delay in the ordinary issues of the Mint, involving silver owned either by Genoese merchants or by Englishmen who had contracted bills for it. And, in fact, the money was repaid promptly.[1] The commercial effects of the move are difficult to appraise. It is possible, for instance, by viewing these events from a modern or nineteenth-century standpoint, to exaggerate the harm done to the credit structure and to mercantile confidence. The seventeenth-century merchant was far more accustomed than his later counterpart to such an arbitrary interference with his assets, and his standards of 'security' were correspondingly lower. In any case, the bullion did not represent, as claimed by some historians, 'a part of the metallic reserve of the London traders'.[2]

On the other hand, such a step was bound to give some pause to commercial activity and to provoke some instability at home, while, as merchants and goldsmiths were quick to point out, aliens, for these reasons, might stop sending bullion to England—although 'the necessity under which his Majesty's affairs labour has not left any room for the consideration of such matters'.[3] Further, where English merchants had exchanged bills for silver they might be hard put to find the cash to meet these bills when they fell due at Antwerp; while, if they had intended to use the coin for the purchase of exports or the payment of debts, its 'seizure' might well have proved directly harmful in, for instance, reducing purchases of textiles. This fear was expressed in a petition from merchants and goldsmiths, who claimed that the delay at the Mint 'will disable your subjects not only from paying their debts, trading and buying of cloths and other manufactures made in this realm. But also from providing goods and shipping for the next vintage.' The Merchant Adventurers protested that they might have to stop buying cloth if they were harmed to any considerable extent by any counter-seizures abroad or by a weakening of the exchange or by the cessation of financial activity on the part of aliens, 'from whom they are always for the most part furnished'.[4] Hence merchants, who at the first news of the 'stop' were 'put . . . into great disorders', might well have found that the delay in issues, by directly and indirectly weakening their credits, adversely affected their ability to finance normal exports to a degree exceeding the initial impact of the temporary abstraction of £40,000 from the money market. In addition these events, together with the later forced loan on

[1] C.S.P.V. 1640–1642, pp. 58–9; Feavearyear, p. 85.
[2] Scott, I, 224.
[3] C.S.P.V. 1640–1642, pp. 58–9; cf. Feavearyear, p. 85.
[4] S.P.D. Chas. I, 461/104, 105.

The Declining Years, 1632–1642   127

pepper, probably aggravated the prevailing 'scarcity of money' which, deriving from an urgent desire for liquidity on the part of merchants, was the bane of economic life in London at the time.[1]

In July and August 1640 there came yet another threat that Charles's financial necessities would force him to adopt a policy which would be disastrous for commercial stability. It was planned to resort to the time-honoured if ultimately self-defeating method of raising money for an impecunious government: debasing the currency. This time there was a detailed plan and a real intention to coin debased money containing some 75 per cent copper.[2] The plan immediately provoked opposition from employees who feared they would be paid in base money and from clothiers who did not wish to exchange their products against adulterated coin. The severity of the proposed debasement would have produced, it was claimed, a great disturbance in domestic and overseas commerce, since owners of coins would 'either keep them in their hands or remit them into other parts while the exchange is high. The very rumour of an intention to coin brass money having laid the grounds of some prejudice already.' Fear was expressed that the step would harm the structure of credit and create adverse terms of trade, and merchants trading to Europe, the Far East and the Mediterranean, dependent as they were to some extent on credit and the exchanges, protested vigorously.[3] There was, in all this, more than the usual hyperbole which accompanied any mercantile opposition to a projected interference with the *status quo*. It will be seen how intimate was the connexion between commercial and monetary stability, and a drastic currency manipulation of the sort planned in 1640 would, inevitably, have lowered mercantile confidence to a dangerous extent. Charles tried to strike a bargain with the London merchants by which he promised not to carry out his intentions and even to waive Ship Money if the City would guarantee a loan of £200,000, but this offer was rejected: 'the citizens pretend great poverty . . . wherefor the brass money is likely to go on.'[4] It was at this point that, having failed to provide increased income by using the debasement as a threat, the royal determination slackened. By insisting upon their gloomy view of the consequences of a debasement, the merchants, with presumably little or no duplicity, led the king to believe that they might, in the last resort, refuse to accept the coins when they were issued. Since the king could

[1] Gardiner, IX, 190; S.P.D. Chas. I, 467/138, 478/86; Rushworth, IV, 233–4; L.J. IV, 576–7, 648; H.M.C. v, 12. For the scarcity of money, see below, pp. 129–31.
[2] S.P.D. Chas. I, 459/77, 78, 460/38; C.S.P.V. 1640–1642, p. 59.
[3] For the opposition, see Gardiner, IX, 171–2; S.P.D. Chas. I, 460/56, 461/32, 77; S.P.D. Jas. I, 104/48 (wrongly calendared); C.S.P.V. 1640–1642, p. 59.
[4] S.P.D. Chas. I, 460/56, 461/32.

only profit from a debasement if the corrupt coin gained currency, nothing could be gained if the opposition was so extreme that the business classes lost confidence in the coinage. It was, indeed, on these grounds that the merchants ultimately won the day: their 'statements ... that they will not take it' led to a permanent shelving of the plans to raise money by what was, at best, a drastic last resort.[1]

The debasement scare, short as it was, coming so soon after the forced loan could not have buttressed commercial confidence at a time when the prevailing tendency was, in any case, towards the restriction of business activity in the interests of liquidity. Although the figures for cloth exports in 1640 are not matched by comparable statistics for the years immediately prior to that date, totals of some 87,000 for London's overall shipments and 45,000 to Germany and the United Provinces are sufficiently low to reaffirm that the year was a bad one for trade.[2] The Crown's attempts to augment its income in the summer were not a propitious start to the insecure years ahead. And their very failure, together with the outbreak of the Second Bishops' War, the City's persistent refusal to back an unconditional loan, and the failure to obtain financial aid from the European Catholic powers, meant that a political step had to be taken which only served to crystallize the anti-royalist ferment and, correspondingly, worsen the environment for mercantile operations: 'all hopes of obtaining [financial] succour without a fresh convocation of Parliament, which is universally longed for, have fallen to the ground.'[3] The only condition upon which the government could secure a voluntary loan from the City was a promise to recall the Commons, and the political forces brought to the fore by the meeting of the Long Parliament meant that constitutional issues began to impinge once again, and even more severely, on economic stability.

It has already been seen how the overwhelming importance of London for much internal trade and for those sectors of the economy which relied upon overseas commerce, meant that a cessation of economic activity in the capital might have drastic repercussions for outlying areas. In the years immediately preceding the outbreak of war, when a major section of the traditional textile industry was already gravely weakened, there was a chronic reaction in the producing districts, which stemmed from the disruption of commerce and credit by political events.[4] In 1640 the

[1] *C.S.P.V. 1640–1642*, pp. 61, 65.
[2] Below, Appendix A, Tables 1 and 3.
[3] *C.S.P.V. 1640–1642*, p. 65; Gardiner, IX, 175, 184.
[4] It appears that the prevailing political and religious atmosphere also led to a significant emigration of textile workers (mainly from East Anglia) to Europe: Robinson, *England's Safety*, pp. 2–3; Roe, p. 10; *C.S.P.D. 1639*, pp. 356–7; Rushworth, IV, 438–51, points 54 and 55 of the Grand Remonstrance.

citizens of London, requesting that a Parliament be called, intimated that 'grievances and fears have occasioned so great a stop and distraction in trade, that your petitioners can neither buy, sell, receive, or pay as formerly, and tends to the utter ruin of the inhabitants of the City, the decay of navigation and clothing, and the manufactures of this kingdom'.[1] Although this type of complaint must, to some extent, be discounted as the use of threatened economic sanctions to alter political policies, the indications were sufficiently insistent to confirm the view that these years saw a crisis of confidence.

Cloth production and the price of wool fell as demand, exerted through London, declined.[2] Money was taken out of circulation not only by English merchants but by aliens: insecurity, it was claimed,

hath been a cause that strangers, who were wont to be lenders, have called in and remitted those monies by exchange into foreign parts. And such of our own nation as were wont to be lenders have called in their monies and stand in expectation of what the issue of things may be. . . . And by our general fears and distractions the inland trade of this kingdom is so far decayed, that country tradesmen cannot pay their debts in London as formerly, and many of them have been ruined.[3]

It was typical of such protests that the suggested remedies all lay in the sphere of political and religious action. Meanwhile, this sort of phenomenon largely accounted for the prevailing contemporary feeling, during 1641 and 1642, that there was a 'scarcity of money'. The money market became excessively tight, and commodity dealings fell off, as Englishmen increased their desire to hold money rather than credit instruments or goods, and as aliens, who normally 'had a great stock here at interest . . . [and] hath supplied the necessities of merchants and helped to drive the trade',[4] withdrew their funds 'out of apprehension of the present conditions of the times'.[5]

England had slipped into yet another depression. Henry Robinson wrote, in 1641, that 'the decay of trade is in everybody's mouth from the sheep-shearer to the merchant, and even a weak statist, without Galileo's prospective glass, may see both our wealth and safety therewith declining'. By the spring of that year the 'scarcity of money' had adversely affected textile production in Berkshire, Wiltshire, Kent, Somerset, Worcestershire, Gloucestershire, Hampshire and Suffolk, whose manufacturers

[1] Rushworth, III, 1263-4.
[2] Rushworth, IV, 33-4; S.P.D. Chas. I, 454/29.
[3] S.P.D. Chas. I, 478/86.
[4] Roe, p. 3. Cf. *Commons Debates, 1621*, VII, 581; S.P.D. Chas. I, 461/105.
[5] H.M.C. v, 12. Cf. L.J. IV, 202, 576-7, 648; Rushworth, IV, 509; S.P.D. Interregnum, 9/61.

complained that they could not sell their cloths 'for ready money as heretofore', or even obtain payment of their debts, the merchants answering 'that this is no time to pay money'.[1] Throughout the winter of 1641-2 various pressure groups utilized the economic depression in an attempt to force the government's hand on questions of popular policy such as a stricter control of Roman Catholics, the elimination of episcopal membership of the Lords, a greater effort in the Irish war, etc. Petitions concerning the dangers of economic distress, whose close resemblances to each other indicate that this was an organized campaign, were presented by London merchants, mariners and seamen, Dorset, Berkshire, Hampshire, amorphous London groups such as tradesmen's wives and widows, and Exeter—which claimed that there was 'great decay and deadness' in the manufacture of serges and perpetuanoes.[2]

Whatever the real intensity of the slump as reported in these petitions, there is little doubt concerning the plight of the Essex textile industry. Seemingly enduring long-term stagnation, it suffered particularly in this period. Its principal petition to the Commons was presented by Grimstone,[3] who spoke feelingly of 'the exceeding great decay of their trade of clothing especially . . . occasioned by the present distractions and distempers of the state', and told a long tale of woe: of weavers leaving their occupations to take up other ways of livelihood, and of the dependent poor being 'brought many of them to beg their bread, and the rest live upon the parish's charge'. Within a week Pym, in a speech before the House of Lords, warned that there was great danger of tumult on a national scale 'by reason of . . . ill-vent of cloth and other manufactures'.[4]

By early 1642, on the very eve of hostilities, the Venetian ambassador wrote that 'the trade of this city and kingdom is stopping altogether. The ordinary course of all trade has been interrupted and those who obtain their daily food by the work of their hands alone are reduced to the limits of despair.' The clothiers of Suffolk and Essex summed up their situation in February: the distractions in the City, 'in whom [sic] the breath of our trade and livelihood consisteth', mean that merchants 'forbear exportation [and] our cloths for the most part, for the space of this 18 months, remain upon our hands, our stocks lie dead therein, and we can maintain our trade no longer'. Berkshire, too, was experiencing just such a textile depression, and in Yorkshire the clothiers disturbed the king's preparations

[1] Robinson, *England's Safety*, p. 17; L.J. IV, 237; H.M.C. IV, 62. The Lords ordered the Merchant Adventurers to buy up the unsold textiles.
[2] See Steele, I, nos. 1972, 1974, 1976, 1996, 2014, 2024; B.M. 669, f. 4/33, 42, 50, 52, 54, 55, 57; J. Somers, *A Second Collection of Scarce and Valuable Tracts* (1750), II, 38-40.
[3] Steele, I, no. 1944; *Mr Grimstone, His Speech in Parliament* (1642), B.M. E. 200 (4). Cf. Rushworth, IV, 506; L.J. IV, 539.
[4] Rushworth, IV, 503-9.

for open warfare with complaints that merchants 'do not take up our cloth as they use to do, but our stocks lie dead in our hands'. In that county thousands of textile workers were said to be 'now at the point of undoing' because so many traders had ceased any commercial activity, 'and others, both merchants and chapmen, do now generally refuse to make payment for goods long since sold and delivered'.[1]

The story of the textile industry during the *ante bellum* years is not a happy one, and it merges into the misery and confusion of the years of Civil War. The depression which settled on the economy in 1641–2 owed little to purely economic factors. In 1642 the 'want of money' was seen as 'an epidemical disease raging like the sweating sickness of late years over the whole land';[2] and it is clear that the constitutional crisis did have precisely this effect. By directly and indirectly reducing confidence it also increased the liquidity preference of merchants, and this must have manifested itself as a shortage of cash, a restriction of credit, and a reduction in demand: 'the tradesman now hath not half that employment, nor is so readily and well paid for his commodities as in former times, there being little store of money.'[3] This situation naturally grew worse when war began, for 'they who have money keep it close'.[4] Economics had finally given way to politics. Trade did not cease entirely, but when James Ashe, a large-scale Somerset textile manufacturer, received (for cloths sold in 1642) payments early in 1643 in the form of £11 'laid out for me in arms' and £3 14s. 0d. 'for 4 muskets',[5] it was obvious in which disastrous way the times were tending.

[1] For all this, see *C.S.P.V. 1640–1642*, p. 291; B.M. 669, f. 3/48, 4/75; Steele, I, no. 1982; L.J. IV, 581; B.M. E. 144 (6); M. James, *Social Problems and Policy During the Puritan Revolution* (1930), p. 60.
[2] *A Caution to Keep Money* (1642): B.M. E. 146 (21), p. 2.
[3] *A Caution to Keep Money*, p. 8.
[4] Somers, IV, 535.
[5] Details from account book ('1631 to 1641', 'The Book of Account of cloths sold') in C. 107/20.

Part II

Years of Change: Real and Monetary Factors

7. A CHANGING ECONOMY: THE OLD AND THE NEW

It is a telling comment on the historian's attachment to change that almost every historical period has, at one time or another, been categorized as 'a time of transition'. And if we view history, or more particularly economic history, as a continuous process, then the recurring platitude becomes at least comprehensible, and any period can be seen, from some viewpoint, as the link between two different sets of economic arrangements. So it is with England's trading economy in the early seventeenth century. The previous hundred years had seen the establishment of a commercial network and an industrial structure which, in spite of many dashing and enterprising exploits, was largely tied to the old draperies and to European markets north of the Mediterranean. When the Hanoverians came to the throne, and even for some years before, it was abundantly clear that businessmen were operating within a new framework—one whose important lines of communication extended westward to America and southward into the Mediterranean, round Africa, and to the Far East; whose trading products had been diversified to a revolutionary degree; and whose industrial underpinning, while it had become somewhat less important to the system's commercial transactions, had evolved away from a unique concern with the traditional woollen fabrics. Concomitantly, the ways in which men thought about economic problems had undergone radical changes. No abrupt revolution had occurred, no class had overnight shaken off its old shackles and assumed new freedoms and powers. Rather, there had been a slow and fluctuating evolution of commerce, industry and private and public economic outlook, an evolution towards a new economic equilibrium. It is, indeed, in this sense that we may speak of the years between the death of Elizabeth and the death of Strafford as comprising that ubiquitous historical prop, a 'time of transition'. But the tendencies which we can see operating manifested themselves when the Tudors were still on the throne and came to their full flowering after Cromwell had died.

The foregoing pages have traced at some length the short-term fluctuations, and have afforded us, from time to time, a glimpse of the more permanent trends in economic development in the early seventeenth century. On the one hand a contraction, as far as English exporters were concerned, of the traditional markets swept the traditional industry, and some of the traditional industrial areas, into a long-term depression. On the other, innovations in the types of cloth produced and in the markets and sources of supply tapped by English merchants were beginning to offer evidence, sparse and limited though it was, of a wholesale shift in economic emphasis. The decline of the old, no less than the first stirrings of the new, merit the historian's study. It will be the task of this chapter to describe the period from both viewpoints.

(i) THE DECLINE OF THE OLD DRAPERIES

Of no time after 1614 can it really be stated that the old draperies enjoyed any sustained prosperity. This long-term development has to some extent already been described and analysed,[1] and the overall decline in the traditional manufacture is now a commonplace of economic history. In the first six years of the seventeenth century London exports of shortcloths had averaged over 100,000 annually,[2] but after 1614 there are only two recorded instances, in 1618 and 1628, of that figure being exceeded, while the only available totals after 1628 demonstrate the low level to which the old cloth trade had sunk:

| 1631 | 84,334 | 1633 | 80,844 |
| 1632 | 99,020 | 1640 | 86,924 |

As the export of shortcloths was largely destined for consumers in northern, eastern and central Europe—to which areas some 84 per cent of cloths were shipped in the early years of the period—so the general fall measures the decline of these lands as markets for the most important of English textiles. Thus Germany and the United Provinces, the two predominant destinations for the English cloth fleets, in 1598 received some 71,300 shortcloths from London, and by 1614 this figure had considerably increased—to some 99,000, as measured in notional shortcloths. But by 1632, which was in any case a good year for total sales, such shipments had fallen below 60,000, and eight years later only 45,000 cloths were exported from London to the Low Countries and Germany.[3] This trend is a precise measurement of the trade of the Merchant Adventurers, who, with the exception of 1632, monopolized cloth exports to these areas. As the trade in the old draperies fell from high prosperity, so the importance of the company declined: from handling some 75 per cent of cloth ship-

[1] Fisher, 'London's Export Trade', *passim*.
[2] For this and subsequent statistics, see the relevant Tables in Appendix A.
[3] Professor Fisher ('London's Export Trade', 153) suggests that port book statistics of 1640 may possibly under-estimate the amounts going to central and eastern Europe, since, in that year, European hostilities enforced an increased use of the trans-Alpine route into those markets.

ments from London the company slipped until it barely controlled half of a much reduced total.

Discontinuous as the available statistics are, we can obtain from them some useful measure of the impact of this decline on the prosperity of the textile industry in the western counties, which substantiates the abundant qualitative evidence of dislocation and stagnation. The basic product of Wiltshire, Gloucestershire, Worcestershire, Somerset and Oxfordshire, was the white, undressed cloth which was the backbone of the old draperies. Since, in addition, these counties were the overwhelmingly principal suppliers of such unfinished fabrics, and since much of their manufacturing potential was given over to white cloth, the export figures are reasonably valid indications of both the fall in demand for their products and the extent to which they bore the brunt of depression:

Exports of undressed shortcloths from London
(rounded to 100)

Year	Amount	Percentage of London's exports
1606	90,700	72·0
1614	87,800	68·7
1620	48,000	56·3
1632	45,700	46·1
1640	30,300	34·8

The slump which had shaken the cloth trade to its foundations in the early 1620's was thus merely a drastic foretaste of the long-term depression which enveloped the traditional industry until the Civil War—and beyond. The contemporary anxiety, which was so unanimously expressed during the great crisis, concerning the Merchant Adventurers' trade, was echoed twenty years later, with no indication that the situation had improved in the interim.[1] In measure as the trade in the old draperies fell off after 1614, the concentration of producing areas, in the West Country, of trading businessmen, in the Merchant Adventurers, and of markets, in northern Europe, were, to a marked extent, deprived of their former predominance.

What was the reaction of seventeenth-century commentators to these developments? In nearly every case the decline in textiles shipments was attributed to the growth of manufacture abroad. 'Dutch, Silesians and Venetians', said Sir Thomas Roe in 1640, 'attempt the making of cloth, and now by experience (I am informed) the half is not vented, that was in the latter age.' The next year Henry Robinson expressed the same

[1] For the 1620's see Add. MSS. 34324, fols. 191, 195; S.P.D. Jas. I, 118/142; Egerton MSS. 33, fol. 44. For the later comments, see *C.S.P.D. 1639–1640*, pp. 234–5, 333–4, 417–18; J.B., *The Merchant's Remonstrance* (1645), pp. 4–5; H. Parker, *Of a Free Trade* (1648), p. 35. Cf. S.P.D. Chas. I (Addenda), 535/32.

feeling: 'We cannot at present vent in Germany and the Low Countries one third part of what we used in former times, being beaten out of it by their subtlety and industry in making the same themselves.' The Merchant Adventurers constantly indicated that the growing manufacture of, for instance, white cloth in the Low Countries had severely reduced their own shipments; and complaints of 'the making of great stores of cloths and other draperies in foreign parts', which had commenced well before 1640, continued in the subsequent years.[1]

These conclusions undoubtedly corresponded with reality. It cannot be argued that the export of English cloth, after decades of growth, had reached a ceiling beyond which it could not rise, that sales, having saturated a static market, could no longer expand. Rather, what happened was that competition developed which English textiles were unable to meet, so that they had to accept a smaller absolute share of total demand. That a full realization of these circumstances did not come until the 1630's does not mean either that competition was absent in the preceding decades or that some men were not able to distinguish its growth. Complaints concerning the development of European textile industries had, indeed, been a marked feature of every period of depression in the years under consideration, and even relatively prosperous years had produced their Jeremiahs. Quite early in the century it was noted that the rapid expansion of Venetian textile production was adversely affecting English exports to the Mediterranean.[2] At the same time, Lionel Cranfield's factors in Germany found that there had been a significant and alarming increase in the manufacture of cheap, coarse cloth in northern and eastern Europe.[3] Even before the Cockayne project added more fuel to the fire, and while the English industry was expanding to its 1614 peak, sharp warnings were uttered concerning Spanish, French, Dutch, Italian and German cloths.[4] In addition, as has been seen, both during the experiment and in the slump which followed it within three years, the threatening industrial developments overseas could not be ignored. By the last decade of the period there could be no excuse for not recognizing that the old draperies had to be sold in a new and highly competitive environment.

It is difficult to adduce any comprehensive explanation of the nature and timing of this powerful competition. There was, for instance, a

[1] Roe, p. 10; Robinson, *England's Safety*, p. 14; S.P.D. Chas. I, 307/76, 449/34; S.P.D. Chas. I (Addenda), 535/32; *C.S.P.D. 1639–1640*, pp. 333–4; Parker, p. 36; Ramsay, 'The Report of the Royal Commission'. For the post-1640 period, see Roberts, *The Treasure of Traffic*, p. 17; *Discourse ... for ... Enlargement ... of Trade*, p. 38; S.P.D. Interregnum, 1/34, 9/5, 15/93, 16/139.
[2] Lans. MSS. 152, fol. 148; S.P.D. Jas. I, 15/4II, 20/9*, fol. 27; Add. MSS. 14027, fol. 287.
[3] H.M.C. *Sackville*, II, 138, 145, 165, 193, 195–6, 203. Cf. S.P.D. Eliz., 283A/51.
[4] Lans. MSS. 152, fol. 229; cf. fols. 205 and 221.

A Changing Economy

generally held opinion during all these years that much of the growth of continental industry should be attributed to the Cockayne experiment, which stimulated rapid industrial developments in Holland and Germany.[1] To some extent there is considerable justification for this view. But it is obvious that other factors must have been at work: a temporary stoppage was too insecure a basis for a rival industry. Clearly the continental manufacture of textiles had very real economic advantages, and artificial interludes such as Cockayne's project merely served to precipitate, not establish, the movement towards effective competition.

In essence the novelty of the situation lay in the cheapness of the foreign product (that is, the relative dearness of English cloth) and in the sharp manifestation of competition in coarser textiles. It was in the manufacture of a cloth of low quality that, for instance, Germany, eastern Europe and France were increasingly able to undercut all sorts of English woollens.[2]

In the general field it is distinctly possible that long-term price developments were working to England's disadvantage. During the early part of the sixteenth century, England, it seems, enjoyed something of a competitive monopoly in the European market for standard woollen textiles, and this was reflected, even later in the century, in an assumption by contemporaries that the domestic product had a scarcity value in world markets.[3] This situation may well have been due to the discontinuity with which American treasure circulated into and through Europe—with a consequent lag between continental and English inflations as the uneven flow of silver pushed continental prices up in the first instance. English prices and costs were, therefore, probably lower. From the end of Elizabeth's reign, however, it seems that home prices rose (under the influence of a further influx of bullion) markedly faster than prices abroad —which soon, in any case, ceased to rise over the long run. Increasingly, therefore, England lost the competitive advantages derived from monetary costs. Overseas costs fell below those of England, which were attuned to a network of relative international prices which no longer obtained; the long-term price-income structure of the home economy fell out of line with that of the rest of Europe and, consequently, English goods became dearer. Continental manufacture was stimulated by the decline in relative costs of production.[4]

[1] See, for examples, Add. MSS. 34324, fol. 191; Hargrave MSS. 321, p. 184; *C.S.P.D. 1619–1623*, p. 387; Misselden, *Free Trade*, pp. 41–2, 126–7; S.P.D. Chas. I, 56/6, 277/124; Sanderson, fols. 241 ff.; Roe, p. 10; Robinson, *England's Safety*, p. 17; J. B[attie], pp. 4–5.
[2] See *H.M.C. Sackville*, II, 193, 195–6; Lans. MSS. 152, fol. 221; Hargrave MSS. 321, p. 87; Culpepper, p. 32; J.B., p. 4.
[3] Below, p. 210.
[4] For a more detailed application of the above argument, see Gould, 'The Trade Depression of the Early 1620's', 86–7.

But the question as to why particular goods, and specifically coarse textiles, should have been affected still needs some explanation. A relatively heavy item in the cost of production of such goods, which used cheaper grade wools and little capital equipment, was undoubtedly the remuneration of the labour involved. Where unskilled labour was inexpensive and abundant, low-quality goods could be manufactured at a low cost. This was especially likely to apply where widespread poverty typified a region in which the production of textiles provided only a by-employment for the labourers concerned. Labour in an employment not expected to produce the wherewithal of total subsistence is normally cheaper than that in a full-time occupation. This was the reason adduced by Adam Smith to explain the historical cheapness of coarse, relative to fine, cloths.[1] In the early seventeenth century economic conditions in eastern Europe approximated to this situation, and this meant that that area was eminently suited to the effective production of cheap cloth if the quality expectations of market demand were lowered. In the event it does seem that with widespread insecurity and economic breakdown accompanying the Thirty Years War in a low-cost economy, the circumstances both of production and demand favoured the cheaper native industries. There is some evidence that such a development ante-dated 1618: one of Cranfield's factors in Europe wrote home in 1608 that a cause of bad markets for English textiles was 'the making of cloth and kersies in Hungary, Silesia and other adjoining parts in such quantity and so good cheap as that the common man desires no better, and the country being so poor can very well miss our English kersies [which are false and] not to be afforded near the price of their own cloth'.[2] These tendencies became even more important after the outbreak of continental war, and when the relatively high costs of English cloth are taken into account it is no surprise that English exports should have been ousted from the European market. Thus the export of northern kersies by London Merchant Adventurers to Germany and the United Provinces fell from 12,186 in 1606 to 1,482 in 1632 and 237 in 1640. A similar, although somewhat less drastic, decline took place in the export of unfinished shortcloths (packcloths).[3] More than this, the relatively depressed state of parts of Europe meant that European consumers tended to substitute coarse cloths for the finer fabrics which they had formerly purchased; and here they would tend to turn to the indigenous manufacturers or the cheaper products of other European countries. England's quality products

[1] *The Wealth of Nations*, I, 227–8.   [2] H.M.C. *Sackville*, II, 195–6.
[3] See Appendix A, Tables 4 and 9. Cf. Lans. MSS. 152, fol. 221: 'In Germany...much coarse cloth is made of their own wool... whereby we are prevented of the utterance of thousands of our packcloths, especially when ours do rise above a certain price.'

A Changing Economy 141

suffered commensurately: 'The Dutch undersell us in our coarser sorts, which is a great part of our trade, and our finer sorts which they cannot make, being unproportionably dear, they will rather make shift with their own meaner cloth than wear our finer at such excessive rates.'[1]

There are abundant indications that a potent stimulus to the growth of competitive industry in Germany and other lands had been provided by the growing supplies of inexpensive native wool.[2] Nevertheless, among many people in England, and not least in government circles, the opinion persisted that foreign manufacture was primarily encouraged by the export of *British* raw materials, and there was, therefore, a long tradition of official complaints and attempts to prevent overseas shipments of wool, fells and fuller's earth. By the 1630's this campaign had become even more intense, in part because the Merchant Adventurers protested vigorously that the current export of wool and fells was sustaining the burgeoning Dutch textile industry.[3] In 1639 this tendency culminated in the drastic decision to ban coastal shipments of fuller's earth lest it be illicitly diverted to European markets. This measure, whose severity indicates the serious view taken of the problem, proved too extreme. Clothiers in Suffolk, Essex, Yorkshire and Lincolnshire sent desperate petitions to London, claiming that overland carriage of earth from Kent would prove prohibitively expensive, and, ultimately, a compromise was arrived at by which regular, although limited and controlled, shipments were allowed.[4]

It is impossible to tell how much wool and fuller's earth was actually smuggled out of British ports. But it is absolutely certain that supplies from these Isles did not possess the strategic importance attributed to them by contemporaries. Besides the coarser varieties deriving from eastern Europe, which were in themselves significant enough to revolutionize the industrial situation, Spanish wool went in increasing amounts to the principal manufacturing centres of Europe. For long in demand in Flanders, it was now sent to Italy, France, the Netherlands and ultimately to Germany;[5] and, as we shall see, it even found a good market in England. In 1610 Richard Gore had warned that Spanish wool was potentially a

---

[1] See Lans. MSS. 152, fols. 273–8.
[2] See, for example, Lans. MSS. 152, fol. 221; S.P.D. Jas. I, 80/126; Culpepper, p. 32; Parker, p. 35.
[3] Steele, I, nos. 1600, 1651; P.C. 2/39, p. 720; P.C. 2/40, pp. 98–100, 244, 245, 392, 412, 452; P.C. 2/41, p. 153; S.P.D. Chas. I, 224/44, 307/76.
[4] *Foedera*, XX, 342–3; Steele, I, no. 1802; *C.S.P.D. 1639*, pp. 379–80, 356–7, 489; P.C. 2/50, pp. 520–1, 630–1; P.C. 2/52, pp. 512–13, 557, 582–4; P.C. 2/53, p. 139; S.P.D. Chas. I, 457/14; *C.S.P.D. 1641–1643*, p. 60.
[5] M. M. Postan and H. J. Habakkuk (eds.), *The Cambridge Economic History of Europe* (Cambridge, 1952), II, 428; Malynes, *England's View*, pp. 137–8; S.P.D. Jas. I, 15/4II, 20/9*, fol. 27, 80/126; S.P.D. Chas. I, 307/76; Lans. MSS. 152, fols. 221, 229; Hargrave MSS. 321, pp. 87, 107; Roberts, *The Treasure of Traffic*, p. 17.

dangerous threat to the English industry: 'If Spain have that abundance of ... good wool for clothing as I believe it hath we ... must be careful lest we put trade from ourselves to our neighbour nations. ... [Spain lies] in wait to take advantage of the dearness of our cloths to have the more vent of their wool.'[1] By the end of the period these forebodings were borne out; Spanish wool was supplying England's strongest competitors, so much so that Henry Robinson could seriously suggest that one means of meeting continental competition would be to 'find means of compassing all the wools of Spain for some years together, whereby Germany, France, Italy and the Low Countries will be necessitated to repair to England for to be set on work'.[2] In this development lay yet another cause of the special problems of English manufacture: Spanish wool, while it was relatively cheap and abundant, was of a reasonably high quality. One commentator reported that 'the chiefest means [of the Dutch] for making fine cloth is the great supply they have in Spanish wools'.[3] Clearly, English fine cloths, which in the past had been considered 'a riches peculiar to this Nation', were now met not only by competitive coarse textiles, but on their own grounds; the continental industry satisfied demands for both quality and cheapness, and as the distribution of Spanish wool was augmented so contemporaries noticed an increased ability (especially on the part of the Dutch) to compete effectively with England in the manufacture of high-quality, expensive woollen textiles.

There has also been an attempt[4] to explain the stagnation of the old broadcloth industry almost entirely in terms of the changing quality of the English wool supply. On this view the Tudor and Stuart enclosures, by improving pasture land, 'made light fleeces heavier, fine wool coarser, and short wool longer'. The result being to render the wool much less suitable for the manufacture of fine broadcloths (and much more adaptable to the production of worsted fabrics and new draperies). The theory is lent further validity by the fact that the only new high-quality cloth which *was* produced in the period utilized fine Spanish wool.[5] There can be little doubt that there was some deterioration of quality in the English wool which during the Middle Ages had enjoyed such a high reputation, and that, especially since foreign supplies of wool were expanding, the English textile industry suffered from some reduction in the supply of

---

[1] Lans. MSS. 152, fol. 221.
[2] *Certain Proposals* (1652), p. 11. Cf. Ramsay, 'The Report of the Royal Commission'; S.P.D. Interregnum, 9/5.
[3] S.P.D. Chas. I, 307/76.
[4] P. J. Bowden, 'Wool Supply and the Woollen Industry', *Econ. Hist. Rev.*, 2nd ser. IX (1956), 44–58.
[5] Below, section (ii).

fine, short-staple raw material and from the necessity to use coarser, inferior wool. But this can by no means provide a universal explanation for industrial stagnation. For one thing it fails to take into account either the expansion of continental industry, against which an inferior product had to be measured, or the remarkable growth in European wool supplies, upon which continental industrialization was based. Further, competition was at its keenest not *directly* in the high-quality market, but in the market for relatively coarser textiles—which presumably expanded to the extent that inferior goods produced abroad were being substituted for the traditional English broadcloth. It was a series of radical changes in the market and in alternative supplies, not solely a deterioration in the English industry, which had such unfortunate repercussions for the old draperies. The resulting economic pressures made for a dynamic and changing industrial environment. Before we consider this, it is advisable to study at some length another factor which some contemporaries viewed as a critical feature of England's industrial situation.

In measure as at intermittent times of crisis merchants had almost unanimously condemned the low standards of textile manufacture as a cause of the decline in sales, so in seeking an explanation of long-term stagnation groups such as the commission which reported in 1640 did not hesitate to turn to 'the false and deceitful making of old and new draperies'.[1] At times these protests seem to have been both honest and indicative of genuine abuses, and then the bitter tone adopted by traders is at least understandable: 'If you had been with me at Amsterdam', wrote one of Cranfield's factors in 1601, 'to have seen some of them [Cranfield's cloths] as I did you would have said it is a pity that such villains as we have in England should live to spoil the drapery of our land in such sort. Some not worth half their money . . . the man cursed me to my face that bought them of me.'[2]

Where corrupt manufacture was not the result of the pressure exerted by a contracting market on prices and costs, part of the reason lay in the organization of the textile industry. With a scattered geographical distribution of the (relatively small) units of production, together with the absence of precision machinery, it was impossible to achieve anything like the standardization of product since secured by the centralized supervision and superior technology of the factory system. Since one prerequisite of a stable trade is that the merchant should be reasonably assured that the products belonging to one group of exports are as near

[1] Ramsay, 'The Report of the Royal Commission'. For a detailed description of the types of deceit practised, see J. May, *A Declaration of the Estate of Clothing* (1613), pp. 24–9.
[2] H.M.C. *Sackville*, II, 91; cf. 15, 32, 34, 39–40, 68–70, 99–100, etc.

as possible identical, any acute differences in quality or measurements would be bound to affect his position and make his trade insecure, while undue variations in quality would tend to reduce the effective market. In the early modern period the function of securing the desired standardization was assumed by the central government, rather than by a rationalized industrial organization, and was embodied in a host of regulatory statutes. Failure to conform to the specified requirements provoked the frequent, although often unproductive, campaigns against 'falsity'.[1] From one point of view, therefore, the problem of corrupt manufacture was essentially one of a lack of qualitative co-ordination between demand and the productive process.

However, the constant coincidence of declining markets and complaints of poor manufacture suggests that it was not always the case that the falsity led to the bad sales, but that it was the repercussion of a contracting market which provoked those attempts to reduce costs under economic pressure which most often led to widespread evasions of statutory requirements. This view derives from the fact that the scope for other forms of cost-reduction was severely restricted by the low standard of living (which meant that wages were near subsistence level to start with), the absence of fixed capital, the nature of industrial organization, and the consequent hindrances to technological or managerial innovations, which meant that the 'textile industry . . . operated under conditions of virtually fixed real costs'.[2] Therefore, when a fall in overseas demand—either in the short run or over a long period—stimulated merchants to demand that English producers accept lower prices for their products, a debasement of quality might be the only way in which the latter could hope to maintain net income. In 1622, for instance, it was said that the 'clothier's conscience is satisfied for he saith that the falsest cloth is answerable to the merchant's best price'; and ten years later it was claimed that 'no country [is] able to make so good and so cheap cloth as England, if the merchant did not, by striving to have it made cheap, cause it to be falsified'.[3] It was for this reason that the Privy Council frequently found itself under twofold pressure, as in 1631 when 'there come daily complaints to the Board, as well from clothiers in divers counties, because the merchants do not take off their cloths, as from the merchants because their cloths are not well and truly made'.[4]

[1] For a sixteenth-century example of the extreme difficulty of securing enforcement even of the simplest laws regulating measurement, see G. R. Elton, 'Informing for Profit: A Sidelight on Tudor Methods of Law Enforcement', *The Cambridge Historical Journal*, XI (1954), 158–60.
[2] Fisher, 'London's Export Trade', 156.
[3] Cotton MSS. Galba, E. 1, fol. 362; S.P.D. Chas. I, 215/101. Cf. S.P.D. Chas. I, 250/53.
[4] P.C. 2/40, p. 323.

The phenomenon might show itself as manufacturers attempted to reduce raw material costs by unduly stretching cloths to statutory lengths or by failing to conform to them. Alternatively, attempts to reduce labour costs—seeking 'amends of . . . bad markets . . . out of the labour of the poor'[1]—might force employees to use deceitful methods in order to maintain their own incomes by saving on raw materials, as happened in the 1590's and in Essex in 1629 where, because weavers were being forced 'to make their cloths longer than they were wont [without a concomitant wage-increase] . . . much of their work is made false and so less vendible'.[2] The reaction of the government to such situations was to attempt to standardize the product and support wages by administrative fiat.[3] In the more general field the commissioners appointed to investigate false manufacture and the decay of trade in 1638 were required to ensure that employees were paid sufficient wages; and in their final report, two years later, they recommended that, in order to prevent deceitful manufacture, the corporations which they proposed be set up be given power 'to settle and provide as occasion offereth, that the poor workmen depending on the said trade . . . may have competent wages for their work'.[4] Laudable as these efforts were, however, it has to be admitted that if the wage reductions and the consequent poor quality were results of an economic depression, then it was impossible, by these means alone, to return in every respect to the *status quo*.

As has already appeared, the early seventeenth century witnessed constant complaints concerning the falsity of cloth, which naturally increased at times of depression. By the 1630's, however, the long-term stagnation of the old draperies had sufficiently asserted itself to be reflected in almost constant pressure on costs, provoking wholesale attempts to debase quality and administrative efforts to maintain it which assumed institutional forms which were, in themselves, indicative of the problem's urgency.[5] Under the stimulus of the Merchant Adventurers, for instance, a commission was issued to Anthony Wither and Samuel Lively in 1630, 'for reformation of the abuses in clothmaking' in the white cloth industry of the West. The detailed story of the commission's activity, which lasted until at least 1636, has already been told.[6] Although Wither's over-eager antics, which provoked violent local opposition, introduced a farcical element into its actions, the commission's work involved

[1] S.P.D. Chas. I (Addenda), 535/32.
[2] Bland, Brown and Tawney, p. 337; S.P.D. Chas. I, 147/43.
[3] P.C. 2/39, p. 399; P.C. 2/41, pp. 440-1. For such a plan in 1636, see above, pp. 122-3.
[4] S.P.D. Chas. I, 398/118; Ramsay, 'The Report of the Royal Commission'.
[5] For a detailed description, see Supple, 'A Comparative Study', pp. 542 ff.
[6] G. D. Ramsay, *The Wiltshire Woollen Industry in the Sixteenth and Seventeenth Centuries* (1943), pp. 87 ff.

important problems, and it served to expose much patent corruption and negligence in local administration, some of which seems to have been improved.¹ The Privy Council instigated other action too, and investigations which started in 1631 led indirectly to the appointment of a subcommittee the next year whose extensive analysis of the textile regulations produced, in 1633, a far-reaching proclamation.² But in two respects the wishes of the government had to be modified, after considerable protest, in order not to disrupt industrial organization in the western counties. It was decided that gig mills, which had been banned as a nefarious means of stretching cloth, could not be so suddenly suppressed, and only their future erection was forbidden.³ Secondly, the original plans to restrict the dealings of market spinners who arranged the production of yarn for sale on the open market to clothiers, and who were reputed to produce two-thirds of the yarn used in the West and to be great 'corruptors' of it, had to be dropped at the insistence of local government officials.⁴ In both cases measures urged by merchants against methods of production which they considered deceitful foundered on the rocks of the necessities of established industrial organization. Five years later there was yet another outcry by overseas traders concerning the low quality of English textiles and the attempts by manufacturers to undercut each other by debasing standards. This led directly to the appointment of the commission of inquiry already mentioned, whose report, not surprisingly, since the body was largely composed of merchants, found the *principal* cause of the decay of trade in deceitful textile manufacture. The remedies proposed were never attempted since by 1640 political events were overshadowing the formulation of economic policy.⁵

To a great extent the issues involved in the falsification of cloth lay at the centre of England's economic difficulties in the early seventeenth century. Although the new draperies suffered from some irregularities, they were not of the order of magnitude (and did not produce the reaction) of those to be found in the manufacture of the traditional white cloth industry. It was the latter which, as has been seen, was under the maximum economic pressure after 1620. It was therefore only to be expected that it was in that sector of the textile industry that the greatest efforts were made to reduce unit costs by debasing quality and that official attempts to

---

[1] C.S.P.D. *1638–1639*, p. 240; P.C. 2/44, pp. 174–9.
[2] P.C. 2/40, pp. 323, 355; S.P.D. Chas. I, 184/95; P.C. 2/42, pp. 160–1, 172, 258–9, 334–6; Steele, I, no. 1657.
[3] See S.P.D. Chas. I, 241/36–7, 244/1, 4, 248/78, 250/53; P.C. 2/43, pp. 167, 199, 372–3, 384.
[4] S.P.D. Chas. I, 14/15, 180/71, 243/33, 248/1, 282/81; P.C. 2/42, pp. 334–6, 484.
[5] C.S.P.D. *1637–1638*, p. 553; C.S.P.D. *1638–1639*, p. 24; S.P.D. Chas. I, 398/118, 409/210, 454/84; Ramsay, 'The Report of the Royal Commission'. The final report, allowing for the change of emphasis, was largely a repetition of the famous report of the 1622 committee.

remedy the situation were largely concentrated in those western counties which had been most severely affected by the changes in the pattern of English trade. Even the most radical of these plans envisaged some retention of traditional forms, some adaptation of old organizations to new functions—as in the case of the reiterated projects to control industry through locally-based corporations.[1] Investigations into the more general question threw light on the industrial tensions arising from the decline of the white broadcloth industry, as factors of production shifted under the stress of long-term changes in overseas demand. Thus the Wiltshire Justices in 1633 wrote that the market spinners gave 'better wages than the clothier . . . in that the market spinners vent much of their yarn to those that make the dyed and dressed cloths (who give better prices than the white men do)'.[2]

Passages like this were indicative of new economic realities. The government, from the start, was presented with a hopeless task. Were legal requirements to be enforced, then costs would rise to such an extent as to augur wholesale unemployment. If a change in production methods was the result of economic depression, as most often seems to have been the case, then it was no answer to the latter to attempt to restrain the former. Given contemporary industrial techniques there might have been some cases where English cloth was losing ground abroad primarily because it was corrupt. But there seem to have been many more instances where the causal process was reversed; and in this case, since false manufacture was only a limited and hopeless form of cutting costs, the answers to England's problems lay in other directions.

Whatever the explanation of the chronic stagnation of the old draperies, the overt manifestation of such long-term depression meant that, except for men living beyond their time,[3] there had to develop a new attitude to the marketing of cloth, a new way of thinking about competition and prices. And whereas in the sixteenth century, partly under the stimulus of a seller's market, unanimity had reigned as to the necessity of maintaining the price of English cloth, of 'selling dear', now a new feeling arose:

---

[1] The early seventeenth century witnessed many attempts to adapt the ancient gild structure and the somewhat newer corporative forms to industrial needs, in an attempt to provide security and channels for investment—not only for regulatory purposes but in order to establish new industries or new centres for old industries. The scheme to utilize county corporations for regulation and expansion in textiles was particularly favoured, although, as with most plans, little success attended the efforts of innovators. See F. J. Fisher, 'Some Experiments in Company Organization in the Early Seventeenth Century', *Econ. Hist. Rev.* IV (1933), 177–94. Misselden, in his *Free Trade*, had also advocated corporations to regulate deceitful manufacture, and in 1622 and 1640 the industrial commissions put forward the same proposals.

[2] S.P.D. Chas. I, 243/33.

[3] Below, pp. 210–11.

that textiles should be sold as cheaply as possible. This keener perception of the competitive environment was, from one point of view, a fundamental departure in economic thought, although the workaday merchant had, of course, always been aware of the relationships between prices, demands and substitutes in the new market conditions.[1] This inevitable change in economic outlook will be dealt with in its place;[2] but it is well to note here that it contained the seed of the ultimate argument against company trading—whose justification had so often been that it kept the terms of trade favourable to England. An institution fashioned to maintain prices to alien consumers could not expect a continuance of the support it had enjoyed under more suitable circumstances once the prevailing mood looked towards the *lowering* of prices as far as possible to meet new competition. The changing climate of opinion is best exemplified in the words of an anonymous critic of the Merchant Adventurers: now that the Dutch manufacture cloth, he wrote in 1645, 'There is far greater necessity of a free trade and selling cheap than heretofore, when the Hollanders made none or but few; for then it was easy to make them give what price we pleased for cloth; but now we must not only endeavour to sell our commodities, but should chiefly aim to sell so cheap, as might cause the Dutch to desist from making of cloth.'[3]

But, as already intimated, the inflexibility of industrial organization in the old draperies imposed a strict and narrow limit on the possibilities of cost-reduction. In addition, the state of Stuart finances rarely allowed a diminution of the financial burdens imposed on cloth, even though the advocates of a lowering of impositions were many and vociferous whenever the competitive situation worsened.[4] The time for intensive adaptation had passed. Undermined by market competition abroad and competition for the factors of production at home, resorting increasingly to the self-defeating form of reducing costs which lay in a debasement of quality, the white broadcloth industry plunged into the turmoils of Civil War—only a weak shadow of what had formerly been England's 'Golden Fleece'. Yet the attitude of mind which was prepared to think in new ways about the price of cloth was also willing to accept novel changes in the overall structure of England's commerce; with the intensive road to adaptation and expansion blocked, men turned increasingly to the possibilities of more extensive change. The solution lay in expanding lines

---

[1] See S.P.D. Eliz., 283A/51; Lans. MSS. 152, fols. 221, 229; Mun, *England's Treasure*, p. 8. Mun suggested that a 25 per cent price-reduction would increase cloth sales by 50 per cent.
[2] Below, pp. 221–3.
[3] *Discourse . . . for . . . the Enlargement . . . of Trade*, p. 38.
[4] See, for example, S.P.D. Chas. I, 282/16, 284/7; Roe, p. 10; Goffe, p. 385; etc. For opinion in the early 1620's, see above, pp. 60–1.

A Changing Economy 149

of goods and of communication: England was manufacturing new products and breaking into new markets even while the old remained depressed and stagnant.

(ii) A QUALITY PRODUCT

Although in general it was true that the manufacturers of old draperies in the western counties were little able to adapt themselves so as to counter the economic forces bringing about their decline, there was a limited field in which they could vary the product to suit the changing times. This was principally in the production of coloured cloth of a very high quality. Thus in the Stroudwater area of Gloucestershire there developed the manufacture of stammells or 'reds'. In 1635 the clothiers concerned claimed that they had begun making that type of fabric, an improvement on the traditional coarse variety, a generation previously, and that over the years they had extended their market from England to the Continent until, at that date, 'we do make of the said cloths near 3,000 every year'. They found a special satisfaction in their achievements because 'the trade of making of white cloths with us is much decayed and thereby many poor weavers want employment'.[1]

But of more significance than the production of stammells was the derivation of a new high-quality cloth which took advantage of the cheap and abundant supplies of wool which were revolutionizing the European textile industry. Spanish wool, as has been seen, served to enhance the quality of some European fabrics; imported into England, it was used in Spanish, or medley, cloths and created an entirely new branch of industry. The manufacture of these high-priced fabrics developed most successfully along the Somerset–Wiltshire border,[2] and also in Devon, and was originally based on the import of dyed wool. Spanish wool was at first principally brought into England for use by felt makers or haberdashers,[3] but as early as 1606 the Merchant Adventurers drew attention to its use in the Somerset textile industry and within a generation it was claimed that the production of fine wool in Herefordshire had declined as a consequence.[4] In time the foreign wool came to be dyed in England and ultimately Spanish cloths were manufactured in part with native wools.[5]

There is no record of any export of Spanish cloths from London in the Port Book of 1622, but by 1628 the equivalent of almost 3,500 shortcloths

[1] S.P.D. Chas. I, 287/77.
[2] Ramsay, *The Wiltshire Woollen Industry*, p. 103.
[3] Bowden, 57.
[4] S.P.D. Jas. I, 20/9*, fol. 27; *C.S.P.D. 1636–1637*, pp. 415–16.
[5] R. Perry, 'The Gloucestershire Woollen Industry, 1100–1690', *Transactions of the Bristol and Gloucestershire Archæological Society*, LXVI (1945), 102. Cf. S.P.D. Chas. I, 380/86.

were being shipped and by the 1630's there was considerable progress with the new product. In this expansion of sales the most significant feature was the extent to which the fabric had invaded those very continental markets which, as far as the white broadcloth industry was concerned, were experiencing the long-term decline:

Export of Spanish cloths from London to northern Europe [1]
(in notional terms)

	1628	1632	1640
Low Countries	2,659	4,153	6,048
Germany	603	1,389	3,954
Flanders and Dunkirk	—	748	3,496
Baltic	84	80	19
Russia	—	6	—
	3,346	6,376	13,517

This expansion in an otherwise contracting market reflected the quality and saleability of the new textile: presumably largely stimulated by the depression in the traditional industry of the early 1620's, by 1640 it comprised over 20 per cent of London's shipments to those areas, while the amounts sent to southern Europe were negligible. In 1631 extended storage space had to be provided in Blackwell Hall for the Spanish cloths coming up to London for export, and two years later it was even claimed that the fall in sales of white and coloured cloths was partly due to 'the growth of an excellent sort of cloth called Spanish cloth, which had grown up since any Parliament took care of the business of clothing'.[2] By 1634 the London clothworkers (finishers) were feeling the pinch of a new development which produced a fully-manufactured article entirely in the rural areas; they protested that 'the one half of [our] trade [is] taken away by the late making of Spanish cloth, being wholly made in the country and dressed there'. On the other hand, the Merchant Adventurers were quick to appreciate the potentialities of the new trade, and in 1634, when they resumed their lapsed privileges, they ensured that Spanish cloth was included among those textiles of which they once again had an export-monopoly in the markets of Germany and the Low Countries.[3] Three years later the company was no less quick to defend its claims against the pretensions of Exeter merchants to handle the new fabrics. The discussions which finally led to a compromise agreement illustrated both the eagerness of the London merchants to control such a prosperous trade when, as they admitted, their standard exports of white

[1] Calculated from E. 190/32/3, E. 190/36/5, E. 190/43/4. See Appendix A, Table 13.
[2] Journals of the Common Council, 35, fols. 346b–7; C.S.P.D. 1633–1634, p. 86. The last cloth statute before 1633 had been in 1623.
[3] S.P.D. Chas. I, 278/106; P.C. 2/44, pp. 89–90; Foedera, XIX, 583–4.

broadcloths were so reduced, and the extent and speed of the growth of the production of Spanish cloths in Devon.[1]

It was generally agreed that Spanish cloths secured their success principally through their fineness and high quality. This, it was said, when combined with their wide variety of attractive colours, opened up a rich market at home and overseas. Yet their high cost meant that they could only have tapped a specialist demand; one contemporary estimate was that 400 Spanish cloths 'usually stand the merchants in more money than 700 white or coloured cloths'.[2] From a surviving account book of James Ashe, of Westcombe in Somerset, who made these cloths,[3] it appears that, with most of his cloths being just over 20 yards in length, they varied in price (to the merchant) from 12s. 0d. to 28s. 0d. per yard. In addition, they came in an astounding variety of colours, ranging from black, 'sad grey', 'stone grey' and 'liver', through 'mussel', 'beaver', and 'partridge grey', to azure, pink, peach, crimson, gold, and silver. In part, therefore, Spanish cloths must have been able to satisfy the same sort of changing fashions which so aided the development of the new draperies.[4] But they were far more substantial than the latter, and there can be little doubt that their real distinguishing feature was their excellent quality. As indicated above, it is possible that part of the difficulties which destroyed the prosperity of England's old draperies stemmed from the deterioration of native wools. If this is so then it was significant that the main adaptation of the textile industry, apart from the use of coarser wools for entirely new products, should have been in a direction which utilized the principal European source of supply of relatively cheap but high-grade wool, and avoided one of the major obstacles in the way of prosperity in England's fine-cloth industry.

Thus, using raw material presumably at a cost which put them on a par in that respect with European manufacturers, and engaged in a productive process which demanded a relatively skilled (and not necessarily a very cheap) labour force, West Country clothiers were able to make a success of the new trade even while the old was under severe pressure. They were able, further, to compete successfully with the manufacturers of the

---

[1] S.P.D. Chas. I, 380/85–8; P.C. 2/48, pp. 476, 516, 535.
[2] S.P.D. Chas. I, 268/5; P.C. 2/50, p. 323; *C.S.P.D. 1640–1641*, p. 370.
[3] The ledger, headed '1631 to 1641' and 'The Book of Accounts of Cloths Sold', is in the Public Record Office (C. 107/20). It provides evidence that Ashe sold on the average at least £3,000 worth of cloth annually in the 1630's, although there are indications that these dealings did not exhaust the extent of his manufacturing activities. On his death in 1646 he left (besides lands and the bequest to his widow) some £6,350 in bequests, besides forgiving debts of £1,000. It was to his son John, of Freshford, and Benedict Webb, of Kingswood, that Aubrey ascribed the development of the manufacture of Spanish cloths (Ramsay, *The Wiltshire Woollen Industry*, p. 103). For Webb, see E. Moir, 'Benedict Webb, Clothier', *Econ. Hist. Rev.* 2nd ser. x (1957), 256–64.
[4] Below, pp. 153–5.

standard old draperies for factors of production, and this in part explains the industrial tensions which were so evident in the western counties during the 1630's.[1] Finally, stimulus must have come, as it seems to have done to the new draperies, from the absence of statutory regulation of the product, which was made 'as any man pleases', (although this occasioned some counterfeiting and friction[2]) and from the fact that customs duties bore proportionately lightly in relation to their value upon such expensive textiles as Spanish cloths.[3] At the end of the period the Privy Council was able to claim, with some justification, that the product, by dint of its high quality, 'is now become one of the best and most requested manufactures of cloth of this kingdom'.[4]

Dyed and dressed in the western textile areas and invading an otherwise depressed market, Spanish cloths were an important industrial departure and afforded some limited economic relief to the older branch of the textile industry. But in their very nature these fabrics could not provide a comprehensive solution to the cloth industry's problems. The scope for a great expansion of output was, with demand, necessarily restricted by the high quality and great cost of Spanish cloths. Such a development was not the sort of extensive adaptation called for by the prevailing commercial environment. This came in a new field and was able to tap a much wider and more volatile market.

(iii) NEW DRAPERIES AND NEW HORIZONS

If our cloth be not vented as in former years, let us embrace some other way to spend and vent our wools. Cloth is a heavy and hot wearing and serves but one cold corner of the World: but if we embrace the new draperies . . . we shall employ all the wool we have, set more people on work than by cloth, and a pound of wool in those stuffs true made will outsell two pounds in cloth, and thus we may supply France, Italy, Spain, Barbary and some parts of Asia by such light and fine stuffs as will fit those warmer regions, and yet have sufficient for the cold climates.

Sir Thomas Roe, his speech in Parliament, pp. 11-12.

[1] S.P.D. Chas. I, 243/23; Ramsay, The Wiltshire Woollen Industry, pp. 96-7.
[2] In the 1630's there were complaints that say-dyed cloths (dyed before the fulling process) were counterfeiting real Spanish cloths, which were dyed in the wool. Say-dyed cloths, or mock-medleys as they came to be called, were made of English wool and the confusion in part arose from their ornamental lists. Following a protest from the Merchant Adventurers, the Privy Council allowed their future production provided they were given distinctive lists and not shipped to Germany or the Low Countries. See Ramsay, The Wiltshire Woollen Industry, p. 104; S.P.D. Chas. I, 268/5; P.C. 2/44, pp. 183-4, 220; P.C. 2/50, p. 323; P.C. 2/51, pp. 382-3; S.P.D. Chas. I, 454/29, 29I, 84; S.P.D. Chas. I, 456/39; P.C. 2/52, p. 549.
[3] It was estimated in 1640 that the impositions on 400 Spanish cloths and 700 white broadcloths (the former being, in value, worth somewhat more than the latter) stood at £200 and £450 respectively (C.S.P.D. 1640-1641, p. 370).
[4] P.C. 2/50, p. 323.

A Changing Economy

There is perhaps insufficient material to write a full history of the rise of the new draperies in England. It has already been made abundantly clear that their development, and the opening of the southern markets which it involved, was largely a response to the stagnation of the old draperies and to economic conditions in the early seventeenth century.[1] In the absence of any significant possibilities of cost-reduction, and faced with a strong and growing continental industry, the traditional manufacture found that it had no effective answer to the shrinking of its markets. Hence innovation, unable to proceed intensively, became extensive, and the new products, originally manufactured in the sixteenth century, were developed for the known markets with warmer climates. Consequently, English capital and labour were diverted to a different type of textile— light, colourful, cheap—in order to tap a new level of demand. The result was a five-fold expansion in the export of these fabrics from 1600 to 1640, so that by the latter date such shipments rivalled, in value, those of the old draperies. With this there went a radical alteration in the pattern of trade. Spain and the Mediterranean were the markets *par excellence* for the new draperies,[2] and by the eve of the Civil War these areas took as much of total London textile exports as the classic markets of northern and eastern Europe.

One 'reason' for these developments lay in the opening of direct trade with Spain in 1604, after years of war-time dislocation in the southern commerce. English goods were once again attracted to the inflationary markets provided by Spain and her dominions; the cessation of war also eased direct commercial communication with the Mediterranean area. Finally, the treaty with France, in 1606, must have aided the sales of new draperies considerably, since bays were important items in Anglo-French commerce. All this is obliquely confirmed by the harmful repercussions, for those English counties which were centres of new drapery production, of the wars against France and Spain in the late 1620's.[3]

Yet it was not merely that England was supplying a pre-existing market, for in one sense an entirely new type of demand seems to have appeared. In some respects the abrupt changes in market demand which stem from wholesale changes in fashion operated no less in the seventeenth

---

[1] Fisher, 'London's Export Trade', 151–61. Professor Fisher's analysis provides a sufficient explanation for the rise of the new fabrics; but it must be pointed out that there was a positive contraction in the market for old draperies. Professor Fisher's arguments at times give the impression that these markets were saturated by English cloth which had come to the limits of its expansion.

[2] New draperies were seen as 'commodities unfit and unapt for those climates [of Germany and the Low Countries]; but made to be exported and vented in the southern parts' (Hargrave MSS. 321, pp. 82–3). Cf. Fisher, 'London's Export Trade', 154; Lans. MSS. 152, fol. 221; *Commons Debates, 1621*, IV, 175; Malynes, *The Maintenance of Free Trade*, pp. 26, 71; S.P.D. Chas. I, 355/144.   [3] Above, pp. 104–7.

century than they do today. In the areas where climatic conditions were favourable, the period saw a swing in favour of the less durable woollen textiles, whose main attraction was not their quality but their vivid colours combined with their cheapness, and, within this, the ability to alter their appearance from year to year in order to meet short-term shifts in the nature of demand. A major reason, for instance, for the decline in the Italian textile industry was its inability, principally owing to stringent gild regulations, to reduce the superior quality of its products. This had become a prerequisite of Italian industrial survival in order to meet the effective competition of the lower-grade, cheaper goods with which the English and the Dutch, and later the French, invaded the markets of the eastern Mediterranean.[1] It was in part as a consequence of this failure to adapt to a changing overseas demand that the Lombardy economy collapsed.

It is difficult to indicate with any certainty what lay behind the changes in fashion which were so important for industrial structure. To some extent it may well have been an increase in general prosperity in southern markets which meant that clothing was no longer bought to last a lifetime. In the same manner in which so much of the modern American consumer market is orientated to short-term obsolescence and replacement, so for some seventeenth-century textile markets durability might no longer have been an important *desideratum*. Clothing-fabrics, since consumers could now afford to purchase them more often, would be bought more with an eye to 'outward appearances and attractive prices'.[2] Where the colours were guileful and the price low, then, as was reported of English cloth in the Levant, the middle and lower classes would be the more tempted to buy.[3] Hence the demand for the traditional hard-wearing cloth, made from carded short wool, gave way to a demand for the more flimsy newer fabrics, which were manufactured from combed long-staple raw material and which consumers were able to purchase at more frequent intervals. Even in England the London drapers noted in 1622 that 'the wonted wearing of gowns and petticoats of cloth both by our women and strangers was no small help to support the draperies of this kingdom, but now swallowed up by an innumerable company of stuffs unprofitable, which after a quarter of a year's wearing are no better than a piece of old painted cloth'.[4] In the main, however, the change took place in southern Europe and the Levant, and its result was the formation of a new type of demand: closely following the volatile course of fashion, and qualitatively

[1] C. M. Cipolla, 'The Decline of Italy: The Case of a Fully Matured Economy', *Econ. Hist. Rev.* 2nd ser. v (1952), 182–5.
[2] See Cipolla, 'The Decline of Italy', 182 n.   [3] *C.S.P.V. 1629–1632*, p. 326.
[4] S.P.D. Jas. I, 130/141. Cf. Lans. MSS. 152, fol. 229.

A Changing Economy

flexible to an unprecedented degree. 'There are many sorts of cloth or stuffs lately invented', wrote John May in 1613, 'which have got new godfathers to name them in fantastical fashion, that they which wear them know not how to name them, which are called new drapery.'[1]

English industry was able to take full advantage of the fresh opportunities now open to it. The other side of the gloomy picture of stagnation in the old draperies was one of expansion and prosperity; the inability to adapt to changing conditions which was so evident in the old industry was counterbalanced by a striking flexibility in the new. The production of new draperies developed above all in East Anglia, but it grew also in many of the large towns of southern England, near the coast from Yarmouth to Plymouth, and in Lancashire, Devon and Kent.[2] One principal advantage which it enjoyed over the Italian industry, with which it competed, was that of being almost entirely free from restrictions, either of the local gild variety, or of the type which derived from governmental attempts to regulate standards, control production, and enforce apprenticeship in other branches of the textile industry. The new draperies came to their maturity after the power of many local gild organizations had been largely dissipated and in areas where there was little chance that they could be extended to the new business. The relative novelty of the industry also meant that the provisions of the Statute of Artificers did not apply to it, since they only had relevance to industries in existence at the time of enactment (1563). The resulting freedom of industrial organization meant, on the one hand, that the new draperies could be produced at a lower price than otherwise might have been possible, and, on the other, that it was far easier to secure the adaptability of production necessary in order to satisfy the ever-changing tastes of overseas consumers.

In the low cost, of course, lay the basic competitive advantage for the English manufacture—a point which was constantly emphasized by Venetian commentators in the eastern Mediterranean. A major possibility is that labour costs were low owing to the long-term depression in the older branches of cloth-making, which liberated a supply of cheap labour. And this argument must have applied to other factors of production to some extent. In any case, the absence of industrial regulation, with its enforcement of a seven-year apprenticeship, greatly facilitated the entry of labour into the new industry. This factor caused some anxiety at times of general slump and debasement of standards.[3] In 1622 it was found that in Essex 'the makers of bays and other the said stuffs which they call new

---
[1] *A Declaration of the Estate of Clothing*, p. 21.
[2] Pilgrim, *passim*; A. P. Wadsworth and J. De L. Mann, *The Cotton Trade and Industrial Lancashire, 1600–1780* (Manchester, 1931), pp. 13, 22; S.P.D. Jas. I, 80/13.
[3] See, for example, *A.P.C. 1621–1623*, p. 156.

drapery, do hold themselves free to use and exercise the making, weaving and dressing of them, albeit they never served as apprentices in that mystery . . . and do also hold themselves not to be within the intent of any statute heretofore made for the making, ordering and dressing of woollen cloth'. Consequently, it was claimed, even farmers entered directly into the industry, while, since the trade was considered to be outside the terms of the Statute of Artificers, journeymen were hired not by the year but 'by the bay or piece contrary to law'.[1] The last process was clearly a method of reducing unit costs of production by converting an overhead into a prime cost; while the lack of strict apprenticeship requirements presumably lowered manufacturing expenses by augmenting the supply of labour to allow for rapid industrial growth in times of expansion. In Suffolk, in the same year, it was estimated that some two-thirds of the manufacturers of new draperies had never been apprenticed. Alternatively, there were, frequently, hirings of so-called 'apprentices' in excess of the legal maximum laid down in the industrial code.[2] Normally these individuals would not qualify by serving out a full term of seven years, but while they could be taken in such numbers, especially where the work was only semi-skilled, they were another potent factor in lowering the costs of the English industry.

In part this lack of regulation was a competitive necessity, for one prerequisite of success in the manufacture of the new materials was that there should be a minimum of rigid standardization, since they were produced for a fashionable demand, liable to sudden vagaries of choice. Regulation was made all the more difficult by the bewildering variety of fabrics involved[3] and the constant variations in pattern and measurement. There were, nevertheless, frequent complaints directed against this lack of standardization, and no less frequent attempts to bring the new draperies into a general scheme of industrial supervision—the most notable of which was that of Walter Morrell, initiated by experiments sponsored by the Earl of Salisbury, to regulate and stimulate the industry by using county-based corporations.[4] In fact it seems possible to detect a move-

[1] S.P.D. Jas. I, 130/65. Cf. S.P.D. Interregnum, 25/48.
[2] S.P.D. Jas. I, 129/59, 130/65. Cf. Essex County Council, *Guide to the Essex Records Office*, Part 1, 103.
[3] For examples of this variety, see Journals of the Common Council, 28, fols. 296-9.
[4] *A.P.C. 1615–1616*, pp. 464–5; S.P.D. Jas. I, 96/39–40; *A.P.C. 1618–1619*, pp. 43–4; *A.P.C. 1619–1621*, p. 132; Hargrave MSS. 321, pp. 199–201; *A.P.C. 1623–1625*, pp. 53–4; S.P.D. Jas. I, 184/44; *C.S.P.D. 1623–1625*, pp. 485, 490; S.P.D. Chas. I, 1/24, 1/62, 10/66; *C.S.P.D. (Addenda), 1625–1649*, p. 430. For other complaints of 'falsity' and plans for industrial regulation, see S.P.D. Jas. I, 19/99*; May, p. 22; S.P.D. Jas. I, 140/82; *A.P.C. 1623–1625*, pp. 40–1, 248; S.P.D. Chas. I, 1/23; *Commons Debates, 1621, passim*; S.P.D. Jas. I, 121/34, 140/82; *C.J.* I, 873; P.C. 2/43, p. 72; P.C. 2/44, pp. 219–20, 424, 512A; P.C. 2/45, pp. 37–8, 435–6; *C.S.P.D. 1635*, pp. 266–7; *C.S.P.D. 1635–1636*, p. 337; *C.S.P.D. 1637–1638*, p. 553.

ment to accept and meet England's new industrial and commercial needs within the framework of traditional forms of organization. But such experiments, which applied to other industries and the herring trade as well as the new draperies, failed, and the new economic developments broke away from the old economic structures.[1] As far as the standards of manufacture were concerned, the absence of effective control must have led to some real abuses; but the stimulus which the new industry derived from its freedom was perhaps an indispensable factor in its growth. In the main, complaints that cloths were falsely made were evidence rather that, in a highly complex trade, production and demand were temporarily qualitatively out of line.

Another important point concerning costs of production can be deduced from the common doctrine of the time that any given amount of wool gave employment to more people, and could be fashioned into end-products of a higher market value, in the new draperies than in the old. It was estimated, for instance, that 84 lb. of wool devoted to the manufacture of a Wiltshire shortcloth would employ only fourteen people, while the same amount would keep forty or fifty persons busy in the new draperies; and another view was that 60 lb. of wool in the form of a Wiltshire shortcloth sold for only £13, while when converted into new drapery it realized £27 or £28.[2] In other words, the cost of raw material relative to that of labour was lower in the new than in the old industry. A concomitant of this was that where wages were rising slower (or falling faster) than the price of wool it would be the more profitable to manufacture new draperies. Alternatively, where English labour costs were lower than, for instance, Italian, the effectiveness of English competition would be proportionately increased by switching to lighter fabrics.[3] Even from the point of view of the cost of wool alone, it is possible that the new draperies secured an advantage from a change in the nature of English wool supplies, which has already been mentioned. The new draperies utilized the coarser varieties of wool, and it is probable that the change-over to their manufacture was both eased and even, in part, enforced by a lowering of the quality of English wools consequent upon persistent enclosure and the better feeding of sheep.[4]

The relatively low cost of the raw material in the new draperies encouraged a development in the organization of their production which became a distinctive feature of the industry: on the whole, the unit of production—the entrepreneur and his immediate economic dependants,

[1] Fisher, 'Some Experiments in Company Organization', *passim*.
[2] S.P.D. Jas. I, 80/16; MSS. of the Library of the Inner Temple, 538, 19, fol. 61.
[3] For the high cost of Italian textile labour, see Cipolla, 'The Decline of Italy', 184.
[4] Bowden, 45–9, 51–6.

no matter how scattered geographically—tended to be small. The basic factor here, for all textiles, was the possible speed of capital turnover and the size of the initial investment. Where, as in the western counties, the final product was expensive and its manufacture a lengthy process, there the organization tended to be 'capitalistic'. That is, production could only be financed by clothiers with abundant capital who would be obliged to employ a multitude of dependent workers specializing in various cloth-making tasks. Conversely, as in the manufacture of kersies in the West Riding, if the final articles, and hence the raw materials involved, were inexpensive and could, individually, be produced in a short period by a small number of employees, the small-scale master was able to subsist by turning over his capital quickly and so deriving his weekly sustenance and that of his very few employees.

Broadly, the new draperies satisfied the second criterion. The wool they used was coarse and therefore relatively cheap;[1] in any case the final product used relatively little wool,[2] so that the cost of the raw material was not prohibitive for the poor man; and the general demands of quality and specifications were sufficiently low to facilitate a reasonably quick turnover of whatever capital was involved. In this arrangement the perpetuation of the small-scale manufacturer was aided by a division of labour, which was geographic as well as functional, between yarn producers and weaver-finishers,[3] and also by the ease of entry (as far as statutory requirements were concerned) into the new draperies. Contemporary observers persistently emphasized the small-scale independence which producers of the light fabrics possessed; and one of its significant consequences was that when, in 1616, wool middlemen came under general attack, special provision was made for the supply of wool by intermediaries to the scattered manufacturers of new draperies[4]—much as in the 1550's the small-scale clothiers around Halifax were given statutory protection against the prevailing anti-middleman policy because they were too poor to establish direct contact with the wool growers.[5]

The new draperies were thus a fresh and progressive force in English industry, and their growth was, in the main, welcomed and encouraged as a departure which could only be beneficial to England. In 1606 the Common Council of London was willing to expend £600 on a gift to any 'noble personage' who would secure an Act for 'the new devised

[1] S.P.D. Jas. I, 80/13; Lans. MSS. 152, fol. 227; A.P.C. 1616–1617, p. 28. Fell-wool was extensively used: A.P.C. 1616–1617, p. 180; Pilgrim, p. 3.
[2] See the patent reprinted in Econ. Hist. Rev. 2nd ser. IV (1952), 353.
[3] A.P.C. 1613–1614, p 8; R. Reyce, The Breviary of Suffolk (1618), pp. 22–3; S.P.D. Jas. I, 130/65; A.P.C. 1621–1623, pp. 295–6, 329, 468–9.
[4] A.P.C. 1615–1616, pp. 624–6. Cf. A.P.C. 1615–1616, pp. 642–3, 669–71.
[5] See 2 and 3 Philip and Mary, c. 13.

draperies and such like stuffs not usually heretofore brought to Blackwell Hall to be all brought to Leadenhall'. By 1611–12 hallage charges were fixed for the new draperies 'appointed to be brought to Leadenhall'. And John May, who had leased the latter market, commented favourably on those resident aliens (in Colchester) 'who now make a commodity among us of our wools, which, by reason of their slightness and small value, might be esteemed unworthy of wearing; yet, by their good observation in making, searching and sealing, it is so upheld and maintained, that it is more vendible than any cloth we make'.[1] By 1615 it was claimed that 'there is more people supposed to be employed in this new manufacture than by all the other clothiers of the realm'; and although, at the time, this was clearly an exaggeration, it reflected the same situation which occasioned the estimate, during a discussion in 1616 of how far the demands of the new draperies were keeping up the price of wool to the old, that a third of English wool supplies was consumed in the production of the new textiles.[2] Although East Anglia received its share of the depression in the early 1620's,[3] the trade in new draperies as a whole was still fairly strong during the slump, perhaps because its principal markets were not influenced by the currency disturbances which so reduced overseas demand for the old draperies. In spite of some dislocation and even, in the 1630's, signs of over-production in Essex,[4] the stature and significance of the manufacture were firmly established in the last decade of the period. By 1640 exports were well above those of the previous generation,[5] and the new draperies had profoundly altered the nature of the English textile industry and the geographical pattern of English trade.

The situation which arose from industrial and commercial adaptation was succinctly described in 1616: 'much wool is employed in new draperies, which occasioneth the making of less quantity of broadcloth. But the English in Turkey, by the cheapness of their cloths, work out the Venetian and all others.'[6] Indeed, the Italian textile industry had been extremely prosperous at the end of the sixteenth and very early in the seventeenth centuries.[7] The cloth industry of northern Italy had, for instance, provided effective and crippling competition for the shipments

[1] Journals of the Common Council, 27, fols. 26, 30, 316; 28, fols. 239b, 296–9; *Remembrancia*, III, 56; May, p. 6.
[2] S.P.D. Jas. I, 80/16; Lans. MSS. 152, fols. 271–2; cf. fol. 251, also *A.P.C. 1616–1617*, pp. 26, 28–9.
[3] See *A.P.C. 1621–1623*, pp. 371–2; S.P.D. Jas. I, 137/13.
[4] Above, pp. 107, 123–4.
[5] See the figures in Fisher, 'London's Export Trade', 154; Pilgrim, p. 204.
[6] Add. MSS. 14027, fol. 282.
[7] Cipolla, 'The Decline of Italy', 178–80; C. M. Cipolla, *Mouvements Monétaires dans l'État de Milan (1580–1700)* (Paris, 1952), pp. 31–2.

of Hampshire kersies to the Mediterranean.¹ But the development of the new English fabrics, often imitative of Italian colours and produced more inexpensively (albeit more flimsily), soon changed this situation. As early as 1610 it was said that, in Turkey, 'the vent of our cloths, kersies, as well as tin and other . . . commodities is more and more uttered'. The eastern Mediterranean provided an excellent market and Mun wrote, most probably in the late 1620's, that 'we have found of late years by good experience, that being able to sell our cloth cheap in Turkey, we have greatly increased the vent thereof, and the Venetians have lost as much in the utterance of theirs in those countries, because it is dear'.²

Venice itself was, of course, soon made aware of this new competition in its eastern markets; its merchants noted despairingly that

Venice was formerly alone in the Levant and exported a great quantity of cloth. Now the French and English bring a great quantity of cloth of Paris and London [sic] respectively. The Londons do the greatest harm to Venetian cloth as they not only imitate its colours, but can sell at a lower price, thus tempting the middle and lower classes to buy them. . . . [It is] impossible to compete with the Londons as cloth like it cannot be made at Venice except at a much higher cost, because wool is so plentiful in England and the Londons are brought by sea at a slight cost.³

Concomitantly with these developments, the Levant Company grew in importance and reputation; although it was not alone the English who penetrated the Mediterranean market: it was a combination of English, Dutch and French textiles—imitative, light, bright and cheap—which defeated the Italian industry, an industry hamstrung by gild and corporative regulation, by high taxation, and by high-cost labour.

But the commercial upheaval of these years was more than a question of increased sales of a new type of woollen fabric. To some extent based on this, there arose a network of English control over a considerable part of general commerce and shipping in the Mediterranean basin. The facilities offered by the free port of Leghorn, which developed into one of the world's great entrepôts,⁴ was a major stimulus to the rapid growth of English participation in the local carrying trades and local commercial

[1] Lans. MSS. 152, fols. 148, 221, 229, 282; S.P.D. Jas. I, 15/4II, 20/9*, fol. 27; Add. MSS. 14027, fol. 287. In 1606 some 10,300 Hampshire kersies were exported to the Levant and Italy (Friis, p. 62), but by 1622 this figure had fallen to some 2,800 (E. 190/25/1).
[2] Lans. MSS. 152, fol. 221; Malynes, *The Maintenance of Free Trade*, pp. 89–90, and *The Centre of the Circle*, p. 107; Mun, *England's Treasure*, p. 8.
[3] C.S.P.V. *1629–1632*, p. 326. For the Constantinople market, see C.S.P.V. *1628–1629*, pp. 54, 83.
[4] Cipolla, 'The Decline of Italy', 186; C.S.P.V. *1628–1629*, pp. 39–40; C.S.P.V. *1629–1632*, p. 326; Roberts, *The Treasure of Traffic*, pp. 13–14, 36.

A Changing Economy

dealings. English merchants exported Italian silks to Constantinople, and dealt with Spanish currency for the products of the eastern Mediterranean. The latter area formed a burgeoning market for the fish of Yarmouth and Newfoundland. English capital at Leghorn grew, and in 1628 it was said that 'the quantity and quality of the English ships in these waters [of the eastern Mediterranean] augment very greatly', while the security provided by English ships was stated to exceed that of the Dutch and the French.[1] By the end of the period trade was thriving: English textiles were exported, and herrings, pilchards, Newfoundland fish, Italian and Russian goods re-exported, to the Levant; the proceeds, in raw silk, cotton wool, mohair, fruits, yarn, etc., went to build up a further trade locally, to supply England, and even to provide some surplus, above these needs, for re-export to the Netherlands, France, Portugal and Germany.[2]

These last developments—the increasing sophistication and the geographical extension of English mercantile operations—were, indeed, not confined to the Levant. On a specific level the similarity to English commercial practice in the trade to the East Indies is immediately apparent. More generally, the trends apparent in English commercial dealings with the Mediterranean areas and the Far East were representative of a wholesale change that was becoming apparent in the relationships between the English economy and the rest of the world. On the eve of the Civil War the home economy was coming to rely increasingly upon entirely new modes of trading, a full description of whose growth lies outside the scope of this work. The economic horizons were lifting. Matching the extension of textile exports from traditional goods shipped to traditional markets, to new products shipped to wider areas, there came increased diversification: in imports and exports, or rather re-exports. By the end of the seventeenth century re-exports comprised 30 per cent of all shipments from London, and they were, in the main, plantation goods: tobacco, sugar and calicoes. By then, too, nearly one-third of England's imports came from outside Europe.[3] In 1640 these developments were still largely in the future, and re-exports were very small in comparison with shipments of English woollens;[4] but it is possible to detect, even in the 1630's, the tendencies which extended trade routes from the near-by continent to the periphery of Europe, to Asia, and to America, and which

[1] C.S.P.V. 1628–1629, pp. 54, 83; C.S.P.V. 1629–1632, pp. 116, 326; Hargrave MSS. 321, p. 86; S.P.D. Jas. I, 15/4 A and B. Insurance rates for English ships in the Levant in the 1620's was said to be 3–4 per cent—as against 8–10 per cent for Dutch, German, French and Italian shipping (S.P.D. Jas. I, 180/74).
[2] C.S.P.V. 1629–1632, p. 473; C.S.P.D. 1650, pp. 71–2.
[3] For this spectacular rise of colonial and re-export trade, see R. Davis, 'English Foreign Trade, 1660–1700', *Econ. Hist. Rev.* 2nd ser. VII (1954), 150–4.
[4] Fisher, 'London's Export Trade', Table 4.

so much increased England's participation in profitable carrying trades. By 1640 re-exports were equivalent, in official valuation, to all nontextile shipments; tobacco imports from Virginia and Maryland rose from 20,000 lb. in 1619 to some 1,000,000 in the 1630's (they were to reach 22,000,000 by 1700).[1] Woollen textiles, of course, still remained the staple items of commerce, but diversification in the economy at large, as well as in the textile industry, had begun to make its mark. The stage was being set for the passing of the Navigation Acts and the clash with the Dutch commercial system. The English economy was still primarily connected to the European by the single strand of the textile trade, yet, to those who had the eyes to see, it was obvious that the future held a much wider promise in Imperial trade and commercial supremacy.[2]

[1] Fisher, 'London's Export Trade', 160; Davis, 152.
[2] For contemporaries who, at the end of the period, urged the necessity of diversification and an entrepôt trade, see below, pp. 223-4.

8. MONETARY INSTABILITY, 1600–1642

The economic world of the early seventeenth century was at the mercy of a host of disturbing factors. In following the course of the fluctuations in the cloth industry we have already seen how arbitrary and random these intrusions could be for the normal course of commercial prosperity. Continental warfare or economic dislocation, the excesses of national economic policy at home, the changes in the organization of trade, mercantile controversies with foreign countries, an outbreak of plague, currency manipulation abroad or the threat of it at home: all these could and did have an immediate impact on the quantities of English textiles exported and, therefore, on the well-being of large sectors of the economy. In the more general field, the short-term instability which derived from the repercussions of monetary factors was an ever-present feature of contemporary economic discussion. However, apart from the direct effect of manipulations for sales of cloth, it is clear that the currency was an outstanding determinant of the course of economic affairs. In the long run, of course, the changing amounts and distribution of supplies of precious metals were not unimportant for European economic development. But by the early seventeenth century the maximum impact of the flood of American silver had passed. On the other hand, this period, no less than the sixteenth century, witnessed the short-run commercial instability resulting from currency manipulations—which to a greater or lesser degree altered the availability and types of money in circulation. This factor was of great significance in an unsophisticated economy dependent on steady supplies of a secure metallic coinage.

In this chapter we shall principally be concerned with the types of monetary phenomena which contemporaries took to be among the most significant constituents of commercial well-being, or its absence. Indeed, writers and administrators concentrated on the technical problems of exchanges and currency valuation to an extent only comprehensible on the assumption of their intimate connexion with the general state of commerce. In Chapter 4 we have already seen how critical could be the role of currency manipulation in determining the flow of goods in the international economy, and how the most severe crisis of the period was largely the result of such manipulations on the Continent. It is now time to turn to a consideration of the contemporary claim that a *direct* result of such alterations abroad was that England lost treasure and coin—with disastrous effect for economic prosperity. After evaluating the recurring complaints of a 'scarcity of money' it will be possible to study in more detail the short-term implications of monetary developments in the early seventeenth century.

(i) BIMETALLIC MALADJUSTMENTS AND A SCARCITY OF MONEY

Any consideration of monetary affairs and international bullion flows in the early seventeenth century must start with an indication of the pitfalls involved in such an analysis. Movements of treasure depended on a variety of circumstances: balances of trade, mint prices, exchange rates, the convenience of merchants, capital flows, treaty arrangements, etc. When a particular flow in one direction has been established, all other possibilities are not exhausted, for gold and/or silver might move simultaneously in different directions for different reasons. One metal might flow out in direct exchange for the other; bullion might temporarily prove the most profitable import for any given trading area while, in fact, that nation was losing treasure on a net basis owing to an overall unfavourable balance of trade; bullion, too, might be coming in under the terms of a treaty such as that with Spain (1630)[1] although it could not necessarily be retained. Finally, the statistics of coining at the Mint are uncertain indicators of bullion flows. On the one hand the Mint could be idle while, in fact, there were reasonable supplies of at least one precious metal in the country: 'silver is continually imported', it was said in 1612, 'and is found stirring amongst the goldsmiths, and otherwise much like as in former times, although in respect of the greater price which it hath with the goldsmith it cannot find the way to the Mint.'[2] On the other hand, as in the early 1630's after the Cottington Treaty, the Mint could be active while a continuous drain created a scarcity of treasure. Mint operations, which in any case might reflect internal redistributions of gold or silver as between plate and coin, were thus no necessary indication of net flows of bullion into or out of England.

With both gold and silver coins circulating, and each type being valued in terms of the money of account, there was an official Mint ratio which was given, and could be altered, by that valuation, or by any other step which changed the amount of gold and/or silver represented by one

---

[1] By the Cottington Treaty silver shipments intended for Flanders were first sent to England. There, part was re-shipped and part was taken by Englishmen (in return for bills on Antwerp) and sent to London for minting. Although this arrangement considerably increased the coining of silver at the Mint, it could not, in the long run and without a change in the balance of payments, augment the effective supplies of silver coin in England.

[2] Add. MSS. 10113, fol. 187. Cf. S.P.D. Jas. I, 104/29.

Monetary Instability, 1600–1642

pound tale. There were also market ratios, both at home and abroad, which were determined by the operations of demand and supply. When official or unofficial ratios abroad differed from those in England the stage was set for an international movement of bullion and specie in response to the profitable opportunities available to merchants. Where continental ratios were higher than the English, i.e. where gold was worth more in terms of silver, the more precious metal would tend to be lost and silver would tend to be imported. These flows would be reversed if the ratio in England was higher than those in Europe. From another viewpoint one could say that bullion and specie moved across frontiers to take advantage of differences in the mint or market prices given to gold or silver. In the main, such movements would be bimetallic—i.e. an efflux of one metal would be counteracted by an influx of the other—but it was quite possible that a sharp increase in the mint prices of *both* metals on the Continent (which meant that specie became worth more than goods since the price rise of the latter lagged behind that of the former) would stimulate a temporary export of gold *and* silver from England.

Over the long run, the influx of American silver had provoked, throughout Europe, a persistent rise in the market ratio, and a consequent threat to the traditional proportion of 12:1. This steady depreciation of silver produced periodic revaluations of gold in order to raise mint ratios and to prevent either a loss of the more precious metal or a cessation in its coining because of the lower valuation given to it at the mints in comparison with the open market.[1] In addition, the various European nations were unable to move together in the alteration of the official prices of gold and silver, and there was, therefore, a need to respond to fluctuations in mint, as well as in market, ratios. Yet great technical and practical difficulties existed: in estimating foreign and market ratios, in fixing a true rating, and in securing approval for any particular policy. There was, indeed, sufficient scope for violent controversies as to the real values of coins, and for the frequent appearance of repetitive manuscript manuals on the problem. It was therefore only to be expected that errors were sometimes made or particular remedies blocked, so that neighbouring lands established mint prices and ratios which differed sufficiently from each other to afford the possibility of a profitable trade in coins or bullion. England in the early seventeenth century suffered from just such a situation.

In 1600 there was some confusion as to the real relationship between English and continental ratios, and the commission which met to discuss the whole question of money and the balance of trade was, in fact, divided

---

[1] For such a process in Holland see Posthumus, I, IV. The same end could be achieved by calling down silver coins, or as gold coins became clipped and worn.

on the question of whether the English ratio was above or below continental levels, although there was agreement that European enhancements of gold coins (which raised foreign ratios) was 'a great cause . . . of the exportation of the monies of this realm . . . and especially of our gold'.[1] This last point should have clearly indicated that the English gold coinage was undervalued. But in 1601 the home ratio was moved down, principally by an enhancement of silver.[2] It soon became apparent that this was a change in the wrong direction: the English proportion fell well below that of the principal European nations, and silver coins, already slightly overvalued, were given an even higher valuation; while silver was attracted, gold tended to flow out in more abundant quantities.[3] As was usual, such bimetallic movements of precious metal were not necessarily in direct exchange for each other: gold being worth so much more abroad, in terms of commodities as well as silver, it was profitable to return it in exchange for commodity imports to England or to export it in order to take advantage of the relatively cheaper (in terms of gold) goods available for import from Europe. 'Those that will take this benefit of our gold', wrote Malynes, 'need not bring silver for that purpose, having foreign commodities ready at hand, in return whereof the gold is very commodious and profitable.'[4] In the other direction, silver came into the country on a comparable basis; and, for instance, it became profitable for the Merchant Adventurers in Germany to return silver coins to England, which they did to such an extent that they provoked a temporary scarcity of liquid funds at Stade.[5] These developments are, in part, reflected in the figures of Mint output: in the three years following the change gold coin dropped to 10 per cent and less of total production.[6]

In 1603 Malynes had advocated the raising of gold to remedy this situation, and late in the next year the government took steps to correct 'this error in the proportion of the gold monies of England to the silver [which] hath been a great cause of the transportation of gold out of this realm'. The ratio was raised to over 12:1 by an increase in Mint prices. The result was 'an evenly balanced coinage, silver being between 50 and 60 per cent of the total issued during the next three and a half years'.[7]

A drain of gold seems, however, to have arisen within a relatively short period, and in 1610, when Holland raised its official ratio to over $12\frac{1}{2}$:1,

[1] S.P.D. Eliz., 279/97.
[2] Feaveayear, pp. 79–80; Gould, 'The Royal Mint', 241.
[3] Malynes, The Canker, p. 79.
[4] The Canker, p. 80. Cf. Malynes, England's View, pp. 180–1.
[5] H.M.C. Sackville, II, 118, 121, 124–5, 141, 153.
[6] Gould, 'The Royal Mint', 248.
[7] Malynes, England's View, pp. 177–8; S.P.D. Jas. I, 10A/19; Steele, I, no. 1005; Gould, 'The Royal Mint', 241.

Monetary Instability, 1600–1642

this loss of the more precious metal grew sufficiently to provoke a deep anxiety in government circles. Discussions of the problem in the Privy Council led to the obvious conclusion that 'in general this is the mischief: that our gold is not so much allowed as our silver and therefore being worth more than silver is bought and carried away'.[1] To prevent this, in November 1611, gold coins were enhanced by 10 per cent. But this move was far too drastic to re-establish an equilibrium. The resulting ratio was over 13:1, which was much too high: silver was now drastically undervalued, and the disparity between the relative valuations of coins, although it brought more gold to the Mint, set up a chronic efflux of silver, which flowed to those European countries where mint prices made it a more valuable commodity.[2] All this, naturally enough, produced a fresh round of official discussion. Sir Richard Martin, the Mint Master, submitted a series of memoranda pointing out that 'as the cause of great plenty of gold brought in since [his] Majesty's proclamation was by raising the price of gold, so the cause of the scarcity of silver, whereof little or none hath been brought into his Majesty's Mint since the proclamation, hath been that the silver is not equally valued with the gold in this realm'. There was, indeed, some suggestion that although the Mint lacked silver it 'is continually imported into the realm', but this could not be a permanent trend, while the disparity lasted, unless the balance of payments was greatly in England's favour. In any case there was a quick dissent from this view: 'since the [proclamation of 1611] great quantities of our silver coin hath been and still is [sic] carried out of the kingdom.'[3]

In spite of many moves in the direction of monetary manipulation, after 1611 until the end of the period the English currency was largely unaltered. Consequently, the bimetallic outflow of silver was semi-permanent for many years and, in addition, it was for ten years under 0·5 per cent of Mint issues, while the absolute and relative amounts of silver coined remained very low until the Cottington Treaty in 1630.[4] However, even while the tendency to lose silver coins existed, England was not entirely drained of her silver currency. Since it was always profitable to clip or sweat full-weight coinage, and since light-weight coinage would tend to stay in circulation, the relatively high European mint prices for silver attracted only the heavier coins. Clipped or worn money stayed in circulation—at least until a fresh round of foreign

---

[1] Add. MSS. 10113, fols. 133, 143, 205–6; Shaw, *The History of Currency*, pp. 69–70; S.P.D. Jas. I, 67/50.
[2] Feavearyear, p. 81; Steele, I, no. 1119; Gould, 'The Royal Mint', 248; Add. MSS. 10113, fol. 141.
[3] Add. MSS. 10113, fols. 170, 178, 187, 200; Add. MSS. 34324, fol. 63; S.P.D. Jas. I, 70/43.
[4] Gould, 'The Royal Mint', 248.

enhancements or debasements made it profitable to export them.[1] The effect of the differentials in international mint prices was, therefore, to deprive England of some of its silver monetary supply and to render the remaining coins less than full weight. The export of silver was especially aggravated from 1615 to 1622, when the Dutch ratio was lower than at other times and when wholesale currency manipulation in northern and eastern Europe accentuated the English undervaluation of silver.[2] Not only was silver likely to be exported to take direct advantage of mint prices abroad, but in any given case it might prove the least profitable way of returning the proceeds of exports, so that other commodities, including gold, would be brought home while silver was diverted: 'when your money is richer in substance and lower in price than that of your neighbour nations, as our silver is than the silver in the Low Countries, how can you expect that the merchant, who only seeketh his profit, will ever bring hither any silver, when he can sell it in the Low Countries at a higher rate, and make more money of it here by returning of it from thence hither, or by exchange, or by commodities?'[3]

It was this sort of phenomenon which underlay most of the monetary discussions of these years: while gold was relatively abundant, silver was, at times, in chronic shortage. Men were not ignorant of the reasons for this situation. 'The advancing of gold', it was said in 1622, 'is the very cause why so much gold rather than silver cometh to the Mint', and Mun, at a later date, wrote that the enhancement of gold in 1611 'carried away all or the most part of our silver (which was not over-worn or too light) ... and the reason ... is, because our silver was not raised in proportion'.[4] The situation was only eased when France and Holland raised their ratios, in 1636 and 1638 respectively, and when the natural depreciation of silver increased market ratios until they more closely corresponded with the Mint ratio. While it lasted, the problems posed by the steady drain of heavy silver coins were intermittently aggravated by an unfavourable balance of trade, which, as was to be expected, turned the exchange rates against England. At such times complaint naturally increased and existing technical knowledge was marshalled in an attempt

[1] For the poor state of the coinage, see Vaughan, p. 42; *A.P.C. 1619–1621*, pp. 190–2; S.P.D. Chas. I, 36/103, 64/41; Maddison, *Great Britain's Remembrancer*, Preface.
[2] For the Dutch ratio see Shaw, *The History of Currency*, pp. 69–70; its raising in 1621 and 1622 gave a sharp stimulus to silver issues in the Royal Mint (Gould, 'The Royal Mint', 248). For the Polish and German manipulations, see above, pp. 76–8.
[3] Vaughan, p. 76. For the attraction of gold, see S.P.D. Jas. I, 118/131; Hargrave MSS. 321, pp. 21–2; Cotton MSS. Galba, E. 1, fol. 364; Add. MSS. 34324, fol. 160; Malynes, *Lex Mercatoria*, p. 208; Misselden, *The Circle of Commerce*, p. 32; Malynes, *The Centre of the Circle*, p. 28; Mun, *England's Treasure*, p. 30.
[4] S.P.D. Jas. I, 131/106; Mun, *England's Treasure*, p. 30. Cf. Add. MSS. 10113, fol. 166; Malynes, *Lex Mercatoria*, p. 207; S.P.D. Chas. I, 124/68, 275/44.

to explain the loss and provide a remedy for it.¹ The most common cry was that bimetallic maladjustments (the gap between English and foreign ratios) were constantly being worsened by the debasing and enhancing of coins abroad, which increased mint prices so as to draw away supplies of English currency. This was especially so after 1618 when, for some five years, in eastern Europe and Holland there were serious currency manipulations—which included a raising of the valuations given to non-native coins.² The merchants of Ipswich were not alone in claiming, in 1621, that major causes for the export of coin were 'the high rates and continual raising of money in the King of Poland his dominions, Germany, and other countries thereabouts'.³

The traditional approach to such a problem had always involved suggestions that silver coins be enhanced and the Mint price of silver raised, or that the seignorage charge at the Mint be reduced, which latter step had exactly the same result: it increased the effective valuation of silver and lowered the Mint ratio. Therefore, in cases of an overvaluation of coins abroad, it was propounded, 'the rule of never-failing profit ... is to raise your coin, and to ease the excessive charge of the Mint'. 'The more the [charge for] coinage is abated,' wrote Misselden, 'the less the coin itself needs to be raised.'⁴ There were, during these years, constant recommendations that the seignorage should be reduced as an answer to the efflux of metal,⁵ but the fear of a loss of royal revenue and the fact that juggling with the seignorage afforded little scope for monetary policy, meant that the most widely canvassed plan was a wholesale enhancement or debasement of silver. That is, in so far as the maladjustment appeared as an undervaluation of the coins of one metal, the traditional proposal was to raise that valuation, and alter the Mint ratio, by direct currency manipulation.

In 1609, when gold was being lost, a committee had been set up partly to see if the enhancement of gold was feasible,⁶ and two years later gold coins were, in fact, raised. After 1611, when the bimetallic trends were reversed, in large part because of this very enhancement of gold, there was a persistent wave of suggestions that silver be enhanced in order to prevent

---

¹ For the history of the successive periods of such anxiety, see section (ii) of this chapter
² S.P.D. Jas. I, 118/114; Misselden, *Free Trade*, pp. 8–10; S.P.D. Chas. I, 70/75.
³ Hargrave MSS. 321, p. 120. Cf. Hargrave MSS. 321, p. 4; Misselden, *Free Trade*, pp. 17–18; Misselden, *The Circle of Commerce*, p. 39; Add. MSS. 34324, fols. 153 ff., 167; S.P.D. Chas. I, 1/85.
⁴ Sanderson, fol. 231; Misselden, *Free Trade*, p. 103.
⁵ For discussions with respect to gold prior to 1611, see Add. MSS. 10113, fols. 119, 133, 135, 143, 205–6. For the consideration of the seignorage on silver coining after that date, see Add. MSS. 10113, fol. 187; *A.P.C. 1618–1619*, pp. 302–3, 305–6; S.P.D. Jas. I, 104/29; McCulloch, *Old and Scarce Tracts on Money*, pp. 136–7; Sanderson, fol. 235.
⁶ Add. MSS. 10113, fols. 205–6.

its outflow. In 1612, 1614, 1616, 1618–22, 1626–9 and 1634 schemes were propounded to alter the silver coinage in this manner by raising its valuation in terms of the money of account.[1] However, in spite of the persistent campaign there was no actual attempt to alter the coinage. Any proposal inevitably provoked the strongest counter-arguments, which were based upon the price rise which would follow any enhancement or debasement, and the consequent harm to recipients of fixed incomes (including the king) and even to wage-earners. In the formulation of policy, the claim that the disadvantages of inflation outweighed the benefits of manipulation was strengthened by the fears expressed concerning the effect of enhancement on the terms of trade, the wealth of Spain, credit and the exchanges. Finally, many controversialists doubted even the direct efficacy of such a policy, and warned that manipulation in England would only provoke retaliatory enhancement abroad—which might easily lead to an endless and disastrous round of coinage alterations. The committee of merchants which met in 1620 presented all these criticisms of the proposed policy, and its conclusion was the hopeless one that 'although the abasing of the said standard . . . is . . . the only way at this present to draw silver into the kingdom, yet we dare not advise to put it into practice'.[2] On the whole, merchants would in most circumstances be opposed to coinage manipulation because of the exchange, monetary and credit insecurity involved, and they would be especially antagonistic if a reasonable portion of their assets was abroad or in the form of debts owing, whose value in real terms would decline as prices rose.[3] In 1626, during the debates on a plan to debase silver, England was contrasted with Holland: the importance, for England, of 'constant reckonings and annual bargains' was brought forward as a major deterrent to manipulation, while it was claimed that people in Holland (a land of 'mechanics or merchants') were more easily able to 'rate accordingly their labour or their wares . . . to the present condition of their own money'. These debates were excellent examples of the strong current of informed opinion which, come what may, refused to approve a policy of enhancement or debasement. 'Experience hath taught us', said Sir Robert Cotton before the Privy Council, 'that the enfeebling of coin is but a shift for a while, as drink to one in a dropsy, to make him swell the more.'[4]

[1] See below, section (ii). For some of these proposals, see Add. MSS. 10113, fols. 159, 166; S.P.D. Jas. I, 67/53, 88/104; Misselden, *Free Trade*, p. 103; S.P.D. Chas. I, 74/33, 103; S.P.D. Chas. I, 124/68; Sanderson, fols. 235–6; S.P.D. Chas. I, 275/44.
[2] *A.P.C. 1619–1621*, pp. 181–2. For another good summary of the dangers of enhancement, see Add. MSS. 10113, fols. 216–17.
[3] For the Merchant Adventurers' opposition to projects in 1622 and 1640, see Add. MSS. 34324, fol. 155; S.P.D. Jas. I, 104/48 (wrongly calendared).
[4] McCulloch, *Old and Scarce Tracts on Money*, pp. 125 ff.

It was, in effect, the fear of 'the loss to all monied men in their debts, gentlemen in their rents, and the king in his customs'[1] which meant that the campaign against the raising of silver was both more vehement and more successful than any against an alteration of the gold coinage. The prevalence of silver coins meant that manipulation of them would have specific and widespread economic repercussions. Gold coins, on the other hand, were by no means such an important element in the circulating medium. A committee pointed out in 1618 that when gold was enhanced there were no inconveniences because it was 'shrouded under silver . . . but if silver be raised the inconveniences of both will be felt' since silver was pre-eminent as a means of payment.[2] With the less precious metal any alteration was far more likely to lead to price fluctuation and thus, while there was little real protest at the raising of gold in 1611, subsequent bitter and sustained hostility prevented any enhancement of silver.[3] Caught in a dilemma, by which the only effective answer to a painful loss of specie was a step which involved an equally painful rise of prices, official policy settled for inaction—preferring deflationary pressure to the realities of inflation. The landed interest and most merchants would clearly find it difficult to stomach proposals for wholesale manipulation of the coinage; both historical and everyday experience led most men to believe that the price, in terms of instability and insecurity, was too great.

We can now consider the question of how far the continuing disparities between the rating of English and European coins did in fact create a shortage of money in England. To some extent a sudden enhancement of gold and silver coins in one country might tend to stimulate a sharp influx of specie—to buy goods. For, as has been seen in connexion with the fall in textile exports in the early 1620's, a raising of the valuation of coins in one country might not be followed by a commensurate rise in commodity prices,[4] and the resulting decline in the amounts of gold or silver needed to purchase goods would make non-native coins of these metals profitable exports from other lands to the relevant areas: their 'price', in terms of commodities, would rise. Therefore it was possible, in certain circumstances, for both types of coins to be lost, as far as England was concerned, when currency manipulation was rife on the Continent.

---

[1] Add. MSS. 10113, fol. 187.
[2] S.P.D. Jas. I, 104/29. Cf. Malynes, *Lex Mercatoria*, p. 257.
[3] In addition to the references already given, see the following for the opposition to manipulation of silver coins: Add. MSS. 34324, fol. 65; Add. MSS. 10113, fols. 159, 216–17; Lans. MSS. 152, fol. 179; A.P.C. *1618–1619*, pp. 318–20; S.P.D. Jas. I, 104/29, 41; A.P.C. *1619–1621*, p. 134; Mun, *A Discourse of Trade from England unto the East Indies* (1621), p. 42; S.P.D. Jas. I, 131/106; Malynes, *The Maintenance of Free Trade*, pp. 94–5; Mun, *England's Treasure*, p. 28; Vaughan, pp. 77 ff.; Maddison, *Great Britain's Remembrancer*, p. 10.
[4] Above, ch. 4.

But in the main the sort of efflux which was consistently present and of which commentators bitterly complained, was more directly bimetallic, i.e. it arose from differences in bullion ratios and was expressed, after 1611, in terms of an outflow of silver and, to some extent, an inflow of gold. It is therefore necessary to distinguish to a finer degree than contemporaries often did between a drain of silver and a net loss of bullion. In the standard example there can be no immediate net loss of both gold and silver: since one metal is only undervalued *in terms of the other*, so this fact and its consequent efflux are matched by an overvaluation and an influx of the other.[1] It was impossible, strictly speaking, to under- or overvalue coins of *both* metals at the same time: 'You cannot advance or enhance the one, but you abate and diminish the other, for they balance upon this parallel.'[2] England after 1611 certainly had a chronic tendency to lose silver, but as long as 'other things' (e.g. the balance of trade) 'remained equal' her total net supply of treasure would not necessarily diminish. To some writers this two-way flow was the final argument against any alteration of the coinage: 'all commodities are priced by plenty or scarcity, by dearness or cheapness the one by the other: if then we desire our silver to buy gold, as it of late hath done, we must let it be the cheaper, and less in proportion valued, and so contrary: for one equivalent proportion in both will bring in neither.... To furnish then this way [by enhancement] the Mint with both is altogether impossible.'[3]

Nevertheless, other contemporary observers readily identified enhancements or debasements abroad with a direct drain on the effective monetary supplies of England.[4] In part this was a general confusion, probably stemming from the conjunction of manipulation abroad and an unfavourable balance of payments at home. On the other hand, many writers, while they fully acknowledged that silver was the only metal which was flowing out and that gold might indeed be coming into the country, tacitly assumed that the net drain of silver was equivalent to a net drain of money. In effect, this was a correct assumption: the fact that, as a consequence of bimetallic flows, total supplies of bullion might not be appreciably reduced did not necessarily mean that the *effective* quantity of money in the economy remained unchanged. For in the operations of the economy

---

[1] Over the long run, of course, this situation (where silver was undervalued) would ultimately effect the net flows of bullion through its encouragement of commodity imports as substitutes for returns of silver. The balance of payments would swing in an unfavourable direction.
[2] Malynes, *Lex Mercatoria*, p. 208.
[3] Debates in 1626, McCulloch, *Old and Scarce Tracts on Money*, p. 139. Cf. Vaughan, pp. 82-5.
[4] See, among many such examples, Hargrave MSS. 321, pp. 4, 444 ff.; Misselden, *Free Trade*, pp. 8-10; S.P.D. Jas. I, 131/55; S.P.D. Chas. I, 1/85.

Monetary Instability, 1600–1642 173

silver was by far the more popular medium of exchange: 'the common payment [is] made in silver . . . payments run betwixt merchant and merchant in silver; in the Customs House in silver; and all petty payments throughout the kingdom in silver.' 'The silver coins', wrote Malynes, 'do rule the market in all places, because of the abundance thereof, being 500 to one of gold.'[1] Silver, in any case, could be coined into units of smaller and more convenient face value than could gold, and so be employed in a much wider range of transactions. Gold, that is, had a much lower velocity of circulation—which was reduced even more by its suitability as a means of holding wealth in an age which placed a great premium on liquidity.

Since, on grounds both of sheer availability and the number of transactions in which one coin could be used, silver was so much more significant than gold, when the latter was imported and the former shipped abroad, a problem of a shortage of *effective* money immediately arose, 'because that the whole body of the land doth stand in continual need of silver monies for their [*sic*] daily traffic, without which our commonwealth can hardly subsist'. There was, that is to say, an incipient scarcity of all but clipped and worn silver coin: 'the scarcity is so great that a man may go into a great many shops in London, of great trade and commerce, before he shall get a 20*s*. piece in gold to be changed into silver. . . . The greatest part of the commerce of the kingdom, and almost all the inland commerce, is made in silver, the want whereof doth greatly prejudice the same.'[2] For many purposes silver *was* 'money', and it did not need a net drain of bullion to provoke monetary scarcity. Although the overall *value* of treasure and coin in England might not be immediately affected by the raising of silver abroad or gold at home, nevertheless such currency manipulation could produce, through its effects on differential ratios, a real loss of effective money—with all the economic difficulties which that loss entailed. This situation obtained after 1611[3] and was particularly virulent in the period 1618–23, at which time monetary anarchy reigned on the Continent and the deflationary

---

[1] S.P.D. Jas. I, 104/29; Malynes, *The Centre of the Circle*, p. 22. Cf. Maddison, *Great Britain's Remembrancer*, p. 11. For the predominance of silver coins in the Netherlands, see Posthumus, lvi–lvii.

[2] Vaughan, p. 42. Cf. Mun, *England's Treasure*, p. 30. In the early 1620's 2*d*. per 20*s*. was given as a premium for silver coins (R. Ruding, *Annals of Coinage* (1840), I, 386).

[3] In 1618 the Privy Council investigated the activity of the Mint in the preceding seven years and in the last seven years of Elizabeth's reign. As far as the production of fresh supplies of money is concerned the results speak for themselves (*A.P.C. 1618–1619*, p. 317):

	Mint output (in £)		
	Fine gold	Crown gold	Silver
39–42 Elizabeth	28,546	75,734	844,433
9–15 James I	11,600	1,534,709	57,689

pressures of the efflux of silver were being aggravated by the manifestations of deep depression. In such circumstances there was an intensification of a prevailing contemporary preoccupation: that which concerned a 'scarcity of money'.

Indeed, there were very few years in the period which were entirely free from complaints of monetary shortage, and one reason for the scepticism on this point of later historians and economists is the bewildering variety of contemporary explanations and descriptions of this particular phenomenon. Whenever the question of a scarcity of money arose contemporaries were able to adduce a host of 'reasons' for an export of specie; for instance, a parliamentary committee in 1621 found it possible to list no less than twenty-one explanations for the loss of coin.[1] On the other hand, there was no standard phraseology for what was *meant* by a scarcity of money. In its most obvious commercial sense, and specifically when used by merchants, it might signify a shortage of liquid loan capital and a consequent tightness of credit.[2] In this sense the 'want of monies' would be the direct cause of bankruptcies: 'The want of money hath caused divers merchants and tradesmen to break, who might have maintained their credits, but that being out of their monies, and the monies out of the realm, maketh them to go out of their credits.'[3] As a remedy for this sort of credit tightness, which men saw as the result of a physical shortage of coin and which increased the rate of interest, both Misselden and Malynes advocated an increase in the supply of money— in part by making bills of debt transferable.[4] In quite another meaning of the phrase a 'scarcity of money', it was applied to the results, for a localized agricultural community, of over-abundant harvests.[5] It might also be employed as a synonym for the presence of poverty in the face of rising prices,[6] or as the result of a slump: 'the trading and commerce among [the king's] subjects', said one M.P. in 1621, 'is much decayed, and his people . . . so impoverished, that the greater part have not wherewithal left to pay, and those that have money will not disburse it upon land or any other commodity whatsoever . . . all which premises plainly show that as a body cannot move without sinews, so a realm cannot prosper or maintain itself without money.'[7] Finally, the terminology was

[1] *Commons Debates, 1621*, II, 212 ff.
[2] H.M.C. *Sackville*, II, 59, 102, 118, 138–9, 213, 228–9; Add. MSS. 10113, fol. 220; S.P.D. Chas. I, 478/86. Also see above, ch. 6, p. 129.
[3] Malynes, *The Maintenance of Free Trade*, p. 102.
[4] Misselden, *Free Trade*, pp. 116–18; Malynes, *The Maintenance of Free Trade*, p. 98. Cf. Roberts, *The Merchant's Map of Commerce*, pp. 110–11, where the low interest rates in Holland are attributed to the abundance of money there.
[5] Hargrave MSS. 321, p. 104; *Commons Debates, 1621*, II, 137.
[6] S.P.D. Jas. I, 123/62, 127/16.
[7] *Commons Debates, 1621*, VII, 581. Cf. Add. MSS. 34324, fol. 179.

used to describe a typically depressed economy, as, for instance, in 1622: 'There is great scarcity of money within all the kingdom, so that any man cannot depend upon any payment or receive any money due to him, and generally all the country is impoverished and good livers cannot make any shift for money. The price of all things except corn is at a very low rate. Tradesmen complain that they cannot get work to employ themselves.'[1] Writers used the phrase in all these meanings, and sometimes more than one in a single passage, but in virtually every case it was seen as the effect of a physical phenomenon: 'The state of England is a decayed state. The nerves are dried up, the money is gone.'[2]

At no time were such complaints more insistent than in the early 1620's. The conjunction of a bimetallic outflow and an unfavourable balance of trade readily explains the contemporary anxiety; but it also served to further confusion as the manifestations of the slump in textile exports came to be blamed directly and solely on to an export of coin. The decay of trade and the 'want of money' were viewed, in fact, as twin problems, or even as two aspects of the same problem. Thus all the outports agreed, in 1621, 'that by reason our English monies are sold for more in other countries than they are valued for here at home, that causes the export of our coins . . . *so that both decay of trade and want of money grew both from one and the same cause, which is undervalue of our money*'.[3] As commentators erroneously equated a lack of confidence, leading to tight credit conditions, with a physical shortage of money, so it became an easy assumption that the cause of the slump, even of unemployment in the textile industry, was basically a loss of coin. Misselden, for instance, wrote that the latter 'is apparently sensible in the drapery of the kingdom . . . and in all the other trades . . . and hath begot that great and general damp and deadness in all the trades of the kingdom, which we do unhappily feel at this day'. And to Malynes it seemed obvious that 'all the . . . causes of the decay of trade in England are almost all of them comprised in one, which is the want of money'.[4]

It is impossible, however, to subscribe to the theory that a spontaneous loss of silver coin produced a deflation which largely or wholly explains the depression of the early 1620's. Whatever the deflationary characteristics of the years 1620–4, the most obvious feature of the slump was a sharp decline in exports. Factors were at work which rendered cloth exports uncompetitive. Whether the causes were internal or external to

[1] Yonge, p. 52. Cf. B.M. E. 146 (21), pp. 2, 8.
[2] *Commons Debates, 1621*, II, 412.
[3] Hargrave MSS. 321, p. 21; my italics.
[4] Misselden, *Free Trade*, pp. 28–9; Malynes, *The Maintenance of Free Trade*, p. 104. Cf. S.P.D. Jas. I, 118/131.

England they could not possibly have included the downward pressure on prices which must have accompanied a scarcity of the circulating medium. For if there had only been a spontaneous efflux of coin, with no other critical change in the economic scene, then the expected result would have been a fall in export prices and a consequent *increase* in textile sales. It is possible, of course, that monetary difficulties adversely affected home demand for cloth and so served to aggravate the industrial depression. Further, the general deflation, which followed the cessation of industrial activity and the rise in food prices, must have been deepened by the bimetallic loss of silver as well as by the export of bullion and specie resulting from an adverse balance of payments. But the undoubted primacy of the fall in overseas sales as a factor in the slump of the early 1620's means that a purely monetary explanation of the crisis must, of necessity, be inadequate. This fact did not escape some contemporaries. 'It is not true', wrote one, 'that the present want of money hath decayed our trade, but rather that the decay of our trade outwards, and excessive consumption of wares brought in have wasted and deprived us of our money.'[1] In this quite valid sense a scarcity of money could be viewed as the result of an unfavourable balance of trade or a general commercial depression.

In spite of the facts of the case in the early 1620's, it does seem that informed opinion at the time and since has done less than justice to contemporary views relating to a shortage of money. In the main it has been held that such complaints only expressed an ever-present and irrational dissatisfaction with things as they were, or that the problem could not long exist without an automatic remedy from the equilibrating and impersonal force of economic processes. Thomas Mun, for instance, claimed that the poor and the rich always complain that they never have enough money: 'I hope it is but imagination maketh us sick, when all our parts be sound and strong.' Josiah Child blamed such views on 'the frailty and corruption of human nature' and went on: 'I can say in truth, upon my own memory, that men did complain as much of the scarcity of money ever since I knew the world.' In the eighteenth century Joseph Harris anticipated the views of classical economists: 'No trading nation can be long in want of money. . . . It is the want of vent and not the want of money that limits trade.' Harris provided a succinct analysis of the self-regulation of the economy operating through price levels and trade balances, and claimed that 'the complaints of particular persons arise not from a deficiency of money or counters in circulation, but from their own want of skill, address, or opportunity of getting more money;

[1] S.P.D. Jas. I, 131/107.

or perhaps only from want of frugality, in spending more than their income or proper share'. Adam Smith, as we should expect, was particularly scathing on this point, and a modern economist—in distinguishing seven possible meanings of a 'scarcity of money'—writes that the complaints arose primarily from 'the confused or inadequate economic analysis ... [a confusion] between money and what could be bought with money or was valued in terms of money'.[1]

In large part the modern approach has been to discount contemporary theories of an independent shortage of currency on the grounds that they were products of a confused mercantilist view of the significance of treasure, and that any economic problems posed by a drain of specie would quite naturally be solved by the speedy readjustment deriving from deflationary pressures on prices, costs and the demand for imports.

But such analyses presuppose economic mechanisms quite remote from the reality of the early seventeenth century. For one thing, the presence of 'constant reckonings and annual bargains'—the importance of prices which were based on long-term contracts or tradition—meant that prices could *not* readjust smoothly to the downward pressure of a reduced supply of money. The operations of the seventeenth-century economy were not frictionless, and economic pressures which, in the perfect models of classical economics, lowered monetary values while maintaining full employment of resources, were likely, in Stuart society, to provoke chronic unemployment or underemployment as they met the relatively rigid line of prices and costs. For an economy whose market values contained a significant traditional element and which depended so much on the availability of metallic coin for its continuing activity, fluctuations in the physical supply of liquid assets could impose long-term strains which cannot be measured by an exercise in formal logic. For this reason it was quite possible, after 1611, for a shortage of money to be the cause of continuing dislocation and incipient deflation. It would therefore be misleading to claim that all such complaints of a shortage arose from a 'confused economic analysis', from an invalid attribution of depression to its most apparent features: that men could not pay their debts, or borrow money, or buy goods, or sell them at profitable prices. Such illogical elements may well have marked much contemporary economic thought on the subject, but the problem was none the less real and urgent. The role which monetary scarcity could play more than justified the anxiety with which writers viewed an export of bullion or specie. The

---

[1] Mun, *A Discourse*, p. 38; Josiah Child, *Discourse about Trade* (1690), Preface; Joseph Harris, *An Essay upon Money and Coins*, Part I (1756), 67, 69–70, 75; Smith, *The Wealth of Nations*, I, 383; Jacob Viner, *Studies in the theory of International Trade* (1937), pp. 88–9.

spontaneous influence of such a factor is well illustrated by the situation in the early 1620's—although that was not the only period in which the repercussions of scarcity were being felt. Arising from the bimetallic movements already described, and coinciding with a fall in exports, a substitution of gold for silver considerably lowered the velocity of circulation of money, while it reduced the amount of coins available for daily commercial transactions and for use as liquid capital. The special difficulties which appeared arose from the fact that the operations of the economy were by no means as flexible as has often been assumed. The price-income structure was sufficiently 'sticky' to throw large sectors of the economy out of gear when the circulating medium was suddenly reduced. A total supply of money below 'normal' might prevail for some time, and the structure of the economy might considerably extend the period which classical economists presupposed to be one of easy readjustment.

When Symonds D'Ewes came to leave college in 1620 his thoughts turned to the possibility of selling his furniture there. According to his own account, he 'laboured much', but it was a considerable time before he was able to 'put off anything save a bedstead'; 'the scarcity of silver everywhere, and especially in the college [made me] ... almost despair of meeting with a chapman.'[1] It was this sort of physical shortage of currency, in addition to net losses of bullion or the general poverty of a slump, whose deflationary influence can be seen operating in certain years, and especially in the period after 1619. The desultory issue of token coins, both privately and under government supervision, did little to alleviate the situation. Certainly from a theoretical standpoint the economic literature which developed from the discussion of specie flows left much to be desired; but we know too much of the difficulties produced by the eighteenth-century shortage of silver coin to ignore what must have been, intermittently, a much more painfully deflationary phenomenon a hundred years earlier.

(ii) THE OFFICIAL APPROACH TO MONETARY AFFAIRS

The motive for most outbursts of official interest in monetary affairs lay in the fear of a loss of bullion or specie and a deflationary scarcity of money. Hence, under the stress of semi-permanent bimetallic bullion flows, of intermittent swings in the balance of payment, and of fluctuations in the ratings of European coins and the course of European exchange rates, the English authorities were nearly always occupied with some aspect of monetary policy. Since, for most practical purposes, the stock

[1] *College Life in the Time of James the First* (1851), p. 120.

of treasure and the actual coinage were nearly identical, it is clear that anxiety concerning the former was really a fear concerning the supply of the latter: the contemporary discussions dedicated to the flow of treasure were an integral part of the approach to the problems of the coinage.

At times it is almost impossible to distinguish any coherent approach to the currency problems of the early seventeenth century. And this is especially true when diverse factors were affecting bullion flows. Thus, anxiety concerning a national shortage of coin jostled with, and was produced by, fear of an inactive Mint and the loss of revenue which this entailed; sophisticated views on the balance of payments competed for official approbation with conspiratorial theories as to the monopolistic influence of continental bankers on the determination of exchange rates; plans for direct currency manipulation were considered as alternatives, at the council table, to projects for governmental exchange control or the nationalization of bullion dealings; and throughout the period there were constant attempts to enforce the network of penal statutes, inherited from a previous generation, which aimed at preventing the export of coins and bullion directly.

The more interesting discussions and the more detailed official approach to questions of monetary policy occurred after 1610. However, at least one important body met before that date: the commission on the export of treasure which reported in October 1600. It included Gerard Malynes, who was possibly its secretary. In a somewhat confused manner the report blamed the loss of treasure on to the erratic tariffs of the bimetallic system, the 'abuse' of the exchange (this was stigmatized, presumably under Malynes's influence, as the 'effective' cause of bullion export), and an unfavourable balance of trade. There was some dissension as to the relative significance of these factors, but general agreement that, in order to prevent the export of money, the Statutes of Employment should be enforced, excessive imports restrained, and the manufacture of import-substitutes encouraged.[1] But in the main little need be said concerning the years before 1611. In only two respects were they significantly representative.

Firstly, there were strong attempts to secure the enforcement of the Statutes of Employment, which stipulated that alien importers should give bonds to disburse the proceeds of sales on commodities for export—in order, it was hoped, to prevent the export of coin.[2] Periods of anxiety concerning the loss of money naturally produced this sort of plan to curb

[1] S.P.D. Eliz., 279/97. Cf. de Roover, pp. 195–7. For Malynes's theories, see below, pp. 201–211.
[2] For the medieval origins of the Statutes, see de Roover, pp. 38 ff.

the activities of aliens by enforcing such laws, which had either been ignored or were being circumvented by allowing exchange by bills to be considered as 'employment'. Aliens, on the whole, tended to import more than they exported and were normally deliverers by exchange in England. Consequently, when a fall in the exchange rates, or a bimetallic disturbance, made the export of specie profitable, merchant strangers were frequently the agents. Thus a merchants' committee in 1602 found that high valuations set on English coins abroad stimulated alien merchants to 'draw all our coins into those parts when the exchange is low and fit for their purpose'. Consequently, in 1600, 1606 and 1607 there were campaigns to tighten the regulations—seemingly without any marked success.[1]

Another way in which the government had traditionally attempted to control the bullion trade was through the Office of the King's Exchanger. The position of Exchanger dates back at least to the reign of Henry III and in the sixteenth century—specifically in 1576—there were plans to use it to control the rate of exchange by endowing the Exchanger with the sole right to arrange bills of exchange. But by the early seventeenth century its advocates mainly considered it (as it was originally founded) as a monopoly of the exchange of coin and bullion in England. The preface to *Cambium Regis*, which was published in 1628 as a defence of plans dating from 1626 to 1628 to establish the Office, claimed that it had never been lawful 'to buy, sell, or traffic gold or silver merchantwise, and so to come betwixt the merchant, or other subject, and the Mint, but to such as were authorized and appointed by the state thereunto: this being the full, proper, and adequate subject of the Office of Exchange'. In this sense writers and administrators from time to time advocated its re-establishment as a means to counteract the 'exchanging goldsmiths', who were accused of facilitating the export of coin, and diverting it from the Mint, by their culling, melting and sale of money, and by offering bullion prices in excess of those at the Mint. Action against these activities were to assume large-scale proportions in the late 1620's, but as early as 1607 there was a possibility that the Office of the Exchanger would become important in the bullion-broking field, and although it does not seem to have had a monopoly, it was certainly active from 1608 to 1611.[2]

From 1608 to 1611 there was extreme concern over the drain of gold which had arisen after the effects of the enhancement of 1604 had worn

---

[1] Hargrave MSS. 321, pp. 144–5; Steele, I, no. 907; Ruding, I, 353; S.P.D. Jas. I, 20/6; Lans. MSS. 152, fols. 181–8, 197, 199, 206, 208, 210–11.
[2] See *Cambium Regis* (1628), Preface; Thomas Wilson, *A Discourse of Usury*, ed. R. H. Tawney (1925), pp. 138 ff.; de Roover, pp. 231 ff.; Ruding, I, 354 ff., II, 149; S.P.D. Jas. I, 28/8; Add. MSS. 10113, fol. 125; S.P.D. Chas. I, 56/6. For the project of 1626–8, see below, pp. 190–2.

off. The goldsmiths came in for sharp criticism, especially 'some few goldsmiths who run betwixt the stranger and the English and gather [coin] together'. In May 1611 a proclamation was published which forbade the melting, culling and exporting of gold and silver coin. But the situation appeared too urgent for such physical controls to provide an effective remedy, and, after lengthy discussions which covered nearly all aspects of the currency question, it was decided in November 1611 to enhance gold coins by 10 per cent in order to retain those coins by raising their valuation to a level nearer that of the Continent.[1] It was apparent that in spite of all laws to the contrary, and all attempts to regulate the bullion trade by physical controls, gold and/or silver would always be exported when there was profit to be made. When, as in 1611, the reason for the loss was a badly tariffed bimetallic system, then the only practical remedy was a readjustment of the Mint ratio by a revaluation of the coinage: 'in all cases of transportation in all countries, the crying-up of the money hath been the remedy.'[2] This was the step taken in 1611 to prevent the outflow of gold; the difficulties after 1611 arose principally because the coinage in question was silver, and an enhancement of silver would have produced a drastic inflation. Thus the characteristic features of the discussions of the monetary problem after 1611 were arguments and counter-arguments on the merits of manipulation, and (when these failed to produce a positive policy) attempts to enforce other aspects of direct currency regulation.

The proclamation in 1611, raising the price of gold, worked too well! The bullion flows were reversed and it was now silver which was undervalued and shipped out of England. In 1612 the new situation was the subject of a detailed official investigation. The Solicitor- and Attorney-Generals, for instance, reported to the Privy Council on the shortage of silver at the Mint. They found that the merchants were strongly opposed to a raising of silver; so much so that even a suspicion of such a policy, they said, would produce 'deadness and retention of money', and they 'were forced to use protestation that there was no such intent'. The report recommended an enforcement of the Statutes of Employment and the penal statutes against bullion export, the easing of the process of bringing Spanish coins to the Mint, and the export of corn for money. Having concluded that other matters, including the question of the balance of trade, were 'commonplaces so well known to your Lordships as it is enough to mention them only', Parry and Bacon categorically rejected

[1] For all this, see Add. MSS. 10113, fols. 64, 112, 114, 116, 122, 123, 127, 129, 131, 133, 135, 138, 143, 198, 205–6, 210, 212, 218, 220–2, 224, 230, 271; Steele, I, nos. 1111, 1119; Ruding, I, 365–6; *Cottoni Posthuma* (1651), pp. 196–200.
[2] Add. MSS. 10113, fols. 220–1.

any policy of direct currency manipulation.[1] Nevertheless, as the economy continued to suffer from a shortage of silver coins, the strongest pressure continued in 1612 for an enhancement.[2]

The issue of farthing tokens during and after 1613 can possibly be considered as one reaction to the chronic scarcity of small change, but all efforts in this direction were unsuccessful, and two years later further suggestions that silver be raised were once again met by a negative response.[3] It was in this context that, in 1614, the government devoted increased attention to the balance of payments as a possible cause of the presumed drain of bullion. 'The true cause of our want of money in England', it was claimed, 'is our importation of foreign commodities more than we export.' Sir Lionel Cranfield, at the same time, asserted that the balance of payments *was* unfavourable and that 'experience hath taught us that base monies have always been found dangerous to our estate'.[4] By May 1615 this line of inquiry had advanced sufficiently far to produce a series of statistical investigations into the balance of payments for 1605–11 and 1613–14. Cranfield's estimates for 1605–11, which were based on the customs figures for London, indicated, after correction for the over-rating of cloth and the differential duties for aliens, that the balance was unfavourable. John Wolstenholme investigated the situation for 1613 and 1614 and both he and Cranfield concluded that England had an export surplus in both years, although the matter was vividly debated before the Privy Council.[5] That anxiety should be expressed concerning the balance of trade when silver was being exported, even if gold was coming into the country, is understandable in view of the results which such a flow had in reducing effective supplies of money. Nevertheless, even more widespread discussions failed to adduce an acceptable solution to the monetary problem, which was still seen as a dual one: an idle Mint and an export of bullion. After more lengthy debate, 'and no resolution yet given for remedy thereof notwithstanding the sundry consultations which have been made thereupon', a committee of Mint experts was

[1] Add. MSS. 10113, fol. 187.
[2] Add. MSS. 10113, fols. 68–72, 104, 178; S.P.D. Jas. I, 70/39–43. For the efforts to enforce the Statutes of Employment, see Add. MSS. 10113, fol. 194; Lans. MSS. 152, fol. 231.
[3] Ruding, I, 369 ff.; Add. MSS. 10113, fols. 166, 216–17.
[4] Add. MSS. 10113, fols. 159, 216–17.
[5] Lans. MSS. 152, fols. 175, 177–8. Cf. the figures for 1613 in Cotton MSS. Titus, B. V, fol. 387. Wolstenholme's figures for 1613 are reproduced in Misselden's *Circle of Commerce*, pp. 121–2. The results of the analyses were:

Balances of Trade (rounded to £1)

	1613 (Lans. MSS.)	1613 (Cotton MSS.)	1614 (Lans. MSS.)
Wolstenholme	+£346,284	+327,000	+413,645
Cranfield	+ 251,233	+368,000	+321,453

For the controversy, see Lans. MSS. 152, fols. 190–1; *A.P.C. 1615–1616*, pp. 188–9.

appointed to consider the best methods 'both for keeping the money in the kingdom and bringing in greater quantity of bullion to the Mint'.[1] There is no further record of this body.

Although, in 1615, contemporaries were reasonably certain that there was no great cause for alarm concerning the overall balance of trade, they were unanimous in thinking that alien merchants imported far more than they exported. One estimate put the deficit, on that account, at some £386,800, and in 1615–16, consequently, there was a sudden increase in the emphasis placed on the enforcement of the Statutes of Employment.[2] Finally, and again with no real effect on policy, the continued differences in currency valuations produced, in 1616, a plan from the Mint officials, whose incomes depended to a significant degree on the activity at the Mint, to reduce the Mint ratio from $13\frac{1}{3}$ to $12\frac{1}{2}$: 1, by lightening the silver coinage.[3]

In 1618 all the old issues were once again brought up for official consideration. Lack of activity at the Mint and a renewal of the fear that bullion was being exported produced another plan to enhance the silver coinage, while the seignorage, bullion-broking, foreign coins, the Statutes of Employment, and the balance of trade for alien and native merchants were all eagerly discussed.[4] Against strong opposition, which seems to have involved a majority of the Privy Council, James I appeared determined to push through a policy of manipulation. The council, in an attempt to counter this threat, met on 18 November, tentatively concluded that 'much silver is brought into this kingdom, but not to the Mint', and ordered a comprehensive statistical investigation of Mint output over the previous seven years compared with the last seven years of Elizabeth's reign, the stamping of plate at the Goldsmiths' Hall for the same periods, the intrinsic worth of the English Jacobus and the Dutch Rider, the balance of trade for the last two years, and the English and European seignorages. The only available results of these inquiries show a fall in the stamping of plate and a rise in total coining which masked a decline in the output of silver coins and a great increase in that of gold. On the basis of its observations the Privy Council urged the king not to continue in his determination to raise silver, since, it was claimed, no evidence could be found of any serious export of treasure or diminution of bullion supplies in England, although the last statement had to be qualified: 'at least of gold'. In fact, of course, the council had to admit to a relative shortage of silver and, therefore, had to base its arguments

[1] *A.P.C. 1615–1616*, pp. 272–3.
[2] *A.P.C. 1615–1616*, pp. 354–5, 477–8, 479–81, 622–3; Lans. MSS. 152, fol. 174b.
[3] S.P.D. Jas. I, 67/53, 88/104.
[4] *A.P.C. 1618–1619*, pp. 302–3; Lans. MSS. 152, fols. 172, 179–80.

against enhancement mainly on the commercial disturbances which would result: 'and because the noise thereof through the City of London, and from thence to other parts of the realm, as we do understand, hath already done hurt, and in some measure interrupted and distracted the course of general commerce, we think it very requisite . . . that some signification be forthwith made . . . that your Majesty hath no purpose or intention at this time to raise your coins.'[1] The merchants themselves made their voice heard in opposition to the proposed policy: a committee composed of traders reported in December and argued cogently against any enhancement although they admitted that, even though there appeared no current shortage of money, 'if there come no more silver to the Mint . . . the kingdom will in time be drained'. They recommended that the penal statutes be enforced and that a King's Exchanger be appointed to control bullion trading.[2] This wave of antipathy did in fact dissuade the proponents of manipulation from carrying out their plans, and, instead, official attention was diverted to more direct action against illegal dealings in coin and bullion in England. Early in 1619 a proclamation was issued reaffirming the laws against exchanging coins for profit, melting currency, and paying bullion prices in excess of those offered by the Mint.[3] In the summer of 1619, in an attempt to attract gold to the Mint, the seignorage on that metal was reduced, but on the whole this move was unsuccessful: 'the quantity of gold is not trebled as the merchants suggested.'[4] In the same year a series of prosecutions was directed against exporters of gold for offences committed at the beginning of the century. It was subsequently reported that these prosecutions were successful, in dissuading bullion exporters from illegally shipping precious metals, since they had been followed by a lowering of the exchange rates produced by a pressure to send money abroad by bills and not in specie.[5] Nevertheless, the basic situation had not been changed: the prevailing Mint prices still provided a strong incentive to the export of silver coins.

By 1620 this incentive had become even more powerful. The currency manipulations on the Continent, which undercut the profitability of English textile exports, had begun to take effect in terms of the bimetallic

[1] *A.P.C. 1618–1619*, pp. 305–6, 317, 318–20; Add. MSS. 10113, fol. 198b.
[2] S.P.D. Jas. I, 104/29.
[3] Add. MSS. 10113, fols. 143, 193; S.P.D. Jas. I, 69/8, 104/41; Steele, I, no. 1240; Ruding, I, 372; Lans. MSS. 162, fol. 230.
[4] *A.P.C. 1618–1619*, pp. 486–7; Lans. MSS. 160, fol. 242; Lans. MSS. 162, fols. 174–5, 180; Add. MSS. 34324, fol. 105; *C.S.P.D. 1619–1623*, p. 60; Steele, I, no. 1254; Ruding, I, 373; Feavearyear, p. 82; Gould, 'The Royal Mint', 246.
[5] Add. MSS. 34324, fol. 155. For the prosecutions, see S.P.D. Jas. I, 104/4; S.P.D. Jas. I, 109/32, 76, 87, 90, 96, 102, 103, 112; S.P.D. Jas. I, 111/34, 62, 66, 67; S.P.D. Jas. I, 112/1, 29; S.P.D. Jas. I, 122/41, 43, 44; *C.S.P.D. 1619–1623*, pp. 165, 169, 173; *A.P.C. 1621–1623*, pp. 2–3; Lans. MSS. 162, fol. 219; Gould, 'The Royal Mint', 243.

movements of bullion, and the drain of silver to Europe became even more acute. From 1 April 1619 to 31 March 1620 no silver was coined at the Mint. Once again all the old controversial grounds were re-trod and the traditional suspicion of the licensed specie exports of the East India Company led to the publication, in the next year, of Thomas Mun's *Discourse of Trade from England unto the East Indies*.[1] All the merchant companies were consulted on 'the means to bring silver more plentifully to the Mint', and in the course of such considerations James once again (this time with the initial concurrence of the Privy Council) decided on a policy of manipulation: the suggestion of the Goldsmiths Company, that silver be enhanced proportionately to gold, was adopted. Plans were well advanced to cut 66s. from one pound of silver and to safeguard the move by requiring the Goldsmiths and the East India Company to pass Court Acts forbidding their members to offer prices for silver higher than the Mint. But in February, when all arrangements for the drastic step had been made, the Privy Council returned to its original attitude on the subject. James received a strong warning of the dangers involved and Cranfield was despatched to Court to explain the technicalities and difficulties of the matter. More than this, yet another committee of merchants was unanimously opposed to any manipulation of the currency, although the report acknowledged that 'the abasing of the . . . standard . . . is . . . the only way at this present to draw silver into the kingdom'. Pointing to the enormous difficulties which would follow an alteration, the merchants advised that consideration of it should be deferred for twelve months to see if the situation could be improved by other means. This report was accepted by the council, and the king, however reluctantly, was forced to bow to the pressure for postponement—which amounted to an effective rejection of the policy. There seems to have been little attempt to revive the plans in 1621.[2]

Within a short period, the monetary difficulties which had given rise to the agitated discussions of 1620 were considerably aggravated by the effects of the continuing manipulation of European currencies and of the depression which undermined English industry and commerce. To the repercussions of bimetallic maladjustments there was added the influence of an unfavourable balance of trade as textile exports slumped and imports increased in value. In this context the anxiety concerning the scarcity of money rose to a new height, and in 1621 Parliament had the matter under permanent investigation, while the Privy Council requested

[1] See, for example, *A.P.C. 1619–1621*, pp. 104–5, 127. For the discussions in 1620, see Lans. MSS. 162, fol. 176; Add. MSS. 34324, fol. 109; Gould, 'The Royal Mint', 248.
[2] For these events, see Add. MSS. 34324, fols. 111, 113; *C.S.P.D. 1619–1623*, p. 113; *A.P.C. 1619–1621*, pp. 100, 119–20, 134, 138, 141, 181–2, 187; Lans. MSS. 162, fol. 179.

the trading companies to give their advice on the best way to attract silver and, in September, sent letters to some twenty outports asking for their views on the scarcity of money.[1] In 1622, however, the debates on monetary affairs took a new turn.

The forces of depression which turned the balance of payments against England had a comparable effect on the rates of exchange.[2] Since most rates were quoted in terms of a variable amount of foreign currency for 20 shillings sterling, a falling exchange was, to many contemporaries, the most significant feature of the monetary problem, and official attention was now increasingly concentrated on the precise technical relationship between the falling exchange rate, the export of bullion and specie, and the deflationary pressure in England. In June 1621 the Privy Council had already evinced some interest in the par of exchange with reference to the outflow of silver. More general inquiries were commenced in November, and by the spring of 1622 James I was moved to order a select body of men to report to him on the exchanges and their alleged 'abuse'.[3] The committee consisted of Sir Robert Cotton, Sir Ralph Maddison, John Williams, William Sanderson and Gerard Malynes. Of these men, a majority (Maddison, Sanderson and Malynes) produced quite independent books or manuscripts at other times which demonstrated their unanimity on analytical questions concerning the determination of the exchanges: they adhered to what might be called the conspiratorial view of the economics of exchange rates.[4] The committee's report was ready on 1 May 1622 and, not unexpectedly, its conclusions were identical with the theories on the exchanges already so amply publicized by Malynes: as foreign currencies were enhanced the expected rise in the exchange rates (since more foreign money of account would have to be given for 20 shillings sterling at par) had not kept pace, principally because European financiers and speculators were keeping the exchange rates below par at a level independent of the operations of the real forces of supply and demand. Hence, it was claimed, English money was 'undervalued' by an artificially low exchange, and this was the real cause of the export of specie, while it was also blamed for adverse terms of trade. The necessary remedy for the loss of money, on this view, was a proclamation that exchange should only take place at par—at the 'true and intrinsic value of

[1] S.P.D. Jas. I, 121/21-2; C.S.P.D. 1619–1623, pp. 254, 259; Add. MSS. 34324, fol. 184; Ruding, I, 376; *Commons Debates, 1621, passim*; Hargrave MSS. 321, pp. 44–5; A.P.C. 1619–1621, pp. 393, 400; 1621–1623, pp. 40, 79–80, 208.
[2] Above, pp. 94–6.
[3] A.P.C. 1619–1621, p. 393; Malynes, *The Centre of the Circle*, p. 76; S.P.D. Chas. I, 14/18; S.P.D. Chas. I (Addenda), 528/84.
[4] For Malynes, see below, pp. 201–11; for Maddison, below, p. 205, and *Great Britain's Remembrancer*; for Sanderson, below, p. 204, and Lans. MSS. 768.

your monies', which, it was hoped, would also help revive trade by *raising* English export prices![1]

Clearly, such views were highly controversial, and there were other economic commentators with sufficient insight to distinguish between primary and secondary causes: another opinion was necessary. Consequently, the manuscript was referred to a rival committee of merchants, which included Thomas Mun.[2] As the views of the first group were identical with those of Malynes, so those of the second group were indistinguishable from Mun's. Their report attacked the concept of an *independent* undervaluation of English currency by exchange and demonstrated that the exchange rate itself was the result of the supply of and demand for currencies in general. They proposed, in effect, an alternative explanation of the variability of exchange rates—an explanation much more akin to that of classical economists, by which the level of the exchanges was dependent upon the relative abundance of funds to be transferred and the relative needs of the contracting parties. A large section of the report was given over to a detailed appraisal of the dangers of an artificial enforcement of exchange at par, by which the assets of Englishmen abroad would decrease in value, the clothier would have to accept lower prices from traders since it was 'very difficult if not impossible' to raise cloth prices abroad, the exporter might stop using the exchanges and so reduce his ability to borrow, and the alien 'being hereby deprived of his accustomed means to return his estate by bills of exchange would be driven to . . . carry it out in coin more than heretofore'. The committee concluded by emphasizing, precisely as Mun was to do in his posthumously published book, *England's Treasure by Foreign Trade*, that for an explanation of net movements of coin and bullion, and for the cause of England's loss of specie, it was only necessary to consider the state of the balance of payments, that if the latter were rendered favourable then all anxiety on the question of monetary supplies would disappear.

In 1622 the exchange controversy was not the only indication of anxiety concerning the currency. For instance, a proclamation was published against the export, waste and consumption of coin and bullion, and there were some efforts in the direction of getting Spanish reals to circulate in England.[3] In addition, the committee on the decay of trade which reported in June, and which—significantly enough—included Thomas Mun, concluded that 'the most important remedy [for the

[1] The report is in Add. MSS. 34324, fols. 153–4.
[2] Add. MSS. 34324, fols. 155–7. Others on the committee were Robert Bell, George Kendrick, Henry Wood, Thomas Jennings and John Skinner.
[3] Steele, I, no. 1332; Ruding, I, 377–8; S.P.D. Jas. I, 132/107 ff., 138/15, 139/5; *A.P.C. 1621–1623*, pp. 403–4, 425.

scarcity of money] ... is to provide against the overbalance of trade ..., for monies must necessarily turn the scale'.[1] Nevertheless, from the point of view of official business the discussion of the determination and effects of exchange fluctuations was highly significant. New participants joined the discussions and when, on the recommendation of the committee on the decay of trade, a permanent trade commission was appointed in the autumn, in part to overlook monetary affairs, the balance of trade and the exchanges, this latter body became the new repository of the manuscript battle then in progress on the subject of exchange rates and bullion flows.[2]

Late in 1622 and in the spring of 1623 there was laid before the commissioners a series of memoranda, principally written by Malynes and Mun, on the problems of exchange rates and trade balances.[3] The arguments need not be described in detail here. In the main they were developments of the original statements of spring 1622 and, although deriving from considerations of a highly practical nature, they tended to develop into a purely theoretical controversy in which Malynes asserted the primacy of a low exchange rate, and Mun the state of international indebtedness, as the determinant of European bullion flows. Both attitudes, nevertheless, closely reflected the contemporary economic scene, which was marked by an unfavourable balance of trade, a falling rate of exchange, and an efflux of specie. These discussions were, indeed, critical for the development of economic thought: they enabled Mun to work out his integrated theory as to the balance of trade and exchange fluctuations, and were carried on in the published works of Misselden and Malynes.[4] But in spite of the fact that the monetary effects of the crisis of the early 1620's played a supremely important role in the development of doctrines which have subsequently been labelled mercantilist, the vivid controversy had little real effect on the formulation of government policy. It was Malynes who was the more able to suggest a single panacea for most economic ills, but the likelihood that there would be any wholehearted attempt to control exchange rates was remote—although James seems fleetingly to have entertained the idea of delegating William Sanderson to appoint five 'exchangers' with a monopoly of bill transactions.[5] On the whole, the controversy may best be viewed as the last

[1] S.P.D. Jas. I, 131/55.
[2] *Foedera*, XVII, 410 ff.; S.P.D. Chas. I (Addenda), 528/84. Besides the two original documents, there is another report dating from the months before the appointment of the commission. Add. MSS. 34324, fols. 159–62 is the answer of the Malynes group to the report of the second committee.
[3] Add. MSS. 34324, fols. 163–4, 165, 167, 169, 171–2, 173, 175, 177–8. For a description of all the MSS. involved in the controversy, see Appendix B.
[4] Below, pp. 205–6. [5] S.P.D. Jas. I, 131/105.

important attempt to secure an official monetary policy based upon manipulation of the rate of exchange in isolation from all other factors; it was the final fling of the school of thought which, at its most powerful, had provoked the unsuccessful nationalization of exchange transactions in 1576.[1] In any case, by 1623 there were already signs which somewhat abated the anxiety over monetary affairs. Burlamachi, the famous financier, 'came into the commission of trade and then affirmed the exchange was amended, being come to thirty-four' which, it was reported, was sufficient to stop the technical discussions.[2] As already seen, the rate of exchange did, in fact, improve as exports picked up and the balance of trade grew less unfavourable. The *raison d'être* of the debates was disappearing, and the increase in the Mint's output of silver coin in 1623[3] was one more slight balm to the Privy Council.

The economy in the period between 1618 and 1622 experienced the most acute monetary difficulties before the middle of the century. The wildly fluctuating valuations of coinage, the outflow of coin and bullion, and the strong deflationary pressures left an obvious imprint on the public and private economic discussions of these years. From the discussions there stem much that has subsequently been termed 'typical' of mercantilist thought, and attitudes towards the supply of money which have unfairly been condemned as fallacious. It was significant, however, that, deep as the official anxiety was, the drastic step of currency manipulation was not actually taken. Neither was it found possible—once the emphasis of official debates had been concentrated on the sagging exchange rates—to return to a policy of pegging the exchanges. Indeed, in spite of the agitated feelings in government circles, no drastic change in policy took place. The government continued to intermingle exhortations with attempts to enforce the laws designed to prevent the export of specie. These statutes had, of course, never been successful in preventing an efflux which was at all profitable. The official dilemma arose because, however anxious the Privy Council was concerning a scarcity of money and however certain it was that it knew why money was drained from the economy, all efforts to render the export trade in bullion unprofitable were hamstrung by the real or threatened results of particular policies. This was further illustrated by the events of 1626 and 1627-8.

By 1625 fears concerning the availability of the silver coinage had returned, in part because the Mint output declined somewhat after the relative peak from April 1624 to March 1625, and there were strong arguments put forward in favour of reducing the fine silver content of

[1] Wilson, *Discourse*, pp. 137-54.   [2] S.P.D. Chas. I, 14/18.
[3] Gould, 'The Royal Mint', 248.

the coinage in order to lower the Mint ratio and stop the bimetallic outflow.[1] In any case, 1625 was a depressed year for commerce and it is possible that the decline in textile exports, which was largely occasioned by an outbreak of plague, combined with an urgent need for imports of grain, produced at least a transitory deficit in the balance of payments.[2] Such a phenomenon augmented the deflationary forces which had already been produced by a textile slump and the drain on silver; but it was the bimetallic maladjustment which received most attention, for, once again, men were attracted to one clean-cut policy which seemed to promise immediate relief for monetary stringency. Therefore, in 1626, plans were put forward, by officials of the Mint, which brought the English currency nearer to drastic debasement than it had been since the middle of the sixteenth century: so much so that, in an effort to attract silver and, it seems, to provide for an increase in the royal revenue, light coin was actually produced before a series of urgent high-level debates defeated the project in a flurry of opposition. There is no need to delineate these events in their entirety,[3] for the discussions merely illustrated an intensification of the traditional arguments against any tampering with silver which might lead to an inflationary disruption of the economy and the activities of landowners and merchants. The crucial debates were held before the king and the Privy Council from the 2nd to the 4th of September. The powerful opponents of the plan, led by Sir Robert Cotton, rejected any currency manipulation as disastrous, and indicated that, while a raising of silver would, in any case, drain away gold, the only effective means of attracting bullion and specie was a favourable balance of trade.

The weight of opposition in 1626 narrowly secured a reversal of the policy of debasement, and with the principal method of reducing the profits of silver exports thus precluded, the government next turned to a plan for exercising physical control over the instruments of that export. In the discussions of 1625–6 the culling and bullion trades had been severely criticized as the means by which the export of coin and treasure was facilitated.[4] In particular the so-called 'exchanging goldsmiths' were accused of 'interloping between the merchants importing bullion and the Mint' and were identified with 'the money-changers in Lombard Street [who] by culling, buying and selling at a dearer rate [than] the king's

[1] Gould, 'The Royal Mint', 248; S.P.D. Chas. I, 1/85, 2/17.
[2] Above, pp. 99–102.
[3] The relevant documents are in McCulloch, *Old and Scarce Tracts on Money*, pp. 121–41; W. A. Shaw, *Select Tracts and Documents Illustrative of English Monetary History* (1896), pp. 3–8. Also see S.P.D. Chas. I, 1/85, 2/17, 23/75, 36/102; Steele, 1, nos. 1488, 1491; Add. MSS. 34324, fols. 67, 68b.
[4] S.P.D. Chas. I, 2/17; Add. MSS. 34324, fol. 67; McCulloch, *Old and Scarce Tracts on Money*, p. 137.

Mint ... have been thereby exceeding great gainers and have sold it again to Dutchmen, by which means they have exhausted many millions of our treasure'.[1] To restrain this development, it was now proposed to re-establish the Royal Exchanger with a monopoly of dealings in foreign coin and bullion and the ability, consequently, to prevent the re-export of such commodities. The first patent was in fact issued (to the Earl of Holland) late in 1626, but the plans were held up by protests from the Mint officials, who claimed that they traditionally held the rights to the Office of Exchanger, and by a strong outburst from the Goldsmiths Company, backed by the City of London.[2] The government set out to satisfy the critics on some points, although not on the central principle, and by April 1627 it was indicated that the goldsmiths could continue their legitimate trade, that dealings in plate were not subject to restrictions, and that merchants were to be allowed to take their coin and bullion directly to the Mint if they wished.[3] On this basis the Privy Council decided to continue in its intention, and on 25 May a proclamation was published which reaffirmed all the statutes concerning melting, export, culling, the sacrosant nature of Mint prices, etc.; gave a monopoly of bullion dealings—apart from those at the Mint—to the Exchanger; and forbade goldsmiths to 'change, exchange, buy or broke, or drive the exchanging, selling or buying of any ... gold or silver in any ... foreign coin, or in bullion or ingots'. It was further made clear that these drastic measures were consciously designed to alleviate the general scarcity, the inactivity of the Mint, and the poor state of the circulating currency.[4]

However, this interference with the untrammelled operation of the bullion market could not proceed unhindered. The profits of the London dealers, the necessities of English merchants, and the feasibility of much international commerce were equally threatened by such control. The goldsmiths' protests continued strong and they succeeded in evading the regulations even though the Office had been opened in June—so that, in the autumn, the regulations were tightened up.[5] By 1628 the government was sufficiently on the defensive to publish a tract in justification of its actions,[6] and, when Parliament convened, the field of attack on the project broadened. In the past the major argument directed against the

[1] S.P.D. Chas. I, 65/74, 43/14.
[2] *Cambium Regis*, p. 28; S.P.D. Chas. I, 56/6, 65/39; Repertories of the Court of Aldermen, 41, fols. 85, 155.
[3] *Cambium Regis*, pp. 30–1.
[4] Steele, I, no. 1512; S.P.D. Chas. I, 64/41; Ruding, II, 151-2. For the planning of the scheme, see S.P.D. Chas. I, 64/41, 75; C.S.P.D. 1627–1628, p. 168.
[5] *Cambium Regis*, pp. 32–5; S.P.D. Chas. I, 79/41, 81/2, 81/18.
[6] *Cambium Regis: or the Office of His Majesty's Exchange Royal; Declaring and Justifying His Majesty's Right; and the Convenience thereof.*

official plan had been that it would discourage the merchant from importing bullion since to accept government prices would mean a reduced profit or even a loss. In the summer, when the goldsmiths and the merchants laid their case before the Commons, it was partly on this basis that the Office was declared a grievance 'both in creation and execution'.[1] The power of parliamentary opposition was sufficient to force a reappraisal of the situation and, once again, a project which was propounded in an attempt to alter international bullion flows more in England's favour was utterly defeated because informed opinion and interested groups concluded that its disadvantages outweighed its supposed benefits.[2]

Thus, after 1625, within the space of three years, attempts on the one hand to manipulate the gains and on the other to control the organization of the trade in coin and bullion had both failed. The government was left with only one course of action, which was tantamount to inaction: the attempted enforcement of the traditional bullion laws. For the rest of the period there was relative quiescence. In the early 1630's the bimetallic drain of silver was still apparent and there was another short-lived plan, which again emanated from the Mint, to raise silver.[3] On the other hand, the disparity between English and European ratios gradually diminished.[4] While there was already an incipient tendency for gold to flow to France, that country enhanced its gold coins in 1636 and the consequent increase in its ratio provoked a chronic outflow of gold from England, and a concomitant anxiety concerning this metal, which involved some punitive action against the exporters.[5] Indeed, the situation with regard to silver within a bimetallic system no longer gave any great cause for alarm. By 1640 debasement had become a policy advocated solely for the purposes of increasing royal revenue, and remote from the realities of the international movements of treasure.[6]

(iii) CONCLUSION

In the context of the early seventeenth century any alteration in bullion flows was likely to affect equally the amount or type of currency, and in an economy dependent upon ready supplies of cash and liquidity of assets

[1] S.P.D. Chas. I, 107/6; S.P.D. Chas. I (Addenda), 528/78; C.J. 1, 917–18.
[2] See the slighting references to the experiment in Mun, *England's Treasure*, pp. 56–7.
[3] Ruding, I, 386; *C.S.P.D. 1634–1635*, p. 31; S.P.D. Chas. I, 275/44, 461/74; S.P.D. Chas. I (Addenda), 528/84.
[4] Above, p. 168.
[5] Shaw, *A History of Currency*, pp. 69–70, 147–8; Violet, *An Humble Declaration*, pp. 2–4; Steele, I, no. 1712; P.C. 2/46, p. 28; S.P.D. Chas. I, 317/10, 339/9; Roe, pp. 1, 3–4; Maddison, *Great Britain's Remembrancer*, pp. 9–10. For the Star Chamber actions against transgressors of the statutes, see S.P.D. Chas. I, 362/103, 406/29; *C.S.P.D. 1636–1637*, pp. 338–9, 402; *C.S.P.D. 1637*, p. 218; *C.S.P.D. 1637–1638*, p. 50; Ruding, I, 389–90; Violet, pp. 5 ff.
[6] Above, pp. 127–8.

Monetary Instability, 1600–1642

it was natural that the authorities should be highly sensitive to such disturbances. On the whole, the supply of currency could be reduced by two phenomena: an unfavourable balance of trade, and a difference in the valuation of silver or gold between overseas lands and England. A sudden enhancement overseas of both sorts of coin might temporarily cause a net export of bullion from England; but in the main it was the relatively higher valuation of one metal in Europe which attracted coins of that metal out of English circulation and produced a counter-movement of the other into this country. The government was understandably sensitive when silver was being lost, because this had a disproportionate effect on the commercial structure. In 1618–23, for instance, the chronic lack of silver, arising from differing bullion ratios at home and abroad, had a marked depressive influence on the economy. When it is remembered that this coincided with an adverse trade balance, it becomes, as for other years during the period, easy to understand, and hard to condemn, an anxiety about the supply of money which frequently bordered on a neurosis. Yet singularly little positive action was taken by the government to reverse currency movements which it judged always to be harmful and sometimes disastrous. This was not through want of trying. But the time was one of constant maladjustment in a bimetallic system and the traditional remedy for such a situation, which was to enhance the undervalued coins and which had been easily done with gold in 1604 and 1611, was ruled out after 1611, when silver was the metal in question, by the fear of inflation and the vehement opposition whenever the step was suggested.

With some significant exceptions most observers compounded nearly all monetary problems in the outflow of silver, and accorded greatest importance to the possibilities of adjusting the tariffs placed on silver coins—although in the last resort it was decided that this course would prove too dangerous. Clearly, not every outbreak of anxiety after 1611 indicated a loss of silver: there was always the possibility that silver might remain in circulation while the output of silver coins at the Mint fell off. But it was frequently just such a decline which provided the immediate provocation for official discussions of monetary problems, and which explains why the Mint officials so often took the lead in sponsoring plans for an enhancement—for in that way they might have hoped for some increase in their declining incomes.

For contemporaries, the technical problems involved in any appraisal of international bullion flows were confused by the phenomenon of a real or imagined unfavourable balance of trade which would aggravate or seem to aggravate the effects of differential mint ratios. In addition there was a widely prevalent myopic view of the specie exports of particular trades—for example, that to the East Indies—which held them in disfavour no matter what their position within overall trends. In any case, most monetary developments were likely to bring into the open an almost hysterical fear of a scarcity of money which was always implicit in the official approach to many economic problems. In most cases it appears that this was a real and not an imagined problem, principally because of the frictions in the English economy which prevented the sort of speedy readjustment to monetary flows which was envisaged by classical economics. In this light 'mercantilism', as it is generally understood, more readily takes on the appearance of a defence-mechanism than an aggressive, fallacious and self-defeating hunt for treasure. Worried by a quantitative or qualitative loss of money, the authorities quite rightly wished to control the outflow before it produced chronic maladjustments in the economy.

Enhancement was ruled out after 1611 by fear of an inflation. Unable thus to make the export of silver unprofitable (the only really effective policy), and with the balance of payments clouded in statistical darkness whose penetration might still not have indicated any feasible course of action, the government was forced into intermittent attempts to control the bullion trade. These failed no less than had the efforts to stabilize the exchanges at par. In the last resort there could only be an attempted enforcement of the existing penal statutes against the export of, or interference with, the coinage. Yet effective readjustment had to await the operation of forces outside England's control. The agitation which marked so much of the monetary discussion of these years led to no changes in a relatively quiescent policy.

Thus, given the bimetallic drain of silver and its consequences, it is clear why the government, grimly on the defensive, was forced to rely upon direct attempts—however wrong-headed or fruitless—to interfere with the natural flow of specie. These piecemeal efforts came directly from an only too rational fear of deflation rather than from a self-defeating appetite for a specious form of wealth. But they have subsequently been stigmatized as 'bullionist', as reflecting a coherent but invalid economic policy solely directed to the accumulation of treasure. This latter-day construction, however, is a policy which contemporary writers and officials, in their real concern for the mundane realities of coinage and currency, would have found difficulty in recognizing as their own.

Part III

The Approach to Economics

No. II.

The Approach to Bombay.

9. ECONOMIC THOUGHT

There seems to be no need for yet another study of the technical writings of the early seventeenth century designed to place them in the context of an intellectual history of economic thought. Most modern attempts to do this are to a considerable extent misleading since, using the concept of a 'theory of international trade' in order to examine a body of writing to which it does not apply, they ignore the sort of short-term problems with which contemporaries were exclusively concerned. As a consequence, many modern commentaries involve interpretations, and even contortions, of contemporary opinion which are likely to be unjustified. The purpose here, even though explanation of a theory will not be confused with justification, will be to relate the views of the leading pamphleteers of the period much more closely to their environment,[1] and to attempt an appraisal of these views in the light of the frequently forgotten fact that they were the products, not of deductive reasoning, but of the impact on men's minds of economic problems which urgently demanded analysis and remedy. From the point of view of the present work it will be necessary to do this for only a few strains in contemporary economic thought.

Thus, in part the story is one of a heightened appreciation of England's changing economic position in an increasingly competitive world. As alternative sources of woollen textiles prospered in Europe and as the European economy began to forge new links with America, Asia and Africa, the market pressures towards diversification in England's international economic and commercial relationships were reflected in and augmented by a changing mode of thought on the role of the native textile industry and the types of trades in which Englishmen should indulge. This development came more towards the end of the period. Prior to the 1630's pamphleteers (although both tendencies were to some extent intermixed in their writings) concentrated largely on short-term problems posed by crises which principally involved the monetary system and the textile industry. And the bulk of their writings was therefore devoted to the interrelationships of currency and commerce. It is, for instance, almost impossible fully to understand the ideas of Misselden, Malynes and Mun apart from the depression of the early 1620's and its

[1] Some aspects of this question have already been ably dealt with in J. D. Gould, 'The Trade Crisis of the Early 1620's and English Economic Thought', *Journal of Economic History*, XV (1955), 121–33.

concomitant problems. Indeed, it is not surprising that there should be a strategic connexion between economic dislocation and the development of economic thought. On the one hand it is often only when a commercial mechanism breaks down that men set about the complex task of investigating its operations, and they do this with an eye to remedying its faults. On the other hand, commercial breakdowns provide the eager audience —both in official circles and in the world at large—which is calculated to stimulate such investigations.

Most of the ensuing discussion will be confined to the crisis of the early 1620's. However, it will also be recognized that some theories were formulated independently of this particular slump, that men's thoughts continued to turn to the longer view of English commerce, and that there were other years when an urgent environment accelerated economic discussion. Nevertheless, in the doctrines of the whole period the part played by the events of the years 1620–4 is crucial, and, significantly enough, the books generally considered to be representative of the period before the Civil War derive in the main from just these years.

(i) THE ECONOMICS OF CRISIS

The outstanding characteristics of the crisis of the early 1620's have already been described in detail. Currency manipulations abroad were aggravating a semi-permanent bimetallic loss of silver, which (because of that metal's normal preponderance as a medium of exchange) amounted to a reduction in the quantity of effective money. Moreover the manipulations, by decreasing continental silver prices, sharply reduced exports, stimulated imports, and therefore led, by way of declining exchange rates, to a heavy net outflow of specie. Internally, the slump in the textile industry, the general depression, and the high corn prices of 1622 and 1623, all combined to reduce economic activity to a catastrophic degree. The deflationary pressures, the poverty, the weak markets, the tightness of credit, and the nature of the widespread complaint, meant that contemporaries were easily led to the conclusion that England's principal economic weakness lay in an actual physical scarcity of currency. Only partly false, this opinion received superficial confirmation from the undoubted efflux of treasure at the time. Most commentators took it for granted that 'the want of money . . . is the first cause of the decay of trade';[1] and nearly all writers were concerned over the 'fearful effect that followeth the want of a convenient stock of money to maintain the prices, and to beat or maintain our home commerce'.[2] For them, con-

[1] Malynes, *The Maintenance of Free Trade*, p. 37. Cf. Misselden, *Free Trade*, pp. 10, 28.
[2] Maddison, *Great Britain's Remembrancer*, p. 15.

troversy only existed with respect to remedying a situation on whose existence and significance all were unanimous: the drain on England's monetary supplies. It is no coincidence that in the crisis of the early 1620's there occurred the well-known flowering of economic literature so largely concerned with monetary problems. For the setting within which some of the typical economic doctrines of the time were worked out was provided by a heightening of urgency in the same question which intermittently agitated the government throughout the period: 'why is England losing treasure, and how can it be regained?'

To some men the answer to this problem, and to the problem of wholesale unemployment, lay in the outflow of silver coin directly consequent upon the enhancements and debasements which demoralized some European currency systems after 1618. Of this group Edward Misselden in his first book, *Free Trade, or, the Means to make trade flourish* (1622), is perfectly representative. Misselden, in this comprehensive analysis of the decay of trade, which adduced ten causes of the 'decay of merchandize', concluded that the want of money (the principal cause) 'is apparently sensible in the drapery of the kingdom . . . and in all the other trades . . . and hath begot that great and general damp and deadness in all the trades of the kingdom, which we unhappily feel at this day'. The principal reason for this loss of coin, he felt, was 'the undervaluation of his Majesty's coin, to that of our neighbour countries', which was produced by European currency manipulation 'whereby abundance of money is drawn into the mints of those countries'.[1] Thus, in his first book, Misselden put most emphasis on the direct loss of silver resulting from natural or contrived maladjustments in Europe's primitive monetary system. For a generation after 1611 this phenomenon provoked plans to enhance the English silver coinage in order to remedy the situation by lowering the Mint ratio. Misselden, therefore, was by no means original in proposing that the valuation of silver and silver coins be raised as a solution for England's economic ills.[2]

Any such proposal had to be justified against the traditional objections that currency manipulations of this sort would be nullified by a vicious circle of retaliatory enhancements throughout Europe and that, in any case, it would produce an internal inflation whose disadvantages would outweigh any beneficial effects it might have on bullion flows. Misselden's answer on the first score was somewhat lame: he sidestepped the main issue by recommending the enforcement of the Statutes of Employment —which were inefficacious and in any case applied only to aliens. But his

[1] *Free Trade*, pp. 7–10, 18, 28–9.
[2] *Ibid.* pp. 103–4, 106–7. For other plans throughout the period, see above, pp. 169–71.

answer to the second point was more cogent and more interesting. He advocated that some protection be given to landlords and creditors by a legal stipulation that existing rents and contracts should be paid at the original *intrinsic* values of the sums involved. His main argument, however, turned on the *advantages* of a price rise: there would be sufficient compensation for the economic friction 'in the plenty of money and quickening of trade in every man's hand', while 'he that buys dear shall sell dear'. So much were Misselden's thoughts influenced by the prevailing deflation and fear of monetary scarcity that he was able to conclude his arguments on a distinctly inflationary note: 'it is much better for the kingdom to have things dear with plenty of money, whereby men may live in their several callings, than to have things cheap with want of money, which now makes every man complain.'

Misselden's analysis in 1622, therefore, was a purely monetary one, and the policy which he advocated looked solely to the direct monetary effects of enhancement, not as has been claimed, to the effects on exchange rates and export prices.[1] As far as it went it was perfectly applicable to a situation where there was a bimetallic outflow of silver. But, like many of his contemporaries, he had been misled by the principal characteristics of the depression (lack of effective demand, pressure on prices, and credit restriction) into thinking that a loss, and physical shortage, of ready money was the prime cause of the accumulation of economic difficulties which they erroneously compounded together as 'a want of money'. Such an approach did not explain, nor could it hope to rectify, the failure of overseas demand which really underlay England's plight. As has been seen, European currency manipulations, by undercutting silver prices in England's principal markets, did in fact play a real and important part in the crisis.[2] But Misselden, although he knew of the connexions between manipulations and exchange rates, between export prices and the exchanges, and between enhancements and a lag in the subsequent price rise,[3] never undertook the next analytical step of connecting the enhancements and debasements with the prosperity of the textile industry and the balance of payments, through the influence of such manipulations on the prices and profitability of exports and imports. He had seized on to the right phenomenon—but for the wrong reason.

Misselden may have confused the cause of the slump with its principal manifestations, and a bimetallic with a net outflow of treasure; but from this confusion, and hence from the depression of the early 1620's with its

---

[1] De Roover, p. 270.   [2] Above, ch. 4.
[3] *The Circle of Commerce*, pp. 17, 25, 39, 102, 107–11.

own intermixture of real and monetary factors, sprang much that is representative of mercantilist writing. Misselden, by comparison with some others of his contemporaries, was poorly equipped for a detailed analysis of the prevailing economic environment. When, in 1623, he wrote *The Circle of Commerce* he shifted his emphasis and found in an unfavourable balance of trade the universal cause of all economic ills.[1] His theories, however, remained superficial, and his presentation was much inferior to Mun's. Nevertheless, the continuing stimulus to thought, the fear of a loss of treasure because of its deflationary associations, remained as his guiding principle.

Gerard Malynes, a bitter antagonist of Misselden, was equally representative of another school of thought which, while agreeing that the cardinal factor was a scarcity of money, interpreted the fundamental cause of the loss as a low rate of exchange. For Malynes the didactic role of the crisis of the early 1620's was negligible. It merely afforded him an opportunity of applying to a new situation analytical tools which he had forged almost a generation previously. His views as exemplified in *A Treatise of the Canker of England's Commonwealth* (1602) were substantially those he held—unaltered and unaugmented—through an ubiquitous career marked by a prolific output.[2] His approach to the problems of the depression was therefore coloured by his permanent articles of economic faith, and these must be dealt with first.

Fully appreciating the nature of the mechanism of specie export points, Malynes took his stand, in all appraisals of bullion flows, on the dogmatic assertion that always and on every occasion the prime and sufficient cause of an export of specie was an exchange rate below par: 'If the exchange with us here be low, so that more will be given for our money being carried in specie, than by bill of exchange can be had, then our money is transported . . . for in truth gain is the cause of exportation of our monies.'[3] Further, in his view, there was a semi-permanent tendency to undervalue English currency in this manner, so that the rate of exchange was sufficiently low to provide an almost constant stimulus to the export of specie. This situation, he claimed, perennially arose as foreign currencies were enhanced without a proportionate decrease in their external valuations. Since the exchanges were so often out of line with the internal valuations of European coin, it was no wonder that England was drained of its money. 'The coins of other nations', he wrote, 'are much enhanced beyond the seas and overvalued unto us in exchange, whereby our monies

---

[1] Below, p. 216.
[2] See the entry in the *Dictionary of National Biography*.
[3] *A Treatise of the Canker*, p. 34. Cf. *The Maintenance of Free Trade*, p. 14.

are become undervalued, and therefore continually transported in specie or bullion.'[1]

Contrary to some views of his principles, Malynes realized perfectly well that rates of exchange depended upon demand and supply, that they varied, in his words, 'according to scarcity and plenty of monies to be taken and delivered'.[2] But he included in these 'monies', funds delivered or taken up for speculative purposes: 'Exchange doth rise and fall according to scarcity or plenty of money, proceeding of the few or many deliverers and takers thereof, in the course of traffic, not by commodities only, *but also by exchange devised upon monies, in nature of merchandise.*'[3] Building on this, he held the unshakeable belief that 'it is an easy matter for these bankers with the money to rule the same [the exchanges] at their pleasure, from place to place, causing ... ebbings and flowings'.[4] The chronic outflow of bullion, he declared, was provoked by a conspiracy of European financiers to keep the English currency permanently undervalued, for 'the great exchangers or bankers invent all the means to compass the [exchange] and to rule the course thereof at their pleasure ... [and] the exchange of England is overruled by the general current'.[5] The remedy at hand, on this view, was patently simple. Since the existence of exchange rates below the intrinsic value of English currency was the sole reason for the export of coin, this loss, Malynes constantly affirmed, could only be prevented by an official enforcement of exchange transactions at par value for English money. His remedy was always, therefore, some means of exchange control by governmental fiat to ensure that no transaction took place 'under the true value of our monies, or par pro pari'—in which circumstances, on his reasoning, there could be no profit in exporting specie.[6]

Apart from the possible connexion with an efflux of treasure, there was a second reason for Malynes's abhorrence of an undervalued exchange. For he believed that a rate of exchange below par shifted the terms of trade against England, and he inherited the sixteenth-century prejudice against selling cheap and buying dear. His arguments for this belief ran as follows:[7] the exchanges 'overruled' commodities in that the prices of the

---

[1] Hargrave MSS. 321, p. 41. Cf. *A Treatise of the Canker*, pp. 98–9; *The Maintenance of Free Trade*, pp. 31–2, 82–3, 88–9; *The Centre of the Circle*, pp. 12, 28.

[2] Add. MSS. 34324, fol. 165. Cf. *The Maintenance of Free Trade*, p. 36; *A Treatise of the Canker*, p. 28.

[3] *Lex Mercatoria*, Part 3, ch. 10 (my italics).

[4] *A Treatise of the Canker*, p. 28.

[5] *The Maintenance of Free Trade*, pp. 36–7. Cf. *A Treatise of the Canker*, pp. 20, 31–3.

[6] Hargrave MSS. 321, p. 42; *A Treatise of the Canker*, pp. 99, 110 ff.; *The Maintenance of Free Trade*, pp. 14, 82 ff.; *The Centre of the Circle*, ch. V.

[7] *A Treatise of the Canker*, pp. 35, 53–4, 109; *The Maintenance of Free Trade*, pp. 25 ff.; *The Centre of the Circle*, ch. III; Add. MSS. 34324, fol. 163.

latter depended on the levels of the former, so that as the exchanges fell English exports were 'undersold', since merchants could now afford to reduce their sale prices, and, conversely, imports rose in price.[1] In addition, Malynes claimed that the initial loss of bullion occasioned by the exchange undervaluation exerted pressures, through changing monetary supplies, which reduced English prices and increased prices in the areas to which the bullion went. Another point on which he was quite vehement was that the shortage of money at home and the ease of borrowing on bills of exchange without surety encouraged 'young merchants' (merchants in the early stages of their career trading without much operating capital) to operate wildly on credit and hence to force down export prices by 'unloading' their stocks when their debts fell due.[2] Malynes also claimed, with some reason, that enhancements overseas produced commodity returns at high prices,[3] while in any case the gains on the direct export of money reduced the purchase, and therefore the prices, of exports. Malynes awarded such an important role to the terms of trade that he claimed that the inflation consequent upon the influx of American silver was, in itself, not significant: the 'true ground must be by making a comparison of the enhancing of the price of commodities of one country, with the price of the commodities of other countries'. Hence the significant investigation is 'whether [countries] do proportionably participate of the general abundance or plenty of gold and silver found nowadays'. He concluded that England did not.[4]

Malynes considered all these tendencies to be disastrous because he identified unfavourable terms of trade with an 'overbalance' of trade. This, he repeatedly emphasized, arose solely from disparate international prices: 'This overbalancing consisteth properly in the price of commodities and not in the quantity or quality.'[5] 'Overbalance', however, was not merely a synonym for 'adverse terms of trade'; it implied a positive loss of treasure and was therefore comparable to an unfavourable

---

[1] This is comparable, of course, to the effects of a modern devaluation. For the long-established recognition that exchange rates affected prices in this way, see the 1564 Memorandum (*T.E.D.* III, 347–50) which argued that an exchange below par encouraged merchants to accept abroad a smaller amount of precious metal in coin than was originally expended by them to purchase the exports in England, because they gained on the return by bills of exchange. The Memorandum claimed that England's loss on commodities was precisely measured by the undervaluation of the exchange; Malynes agreed with this view.

[2] For Malynes's strictures on young merchants who 'run by exchange upon bills to maintain their trade, paying great interest for money, which they cannot take up at use upon single bond, as they can do by a bill of exchange, without sureties', and who, he thought, sold English cloth too rashly, see *The Maintenance of Free Trade*, p. 23; Add. MSS. 34324, fol. 163; *A Treatise of the Canker*, p. 53.

[3] See above, pp. 89–92.

[4] *England's View*, pp. 78, 104, 109, 118.

[5] *A Treatise of the Canker*, pp. 12, 17, 39–40. Cf. *The Maintenance of Free Trade*, p. 22.

balance of trade as that concept was used by Mun. A loss of treasure was involved, on Malynes's view, because with higher import prices, more *in value* would be purchased by England, and with lower export prices, less *total income* would be derived from sales. Malynes's writings were quite straightforward on this point; it was, he claimed, unfavourable terms of trade 'wherein chiefly consisteth the aforesaid overbalancing, which is the cause of inequality, we giving in effect both money and commodities to have foreign commodities for them'.[1] Within strict limits, of course, the theory that unfavourable terms of trade lead to an unfavourable balance of payments might well be true. But the necessary assumption is that demand be inelastic. If, for instance, demand for English textiles had been perfectly inelastic—had an increase in selling price made no difference to the amount sold—then it would indeed have been true that England was losing income in direct proportion to the low price of her cloth. If, on the whole, the demands for both imports and exports are inelastic then, up to a point, the higher the price of exports and the lower the price of imports the more favourable will be the balance of trade. Malynes certainly seems to have known this and to have made the necessary assumptions of actual inelasticity. This especially applied to his consideration of exports: 'Our home commodities being also so needful, and of continual request, that at all times they are most vendible.'[2] And he reserved special vituperation for the sale of English cloth at low prices. On general grounds Malynes's view of an overbalance of trade is much more logical and consistent than some modern writers are prepared to allow.[3]

Thus it is plain that in all circumstances Malynes considered a low rate of exchange disadvantageous in the extreme. In this he was not alone, for men commonly confused the means by which the export of specie was rendered profitable with the cause of that export. William Sanderson, for instance, who was with Malynes on the committee which considered exchange problems in 1622, wrote a manuscript treatise on the subject[4] which to a considerable extent appropriated some of Malynes's ideas and even whole passages from *A Treatise of the Canker*—although some parts of Sanderson's work are undoubtedly original. He was designated by James I to choose the officers for the Royal Exchanger in an abortive attempt to control the exchanges in 1622.[5] But Malynes was almost alone

[1] *A Treatise of the Canker*, pp. 3–4, 53–5. Cf. *England's View*, pp. 15, 149; *The Maintenance of Free Trade*, pp. 5, 22.
[2] *A Treatise of the Canker*, p. 106. Cf. ibid. pp. 49, 117–18; *England's View*, pp. 139 ff.
[3] See, for instance, de Roover, pp. 246–9.
[4] Lans. MSS. 768.
[5] S.P.D. Jas. I, 131/105. For other manuscript works by Sanderson, see S.P.D. Jas. I, 140/61; Cambridge University Library, MS. Gg. v. 8.

in adducing such a comprehensive published version of this theory. Sir Ralph Maddison was his only rival in this respect. In *Great Britain's Remembrancer*, which he wrote in 1640 and augmented for re-publication in 1655, Maddison gave lip service to the more common view of the balance of trade. But in addition, and at greater length, he claimed that English currency was undervalued by exchange relative to the enhancement of coins abroad, that European bankers controlled and directed the exchange, that the undervaluation was the efficient cause of the export of specie, that the low rates of exchange shifted the terms of trade against England, that such adverse trade terms produced an 'overbalance' of trade and a loss of specie, and that the only effective remedy was to stabilize exchange rates at par by official intervention.[1] Maddison, according to his own account, played a crucial part in initiating the consideration of the low exchange in 1622,[2] and he, like Sanderson and Malynes, sat on the first committee. In many ways, and especially during the Interregnum, Maddison was an important writer on economics and a quasi-official government adviser,[3] but it is most likely that he learned most of his doctrines from Malynes and they do not differ from the latter's to any significant extent. Before we can appraise Malynes's theories properly, it will be helpful to consider his role in the crisis of the early 1620's.

The depression afforded Malynes a magnificent opportunity for presenting his theories in the highest official circles. With treasure flowing out and the exchanges obviously below specie export point he was able, in the words of an acrimonious antagonist, to revive 'an old soiled project of his, of 22 years' growth',[4] and to explain, at least to his own satisfaction, all England's economic ills in terms of an 'undervalued exchange'. His first book dealing with the crisis, *The Maintenance of Free Trade*, was provoked in 1622 by Misselden's *Free Trade*. In the latter, Misselden had insultingly dismissed Malynes's theories when dealing with the desired aims of getting and keeping money:[5]

neither of which can be done by that par of exchange, which is now again in agitation, and hath taken more than twenty years to bring it to perfection. Wherein . . . there is neither parity nor purity. For it is not the rate of exchange but the value of monies here low, elsewhere high, which cause their exportations: nor do the exchanges, but the plenty or scarcity of monies cause their values.

[1] For all this, see *Great Britain's Remembrancer*, pp. 8–9, 13, 14, 17, 20, 21–4, and *passim*.
[2] S.P.D. Chas. I, 14/18. See Appendix B.
[3] See S.P.D. Jas. I, 131/106; Add. MSS. 34324, fols. 173, 179; S.P.D. Chas. I, 461/74; C.S.P.D. 1649–1650, pp. 284, 456; S.P.D. Interregnum, 16/106.
[4] Misselden, *The Circle of Commerce*, p. 92.   [5] *Free Trade*, p. 104.

Malynes returned the attack and admonished Misselden for failing to handle correctly the 'predominant' part of trade, i.e. the exchanges. He criticized Misselden's views of the importance of enhancements in determining the flow of bullion and specie, on the grounds that no analysis was valid, and no remedy could be satisfactory, which left out of account the need for exchange at par:

The efficient cause of the transportation of our monies is gain, and this gain ariseth by the undervaluation of our monies, in regard of the enhancing and overvaluation of foreign coin; so that the cause is extrinsic and comprised under the said exchange of monies, and not intrinsic... thereupon it followeth, that neither difference of weight, fineness of standard, proportion between gold and silver, or the proper valuation of monies, can be any true causes of the exportation of our monies: so long as a due course is holden in exchange, which is founded thereupon.[1]

In Malynes's view, and to this there was little opposition, the chronic depression stemmed from a loss of treasure. For the explanation of this, and of all the concomitant economic troubles, he had his pre-formulated framework, into which he now fitted the new situation. Since 'all the ... causes of the decay of trade are almost all of them comprised in ... the want of money, whereof we find the abuse of exchange to be the efficient cause', so the fixing of exchange rates at par by proclamation 'is the only mean and way to restore England's wealth by importation of money and bullion, advancing the price of our native commodities, and to prevent the transportation of our monies: and all other remedies are defective'.[2] Like every important writer of these years Malynes propagated his theories not *in vacuo*, but in an attempt to explain an efflux of bullion which, rightly or wrongly, was seen as the 'cause' of a slump because that slump appeared as a deflation, i.e. as a 'scarcity of money'.

Besides publishing *Consuetudo, Vel, Lex Mercatoria* in 1622 and *The Centre of the Circle of Commerce* in 1623, Malynes was also occupied in bringing his views more directly to the notice of the authorities. He took an active part in the controversy on bullion flows and exchange rates which commenced at the government's behest early in 1622 and moved into the meetings of the commission on trade later in that year.[3] In part

[1] *The Maintenance of Free Trade*, pp. 82–3. He had written almost the exactly the same thing twenty years before (*A Treatise of the Canker*, p. 99). Cf. a similar passage in the report of the 1600 commission (on which he sat) (S.P.D. Eliz., 279/97).
[2] *The Maintenance of Free Trade*, pp. 89, 104–5. Cf. Hargrave MSS. 321, p. 43: the enforcement of par, wrote Malynes, 'will ... restore England's wealth, and cause importation of bullion and monies as in times past, and prevent further transportation ... and also advance the price of our home commodities and abate the price of foreign commodities'.
[3] Above, pp. 186–9, and below, Appendix B.

Economic Thought

the vitriolic debate with Misselden, which was carried on into 1623 with the latter's *The Circle of Commerce* and his own book of that year, must have stemmed from the officially inspired clash of doctrines. In any case Malynes was obviously a leading member of the original committee, whose report coincided exactly with his views and clashed directly with those of Mun.[1] And he wrote subsequent summaries of the points at issue, when his theories were attacked by Mun's group, and assumed ultimate responsibility for continuing the paper debate with Mun himself.[2] Nothing of fresh theoretical interest emerges from these manuscripts which cannot be gleaned from the published material already described. Indeed, at the time of the crisis Malynes used several passages which he included in his official memoranda to compose sections of *The Maintenance of Free Trade*.[3] Malynes's theories had long been available in print; the crisis merely meant that he was led to state certain parts of his general thesis with increased emphasis. Thus, since his antagonists relied so much upon the balance of payments as an analytical tool, he had to assert the more plainly his own version of an overbalance of trade.[4] Further, given his ideas on the terms of trade, he could not but find fault with those who were already advocating lower prices as a competitive measure. In his view, to attempt to reduce cloth prices in order to increase sales and in that way redress the unfavourable trade balance would be ineffective and disastrous:[5] the only true remedy was a high exchange. In the following appraisal of his writings it will be seen that Malynes's views had an ancient pedigree, but were, in the context of the early 1620's, hopelessly archaic.

The bulk of Malynes's writings, like Misselden's, concentrated on the mechanism by which it was thought bullion and specie flowed overseas. In paying so much attention to the specie export point, however, he did not have even the meagre satisfaction of fully appreciating the bimetallic maladjustments rife at the time. In general, of course, Malynes mistook the means by which basic factors caused movements of specie for the cause itself. Against his view that the rate of exchange was an extraneous and independent arbiter of bullion flows, terms of trade, and the balance of trade, Mun's logical arguments still hold good. The rate of exchange is a price, and is determined by the demand for and supply of currencies, i.e. the balance of payments. In this determination the normal market

[1] Above, pp. 186–7.
[2] Add. MSS. 34324, fols. 159–62, 163–4, 165, 167. See below, Appendix B.
[3] Cf. Add. MSS. 34324, fols. 161, 163, 164 and *The Maintenance of Free Trade*, pp. 91–2, 22–5, 89–90, respectively.
[4] Below, pp. 216–7.
[5] See, for example, *The Maintenance of Free Trade*, pp. 46–7, 56, 75–6; Add. MSS. 34324, fols. 161, 164, 165, 167.

forces are, over the long run, much stronger than the speculative: manipulation of rates of exchange can normally only be effective over the short run. It is, in any case, useless to propose fixing the exchange rate at par unless there is an effective and comprehensive control of demand and/or supply. As twentieth-century experience has taught, official speculation can only counter very short-term fluctuations; any wish to stabilize exchange rates over the long run needs a complicated but efficient network of control which must take into account the real causes of normal variations in the rates. Malynes did not appreciate this point—although many of his opponents did to some extent[1]—because he did not appreciate that an exchange rate below specie export point was not the cause of an outflow of coin, but merely a facilitating prerequisite; and both were produced by the same causes. It was consistent, but entirely misleading, for him to claim that as long as the exchange was at par no bullion would flow out, whatever the variations in coins or their valuations.[2] Factors such as these, by putting market pressure on exchange rates, would tend to alter those rates, and an official proclamation as to exchange rates alone could only lead to direct export of specie or a circumvention of the law. Also, it is difficult to see how a mere proclamation could have secured the 'par pro pari' if, as Malynes claimed, international banking houses were still able to dispose of the funds with which they ruled European exchange rates.[3]

Quite apart from all this, Malynes was not consistent when he came to consider the reverse case. Although he acknowledged the influence of specie export points his analytical insight, such as it was, failed him when it came to specie import points: he disliked a high exchange almost as much as a low one. Par, for him, was economically the optimum level and ethically the prime objective; with Maddison he believed that 'only a mediocrity is best'.[4] A high exchange, Malynes claimed, would not cause an import of money because of 'the toleration of the monies to go current far above their value beyond the seas'. But if a true par is exceeded, then, on his own reasoning, such a 'toleration' is irrelevant—gain is still to be had by shipping specie out of these countries. He also had some

---

[1] See Add. MSS. 34324, fols. 171, 155–7; Misselden, *Free Trade*, pp. 104–5; *The Circle of Commerce*, p. 110; Mun, *England's Treasure*, pp. 41–2; Vaughan, pp. 96–7. Their arguments were: if the exchange is raised to par by proclamation then takers in England will find their transactions less profitable. Some will therefore cease business and this decrease in the supply of foreign currencies (by bills) will oblige the deliverers to send specie abroad (or, it may be added, establish a clandestine rate below par in order to obtain bills of exchange).

[2] *The Maintenance of Free Trade*, pp. 82–3.

[3] Cf. Robinson's plan to post agents with abundant funds at 'Paris, Antwerp, Amsterdam, and in such like principal places of trade' (S.P.D. Interregnum, 9/64); *Certain Proposals* (1652), pp. 15–18.

[4] Maddison, *Great Britain's Remembrancer*, p. 21.

insubstantial theories that a high exchange turned the terms of trade against England: by encouraging exchange transactions for profit and lessening the purchase of English goods; by forcing merchants to return goods to England at high prices; by producing rash sales of exports owing to the cost of borrowing as measured by the high exchange.[1] He surely ought to have realized that this high exchange ('high' from England's point of view) was, in fact, a 'low exchange' when seen from the viewpoint of European countries. What in the case of England had stimulated an outflow of bullion and provoked unfavourable terms of trade should, when it applied to other lands, have had the same effects for them. On Malynes's own arguments a high exchange should have produced an inflow of treasure and favourable terms of trade for England.

It is difficult to say, for all periods, how much truth lay in Malynes's claim that the English currency was permanently undervalued. Given the complexity and confusion of monetary systems at the time, the determination of what parity was could be an extremely controversial process, and Malynes's antagonists always claimed that he either invented or vastly exaggerated the undervaluation.[2] However, for various reasons it is distinctly possible that the exchange as far as England was concerned was frequently below parity. Firstly, after 1611 there was a tendency to lose silver for gold. Since exchange transactions were made according to and with the silver coinage, the pressure to export silver would initially force down the rate of exchange. Ultimately, however, full-weight silver coins disappeared and exchange rates would depend on the actual (light) coins in circulation: *effective* par would be below Mint par: English money would be worth less than its supposed intrinsic content because, in fact, the coins remaining in circulation contained less silver than they ought. Secondly, in the circumstances of the time, since the high legal and physical risk of exporting bullion substantially increased the cost of shipment, i.e. widened the gap between the specie points, adjustments of international balances and flows of purchasing power were more likely to take place by means of hectic fluctuations in exchange rates, than through shipments of coin and bullion. This meant, in England's case, that the exchange might appear dangerously below par while, in fact, it was still above the specie export point.[3] The exchange would have to suffer an exceptional decline below par, by nineteenth-century standards, before it became profitable to ship specie instead of buying bills. Finally, there is no doubt that the crisis of the early 1620's caused a sufficiently

[1] *A Treatise of the Canker*, pp. 39, 40–1, 43–4, 47–8; *England's View*, p. 190.
[2] It was said that merchants 'of great worth and experience' disagreed with each other as to whether or not there was a deviation from par (Vaughan, p. 103).
[3] Such a situation is described in Robinson, *England's Safety*, pp. 52–4.

sharp fall to move exchange rates below the specie export point, and
Malynes's insistent warnings at the time were in a long line of such
anxieties; indeed, it was only to be expected that economic crisis and
exchange depreciation should have been virtually conterminous.[1]

It remains to consider the significance of Malynes's approach to the
terms of trade.[2] As was seen, he persistently advocated buying cheap and
selling dear: any failure to do so, he imagined, would ruin the economy,
and some of his angriest invective was hurled at the advocates of lower
textile prices during the depression after 1619. At the basis of this belief
lay the assumption that England, as long as her cloth was of a high
quality, could, within reason, demand what price she liked for it. In this,
as in other matters, Malynes was the heir of sixteenth-century economic
thought. A hundred years before he wrote, England faced a seller's
market for textiles in Europe; and when, in the late 1550's, the export of
cloth fell off, the decline in total value was not too serious[3]—which
suggests an inelastic demand. Certainly, it took some little time for the
continental textile industries to provide significant competition for
English cloth. Combined with the belief that England had a virtual
monopoly of wool suitable for standard textiles, this led to strong claims
that English textiles had a distinct scarcity value.[4] Since, in the sixteenth
century, it was also a commonplace of policy that England should buy
cheap and sell dear it can be no surprise that Malynes's theories were
often remarkably foreshadowed. For example, by William Cholmeley
in 1553, with respect to the overbalance: merchants 'sell our English
cloth as good cheap in Antwerp and in Spain at this time as ever they
did . . . and pay double for all things that they bring us thence. So that
the cloth which they carry out will not answer in value those things
which are yearly brought into this realm.' Or in the memorandum on
exchanges of 1564: 'if the exchange . . . may be kept up, as the proportionated values of monies of either realm doth duly require, then will the
price of English wares so rise beyond the seas, and the price of strange
wares so fall in England, that our overvalue gained thereby in our interchange of merchandise will bring in or save a great deal of treasure that
the falling of the exchange too low doth defraud and spoil us of.'[5] But by
the early seventeenth century, irrespective of the situation under the

[1] See, for the sixteenth century, de Roover, pp. 200 ff.; Fisher, 'Commercial Trends', 105.
[2] For a similar analysis of Malynes's views and their origins, see Gould, 'The Trade Crisis of the Early 1620's and English Economic Thought', 127-9.
[3] Fisher, 'Commercial Trends', 104.
[4] *A Discourse of the Commonweal of this Realm of England* (ed. E. Lamonde, 1893), pp. 46-7, 51, 92; T.E.D. III, 134-5, 139, 141.
[5] T.E.D. III, 140, 355.

Tudors, the economic reality was very different from that envisaged by writers such as Malynes. England was only one among many suppliers of wool; any differential cost-price advantages she might have had were being eliminated; and the manufacture of woollen textiles was booming on the Continent.[1]

The complaints of foreign competition which persisted throughout our period bear witness to the fact that England now had to subsist in an entirely new world. Of this Malynes, along with those like him who claimed that 'all is one, to import more than transport, or to buy dear and sell cheap',[2] was blithely unaware. There *were* men who more realistically argued that lower prices were essential and even that the effects of a low exchange on the terms of trade would be beneficial for English trade.[3] But Malynes ignored, or was unable to appreciate, the new alignments of demand in European markets which would have made a complete mockery of his plans to raise exchange rates and increase English export prices. Few theories could have been less appropriate to the economic conditions of the early 1620's. Malynes was a man living well beyond his time, for he took his sixteenth-century ideas, pristine and uncompromised, into the controversial arena at the very moment when it first became disastrously clear that England was facing a buyer's market.

From the economic debates in which Malynes played such an important role, there also emerged a new formulation of another theory concerning the flow of bullion. In the history of economic thought Thomas Mun is usually credited with the significant statement of the 'mercantilist' theory that the balance of trade[4] alone determines net bullion movements, and that all other factors are entirely subordinate to it. These views were fully worked out in *England's Treasure by Foreign Trade*. Published posthumously in 1664, its date of composition has been uncertain, although in the past it has normally been attributed to the 1630's. But it is now clear that the most important parts of Mun's theoretical analysis derive directly from the 1622-3 controversy on treasure and the exchanges. He was a member of the second committee which, in spring, 1622, sharply criticized Malynes's theory as to an independent exchange undervaluation: 'as the balance of trade swayeth,' they wrote, 'so necessarily and so only must the exportation and importation of treasure proportion itself for the evening of the said balance.' After the initial clash Mun submitted a

---
[1] Above, pp. 137-42.
[2] Add. MSS. 10113, fol. 159.
[3] Robinson, *England's Safety*, p. 55; below, pp. 222.
[4] I shall often use the phrase 'balance of trade' synonymously with 'balance of payments'. Contemporary writers were often well aware of the importance of invisible items.

further series of memoranda to the trade commission in 1623.[1] In these manuscripts are the arguments, the technical advice, and much of the wording which comprise the significant portions of the later book—so that there can be no doubt that the originals were used in compiling the book, and that the views found there were first formulated in response to the problems posed by the prevailing crisis.[2]

Mun's theories are sufficiently well known, but their development becomes more comprehensible when seen in this light. For, like Misselden and Malynes, although his analysis led to entirely different conclusions, Mun was aiming at an explanation of, and remedy for, the export of treasure which was identified with England's *malaise*. In this sense, as has been already indicated, some of the most representative of 'mercantilist' doctrines were reactions to a particular economic situation; more than this, they were not initially indicative of a desire to amass bullion, but of a wish to explain how its loss was brought about.

As late as 1621, to judge by his opinions in 1623, Mun's approach was hesitant and confused. In his defence of the East India Company against the charge that it drained England of bullion,[3] he briefly examined 'the true causes of those evils which we seek to chase away'. He then attributed the export of treasure to a variety of causes. For instance, like Misselden in 1622, he blamed European currency manipulation for a (bimetallic) loss: 'by which courses . . . there is greater cause given of exportation of monies of this realm'—although he was less sanguine than Misselden concerning the dangers of enhancement by England (inflation and a fresh round of retributive enhancements abroad). Like Malynes, on the other hand, he saw the low exchange as a cause of the bullion efflux, criticized the 'abuse of the exchange', and complained that 'the exchange is . . . become rather a trade for some great monied men, than a furtherance and accommodation of real trade to merchants'. In addition, he blamed the drain of money on to the neglect of their patriotic duties by subjects of the Crown who exported full-weight coin, the nefarious activities of goldsmiths, and the non-enforcement of the Statutes of Employment. Finally, his main reasons for the efflux were the particular lack of mercantile expertise and a general excess of imports over exports, which cannot otherwise come to pass, than with a manifest impoverish-

[1] See Add. MSS. 34324, fols. 155-7, 169, 171-2, 175, 177-8; below, Appendix B.
[2] See B. E. Supple, 'Thomas Mun and the Commercial Crisis, 1623', *Bulletin of the Institute of Historical Research*, XXVII (1954), 91-4. Parts of the book were, on the basis of internal evidence, obviously written at a somewhat later date (J. D. Gould, 'The Date of England's Treasure by Forraign Trade', *Journal of Economic History*, XV (1955), 160-1), but the important theoretical departures are all to be found, in embryo or *in extenso* in the 1623 manuscript.
[3] *A Discourse of Trade from England unto the East Indies*.

ing of the commonwealth'.[1] This was a confused amalgam of 'reasons' quite typical of much contemporary writings on the subject and analytically trivial when compared with Mun's other work. Yet within two years he had explicitly rejected the possibility that any of these factors, other than the last, had any influence on treasure movements—and had proceeded to erect his theories on the balance of trade into the most influential economic doctrine before Adam Smith. This fundamental change in economic doctrine was the direct result of the events of the 1620's and the controversies which they stimulated.

In 1622 Mun sat on two committees, both of whose reports urged that the balance of trade was the sole effective arbiter of net flows of bullion and specie. Thus, the committee investigating the decay of trade held that 'the most important remedy [for the scarcity of money] is to provide against the overbalance of trade, for if the vanity and superfluity of our importation be greater than the exportation of our home commodities will bear, the stock of this kingdom must need be wasted, for money must necessarily turn the scale'.[2] In 1623, debating the question with Malynes, he produced his own coherent body of doctrine. Having to answer the thesis that there was a 'spontaneous' undervaluation of English currency by exchange, he demonstrated by logical steps that import surpluses cause 'plenty of money to be delivered by exchange' (i.e. an increased demand for foreign currency), that *this*, in its turn, produces the undervaluation, and that 'where our monies are undervalued in exchange, to those particular places are our monies exported'—and then only in amounts sufficient to make up the trade deficit. This would happen, he claimed, 'although the rate of our exchange be high or low or at par or put down altogether'; and his conclusion was one which he continually urged against Malynes's views: that the mechanisms of international indebtedness were impersonal, 'that it is not gain but it is necessity which is the efficient cause to carry away our money.' In the same vein, in his subsequent book, he countered Malynes's claim that European bankers ruled the exchanges: 'I have lived long in Italy, where the greatest banks and bankers of Christendom do trade, yet could I never see nor hear, that they did, or were able to rule the price of exchange by confederacy, but still the plenty or scarcity of money in the course of trade did always overrule them and made the exchanges to run at high or low rates.'[3]

Thus Mun was able to show that exchange fluctuations merely reflected

[1] For all this, see *ibid*. pp. 42–5; cf. pp. 5–6.
[2] S.P.D. Jas. I, 131/55. The other committee answered Malynes's group on the question of exchange rates: Add. MSS. 34324, fols. 155–7.
[3] Add. MSS. 34324, fol. 169; *England's Treasure*, p. 51.

changes in the demand for and supply of currencies. In a memorandum of April 1623 he wrote:

The gain or loss which happeneth in merchants' exchange by bills is ruled by the plenty or scarcity of money in the places where it is delivered out and taken up, and this plenty or scarcity of money is caused only by the over or underbalance of our commodities in the respective places of our foreign trade. For it is a certain rule that in those countries beyond the seas which send us more of their wares in value than we carry unto them of our commodities, there our monies are undervalued in exchange, and in other countries where the contrary of this is performed, there our money is overvalued: if it be considered according to the par of the respective standards.[1]

Correctly considered, therefore, exchange fluctuations were the means and not the cause of the loss of treasure and 'it is not the undervaluing of our money in exchange, but the overbalancing of our trade that carrieth away our treasure. . . . In vain therefore hath Gerard Malynes laboured so long, and in so many printed books to make the world believe that the undervaluing of our money in exchange doth exhaust our treasure, which is a mere fallacy of the cause, attributing that to a secondary means, whose effects are wrought by another principal efficient, and would also come to pass although the said secondary means were not at all.'[2] Mun also attempted to show that while the size of the unfavourable balance precisely determined the final movement of specie, the resulting undervalued exchange meant that in fact *less* ready money would be lost since more of the proceeds of imports would be absorbed in the exchange transactions.[3]

Mun was able to fit this analytical framework to the prevailing crisis. Money was being lost because the balance of trade was unfavourable, and the undervaluation by exchange 'is in truth nothing else but the declination of our trade which vents not half so many cloths, and yet spends twice as much lawns, cambrics and the like as in times past'.[4] Further, through his opposition to Malynes's plan to increase the rate of exchange he was able to demonstrate the relationships between exchange rates, prices and demand. If, he explained,[5] the level of the exchanges were raised 10 per cent then, in the first instance, the likely reduction in import prices would cause a more than proportionate increase in England's

[1] Add. MSS. 34324, fol. 171; cf. *England's Treasure*, pp. 39–40.
[2] *England's Treasure*, pp. 41–2.
[3] Add. MSS. 34324, fol. 171. The reasoning here is somewhat doubtful.
[4] Add. MSS. 34324, fol. 175.
[5] The following account is taken from Add. MSS. 34324, fol. 171.

expenditure on foreign goods: he estimated that a 10 per cent price reduction would provoke a 20 per cent increase in consumption. So on this account the move would 'prove directly against the balancing of our trade'. On the other hand, the English cloth exporter would either have to increase his sale price abroad—in which case, Mun thought, textile sales might be reduced by as much as 40 per cent—or, what was more likely, be forced to pay the clothier correspondingly less for the latter's products, which would be equally disastrous at such a time of depression. This argument, which is paralleled elsewhere,[1] establishes a clear distinction between its author and Malynes: Mun was well aware of the potential importance of demand elasticities; unlike his antagonist he realized that to buy imports cheaply would increase the amount purchased. Similarly, his view of what was a feasible price level for cloth exports was naturally coloured by his opinion that at a time of depression and threatening competition England could simply not afford to increase export prices. He was thus the economist of a competitive era in a sense in which Malynes was not, and there can be no doubt that his assumptions were closer to reality than those of Malynes. While the latter protested bitterly at any moves to reduce export prices, Mun continually advocated cheap exports[2] and waged battle, as did Keynes 300 years later when attacking the return to the gold standard in 1925, against an unnecessarily high rate of exchange, because of the dislocations which would arise in England's staple export industries operating in a competitive world economy.

Clearly, by 1623 Mun, developing his analysis under the influence of the crisis, had completely rejected some of his opinions of 1621. Then he had attributed some real importance to the 'abuse' of the exchange and the operations of 'mere exchangers'; now he relegated them both to secondary positions as effects or means and not causes of the outflow of treasure. Then he had considered currency manipulation as an active determinant of bullion flows; now he completely discarded this theory on the grounds that prices and exchange rates would make immediate, smooth and proportionate adjustments to the changing valuations of foreign coinage;[3] and his views of the efficacy of the Statutes of Employment had radically changed. In the pride of possession of a seemingly omnipotent analytical tool, Mun pronounced authoritatively that almost every aspect of government economic policy and any sort of action by individuals could have no effect whatsoever on the course of net bullion flows, for treasure only moved according to the balance of trade: 'all

---

[1] Add. MSS. 34324, fols. 155–7; Misselden, *The Circle of Commerce*, pp. 107–10.
[2] See, for example, *England's Treasure*, pp. 8, 12, 17.
[3] Add. MSS. 34324, fols. 171, 175; *England's Treasure*, ch. VIII. Mun was clearly wrong on this point: prices rose neither as fast nor as far nor as painlessly as he assumed.

other means which are commonly supposed to enrich the kingdom with treasure are altogether insufficient and mere fallacies.'[1] Look after the balance of trade, Mun preached, and all else will look after itself: 'I never knew as yet, a decay in our trade and treasure . . . but . . . by excessive consumption of foreign wares at home, or by declination in the vent of our commodities abroad.'[2]

It is, of course, common knowledge that the balance of trade was accorded prime importance in technical memoranda and pamphlets for long before Mun wrote, and in 1612 the state of the balance of trade as an influential factor in the loss or gain of treasure was listed among the 'commonplaces so well known . . . as it is enough to mention them only'.[3] But there had been nothing in English[4] to rival his singleness of purpose, logical analysis, and accomplished manipulation of the economic variables. The troubled 1620's produced similar thoughts in other men who saw the balance of trade as playing the critical role in treasure flows and directly controlling exchange fluctuations.[5] In addition, Misselden, who in 1622 had given pride of place to currency manipulation and only gave to the balance of trade the lip-service due to a time-honoured truism,[6] by 1623 was almost lyrical in his statements of the latter factor's all-embracing significance: 'all the mysteries of other exchanges are hid in this mystery, all the knowledge of commerce is presented and represented to the life in this story, in this history. All the rivers of trade spring out of this source, and empty themselves again into this ocean. All the weight of trade falls to this centre, and comes within the circuit of this circle. . . . This is . . . the very eye of the eye . . . the beauty, the ornament, the complement, the accomplishment of commerce.'[7]

Malynes, as was seen, agreed with the concept of a balance which entailed flows of treasure[8]—but his rule of the thumb in this matter was the state of the terms of trade, as affected by the level of the exchanges. He could not, in these circumstances, attack Mun's ideas directly; indeed he made similar statements with regard to the need for a favourable balance.[9] But he did stigmatize his opponents' plans to swing the trade

[1] *England's Treasure*, p. 6. On the basis of these opinions Mun was able to argue, quite self-consistently, that it was perfectly safe to allow particular exports of treasure and, conversely, entirely useless to attempt to force treasure into England (*ibid.* pp. 14–15, 19, 34–7).
[2] *Ibid.* pp. 59–60.
[3] Add. MSS. 10113, fol. 187. Also for early formulations of the doctrine, see de Roover, pp. 260–1; Viner, pp. 6–7.
[4] For Antonio Serra's statement of the balance of trade doctrine, see Joseph A. Schumpeter, *History of Economic Analysis* (New York, 1954), pp. 194–5, 353–5.
[5] S.P.D. Jas. I, 121/22, 131/107.
[6] *Free Trade*, pp. 12–13.
[7] *The Circle of Commerce*, p. 142.
[8] Above, pp. 203–4.
[9] *A Treatise of the Canker*, p. 2; *The Maintenance of Free Trade*, p. 5.

balance by reducing cloth prices as 'hunting after shadows',[1] and he sharply questioned the technical feasibility of drawing up any useful totals: 'we all agree that there is an overbalance, which must be remedied by the redress of the causes and not by the study of balances, which demonstrate little in truth and certainty, but much in imagination and conceit.'[2] Basically, the real measure of the cleavage of opinion is that Malynes's reasoning started from a low exchange (whose redress, he supposed, would therefore be an effective anti-crisis measure) and worked towards an overbalance, while Mun's causal analysis proceeded in the reverse direction. We have already seen the weak spots in Malynes's arguments. We can now appraise the validity and significance of Mun's views.

Of the three best-known economists of the early seventeenth century, Thomas Mun is most applauded by modern students of the discipline, although their criticism remains harsh. Certainly Mun's theory is more logical than the others, and his perception of the operations of the exchange rates has a deductive clarity which is very rare in contemporary polemical writings. For this part of his doctrine the crisis of the early 1620's was most stimulating: it exemplified the crucial parts of the mechanism of international exchange and gave him the strong incentive to question Malynes's myth of the arbitrary determination of exchange rates.

Mun was well aware of the effects of price variations on exports and imports, and of the effects of treasure on prices; indeed, he specifically argued against having 'plenty of money' in the realm on the grounds that the price rise would reduce exports.[3] But one of the major theoretical flaws in his system is precisely that he did not acknowledge the ultimate tendency to equilibrium which derived from the repercussions of specie flows on trade balances through international prices. That is to say, he did not deal with the ultimate effects of a favourable balance which would have imposed inflationary pressure at home and deflationary pressure abroad. Yet this was an omission which was in part justified by the circumstances at the time of writing. Mun was then concerned, above all, to investigate the short-term efflux of specie about which there was so much contemporary anxiety. And there was nothing logically wrong with his explanation: the balance of trade *was* unfavourable—although that was by no means the whole story. Mun was arguing against other explanations and presumed remedies which he considered false and

---
[1] Add. MSS. 34324, fols. 161, 164, 167.
[2] *The Centre of the Circle*, p. 60. For his detailed technical objections, see *ibid.* pp. 55 ff. Cf. Maddison's objections in Add. MSS. 34324, fol. 173.
[3] *England's Treasure*, p. 17.

mischievous,[1] and it is unfair to criticize him, by applying a modern long-run view, as a writer who did not appreciate the contradiction of a steady influx of gold and silver. For, in fact, like government officials at the time, he was motivated not so much by an independent desire to achieve this as by a need to describe the forces which were temporarily producing the reverse situation.[2]

Nevertheless there was a basic invalidity in his approach, even to the short-run situation, for it is entirely misleading to view the balance of trade as a 'cause' of the movement of treasure. To emphasize, in this exclusive way, the relationship between an unfavourable balance and an outflow of specie is to perpetuate a tautology rather than to advance a causal analysis. Mun was logically at fault here, because the unfavourable balance and the export of money to fill the gap are merely two sides of the self-same phenomenon; the 'theory' is true by definition since the concept of an efflux is built into the concept of an unfavourable balance at the outset. One is reminded of Mun's own criticism of the theory of an undervalued exchange as ignoring primary causes: the reasons for the gap between international demands for and supplies of currency have still to be investigated in any situation. This error on Mun's part led him to miss some of the most significant factors in the contemporary crisis. It was with misplaced arrogance that (claiming universal primacy for the state of international indebtedness in the determination of specie exports) he contrived to dismiss as at best irrelevant and at worst pernicious all other factors: currency manipulation, exchange fluctuation, administrative action, private speculation, etc. Some of these factors in themselves could alter the demand and supply relationships which went to comprise a balance of payments. No explanation of bullion flows could be complete without taking them into account.

Thus Mun perhaps missed the point that while exchange rates can alter under the influence of speculative activities, so gold and silver could flow from country to country in the form of (short-term) capital imports and exports. But far more important than this was the fact that imports and exports were themselves determined, given the state of demand, by the relationships between nominal prices, the metallic content and valuation

[1] The 1626 debates on the proposal to manipulate currency also produced strong counter-statements of the balance of trade doctrine: 'if we desire both [gold and silver], it is not raising the value that doth it, but the balancing of trade; for buy we in more than we sell of other commodities, be the money never so highly priced, we must part with it to make the disproportion even. If we sell more than we buy, the contrary will follow' (McCulloch, *Old and Scarce Tracts on Money*, pp. 139-40; cf. pp. 131, 136).

[2] For the view that Mun appreciated the inflationary dangers of an influx of silver, but was not led to adopt the self-regulating hypothesis because of the possibility that an increase in monetary supplies would be used as liquid capital to finance a greater volume of trade, see Gould, 'The Trade Crisis of the Early 1620's and English Economic Thought', 131.

Economic Thought

of currencies, and the level of the exchanges.[1] In addition, as imports or exports rise or fall, so the first and last of these change, and with this alteration themselves affect the demand for goods and services entering into international trade. The 'balance of trade' is, in fact, a nice process of continuous adjustment. Further, and most significantly, any manipulation of the amount of metal (more especially silver) represented by a given nominal unit of currency could, by itself, have an all-important role to play in the determination of the balance, through its volatile effects on prices, exchanges and profits. This factor, as has been seen, actually turned the balance of trade against England in the early 1620's. Mun's equation—net loss or gain of bullion *equals* gap or surplus in balance of trade—was therefore an *a priori* statement which could tell him very little about the real forces at work. Indeed, it led him to dismiss the very factors which contributed to the dynamic process of international trade, and to discount the factor (European currency enhancement) which had in fact altered the relationships between exports and imports.[2]

It was left to Rice Vaughan to synthesize the traditional doctrine of the balance of trade with an appreciation of the effect that currency factors could have on prices and sales. In *A Discourse of Coin and Coinage*[3] Vaughan presents a very able summary of monetary questions in the early seventeenth century. He was, for instance, fully aware of the loss of silver in exchange for gold as occasioned by its low price—i.e. by the high English Mint ratio—and of the mechanism by which this drain operated: 'whatsoever laws are made against transportation of our monies, if our silver be so rich as the merchants by transporting it into the Low Countries, or elsewhere, can make profit by returning it in commodities, or by exchange; or that which is yet more clear and evident, by returning it in gold, must not our silver be inevitably exhausted?'[4] Even though silver is exported in return for gold, he also recognized that, given the normal importance of silver, the change in the composition of the currency could

---

[1] Misselden realized that a merchant must study all these factors, 'otherwise if the money rise in denomination above its true worth in valuation, and the exchange also rise accordingly: if this merchant do not raise the price of his commodity thereunto, he shall be sure to come home by weeping cross, however he make his return, whether by exchange, or in money, bullion, or wares' (*The Circle of Commerce*, p. 17).

[2] It is particularly disappointing that Mun dismisses, so peremptorily, the possibility that currency enhancements could be in any way important. He does so on the quite fallacious grounds: (1) that, where the manipulations took place abroad, there would be a corresponding increase in English export prices with, presumably, no consequent decline in sales; (2) that there would be an equivalent rise in internal prices. See Add. MSS. 34324, fols. 171, 175; *England's Treasure*, ch. VIII.

[3] Published 1675, but a statement on page 42 (in McCulloch, *Old and Scarce Tracts on Money*) that 'now very lately' for the first time since 1611 a reasonably large amount of silver was being coined would place its compositions in the mid-1620's. See the figures in Gould, 'The Royal Mint', 248.

[4] Vaughan, pp. 28–9, 42, 76–7.

have distinctly deflationary effects. He provided an able analysis of the harmful repercussions of European currency manipulations, and of the arguments for and against England following suit. He knew too that juggling with the valuations set on coins and precious metals could not *directly* provoke a loss of both gold and silver to any significant degree, and that in the last resort the balance of trade determined the net flow of bullion. But, unlike Mun, he was not content to leave the matter there: he continued his analysis to see what connexion there could be between currency alterations and the balance of trade through the indirect effects of the former. The relevant passage in the book is by no means comprehensive in its treatment of the subject, but it is sufficient indication that Vaughan had mastered the essential feature of the role of enhancements and debasements. He supposed exports to be £1,000,000 and imports £900,000:

Then of necessity, it follows, that an hundred thousand pounds must be brought in, in gold and silver, what price so ever money bear. But if it shall appear that the low values of our money doth cause the kingdom to vent more foreign commodities than otherwise it would vent; and that where otherwise it would vent 900,000 pounds, the low values of money cause it to vent a million or more: then is the force of the argument lost; and it follows that *the low values are the cause why the materials of gold and silver, or less of them than otherwise would do, come not in.*[1]

Vaughan also showed that a stimulus is, in fact, given to the purchase of imports by the differential valuations set on coins.[2] Although he was not alone in recognizing the obvious relationship between currency enhancements and the incentives to increase import, Rice Vaughan was the most apt commentator to describe this in terms of the balance of trade, and thus to turn Mun's static truism into a dynamic analysis.

An examination of the economic background to early mercantilist thought can never confer validity on views which are manifestly erroneous. It can, however, bring a better understanding of why those views were held, and make the men who held them seem less like disingenuous economic innocents. The foregoing pages have attempted to show that the works of all three of the leading mercantilists of the period are initially best judged as responses to an economic crisis rather than as intellectual exercises intended to deduce a 'theory of international trade'. Contemporaries showed very little interest in the latter approach. Misselden, Malynes, Mun, Maddison, Vaughan and a host of other

---

[1] Vaughan, pp. 83–4 (my italics).   [2] Vaughan, pp. 84–5.

writers were at times almost exclusively concerned with the problems of an efflux of treasure because these problems demanded urgent attention: to contemporaries the loss of bullion was the central feature of the most serious crisis of the early seventeenth century. Their theories may have been inexact or inappropriate, and their grading of phenomena in order of importance may have been misleading. Yet no student who hopes to understand the relationships between commerce and currency, or who wishes to appreciate the intellectual approach to economic problems, can afford to ignore these theories and the processes by which they were derived. Such a study is also useful in another respect. It demonstrates the inadequacy of an approach which holds that for mercantilist thought 'the circumstances of the time were not decisive' or that the assumed scarcity of money played no essential motivating role in mercantilism as a monetary system.[1] There is incontestable evidence that it is impossible to dissociate some mercantilist writing from the problems of the day, and that it was usually a time of economic distress which provided an environment of urgency within which economic views first became fully articulate. Whatever the theoretical shortcomings and blatant oversights of contemporary pamphleteers, their appreciation of the significant areas for economic investigation cannot be questioned. If these men had their faults then they are largely those of any group desperately involved in an economic crisis. The whole tenor of what has come to be known as mercantilist literature owes not a little to this involvement and to the sincere attempts of the men concerned to extricate England from her precarious position within the European economy.

(ii) THE ECONOMICS OF DIVERSIFICATION

The troubled years 1640–1 coincided with another small output of economic literature. In the writings of Sir Ralph Maddison, Sir Thomas Roe, Lewes Roberts, Henry Robinson and William Goffe there is an accentuation of the change in attitude and emphasis which mirrors England's evolving relationships with the international economy. The exception in this respect is Maddison's *Great Britain's Remembrancer*, which is of little real importance or interest: he simply retailed sixteenth-century ideas gleaned from Malynes some twenty years before, when they were already hopelessly inappropriate.

By the eve of the Civil War the lesson which had first been fully brought home in 1620 was now an accepted doctrine: England had to earn her keep in a newly competitive world; the textile industry, in the

[1] Eli F. Heckscher, *Mercantilism* (rev. ed., 1955), II, 177, 221–4.

face of growing European manufacture, no longer had a prerogative of sale without a careful scrutiny of prices. Hence the opinion that cloth, of necessity, had to be cheap, which had so alarmed Malynes when propounded by Mun in the early 1620's, was, to Henry Robinson, a cardinal basis of economic policy. 'The rather it concerns us to sell good cheap', he wrote, 'in that all other nations now almost make cloth of their own, or other clothing which may serve near as well.'[1] Within four or five years the need to undercut foreign industries had moved men to attack the trading companies for perpetuating the very policies—of market manipulation aiming at price maintenance—which formerly had been viewed as their supreme justification; the old bugbear of a 'straggling trade' was now a *desideratum* of commercial policy: to beat the European manufacture out of overseas markets, wrote one anonymous pamphleteer, 'There is no way under Heaven . . . but by devising ways to sell our manufactures at cheaper rates, and dispense them more up and down the country.' By contrast, forty years earlier Sandys, in his opposition to company trading, argued that the abolition of companies would *not* reduce prices.[2] The whole attitude of men like Henry Robinson to economic affairs was coloured by a desire for competitive cheapness. By means of an undervalued exchange, he claimed, 'we are enabled to sell our cloth and other commodities the cheaper'. Any raising of the exchange would decrease import prices and so increase purchases by England, while it would 'raise the price of our commodities sold abroad, and diminish their vent'.[3] For reasons which someone like Malynes would have been unable to grasp, Robinson, and others like him, completed the overthrow of generations of unquestioned doctrine, and because undervaluation of the English currency lowered prices and augmented sales, it seemed to him to be 'the most beneficial state'.[4] So far did Robinson carry his ideas on the need to sustain overseas sales that, on the grounds that European purchasing power must be maintained, he opposed policy directed at the wholesale accumulation of treasure: 'it is to our benefit that monies be plentiful also in countries where we carry

---

[1] *England's Safety*, p. 56. Cf. pp. 10, 14.
[2] *A Discourse . . . for the Enlargement . . . of Trade*, p. 38. Cf. Thomas Johnson, *A Plea for Free-Men's Liberties* (1646), p. 3. Bland, Brown and Tawney, p. 447.
[3] *England's Safety*, p. 55.
[4] Robinson knew that a very low rate would lead to an export of specie, but argued—in 1641—that although the rate of exchange was below par it had not yet reached specie export point (*England's Safety*, pp. 52–4). He also knew that official stabilization at par would necessitate some control over the demand and supply of currencies, and was opposed to such a policy because of its inherent difficulties and the competitive advantages of a low rate of exchange (*England's Safety*, pp. 54–6, 60). But in 1650 and 1652 he favoured some control and suggested a detailed plan, involving goverment agents in the principal European money markets (S.P.D. Interregnum, 9/64; *Certain Proposals*, pp. 15–18).

our commodities to sell.'[1] In the sphere of economic policy an intellectual revolution was under way. 'Cheap wares', wrote one observer, 'do increase trade, and dear wares do not only cause less consumption, but also decline the merchant's trade, impoverish the kingdom of treasure ... and abate the manufactures and employments of the poor in shipping, clothing, and the like.'[2] The constant pressure for low prices and low costs which was to be an outstanding characteristic of post-Restoration writings,[3] was clearly anticipated in the pamphlets of these last years of Charles I.

But cheap cloth exports in themselves would not suffice. As has already been seen, by the 1630's England's future economic well-being could no longer be exclusively tied to the old draperies. Part of the traditional market had been irrevocably lost: 'we cannot at present vent in Germany and the Low Countries one third part of what we used in former times', and even the expanded Turkish market is threatened, Robinson wrote, because West Indian cotton will soon deprive England of return goods from the Levant. He argued that the actual or threatened unemployment of men and capital should be alleviated by the development of other types of economic activity. Like others of his generation, who recognized the weaknesses of economic and commercial specialization, Robinson preached the gospel of diversification and adaptation to new conditions. For instance, security and trade ought to be established on England's own basis: fishing. Further, new manufactures (coarse and fine linens, salt, cordage, etc.) should be encouraged, the re-export trade ought to be expanded, and the East India trade cherished.[4]

Such doctrines were widely accepted. Sir Thomas Roe praised re-exports from the Indies as the only means of ensuring a favourable trade balance: 'nothing exported of our own growth hath balanced our riotous consumption at home, but those foreign commodities which I call naturalized, that is the surplus of our East India trade, which being brought home in greater quantity than are spent within the kingdom, are exported again and become in value and use as natural commodities.' Roe also saw in fishing a stimulus to a carrying trade potentially as prosperous as the cloth industry; he was 'confident [that, by attracting Dutchmen to sow flax and hemp,] we may make and undersell in all linen cloth in all the

---

[1] *England's Safety*, pp. 56–7. Cf. p. 9.
[2] *Decay of Trade. A Treatise against the abating of interest* (1641), p. 9. Quoted in Viner, pp. 34–5.
[3] See E. S. Furniss, *The Position of the Labourer in a System of Nationalism* (Boston and New York, 1920); T. E. Gregory, 'The Economics of Employment in England, 1660–1713', *Economica*, I (1921), 37–51. However, some of the old attitude to the terms of trade survived the Civil War; for instance in Locke (Heckscher, II, 239–40), and Fortrey (Viner, p. 35 n.).
[4] *England's Safety*, pp. 14, 18–25, 49.

nations of Europe'; and he saw the new draperies and their new markets as the real salvation of the declining textile industry.[1] Lewes Roberts argued that England should imitate Tuscany: secure herself as a customs-free staple, allow an unrestricted trade in bullion, and so ensure an entrepôt trade which would confer untold economic benefits.[2] Finally, William Goffe, about 1641, in his anxiety over the underemployment in England and 'the manufactories which we are overstocked with already ..., the woollen manufactures or any other where the price is beat down to so low a rate that the slow workmen cannot maintain themselves', put forward a remarkable scheme for industrial development based on community enterprise in fishing and its associated manufactures: hemp, flax, timber, metals.[3]

That cloth prices ought to be low or lower, that fishing, the East India trade, and re-exports should be encouraged, and that a new range of industrial products should be developed: all these were opinions which had some roots in the past. But the conscious orientation was relatively new—perhaps only dating from the early 1620's. There was a fresh economic orthodoxy on the eve of the Civil War which was willing to accept a decline in the importance of England's traditional industrial staple,[4] and was busy planning a new equilibrium along the lines which ultimately proved most fruitful. It is surely not too fanciful to see, in these faint intimations, a reflection of, and encouragement to, those changes which were already taking place: there was an absolute decline in the old draperies; newer fabrics were stimulated and different markets were tapped; re-exports were becoming an increasingly important element in English trade and the carrying trade was being developed in the Far East and the Mediterranean; England's commercial outlook was becoming slightly less myopic as economic diversification made its mark and as America and Asia loomed larger on the economic horizon. These were tendencies which matured only after 1660, but they were sufficiently strong before the Civil War for men to notice which way the wind was blowing and to trim their sails accordingly.

[1] Roe, pp. 7, 8, 11-12.
[2] Roberts, *The Treasure of Traffic*, passim.
[3] Goffe, *How to Advance the Trade of the Nation*.
[4] One should differentiate between an attitude which accepted the inevitable growth of European industry and positively looked for other industrial and commercial uses to absorb England's idle labour and capital, and one which wished to restrict the English textile industry (in favour of agricultural employment) because intermittent textile slumps were a threat to national security. For the latter, which was best exemplified in the sixteenth century, see Burghley's memorandum in *T.E.D.* II, 45, and Fisher, 'Commercial Trends', 109-12. Mun also favoured this view to some extent (*England's Treasure*, p. 73).

10. THE GOVERNMENT AND THE ECONOMY

(i) THE ASSUMPTIONS OF ECONOMIC POLICY

After the foregoing treatment of the economic thought of the pamphleteers, the present chapter would appear to be a natural place for a lengthy disquisition on 'mercantilism'. Such, however, is not the intention here. The primary emphasis of this book would make such a dissertation almost anachronistic. For either it would be based on the view that there existed a mercantile *system* whose significant and coherent unity pervaded government thought in the early modern period, or the burden of the argument would be that there was in reality no consistent long-term policy divorced from the reality of temporal economic conditions. The former possibility has, it is hoped, been excluded by the content of the foregoing chapters. And the latter has already been implied throughout most of this book, while it is a viewpoint which has already been cogently and ably propounded.[1]

Therefore, instead of a detailed analysis and critique of the historiography of mercantilism, we may more usefully begin an analysis of the government's approach to economic problems with a briefer exercise: a statement of the traditional appraisal of mercantilism and a proposal, by way of contrast, of another view of the origins, content and attitudes of economic policy during the early seventeenth century.

The leading proponents of the existence of a mercantile system—however much they disagreed on its content, its theoretical validity, or its practical usefulness—combined in attributing to government policy in the sixteenth and seventeenth centuries an overall and integrated content based upon conscious thought and primarily directed towards the creation of some ideal economic or political society. On this view, specific government actions were very much parts of a whole, and aimed at more than the solution of short-term problems or the effecting of partial changes in economic structures. Adam Smith, for instance, in his biting attack on mercantilism, held it to be founded on a basically invalid principle which identified national wealth with treasure and which guided official action

[1] For critiques of traditional views of mercantilism—specifically that of Eli Heckscher—see D. C. Coleman, 'Eli Heckscher and the Idea of Mercantilism', *Scandinavian Economic History Review*, V (1957), 3–25; Herbert Heaton, 'Heckscher on Mercantilism', *Journal of Political Economy*, XLV (1937), 370–93; A. V. Judges, 'The Idea of a Mercantile State', *Trans. Roy. Hist. Soc.* 4th ser. XXI (1939), 41–69. Also, see Wilson, 'Treasure and Trade Balances'. Cf. C. Wilson, ' "Mercantilism": Some Vicissitudes of an Idea', *Econ. Hist. Rev.* 2nd ser. X (1957), 181–8.

towards the unbounded accumulation of money by manipulation of the balance of trade. By the German historical economists of the late nineteenth century, mercantilism was gratefully and approvingly reinterpreted in political terms: as a centralized policy directed towards the building of nation states and the concentration of national power. In this century Eli Heckscher found in the mercantile system concepts of unification, national power, protection, money, and society; these he systematized and, measuring them against the tenets of *laissez faire*, found wanting.[1] Whatever the particular emphasis, however, traditional views of mercantilism as a system of policy have held it to be rooted in consciously articulated doctrine, with the result that a significant number of official economic measures over an extended period of time could be seen as component parts of a larger plan. Further, on this view, it is normally held that the mercantilist doctrines were propounded with more reference to an ideal economic or political state than to the prevailing economic conditions. Most extreme of all, Heckscher denied any possible influence of economic environment on government policy.[2] To all these views we can reasonably take exception on the basis of the processes already described.

Nearly every detailed study of particular aspects of economic policy in the sixteenth and seventeenth centuries has, inevitably, been forced to deal with the economic environment within which that policy has been shaped, and it has been the rule rather than the exception that the conclusions of such studies point to a crucial relationship between actual events and government actions.[3] It will be the argument here that 'mercantilist' doctrine was not the spontaneous product of an ideal of society nor is it evidence of the momentum of medieval concepts. Instead, officials in the early seventeenth century had in mind quite unexceptionable ends whose simplicity contrasts sharply with those so often attributed to 'mercantilism'.

On the whole, Tudor and Stuart governments directed their regulatory efforts to the maintenance of social order, public peace, national security and the achievement of economic prosperity—simply defined. Certain policies had obviously strategic roots. They were directed towards the encouragement of shipping, of the provision of naval supplies, armaments and necessary foodstuffs. These doctrines and actions do not need investi-

[1] For the development of the idea of mercantilism, see Wilson, ' "Mercantilism": Some Vicissitudes of an Idea'.
[2] Coleman, 'Eli Heckscher', 12–13.
[3] To take two examples out of many, see Professor Fisher's analysis of the relationship between the textile depression of the 1550's and the code of industrial regulation of the mid-sixteenth century ('Commercial Trends and Policy'); also, for the necessity of appreciating actual economic conditions in order to understand the development of the official plans for poor relief, see Leonard, *passim*.

gation here: the prevailing international political climate was one of warfare and it was therefore only natural that some attention should be given to the military and civil preparation for such an environment. And particular variations in the frequency, nature and sincerity of policy measures are to be explained only in terms of the personalities and politics involved, the dangers threatening, and the funds available. We can also exclude from consideration another aspect of policy: that whose *raison d'être* was a prohibition of some form of economic activity merely in order to derive an income from licensing exceptions to it. Indeed, the altruistic light in which we shall view attempts at economic regulation did not distinguish all government activity at the time. The policies which provoked the maximum public criticism were precisely those which reflected the worst features of the Stuart Court: plagued by impecunious parasites and desperately anxious for new sources of income and new possibilities of corruption. Thus industrial intervention was only too frequently the result of attempts to satisfy the greed of the hanger-on at Westminster or the extreme financial needs of government itself. The patents and monopolies, the cloaking of selfish aims beneath verbose platitudes, were an integral part of the fabric of Stuart government. And the fate of many seemingly sincere policies was to degenerate into inefficient taxes on enterprise: taxes which rarely reached the royal coffers.[1] This is a feature of policy with which we shall not be concerned. It is with other aspects of official action that we shall deal; with the more purely economic measures and with those adopted in some way to preserve order or maintain the social fabric.

The outstanding feature of such policies, it will be argued, was that their timing and content were explained above all by the context within which they were promulgated and the urgency with which economic problems were brought to the government's attention. An understanding of the economy and the nature of its day-to-day workings is essential to an understanding of economic policy. From this point of view it is far from a useful procedure to cloak generations of policy under one term, and the methodological concepts of those historians who believed in a 'mercantilist system' are decidedly not the most useful tools for appraising official action. Instead, even at the risk of economic determinism, we must conclude that while economic conditions shaped the course of economic

[1] See Heaton, 'Heckscher on Mercantilism', 385; M. W. Beresford, 'The Common Informer, the Penal Statutes and Economic Regulation', *Econ. Hist. Rev.* 2nd ser. x (1957), 237: 'The penal statutes thus emerge not as efficient weapons of despotism, revenue-raising or economic planning but rather as a political irritant; a means of private profit and lawyers' fees; and an irregular charge on manufactures and trade; in short, a leading example of the discredit into which need so often drove official economic policy.'

doctrine and regulation, it was the more violent short-run variations in the economic environment which best explain the dynamic components of policy. On this basis the continuous recurrence of various *motifs* in official action (for instance, bullion laws, wage-regulation, plans for exchange control, and anxiety concerning the balance of trade) is evidence not so much of a continuity of ideas *per se* but of a not surprising recurrence of short-term situations, and specifically depressions, within the framework of an economy whose essential characteristics were slow to change.[1]

Even more than this: economic policy was attuned most exactly to *downswings* in economic activity, and there is hardly an important government measure during the period—with the obvious exception of the strategic policies and the strange Cockayne plan—which was not stimulated by the urgent demands of a period of short-term (if recurrent) dislocation. In the words of a critic of Heckscher's views of mercantilism, 'I have long felt that a graph showing business fluctuations should be a compulsory frontispiece for every historical study of commercial policy. ... The relationship between depression on the one hand, and discontent, drastic demands, concessions to the vociferous, and great changes in policy, on the other hand, is intimate.'[2] This lesson, it is hoped, has already been made apparent in the foregoing chapters: the most powerful type of stimulus to the formulation and application of a body of government policy—however we baptize it—was precisely the sort of economic fluctuation which has been the subject of this book. And the inevitable result was that the emphasis of this policy was defensive.

The previous chapter has already dealt with the economic doctrines of the pamphleteers of the time from the viewpoint of fluctuations in commercial and monetary affairs. It was there seen that the writings taken by later observers to be *typical* of generations of commentators belonging to one school of economic thought were in fact the result of painstaking deliberation on the vagaries of short-run crises, and were directed towards a solution of the problems they raised. In calling such authors 'mercantilist' there is the danger of implicitly attributing to them a continuity of doctrine, based on a set of supposedly logical principles, which was not theirs. Neither in aim nor achievement were their theoretical arguments timeless. Through the years, of course, various themes recur in the writings of many men. An outstanding one, for example, was the argument that a favourable balance of trade, and the different ways to achieve it, were significantly conducive to England's economic welfare. But this, and the theories which refer to the significance of particular bilateral

[1] See Coleman, 'Eli Heckscher', 18–20.
[2] Heaton, 'Heckscher on Mercantilism', 386.

flows of international trade and payments,[1] should be seen in the light of England's relatively unchanging position within the European economy, combined with a recurrent balance-of-trade crisis.[2] Nevertheless, bearing all possible dangers in mind it is surely possible, as a convenient shorthand, to refer loosely to this group of writers as mercantilist on the grounds that their immediate concern was with questions of a *mercantile* nature, their writings displayed a sufficiently common ground of anxieties and modes of discussion, and that to use the widely accepted term does not confuse too many issues.

The connexion between economic thought and economic policy is at best debatable. One recent critic of Eli Heckscher has argued, with some reason, that in the early modern period there was little logical or necessary relationship between economic ideas and policy,[3] and it was certainly true that under James I and Charles I the policy suggestions of the outstanding pamphleteers were rarely put into practice. But in any case, even though the assumptions with which writers and government officials approached the economic problems of their day were often indistinguishable, and official action itself had a strong orientation towards commerce and international economic relationships, there is a much greater risk, when dealing with government policy, in employing the 'convenient shorthand' of 'mercantilism'. For this would be tacitly to assume a full-blown system of doctrine and policy, so that the use of the term mercantilism would not only confuse the issue by its historical identification with definite concepts of policy which we may feel did not exist, but would imply a continuity and momentum in official outlook which have been more conspicuous in history books than history.

Although there was no such thing as a mercantilist *system* of economic regulation, it is possible to distinguish, at a less complex level, some common attributes of policy during the early seventeenth century. But, as might be expected, these spring less from a continuity of administrative outlook than from the nature of the economic environment within which men thought out their actions. For, given the general economic structure at the time,[4] men fashioned policy under the sharp stimulus of short-run dislocation in the hope of reducing the harmful effects of the type of disturbance which was likely to arise in such an economy. In the last resort, as we shall see, the mass of official regulations aimed at alleviating those situations from which food riots might result. Thus the

[1] See Wilson, 'Treasure and Trade Balances'.
[2] Compare the economic background to labour policy (Coleman, 'Labour in the English Economy').
[3] Coleman, 'Eli Heckscher', 22–3.
[4] See Introduction.

maintenance of public order was among the primary ends of government action. Since the commercial disturbances which threatened public order were comparable in the effects they had, it is not surprising that the official reaction to them should itself display some continuity over the years. There was, in addition, another feature which distinguished official action at the time, and it is possible that herein lies the real distinction between mercantilism and *laissez faire*:[1] policy was formulated with a specific and unquestioned assumption as to the necessary role of the government in the economy. With this assumption we may usefully start our analysis of economic regulation during the period.

More than most other periods of English economic history the sixteenth and seventeenth centuries illustrate the acceptance of government participation in and regulation of economic affairs. Official willingness to shape economic and social institutions and the course of economic change has rarely been greater, the framework of laws and administrative edicts propounded as a result has rarely been more complex, and this was more than matched by an almost universal faith on the part of contemporaries that this arrangement, rather than the free play of market forces, was the natural order of things. The validity which was imputed to the government's far-reaching role was little affected by the constant demonstration of its failure to do what it proposed to do, or its success in aggravating the very problems which it had set out to solve! Of course, there were always those who argued that some aspect of the economy—usually one in which they themselves were busy seeking a profit—would be better off without regulation, or with a laxer system of official controls. But such pragmatic approaches were rarely couched in terms of a general principle, and were virtually never based on a broad theoretical foundation. Views as heretical as those of Adam Smith would have received short shrift from the economic orthodoxies of the seventeenth century. Whatever the level of inspired inefficiency with which government policy was applied to the intransigent facts, no one thought to question in any serious way the government's right, whether by prerogative or parliamentary approval, to extend its influence over everyday life. Nor was there any real opposition to the view that disaster would attend any experiment by which the government abstained entirely from participation in economic affairs.

The actual formulation of policy during the early seventeenth century was principally the responsibility of the Privy Council. True, the House of Commons was always a sounding board for possible government action, and its members, representative of widely diverse economic interests and areas, were never loath to give their opinions on the state

[1] See Heaton, 'Heckscher on Mercantilism', 390-2.

The Government and the Economy

of the economy or to attempt to advance relevant legislation. In addition there were some not unimportant instances when Parliament took the initiative in framing, or breaking down, a particular code of commercial regulations. Important in these respects were the 1604 debates on free trade, the 1606 Act ensuring an unregulated trade to France, Spain and Portugal, the urgent considerations of 1621, and the pressure then and in 1624 which produced a significant liberalization of the organization of the trade to Germany and the Low Countries.[1] But in the main, and not least because of the discontinuity of parliamentary sessions, government policy in the period was determined, enforced or delegated by the Privy Council.[2]

One other reason why the legislature took second place to the executive in this matter lay in the fact that, given the contemporary reaction to economic crisis, except in relation to the potentialities of an unregulated trade, there was relatively little scope for fresh economic legislation. On the whole, the tendencies of policy, even in the face of a continually changing commercial scene, could ideally be satisfied by the selective application of existing laws. In other words, there was no great demand for institutional revolutions. For the men concerned with government, regulation was best carried on by the administrative organ: it was the council's responsibility to emphasize those aspects of the inherited framework of statutes which it imagined best fitted the needs of the economy. If, for example, the desire was to prevent the export of money then contemporary policy-formulation demanded no more than could be satisfied by the prevailing penal statutes against the shipment of coin or by the unquestioned right of the executive to manipulate Mint prices. If anxiety was expressed concerning the low quality of English textiles, then the requisite regulatory laws were on the statute books and it was open to non-parliamentary powers to set up commissions to investigate, or corporations to control, the processes of manufacture. In questions of poor-relief, of anti-unemployment policies, of wage regulation and industrial codes, and of monetary affairs the power and prerogative of the Privy Council were, in theory at least, sufficient unto the day.

It was, then, the council which attempted to enforce old laws, promulgated new proclamations, took far-reaching administrative action, issued commissions for a host of purposes, and acted as the energizing force for local authorities whose all-important task it was to administer the day-to-day requirements of policy. The political configurations which went far

[1] Above, pp. 68–71. It is typical that these proceedings should have represented the viewpoint of outport traders, for which purpose the Commons was ideally constituted.
[2] The council normally acted independently, but in at least one instance, the ill-advised and badly executed Cockayne project, it came reluctantly under headstrong royal pressure.

to explain the position of the Commons need not be considered here. But it is abundantly clear that parliamentary supremacy might have made little difference to economic regulation. The principal exception in this respect is probably in the field of the award of privileged areas of trade and strict rights of self-government to London mercantile companies—the economic interests in Parliament consistently displayed the strongest suspicion of these metropolitan cartels. Yet even on this point the council, although in the long run content to maintain the fabric of regulation, frequently demonstrated that it was not irrevocably committed to the concept of regulated commerce, and in 1621 and 1624, when the parliamentary pressure groups succeeded in throwing open large portions of the Merchant Adventurers' trade, this step was taken with the not unwilling concurrence of the Privy Council. In most other matters, however, it is doubtful if there existed even the possibility of a cleavage on matters of economic regulation in the face of commercial crises. Commons' debates and suggestions arising from economic troubles display no great deviation from those which came before the privy councillors. This was true with respect to currency problems, unemployment measures, poor law enforcement, the regulation of the cloth industry, and the attitude towards sharing the burden of depression between labour and capital or industry and trade. The real break between Parliament and Crown came on matters remote from the critical attributes of the commercial fluctuations which intermittently disturbed sectors of the English economy. It was reserved for questions of politics and religion, and in so far as it concerned economic matters, it dealt in the main with taxation, patents and agriculture, and with questions of principle as to *who* should determine the national destiny, and by what authority.

As far as possible the Privy Council attempted to give direct attention to important matters: it was rarely reluctant to exhort local officials to positive action in any matter which it felt to be important, or to call to account those who too blatantly went against its will. But as the burden of necessary work accumulated it was only to be expected that there should be some delegation of the responsibility for sifting and evaluating evidence, and even for some decision-making. The result was an informal and ever-changing structure of committees and commissions. As exemplified already, the investigating committees might be completely independent groups representing one particular viewpoint; for example, the merchant committees that investigated projects for currency enhancement in 1618 and 1620, or the special committees appointed in 1622 to appraise the collapse of the exchange rates. On the other hand, these committees might be quasi-official bodies, whose task it was to present a balanced view of a particular problem and suggest remedies for it. The outstanding example here was the group that considered all aspects of the commercial depression in 1622. One result of the deliberations of this committee was the appointment of a more permanent commission, and in this sort of appointment we can see another fundamental development of policy delegation.

There were clearly many matters that the council wished to control but which might evade its own oversight by reason of the pressure of work or the need for its members to be in London. In these circumstances it could at best issue a commission for the specific task in mind, and delegate administration to a chosen body of men. Thus in 1631, at a time of widespread poverty and famine, a general commission was set up to enforce relief measures throughout the country, and in the early 1630's a commission was active in the western counties 'for reformation of the abuses in clothmaking'. It was, however, in the autumn of 1622 that the most significant departure took place. As a consequence of the prevailing depression and the recommendations of the investigating committee earlier in the year, a large commission was appointed to investigate and oversee most crucial questions of commercial and industrial policy.[1] In effect this move amounted to the delegation of an enormous area of economic supervision, and subsequent commercial and industrial controversies frequently came before the commission directly. Thus, the critical debates on the mechanism of the exchanges were held under its auspices in 1622 and 1623. In this respect the great depression of the early 1620's, which did so much to shape economic thought and policy, served to mark a turning point in the evolution of government institutions. For the body appointed in 1622 was revivified in 1625 and in its operations and scope one can detect the origins of the later Board of Trade.

(ii) THE NATURE OF ECONOMIC POLICY

The thesis has already been proposed that the most significant aspects of government policy during the early seventeenth century are best explained in terms of an attempted defence against the vagaries of economic dislocation. Governments reacted to the intermittent commercial crises which afflicted the economy in a manner primarily calculated to alleviate the worst effects of depression or to alter the arrangements of factors of production so that another crisis would be less harsh. Only rarely was there any attempt to propound policies primarily designed to get to the roots of potential dislocation.

[1] Above, p. 67.

The most critical element of instability as far as the government was concerned was the possibility of chronic unemployment. And it has already been indicated that in this last respect the textile industry played an almost unique role at this time. Thus variations in the effective demand for cloth were the principal causes of outbreaks of unemployment for people who might, at such times, find few alternative sources of income. England, like the neighbouring lands, was a poor nation whose population lived, for the main part, close to a subsistence level. Even when he was employed, the average textile worker had little enough income to buy his basic necessities, quite apart from any possibility of his saving enough to establish a buffer between slump and starvation. Consequently, the unemployed weaver was even less tender than the underprivileged farm labourer of the rights of property or the king's peace, and when—as was normally the case—the looms stopped in areas where cloth manufacturing was a concentrated industry, the result might not be far from anarchy. The potential barriers between unalleviated unemployment and a dangerous outburst of rioting were only two (if we exclude the possibility of superhuman patience in the face of starvation): social welfare measures, which served to redistribute income by means of poor-relief, and the exercise of an efficient police power. In both respects Stuart England was poorly equipped to meet the urgent problems of a depressed area; any except the slightest disruption could pose alarming threats to social peace. The poor-law will be dealt with below, but in general it was true that the paucity of resources, the inefficiencies of local administration, and the opposition of local propertied interests to the necessary taxation, hamstrung all but the most determined efforts to organize relief. On the other hand, a ramshackle administrative system, poor communications, and financial stringency kept everyday police powers close to the ludicrous—Dogberry and his men were no more than the inspired exaggeration of a cruel truth which lasted well beyond Shakespeare's time. Clearly, no Stuart government could look with equanimity on the possibility of a declining cloth market putting local resources and aptitudes to the test. If one had to choose, it would be fear of the bread riot rather than adherence to a medieval philosophy of social harmony which went furthest to explain measures directed at the maintenance of economic peace and stability in local communities.

Since the prevention of social unrest by the maintenance of employment in textiles was a major aim of policy, governments were clearly forced to consider the relationship between commercial crises and the structure of the cloth industry. Indeed, in the sixteenth century such considerations, as has already been intimated, led to the emergence of a school of thought that was opposed to industrial development in textiles precisely because it felt the price—measured in intermittent bouts of chronic unemployment —was too high. To quote Lord Burghley's words again: 'it is to be thought that the diminution of clothing in this realm were profitable to the same . . . first, for that thereby the tillage of the realm is notoriously decayed. . . . Secondly, for that the people that depend upon making of cloth are of worse condition to be quietly governed than the husbandmen.'[1]

Although such views were not confined to any one brief period of time, it is abundantly clear that they derived their strength from appraisals of specific depressions in the course of the mid-sixteenth century. They were the horrified reactions, of men who appreciated only too bitterly the danger of tumultuous poverty, to the intrusion of a complicated and unstable industrial development into an agrarian economy. And they were embodied in a framework of regulation whose aim was, in part, 'the diminution of clothing in this realm'. The Cloth Acts of the mid-sixteenth century, and even the Statute of Artificers, were directed towards the restraint of unbridled industrial expansion in order to guard against the impact of potential contractions in demand. Laws were passed which aimed at the maintenance of quality in English woollens, which confined the manufacture of cloth to those who had served an apprenticeship of seven years in the industry (although this requirement was subsequently relaxed for towns and cities), and which limited the number of looms and apprentices which even a qualified rural manufacturer might employ. And the great Statute of 1563, by its apprenticeship, wage and labour-contract clauses 'made illegal that mobility of labour without which rapid industrialization and spectacular commercial expansion are impossible'. Behind this series of enactments lay not a medieval ideal of a stable agrarian society but the reality of a disastrous slump. The significance as well as the timing of some of the outstanding sixteenth-century measures of economic regulation are explained by the prevailing economic environment.[2]

But, although anxiety on the score of dangerously concentrated pockets of industry was still evident in the early seventeenth century, by that time, as far as official doctrine was concerned, all thoughts of unduly restraining the processes of industrialization had disappeared. As previously mentioned,[3] men's attention now increasingly turned to the possibilities of

[1] *T.E.D.* II, 45. The third reason was the consequent shortage of artificers and common labourers.
[2] See Fisher, 'Commercial Trends and Policy', 110–13. Significantly enough Professor Fisher's name does not appear in the index to Heckscher's work.
[3] Above, pp. 71–2, 160–2, 221–4.

expansion rather than contraction. England's industrial destiny, as much as it was then apparent, was the accepted starting point for policy discussions. And this change in outlook had a twofold origin. First, market forces were doing more than the Elizabethan government ever could to prevent the undue expansion of the traditional broadcloth industry. Second, the beginnings of a new international economic order were affording opportunities of commercial diversification into textile innovations, new markets and new trades.[1] Rather than concentrating on preventing factors of production from entering a burgeoning old-drapery industry, the government now attempted to facilitate their entry into fields of endeavour which compensated for industrial decline in the traditional manufacture. The new 'economic gospel'[2] banished thoughts of a primarily agrarian society. Government planning was too busy investigating the potentialities of new demand.

Nevertheless, the problem of critical fluctuations in the demand for textiles remained a pressing one. And, correspondingly, the government now felt its task to be not to reduce the relative importance of the industrial sector of the economy but positively to buttress that sector against the vicissitude of market forces. Yet there was little sign that those in office had sufficient analytic skill or the effective power to countervail directly the principal causes of decline in the overseas demand for English cloth. For example, in the early 1620's there was virtually no appreciation, in government circles, of the essential relationship between currency manipulations abroad and declining cloth output at home. And even if the connexion had been proved beyond all question it is doubtful—to judge by the passivity in the face of pressure on other grounds to manipulate the English coinage—if a policy of devaluation, in order to increase demand for exports, could have been effected. In any case, in so far as the principal causes of abrupt depressions in English industry derived from the European scene, the government was normally powerless to prevent them. It is true enough that there were attempts to counter European developments—e.g. the frequently reiterated prohibition of the export of raw materials to feed the growing continental industry—and that at each fresh crisis there was a frenzied effort to get to its root causes. But the fact remains that nearly every onslaught of depression caught the government unawares and ran its course independently of official action.

Clearly, therefore, it was not unreasonable that the government should devote its principal attention to those phases of economic dislocation where its authority could be most directly exercised and where, to

[1] Above, ch. 7.
[2] The phrase is Professor Fisher's ('Some Experiments in Company Organization', 185).

The Government and the Economy

unsophisticated eyes, it seemed easiest to alleviate the rigours of a slump. Hence the council, unable effectively to alter the forces which reduced the overseas demand for English cloth, concentrated its efforts on the intermediate demand exerted by exporting merchants, on the possibilities of owners of capital assuming more of the financial burden of a slump, and on measures of poor relief. From this willingness to manipulate economic structures in order to maintain employment, either in anticipation or, more often, in the face of a depression, there sprang some of the most representative of contemporary policies.

At times of extreme crisis the Privy Council might seriously discuss, as it did in 1616, the possibility of enforcing the participation in trade of non-mercantile capital in order to take unsold stocks off clothiers' hands.[1] But in the main, official attention was confined to merchants. In attempting, with varying degrees of success, to find some means of persuading traders to continue buying cloth at a time when they claimed that they were unable profitably to sell it abroad, the council found itself in a hornets' nest of controversial issues. Questions of immediate significance concerned the organization of trade in regulated companies as against more freedom to individual merchants to choose the time and destination of their shipments; the supply and turnover of mercantile capital; the clash of economic interest between industrial entrepreneurs and merchant exporters; and the extent to which different economic groups should bear or transfer the brunt of the effects of industrial deflation. Such matters in the main were not discussed with grandiose 'mercantilist' concepts of society in mind, but on the basis of an urgent quest for measures to relieve short-term exigencies. Although special interests—such as the outport merchants who pleaded for free trade in 1604, or the Staplers who perpetually tilted at the Merchant Adventurers' privileges—rarely ceased their quest for a favourable re-alignment of policy, it is evident that on the whole the government was willing to envisage the most extreme experiments only at times of the most extreme economic fluctuation.[2]

The initial government reaction to almost every outbreak of unemployment in cloth manufacturing was to call before the council the merchants or representatives of the companies normally concerned with the export of the relevant textiles. This was as true of crises provoked by an experiment in commercial organization such as that of 1614–17 as it was of the industrial depressions resulting from the sudden collapse of European

---

[1] There was then some thought that James I, the nobility, the council, and the leading citizens of London should contribute capital for this purpose. Above, p. 48.
[2] The principal exception here was the Cockayne project; see above, ch. 2, and below, pp. 247–8.

markets. Thus the Merchant Adventurers came before the privy councillors in 1620 when reports of unemployment flowed in from the broadcloth industry of the West, and English and foreign merchants exporting to France were interviewed in 1629 when depression settled on the East Anglian new drapery manufacture. In nearly every case the council demanded from the merchants an explanation of their failure to maintain purchases and ordered or exhorted them, sometimes on the direct promise of government action to improve the situation, to recommence their buying.

To such requests that they assume more of the burden of a depression, either by bearing the cost of unsold stocks or running the likely risk of falling prices, the traders might well answer that their capital was exhausted or tied up in existing stocks of their own, or that the market was so bad that they could see no reason in such a procedure. As with the Adventurers in April 1622,[1] they might be pushed to the point of at least claiming that they would withdraw from their trade, never to return, rather than be forced to continue to do business unprofitably in order to satisfy the clothing counties. The Privy Council, on its side, might threaten to withdraw the privileges of the company and throw the trade open to all comers if its request was not complied with. Thus early in 1622 —even while debates were proceeding which gave them an increased control of Baltic imports[2]—members of the Eastland Company exporting cloth through the Sound were told that if they did not maintain their purchases of East Anglian textiles their trade would be thrown open to the manufacturers who had such a 'great quantity of cloths lying upon their hands'. Indeed, some Suffolk clothiers used this instance as a defence against subsequent charges of having traded in the privileged areas.[3] In cases like this it was not so much that the government felt that a regulated company was positively hindering trade recovery: such threats were used as incentives to merchants to assume costs which the council felt they ought to bear in order to guard against the greater dangers of chronic unemployment. The best illustration of this tendency was the assumption by the government of its right to enforce a quota system by which individual merchants were obliged to purchase stipulated amounts of cloth. This happened with the Cockayne adventurers in 1616, and with the Merchant Adventurers, who were otherwise threatened with disenfranchisement, in February 1622, and with the merchants dealing in new draperies in 1629.[4] At the root of such a development in government

---

[1] Above, pp. 65–6.   [2] Above, pp. 87–8.
[3] *A.P.C. 1621–1623*, pp. 223–4 and E. 134/5 Charles I/Easter 1 (1629).
[4] Above, pp. 47–8, 65–6, 107.

policy lay an attitude to property which would be almost unthinkable in the twentieth century. For it assumed that the government might exercise direct command over the distribution of private traders' capital with no regard for compensation and no possibility of alternative uses.

The companies' trading policies could also be manipulated in another direction by forcing merchants to ship goods at a time when they were reluctant to do so on non-economic grounds. Thus, the Adventurers in 1627 were trying to bring pressure to bear on the Dutch by abstaining from shipments to the United Provinces. The council, in its anxiety to preserve industrial peace, was forced to order the company to send off its convoys notwithstanding the demands of private economic policy.[1]

There was, however, a limit to the extent to which the merchant groupings could be bullied into adopting policies repugnant to their members. The threat to throw open a trade might not always be matched by the availability of alternative supplies of trading capital. If a trade were opened to the generality, and if the established merchants then withdrew from active business, the likelihood was that there would not be sufficient entrepreneurial skill or working capital to maintain commerce even at the low level which had originally occasioned the pressure on the existing traders. The primary example of this had occurred during the Cockayne experiment, which had been effectively sabotaged by the refusal of leading Merchant Adventurers to participate.[2] And in the previous reign, when, in response to a slump, Blackwell Hall had been opened to all in 1587 and the Adventurers had refused to co-operate, the lesson had been that the remedy was worse than the disease: the company was speedily reinstated.[3] Yet whatever the final outcome of such policies, the government more often than not put its own estimation of social peace higher than its regard for commercial property.

The official attitude towards industrial capital was no less marked by a solicitous regard for the maintenance of employment in the textile areas. Of course, clothiers could always claim with some justice that all their capital was tied up in unsold stocks so that, without help from mercantile capital, it was absolutely impossible for them to maintain production. This was, for instance, the almost unanimous complaint of manufacturers in 1622,[4] and was the argument put forward by Surrey clothiers in 1630.[5] Nevertheless, there were times when the Privy Council was as firm with clothiers as it was with merchants: commanding them, on the threat of extreme displeasure or the promise of government efforts to stimulate mercantile purchases, to continue to provide work for their employees.

[1] Above, p. 112,.   [2] Above, pp. 37, 39.   [3] Wheeler, p. 376.
[4] Above, pp. 55–6, 65, 69–70.   [5] S.P.D. Chas. I, 177/56I.

This attitude, as well as that towards overseas traders, is best exemplified by the letter which was sent to the J.P.s of the ten leading clothing counties in 1622, in the course of which entrepreneurs were treated to a disquisition on the duties as well as the rights of industrial and commercial enterprise:[1]

as upon calling of the merchants here before us and due examination of the state of their trade at this present, we have taken order in the behalf of the clothier for the taking off (as far as may be) of such cloth as now lieth upon the clothiers . . . so we do hereby require you to call before you such clothiers as you shall think fitting and to deal effectually with them for the employment of such weavers, spinners, and other persons as are now out of work . . . so may we not induce that the clothiers in that or any other county should at their pleasure and without giving knowledge thereof unto this Board dismiss their workfolks, who, being many in number and most of them of the poorer sort, are in such cases likely by their clamour to disturb the quiet and government of those parts where they live . . . wherein if any clothier shall after sufficient warning refuse or neglect to appear before you or otherwise shall obstinately deny to yield to such overtures in this case as shall be reasonable and just, you shall take good bonds of them for refusing to appear before us and immediately certify their names unto this Board. [A general rule for woolgrowers, merchants and clothiers is that] whosoever had a part of the gain in profitable times since his Majesty's happy reign must now in the decay of trade (till that may be remedied) bear a part of the public loss as may best conduce to the good of the public and the maintenance of the general trade.

The government's main aim in all of this was to keep the wheels of industry turning by encouraging or enforcing the circulation of capital. Hence there might even be successful attempts to protect debtors who were temporarily short of funds where those debtors were manufacturers whose businesses might otherwise cease. This happened in the early 1620's when the council used its powers to protect insolvent clothiers in Suffolk and Devon.[2]

Such direct interferences with the processes of private business and the flows of private capital were not the only reflection of government anxiety concerning the disastrous repercussions of large-scale unemployment. Intermittent depression time and again had forced men to question the wisdom of prevailing modes of trade organization. And an economic crisis was in almost every case the cue for bitter discussion on the rival

[1] *A.P.C. 1621–1623*, pp. 131–3.
[2] S.P.D. Jas. I, 130/97, 131/95, 134/94; *A.P.C. 1621–1623*, pp. 278, 313–14, 381–2

The Government and the Economy

economic virtues of a regulated as against a free trade. In the main the government was concerned to investigate the repercussions of different trading arrangements on the effective demand for English cloth and therefore on the state of public order.[1] Parallel with this tendency, and, for obvious reasons, much more continuous than the anxiety of privy councillors on the subject, was the opposition of important groups in the Commons to any company which tended to concentrate trade in London to the detriment of the provincial ports or whose control of the timing of and destination of exports militated against the provincial merchant with his small stock of capital and his need for a rapid turnover. Nevertheless, the free trade movement in the Commons, which was almost directly representative of the outports, had little hope of shaping policy unless the executive concurred. And the only time at which there was a possibility of such concurrence normally came during a slump. Thus, the outstanding example of a variation in a government policy during the period came as a result of the crisis of the early 1620's.

The Merchant Adventurers, who normally handled almost three-quarters of London textile exports, came under severe criticism as a result of the depression, as did most of the mercantile cartels.[2] Parliamentary pressure, with the connivance of the council and the reluctant acquiescence of the company itself, secured an important liberalization of trading arrangements: the council clearly anticipated—or hoped—that the unsold stocks of manufacturers might be disposed of more easily if more merchants were allowed to participate in the trade. Consequently, in a drastic policy-change of 1621 and 1624, membership in the Merchant Adventurers was thrown open, all non-members were allowed to trade in kersies, dozens and new draperies, and, in addition, provincial merchants were given permission to export coloured cloths to the company's privileged areas.[3] Practical expediency had at last rendered effective the traditional jealousies of provincial merchants; although ten years later the Privy Council revoked this freedom, in response to another period of poor trade and without the benefit of parliamentary advice or the stimulus of parliamentary harrying, at the request of the company, and committed itself once again to the concept of a strictly regulated trade.[4]

It was, however, not only at times of economic depression that the government was called upon to adjudicate the controversy between

---

[1] The Cockayne project might seem to be an exception to this rule since the old company of Merchant Adventurers was deprived of its privileges at the peak of a boom in exports. But, in fact, the new traders who came in were similarly organized: the experiment (which was largely one with personnel and techniques) took place *within* the traditional framework of company organization.

[2] Above, pp. 62–4.   [3] Above, pp. 68–71.   [4] Above, pp. 121–2

supporters and opponents of a regulated trade. Provincial merchants and interlopers, who could not or would not keep to company rules regarding shipments, were permanently opposed to this method of organization. Clothiers, on the other hand, would normally be unconcerned with such matters while demand and prices held up; only during a crisis would they tend to demand more buyers. Finally, there were those who sincerely felt that it would be to England's economic benefit to dispense with trade regulation. And as the realization spread that English textiles could best subsist in a competitive world by competitive pricing, so this last viewpoint increased in importance.[1] All critical arguments emphasized that the original basis of company organization—the limitation of competition between English exporters, the attempts to create a seller's market abroad—was not suited to a continued and prosperous demand for the products of England's export industries. Commercial expansion, critics argued, could be the welcome result of a destruction of corporate monopolies and a liberalization of the conditions of trade. The defenders of the regulated companies, on the other hand, usually claimed that the organizations benefited the nation as a whole by successfully maintaining export prices, by keeping the costs of imports low, by defeating the attempts of aliens to arrange commerce to England's disadvantage, and by generally supporting industry at a prosperous level and stimulating high-quality production.[2] However, in addition to these arguments on principle, the companies were frequently forced to state their case on a specific issue. When answering the bitter attacks during a depression, adherents of a regulated trade indicated the poor trading conditions already existing as a strong reason against allowing more merchants into the trade. More consumers rather than more dealers would be the answer to the depression, they said: 'what needs that [more exporters] when there are already ten times as many Merchant Adventurers as the quantity of the trade will employ?' 'To add more persons to be Merchant Adventurers, is to put more sheep into one and the same pasture, which is to starve them all.'[3]

Since a free trade was the exception in the significant commercial areas during the sixteenth and seventeenth centuries, it would be undeniably true to say that in the last resort the government favoured the system of company regulation. But this was principally because it was an arrangement which men in power considered best suited to the prevailing conditions. Of course, this might merely mean that a privileged company

[1] Above, pp. 221–3.
[2] The classic defence of a regulated company is John Wheeler's *A Treatise of Commerce* (1601).
[3] Both quotations derive from the slump of the early 1620's (*Commons Debates, 1621*, VII, 225; Add. MSS. 34324, fol. 195).

was one of the best means of securing to government officials non-salaried incomes which a more circumspect age had labelled bribes. But on the whole, it could be argued that such an organization fulfilled various important functions: it acted as a quasi-official protective and representative agent abroad, much as later consuls did; it was a strategic source of royal loans and a convenient site for discontinuous taxation; its control of trade facilitated the collection of customs; it was, in the bellicose conditions of the time, a useful agent for the organization of convoys and the protection of shipping; and, in a period which, to a considerable extent, still viewed trade as an extension of warfare by which one country's gain was another's loss, a strong company was held to be the best means of ensuring England's interest against the European countries, of maintaining export prices and reducing import prices, and of carrying on that extensive economic war of ban and counter-ban, which passed for peaceful commerce at the time.

There are also examples of official protection to company trading which stem directly from an employment policy—although they bear the superficial marks of being concerned solely with private or strategic interests. Outstanding in this respect was the order of 1622 which confirmed the Eastland Company's monopoly of Baltic imports. At first glance this appears as a forerunner of the Navigation Acts in so far as they aimed at stimulating English shipping and countering the mercantile strength of the Dutch. But closer investigation has shown that in fact the order was a direct response to the complaints of the company that competition (from the Dutch) in imports was seriously reducing the capacity of English exporters to buy up the products of the depressed East Anglian cloth industry. It was hoped that by ensuring Englishmen the control of their returns from the Baltic, the export of cloth would be stimulated at a time of slump.[1]

There was yet another reason why, over the long run, the privileges of the leading companies were very little impaired. This derived from a practical factor already mentioned: the nature and sources of the risk capital available for investment in specific lines of commerce. As in the case of its ability to bring pressure to bear on merchants to buy up stocks, the council was limited in its attempts to experiment with the structure of trade by reason of the danger of alienating the existing participants. In 1614–17, for instance, it was found that the abstention of the leading Adventurers, with their capital, had reduced the trade to northern Europe to near chaos. In the subsequent words of the company: 'ignorant, weak newcomers . . . with all the spurs that were almost weekly put

[1] Above, pp. 87–8.

into them by the complaints of the clothiers . . . and by their orders enforcing the particular brethren to buy up the cloth . . . yet were not able to buy up the cloth or maintain the markets in any good measure.'[1] To throw open the trade, on the pretext of expanding demand, with no assurance that company members would remain active, might only aggravate the slump. There were obvious economic limitations to a policy which contradicted the expectations of private capital.

In fact, in nearly every severe crisis the government found that its powers to affect demand were exhausted at an early stage. But even before this point had been reached it was the general practice to bolster these attempts to maintain private industrial activity with other measures, which tried much more directly to alleviate distress at the local level. Indeed, it was for just such a purpose that the Elizabethan Poor Law had been designed, and the government was never reluctant to use its powers in the cause of protecting living standards by the enforcement of general poor relief, price control, and minimum wage supports. The practices of Stuart officialdom in this regard, however much they reflected a sophisticated social conscience, were marked by a practical expediency. For they were an integral part of the overall effort to keep the populace in a quiescent frame of mind. Clearly, this aim would be strongest when the council was trying to dispense with parliamentary aids to government and therefore desired to offset any distress which might lead to an irresistible popular demand to recall Parliament. It is this which explains the reputation of the personal government with regard to the efficiency of its central administration. And to judge by the experience of the years after 1628, official attempts at poor relief were as sincere and wholehearted as was then humanly possible.

The narrative sections of the earlier chapters of this book have already illustrated how it was in the face of textile depression that the government attempted to secure a more than normally efficient enforcement of the requirements of the Elizabethan Poor Law. This applied as much to the provisions for 'setting the poor on work' with capital derived from local taxation, as it did to those which aimed at more direct relief. Thus in the early 1620's the Privy Council exerted considerable effort in exhortations to J.P.s in the western counties to enforce the Poor Law, 'because we have been informed of diverse tumultuous assemblies and riots in some of those western parts occasioned partly through want of employment for the poorer sort by the decay of clothing'.[2] The situation seems to have been

[1] Hargrave MSS. 321, pp. 186–7.
[2] *A.P.C. 1621–1623*, pp. 224–5. This, of course, is just one example of many such efforts in the 1620's.

even more urgent after 1628, and the closest attention was given to problems of poor relief in East Anglia, which ultimately led to the issue of a special commission in 1631. It was, indeed, at the latter time, in the textile-producing counties, that the principal efforts were made, and most success attained, in easing the burden of the slump for the distressed weavers and spinners and their families. The depressed years after 1628, in their effects upon the stimulation of poor relief by the central government, were a fitting prelude to the period of Caroline paternalism.[1]

In conjunction with these moves to redistribute income to the benefit of the poor, a slump which coincided with a bad harvest would normally provoke far-reaching government efforts to facilitate the supply of food and lower the price of bread. At times this might be almost impossible. But, given the normally poor system of transportation and distribution, there was often scope for price reduction through an easing of the processes of immediate supply of grain and an elimination of its more frivolous uses. On this basis the government moved not so much with some ideal of a consumer society in mind, as with a positive fear of starvation and the unrest which accompanied it. And it was in just such a context that the anti-middleman policy, which has been held to be a marked feature of internal trade regulation, was bolstered and applied. The roots of such a policy lay in the fear of the effects of the high price of necessities upon economic and social well-being, and a depression was most likely to bring this fear into the open. Thus during the crises of the early 1620's and the early 1630's the government moved as firmly as it could to control the supply of grain, eliminate speculators and hoarders, avoid unnecessary processing of barley, and bring down the current price of bread. By January 1631 the Book of Orders, which outlined the requisite regulations, was issued on a permanent basis.[2]

Finally, in the way of direct local efforts to improve the lot of the poverty-stricken textile workers, it was natural that the government should now and then feel stirred to interfere in the free play of market forces which, no matter what their beauty or inevitability, were combining to reduce real wages. Government wage policies in the sixteenth and seventeenth centuries were ambivalent. On the one hand, the Statute of Artificers and many local wage assessments aimed at a ceiling for wages which might limit industrial mobility and/or keep down industrial costs. On the other hand, there were times when the short-run effects of fluctuations in demand and supply put a pressure on wages sufficient to threaten social disturbance. In these latter circumstances the official

[1] For the details, see above, pp. 108–10, 117–18.   [2] Above, p. 117.

reaction was to intervene in order to establish minimum rates of pay at least at subsistence level. Examples of this occurred in 1603-4, when statutory power was given to the assessment of minimum wages; in 1629, when Essex J.P.s were ordered to maintain the wages of employees in the bay-making industry; in 1630 and 1631 generally throughout East Anglia; and in 1636, again in Essex.

The lesson was obvious: industrial no less than commercial regulation had to be an essential attribute of a government policy whose primary aim was the continuity of employment. With respect to the textile industry government policy, no less than in regard to the commercial structure, illustrates a search for stability which should be distinguished from the sixteenth-century emphasis on the passive ideal of an agrarian society. The prevailing fear was of unemployment or excessively low standards of living, and any move which might guard against such eventualities was favourably considered. It was for this reason that frequently there were conscious attempts *not* to enforce aspects of the Elizabethan code of industrial regulation. This applied, for instance, to the legal requirements of a seven-year apprenticeship before practising the trade of cloth-making. For by the early seventeenth century there were sufficient unapprenticed weavers, clothiers and the like to make the enforcement of such a provision a dangerous prelude to unemployment for a host of textile workers.[1] The same principle—that a conflict between the law and the desire to maintain employment should more frequently be decided in favour of the latter—was applied in the case of laws or proposed edicts towards the improvement of the quality of English textiles.

The recurrent campaigns against false manufacture can themselves be seen as integral parts of a policy designed to increase the demand for English cloth: certainly this was the burden of most complaints by merchants at times of depression.[2] It was felt that if the quality could be improved then cloth would secure a better sale abroad. Consequently there were intermittent attempts throughout the period to enforce the laws designed for this purpose.[3] But the fact, not entirely appreciated at the time, that low-quality manufacture was more often a sign of cost-reducing measures than a proof of original sin, meant that a strict application of the law, by increasing costs, might put the marginal operator out of business. And when the realization came that this was more than just a remote possibility, the government was forced to compromise with its legalistic principles. This happened, for example, in the 1630's when strong efforts to experiment with the arrange-

[1] Davies, 226-7. [2] Above, pp. 143-6. [3] Above, pp. 120, 144, 145-6.

ments for textile production in the West were abandoned as it came to be recognized that an elimination of the notorious gig mills or of the specialist market spinner, whatever their effects on quality, would only serve to provoke a crisis of unemployment.[1]

Hence the government's approach to the industrial structure of the old draperies was determined in the last resort by a desire to guard against those periods of distress and tumult, fear of which in the sixteenth century had produced legislation designed to restrict industrialization. However, by the early seventeenth century the primary emphasis had been concentrated on at least sustaining the level of employment, and possibly increasing it. There was no thought of enforcing any policy which, no matter what its effect over a long period of time, might throw people out of work in the short run. However, there was no way of telling which way the government might act with these feelings in mind. Thus in 1615 and 1616 there was a renewed campaign against that bane of the sixteenth-century humanist, the middleman. Out of the controversy which accompanied the stoppage of trade consequent upon the Cockayne project emerged a theory that the price of English wool was too high. As was normal in such circumstances, it was widely felt that elimination or control of the despicable wool brogger would go far to reduce prices, and therefore make English textiles more competitive in European markets. As a result, an extensive survey of the mechanism of the internal wool trade in 1615 and 1616 was followed by orders designed to restrict the activities of wool broggers in all areas except those where small-scale producers of new draperies were dependent on middlemen the year round.[2] On the other hand, the crisis of the early 1620's saw an attempt to raise the price of wool by a repeal of the 1552 statute against wool middlemen (21 Jac. I, c. 28). And modern research has indicated that industrial regulation, in all the variety inherited from the sixteenth century, was not, by the early seventeenth, considered to be anything more than peripheral to the central concerns of government. As far as positive industrial policy went, it concentrated on the problems which most immediately might effect the peace and livelihood of local communities.[3]

It is possibly this which goes furthest to explain a new aspect of industrial policy: one which reflected the expanding possibilities of a more diversified economy and, ultimately, the economic reality of a decline in the traditional textile manufacture. Government intervention turned in the direction of industrial expansion.

As far as the government itself was concerned this was the real motive behind the Cockayne experiment. The adventurers themselves, as we saw

[1] Above, p. 146.   [2] Above, pp. 45–6.   [3] Davies, pp. 244–58.

in Chapter 2, far from embodying a sincere desire to create a large-scale finishing industry, concentrated their efforts largely on the hope of forcing the old company to share its profitable privileges with respect to unfinished broadcloth. But for the privy councillors the project, quite apart from the bribes which they received, provided an opportunity of satisfying what has subsequently been thought of as typically 'mercantilist' desire: to increase the value of exports and raise the level of employment. This, they hoped, might be done by converting the preponderant export of white broadcloth into the sale of dyed and dressed textiles, with a consequent increase in values and the growth of a domestic finishing industry capable of beating the Dutch out of the market. The experiment was a dismal failure. Its main interest from the point of view of government policy, however, resides in the fact that such a horrendous and arbitrary alteration of the established structure of commerce should have taken place when, far from there existing the urgent environment of a slump, the woollen trade to northern Europe was at the height of its prosperity. Whatever the other reasons for this departure, it is clear that the council was only finally persuaded to support the project, against its better judgement, by pressure from the Throne and extreme duplicity on the part of the projectors. It needed the exercise of extraordinary power to instigate an extraordinary experiment.

Less extraordinary, although in final effect they were much less important than Alderman Cockayne's plans, were those projects, favourably considered or even stimulated by the central government, for a different type of industrial expansion. In the main, government officials did little more than look with benign satisfaction on the developments which were beginning to make their mark in the early seventeenth century. But in some areas more positive steps were taken in an effort to promote economic growth.[1]

In its efforts to encourage the influx of new capital into old industries (e.g. the manufacture of soap, salt and starch) or to stimulate in new ways such pursuits as fishing or the manufacture of new draperies, it was natural that the government should envisage an adaptation of the traditional corporate and gild organizations. The result was a series of unsuccessful experiments in economic development, whose structure ranged from an industrial monopoly to a network of regional joint-stock organizations, and whose aim was more often the establishment than the regulation of a particular industry. With respect to the new draperies there were two main efforts to set up a system of quasi-public corpora-

[1] The following account is taken largely from Fisher, 'Some Experiments in Company Organization', 177–94.

tions, the second of which emerged from the confusions of the crisis of the early 1620's. These bodies were to be based on county administrative units and in part integrated with the poor-law system. They were intended to stimulate, and also exert quality control over, a growth in the new manufacture. In the end, these plans, like all the others, came to nothing. Their failure has been attributed to a fatal rigidity in the gild system itself and to the lustiness of new competition: the powers of the corporations, it has been said, bore no relation to the problems they had to solve.[1] In the main, therefore, the government was forced to let the principal elements in economic growth go their own way, and in the event it was even found impossible to regulate the quality of the new manufacture. Once more the government was forced back to a short-term approach to economic regulation. This was even more evident, to take another example, in its relationship with the monetary system.

The concern to alleviate dislocation which directly or indirectly shaped almost every important measure of industrial and commercial policy during the period, was an equally marked feature of the official attitude to the national and international currency system. As has already been abundantly shown, the economic fluctuations which so shook the economy of the early seventeenth century were to a significant degree intermingled with the general repercussions of an unstable monetary system. At one level variations in the prices of gold and silver provoked abrupt shifts in the flow of commodities, the balance of trade, and industrial prosperity. More basically, such variations stimulated even more violent ebbs and flows of bullion and ready money. It was therefore quite natural that so much government time and energy, in the line of economic policy, was devoted to questions of coinage valuations and monetary supplies. From this background, as we have already seen in Chapter 8, there emerged the framework of official discussion and activity so familiar to historians of 'mercantilist policy'.

There is no further need to outline the details of proposed and accepted policy which demonstrate, beyond all doubt, that the stimulus to government action lay immediately in the desire for an adequate supply of money in the kingdom—and that this found its origin in the painful experiences of intermittent monetary shortage. The role of liquid capital as a stimulant to continuous, diversified productive effort and the importance of a steady supply of cash in an underdeveloped economy deprived of the benefits of a sophisticated banking structure and widely circulating fiduciary instruments, do not need re-emphasis either. Threats to the monetary supply struck at the basis of an enormous range of internal

[1] Fisher, 'Some Experiments in Company Organization', 194.

economic activity, and, therefore, the *defensive* note which runs through other aspects of policy was more than ever evident in the official approach to monetary affairs.

It is not too difficult to recognize, in government attitudes and actions, widespread feelings concerning the wisdom of accumulating treasure and the economic and strategic strength which, it was felt, England might derive from such a process. These concepts, indeed, viewed by Adam Smith as a systematization of thought and policy, were those which he identified with mercantilism and ridiculed so ably on theoretical grounds. But it has already been argued in these pages[1] that it would be misleading to attempt to understand policy solely in terms of a spontaneous regard for the unlimited acquisition of treasure. In any case, it is likely that such views envisaged the inflow of bullion not so much as an augmentation of monetary supplies—which would be inflationary and self-defeating—but as an increase in the supply of capital, to be absorbed into an expanding economic system.[2] But quite apart from such arguments, the fact remains that it is possible to see every policy measure in the light of the prevailing economic conditions which posed direct and indirect threats to England's monetary supplies and forced the government on to the defensive and into policy discussions primarily intended to reduce an outflow rather than augment an inflow of money. This was equally true, although in each case little positive action resulted from them, of all considerations of monetary policy: the proposed enforcement of statutes prohibiting the export of coin and commanding the 'employment' of the proceeds of imports by aliens; the plans for government monopolies of money-changing and exchange transactions; the projects for currency manipulation and export- and import-control. In the event the government was forced to leave the determination of bullion flows to market forces operating within the framework of established mint prices, supplemented by the intermittent enforcement of pre-existing laws. And, not surprisingly, the criterion used to defeat great plans for monetary experiments was comparable to that which occasioned the initial discussions: the reverence for economic stability. In the last resort the government concluded, or was reluctantly persuaded, that the cost of projects to maintain monetary supplies—measured in economic dislocation at other points—was too great to justify experiment. At all points the delicacy of the economic and social mechanism was appreciated as perhaps the most important consideration in shaping policy.

[1] Above, pp. 192–4.
[2] R. W. K. Hinton, 'The Mercantile System in the Time of Thomas Mun', *Econ. Hist. Rev.* 2nd ser. VII (1955), 282–3; Gould, 'The Trade Crisis of the Early 1620's and English Economic Thought', 130–2.

We have seen that government action in the early seventeenth century was marked by a search for stability: by a valid fear of unemployment and economic instability. Contrasted with the sixteenth century, which had the same ends in view, the period under discussion demonstrated that industrial restrictions were not the only possible outcome of such an attitude. The aim was, instead, to protect England against the harsher repercussions of economic fluctuation without regressing in terms of the industrial and commercial structure. And the urgency of this aim explains the assumption that, in its cause, the rights of private property and of established organizations could be abrogated without further thought. In its fear of the bread riot the government, short of shattering the very bases of society, was willing to entertain virtually any idea. Indeed, among the primary motives of the quest for expansion and diversification, which was a feature of long-term developments, was a desire to compensate for the decline in the traditional industry and provide outlets for unemployed factors of production. This last attitude ultimately shaded imperceptibly into a new appraisal of the role and value of competition for English trade and industry. It served to set the stage for those revolutions in policy and more especially in outlook which became so evident in the generations after the Restoration.

Thus the setting within which it is absolutely necessary to study the formulation of government economic policy is that which has been the general subject-matter of this book. Policy and intermittent trade crisis are historically inseparable. This is true to the extent that we can never consider in isolation those elements of official policy which so many students of the period have called 'mercantilist'. The desire to prevent or alleviate undue commercial fluctuation is surely not a remarkable or exceptional administrative viewpoint. Yet it is the only element which really binds together generations of policy; and reasonably consistent and pragmatic responses to consistent fluctuation in an economic environment whose basic elements were slow to change hardly merit treatment as a full-blown system. Disparate official measures were not meaningful and complementary parts of any 'plan' greater than a pressing need to maintain the economy on at least an even keel. In any case, few statesmen had the inclination or the ability to formulate an ideal image of economic society and the policy which would bring it into being.

However, few processes could be more misleading than to measure the extent of the Stuart government's economic participation by the number and range of the laws in existence, by edicts promulgated, or by the formal exhortations to action which proceeded, with such monotonous regularity, from the Privy Council. Historians by now are quick to appreciate that a plethora of regulations may well be, by the very frequency of the latter, a better indication of what was *not* done than of what was. For we are dealing with an age in which the formal ability to articulate policy had developed well beyond the administrative capacity to enforce it: an England all of whose economic regulations were fully in force would have been unrecognizable as well as unthinkable.

This inability to shape the larger economic developments closer to the government's heart's desire went along with a relative failure to alleviate more directly the impact of depression. The government failed to control, as far as England was concerned, the international flows of bullion. It was unable to come effectively to grips with the principal causes of commercial fluctuations and its attempts to sustain demand by pressure on English capital had obvious limits beyond which they could not go. The grand design for finishing cloth was a dismal holocaust of official expectations. The most that industrial policy could do was to abstain from those measures of interference (for example the enforcement of quality requirements) which might have provoked further unemployment. The dynamic elements in economic development during the early seventeenth century were moulded by market forces, and the government's relation to the economy—although its extent was admittedly wide—was effectively confined to sustaining some of the commercial and industrial organizations destined, in the long run, to survive or perish more by dint of their economic usefulness. The period, as far as the government was concerned, was marked by no revolution in the institutional framework within which economic fluctuations and developments took place. There is nothing to compare with the sixteenth-century economic statutes or the eighteenth-century Enclosure Acts. Adherents of government action must have derived most satisfaction from an appreciation of the direct relief organized and stimulated by the central government. The poor laws and the regulations for grain markets, although they were to some extent hamstrung by an impecunious and ramshackle administrative structure, were frequently marked by a sincerity and doggedness of purpose which served as a peripheral defence for some communities during the starvation-ridden horrors of a seventeenth-century slump.

These concluding remarks are not intended to be either a proof of the inevitability of governmental inefficiency or a further indication of the poverty of talent under the first two Stuarts. In large part the absence of any wholesale social engineering reflects the government situation during a period in which administrative structures were too weak to carry into effect the tasks which might have been entrusted to them. Yet the absence of any real tendency in this direction also needs explanation. Even the relaxations of trade regulations in 1621 and 1624, which might be taken as evidence of a less conservative approach to commercial problems, ultimately, by the tentative nature of their application and the relative speed of their revocation, only serve to underline the fact that the time was one which was far less 'heroic' in its approach to commercial problems than, for instance, the mid-sixteenth century. To some extent this may have been due to a distinct decline in the standards of administrative ability under the first two Stuarts. Men of vision and executive power were markedly absent from most of the deliberations on commercial affairs at the time, while James's most important contribution merely led to the disasters of the cloth-finishing project and Charles's attempts at direct economic interference too often produced only extreme mercantile insecurity. But quite apart from the low calibre of men of affairs the official approach to trade and industry primarily derived its character from the fact that the early seventeenth century marked one of the many transitions in English economic life. It bridged a gap between an England whose typical statutory products were the Cloth Acts of the 1550's and one whose significant legal expressions lay in the Navigation Laws. Operating when the established framework of industrial England was no longer seriously questioned and before the new developments had become sufficiently important to be candidates for significant legal buttressing, the administrators of the first forty years of the seventeenth century were in no position, and did not possess a sufficiently forthright philosophy, to attempt to interfere spontaneously and effectively in the course of economic events.

It was for this sort of reason that the government's main problems were those of day-to-day administration. And in this respect, although part of its emphasis was novel, it added little to the inherited official tools of policy. This was perhaps more because the sixteenth century had exhausted the possibilities of administrative enactment, than because the seventeenth was particularly unimaginative. That most of the official efforts positively to participate in the economy were failures is no reason to ignore the implications of government policy. For policy and official discussions were directly involved with economic change, and an appreciation of them, while it demonstrates their specific inability to direct the course or guard against the consequences of change, can tell us a great deal about the obdurate economic facts with which they so unsuccessfully tried to deal.

Appendixes

Appendices

APPENDIX A

STATISTICS OF THE CLOTH TRADE

The data on the following pages derive partly from a study of port books by the present writer, and partly from figures already available in secondary authorities. Where the source for any table is not specified, the relevant statistics have been adduced from one of two bodies of information.

(i) For the years 1606, 1614, 1616 and 1618: Astrid Friis, *Alderman Cockayne's Project and the Cloth Trade*.
(ii) For the years 1620, 1622, 1628, 1632 and 1640: E. 190/23/3; E. 190/25/1; E. 190/32/3; E. 190/36/5; E. 190/43/4.

All the figures have been converted into notional shortcloths. Customs authorities at the time circumvented the difficulties involved in taxing the great variety of types of old draperies by propounding a fictional 'cloth' of 24 yards into which all these woollens were translated according to a standard table. This enabled the standard (old) custom of 6s. 8d. per 'cloth' to be levied on the most disparate goods exported by Englishmen. It also means that the historian is provided with an effective measure by which to compare and collate statistics initially applicable to a bewildering multitude of textiles. The main types of cloth, with their 'notional' equivalents in shortcloths, are given in the following table:

Cloth	Notional equivalent
Longcloths (e.g. western, dressed and undressed; Kent and Reading, dressed)	One and one-third 'shortcloths'
Shortcloths (mainly western)	One and one-sixth 'shortcloths'
Suffolk shortcloths, dressed	One 'shortcloth'
Northern dozens (single)	One-half 'shortcloth'
Kersies (all sorts)	One-third 'shortcloth'
Devon dozens (narrow)	One-quarter 'shortcloth'
Spanish cloths	In direct proportion to length

The countries here noted as 'markets' are, in fact, merely the *immediate destinations* of the cloths (as noted in the port books). This information does not, therefore, necessarily tell us anything concerning the final centres of consumption. All the figures have been rounded to the nearest 'shortcloth'; hence the totals need not necessarily coincide with the sum of the individual figures reproduced in any one table.

Table 1. *Export of shortcloths from London by English merchants, 1598–1640*

Year	Cloths	Year	Cloths
1598	100,551	1620	85,517 (85,741)
1598–1600 (Av.)	97,737	1622	75,631 (76,624)
1601	100,380	1626	c. 91,000
1602	113,512	1627	c. 88,000
1603	89,619	1628	c. 108,000 (108,021)
1604	112,785	1631	84,334
1606	126,022	1632	99,020
1614	127,215	1633	80,844
1616	88,172	1640	86,924
1618	102,332		

Sources: 1598: S.P.D. Eliz., 268/101.
1598–1640: F. J. Fisher, 'London's Export Trade in the Early Seventeenth Century', *Econ. Hist. Rev.*, 2nd ser. III (1952), 153.

The figures for 1620, 1622 and 1628 in brackets are those compiled by the present writer from the port books. They differ from those published by Professor Fisher, but this is an expected state of affairs when dealing with statistics as detailed as these.

For a tentative estimate, derived from the accounts of the Great Farm of the Customs, for the years 1605–1611, see above, ch. 1.

Table 2. *Export of notional shortcloths to certain areas for selected years by English merchants from London*

A. *Numbers of cloths*

	1598[1]	1606[2]	1620	1622	1628	1632	1640
Germany and the United Provinces	71,327	95,608	58,051	50,187	96,462	59,478	45,140
Eastland	11,932	8,255	2,848	4,054	2,359	2,469	4,507
Russia	1,863	2,416	1,492	1,606	3,587	3,910	4,662
France	6,252	6,401	1,934	839	nil	*	*
Levant and Italy	8,833	8,291	9,501	8,036	2,034	*	*
Spain and 'Islands'	nil	3,110	4,320	3,413	nil	*	*
Africa (mainly Barbary)	2,394	1,942	237	370	1,637	*	*

B. *Percentages of total exports*

	1598	1606	1620	1622	1628	1632	1640
Germany and the United Provinces	70·9	75·9	67·7	65·5	89·3	60·1	51·9
Eastland	11·9	6·6	3·3	5·3	2·2	2·5	5·2
Russia	1·9	1·9	1·7	2·1	3·3	3·9	5·4
France	6·2	5·1	2·3	1·1	—	*	*
Levant and Italy	8·8	6·6	11·1	10·5	1·9	*	*
Spain and 'Islands'	—	2·5	5·0	4·5	—	*	*
Africa	2·4	1·5	0·3	0·5	1·5	*	*

[1] 1598 figures are in S.P.D. Eliz., 268/101.
[2] The 1606 figures have been reproduced as Friis printed them. However, if the amounts for different types of cloths, which she gives in an appendix, be converted into shortcloths they give a larger figure for the Merchant Adventurers—this latter conversion is used for the figures of the Adventurers given below, Tables 3–6.

Table 3. Cloth exports from London to privileged areas of Merchant Adventurers (excluding Calais and Dunkirk)

	1598 Amount	1606 Amount	%	1614 Amount	%	1616 Amount	1618 Amount	%	1620 Amount	%	1622 Amount	%	1628 Amount	%	1632 Amount	%	1640 Amount	%
United Provinces	*	(30,377) 36,170	35·7	(34,462) 42,862	43·3	*	(c. 31,500)	46·4	35,716	61·5	26,518	52·8	65,597	68·1	36,425	61·2	24,377	5·9
Germany	*	(55,858) 65,166	64·3	(46,278) 56,046	56·7	*	(c. 35,000)	51·6	22,336	38·5	23,668	47·2	30,865	32·0	23,053	38·8	20,763	46·0
TOTAL	71,327 plus 8,347 by interlopers	(86,235) 101,337	100·0	(80,740) 98,908	100·0	51,564	(67,853 sic)		58,051	100·0	50,187	100·0	96,462	100·0	59,478	100·0	45,140	100·0

The figures in brackets are those given by Friis. There seems, however, to be some confusion; for if one reduces the amounts of different *types* (given in her appendix) to notional equivalents, then one obtains a larger total figure (given for 1606 and 1614 without brackets). Friis seems, in fact, to have added all types of the main varieties of cloth together without weighting. The figures for 1598 come from S.P.D. Eliz., 268/101.

Table 4. Main types of cloth exported from London to Germany and the United Provinces
(reduced to notional terms)

	1606 Amount	%	1614 Amount	%	1620 Amount	%	1622 Amount	%	1628 Amount	%	1632 Amount	%	1640 Amount	%
Undressed shortcloths	79,475	78·4	57,599	58·2	31,061	53·5	23,721	47·3	43,070	44·7	34,127	57·4	23,488	52·0
Undressed longcloths	6,730	6·6	29,521	29·8	16,954	29·2	14,730	29·4	20,434	21·2	10,836	18·2	6,021	13·3
Undressed coarse shortcloths	970	1·0	225	*	nil	—	1,570	3·1	nil	—	nil	—	nil	—
Long Kent and Reading cloths, dressed	7,384	7·3	6,266	6·3	8,116	14·0	7,443	14·8	12,584	13·1	4,055	6·8	3,187	7·1
Suffolk shortcloths, dressed	484	*	183	*	1,140	2·0	703	1·4	665	*	261	*	72	*
Dressed shortcloths	89	*	11	*	nil	—	50	*	287	*	2	*	20	*
Dressed longcloths	281	*	2,103	2·1	49	*	81	*	1,537	1·6	362	*	859	1·9
Devon dozens (narrow)	1,502	1·5	1,512	1·5	697	1·2	957	1·9	7,439	7·7	3,042	5·1	915	2·0
Northern dozens (single)	139	*	nil	—	248	*	369	*	1,359	1·4	102	*	26	*
Northern kersies	4,062	4·0	1,002	1·0	84	*	99	*	2,515	2·6	494	*	79	*
Hampshire kersies	225	*	11	*	nil	—	nil	—	315	*	3	*	57	*
Spanish cloths	nil	—	nil	—	nil	—	nil	—	3,262	3·4	5,542	9·3	9,996	22·1
TOTAL (including other cloths)	101,337	100·0	98,908	100·0	58,051	100·0	50,187	100·0	96,462	100·0	59,478	100·0	45,140	100·0

Table 5. *Main types of cloth exported from London to Germany (reduced to notional terms)*

	1606 Amount	%	1614 Amount	%	1620 Amount	%	1622 Amount	%	1628 Amount	%	1632 Amount	%	1640 Amount	%
Undressed shortcloths	50,190	77·0	37,451	66·8	13,815	61·9	11,946	50·5	16,978	55·0	14,671	63·6	11,106	53·5
Undressed longcloths	2,791	4·3	11,893	21·2	5,133	23·0	6,134	25·9	6,251	20·3	4,189	18·2	3,641	17·5
Undressed coarse shortcloths	870	1·3	161	*	nil	—	1,307	5·5	nil	—	nil	—	nil	—
Long Kent and Reading cloths, dressed	4,996	7·7	3,713	6·6	1,879	8·4	2,272	9·6	3,042	9·7	1,641	7·1	717	3·5
Suffolk shortcloths, dressed	424	*	178	*	1,068	4·8	675	2·9	488	1·6	233	*	nil	—
Dressed shortcloths	88	*	11	*	nil	—	nil	—	195	*	nil	—	20	*
Dressed longcloths	225	*	276	*	49	*	48	*	1,104	3·6	349	*	799	3·8
Devon dozens (narrow)	1,239	1·9	1,014	1·8	556	2·5	673	2·8	1,329	4·3	582	2·5	511	2·5
Northern dozens (single)	108	*	nil	—	248	1·1	367	1·6	607	2·0	58	*	2	*
Northern kersies	4,013	6·2	888	1·6	60	*	93	*	143	*	20	*	55	*
Hampshire kersies	225	*	11	*	nil	—	nil	—	8	*	nil	—	57	*
Spanish cloths	nil	—	nil	—	nil	—	nil	—	603	2·0	1,389	6·0	3,948	19·0
TOTAL (including other cloths)	65,166	100·0	56,046	100·0	22,336	100·0	23,668	100·0	30,865	100·0	23,053	100·0	20,763	100·0

262 Appendix A

Table 6. *Main types of cloth exported from London to the United Provinces (reduced to notional terms)*

	1606 Amount	%	1614 Amount	%	1620 Amount	%	1622 Amount	%	1628 Amount	%	1632 Amount	%	1640 Amount	%
Undressed shortcloths	29,285	81·0	20,148	47·0	17,246	48·3	11,775	44·4	26,092	39·8	19,447	53·4	12,382	50·8
Undressed longcloths	3,939	11·0	17,628	41·1	11,821	33·1	8,596	32·4	14,183	21·6	6,647	18·2	2,380	9·8
Undressed coarse shortcloths	100	*	64	*	nil	—	263	*	nil	—	nil	—	nil	—
Long Kent and Reading cloths, dressed	2,388	6·6	2,553	6·0	6,237	17·5	5,171	19·5	9,542	14·6	2,414	6·6	2,469	10·1
Suffolk shortcloths, dressed	60	*	5	*	72	*	28	*	177	*	28	*	72	*
Dressed shortcloths	1	*	nil	—	nil	—	50	*	92	*	21	*	nil	—
Dressed longcloths	56	*	1,827	4·3	nil	—	33	*	433	*	13	*	60	*
Devon dozens (narrow)	263	*	498	1·2	141	*	284	1·1	6,110	9·3	2,460	6·8	404	1·7
Northern dozens (single)	31	*	nil	—	nil	—	2	*	752	1·2	44	*	24	*
Northern kersies	49	*	114	*	24	*	6	*	2,371	3·6	474	1·3	24	*
Spanish cloths	nil	—	nil	—	nil	—	nil	—	2,659	4·1	4,153	11·4	6,048	24·8
TOTAL (including other cloths)	36,170	100·0	42,862	100·0	35,716	100·0	26,518	100·0	65,597	100·0	36,425	100·0	24,377	100·0

Table 7. *The export of cloths by Englishmen from London to Eastland*[1]
(*reduced to notional terms*)

	1606		1620		1622		1628		1632		1640	
	Amount	%	Amount	%	Amount	%	Amount	%	Amount	%	Amount	%
Suffolk shortcloths, dressed	6,885	83·4	2,297	80·7	3,247	80·1	1,562	66·2	2,142	86·8	4,391	97·4
Longcloths, undressed			220	7·7	227	5·6	nil	—	40	1·6	nil	—
Devon dozens (narrow)			166	5·8	293	7·2	174	7·4	61	*	18	*
Longcloths, dressed			64	2·3	132	3·3	245	10·4	69	*	40	*
Shortcloths, dressed	1,370	16·6	64	2·3	12	*	37	1·6	nil	—	2	*
Shortcloths, undressed			nil	—	11	*	nil	—	nil	—	nil	—
Long Kent and Reading cloths, dressed			19	*	37	*	130	5·5	19	*	nil	—
Spanish cloths			nil	—	nil	—	84	3·6	80	3·2	19	*
Others			19	*	95	2·3	125	5·3	58	2·3	37	*
TOTAL	8,255	100·0	2,848	100·0	4,054	100·0	2,359	100·0	2,469	100·0	4,507	100·0

[1] Friis also gives the following totals: 1614: 7,700; 1616: 8,713; 1618: 7,843.

Table 8. *The export of cloths by Englishmen from London to Russia (reduced to notional terms)*

	1606		1620		1622		1628		1632		1640	
	Amount	%	Amount	%	Amount	%	Amount	%	Amount	%	Amount	%
Suffolk shortcloths, dressed	2,103	87·0	1,111	74·5	1,079	67·2	1,667	46·5	2,084	53·3	1,367	29·3
Hampshire kersies			180	12·1	43	2·7	29	0·8	19	*	nil	—
Shortcloths, dressed			99	6·6	257	16·0	211	5·9	86	2·2	120	2·6
Longcloths, dressed			48	3·2	212	13·2	1,617	45·1	1,473	37·7	3,027	64·9
Yards of broadcloth			28	1·9	15	*	nil	—	nil	—	nil	—
Long Kent and Reading cloths			3	*			12	*	12	*	nil	—
Bridgwaters, dressed			22	1·5			nil	—	nil	—	nil	—
Ilminster kersies	313	13·0							6	*	45	1·0
Long stammell cloths					nil	—			9	*	nil	—
Spanish cloths									6	*	nil	—
Pennystones unfriezed									49	1·3	20	*
Northern dozens (double)			nil	—					15	*	19	*
Northern dozens (single)							42	1·2	47	1·2	nil	—
Northern kersies							nil	—	103	2·6	60	1·3
Northern plains							8	*	nil	—	3	*
Flannel									nil	—	nil	—
TOTAL	2,416	100·0	1,492	100·0	1,606	100·0	3,587	100·0	3,910	100·0	4,662	100·0

Table 9. *Total exports of undressed cloths by Englishmen from London (reduced to notional terms)*

	1606		1614		1620		1622		1628		1632		1640	
	Amount	%	Amount	%	Amount	%	Amount	%	Amount	%	Amount	%	Amount	%
Shortcloths	82,500	91·0	57,600	65·9	31,060	64·4	23,732	58·9	43,332	67·9	34,489	75·5	24,150	79·8
Longcloths	7,212	8·0	29,521	33·8	17,175	35·6	14,957	37·2	20,483	32·1	11,164	24·5	6,107	20·2
Coarse shortcloths	971	1·1	225	*	nil	—	1,569	3·9	nil	—	nil	*	nil	—
Miscellaneous	nil	—	nil	—	nil	—	nil	—	nil	—	22	—	24	*
TOTAL	90,683		87,346		48,235		40,258		63,815		45,675		30,281	
Undressed exports as percentage of total exports	72·0%		68·7%		56·3%		52·5%		59·1%		46·1%		34·8%	

The figures for 1606 and 1614 have been deduced from the details of types of cloth exported printed in Friis, pp. 453–6. I have translated them into notional shortcloths according to the practice of the customs authorities. However, Friis (p. 129) gives figures of undressed exports which are adduced by merely adding together all types without weighting. The resulting totals are therefore lower than mine (1606: 76,123; 1614: 71,539), as are the percentages which these bear to total exports (1606: 60·4 per cent; 1614: 56·2 per cent). In fact, comparing my figures with Professor Fisher's statistics of total exports (above, Table 1), mine seem an over-estimate. But the process of translation into 'shortcloths' is still useful for comparison with later years.

Appendix A

Table 10a. *The distribution of the main types of cloth exported by English merchants from London, 1622 (reduced to notional terms)*

	Germany and the United Provinces	Eastland	Russia	Remainder (mainly south Europe and Mediterranean)	TOTAL	Percentage
Undressed cloths (mainly West Country)	40,020	238	nil	nil	40,258	52·5
Suffolk shortcloths, dressed	703	3,247	1,079	4,794	9,823	12·8
Long Kent and Reading cloths, dressed	7,443	37	nil	1,915	9,395	12·3
Devon dozens (narrow)	958	293	nil	4,897	6,148	8·0
Longcloths, dressed (mainly Gloucestershire)	81	132	212	4,755	5,180	6·8
Northern kersies	99	85	nil	1,877	2,061	2·7
Hampshire kersies	nil	nil	43	755	798	1·0
TOTAL	—	—	—	—	76,624	

Table 10b. *Main types of cloth exported by Englishmen from London to northern Europe (Germany, United Provinces, Flanders, Russia, Eastland) (reduced to notional terms)*

	1606	1620	1622	1628	1632	1640
Undressed cloths (mainly West Country)	90,683	48,235	40,258	63,553	45,675	30,281
Suffolk shortcloths, dressed	9,521	4,632	5,066	3,894	4,599	5,839
Long Kent and Reading cloths, dressed	13,000	8,225	7,803	12,726	5,394	4,535
Devon dozens (narrow)	c. 2,000	c. 863	c. 1,250	7,613	3,283	1,112
Longcloths, dressed (mainly Gloucestershire)	c. 300	c. 161	c. 450	3,399	1,906	3,926
Northern kersies	4,062 (Adventurers only)	c. 85	c. 100	2,647	628	161

Table 11. *The export of Suffolk shortcloths dressed from London by Englishmen*

	Totals	Percentage of total exports
1565	9,745	?
1606	14,507	11·2
1616	11,599	13·1
1618	12,109	11·8
1620	11,687 (11,494)	13·6 (13·4)
1622	8,895 (9,910)	11·6 (12·9)
1628	5,089	4·7
1631	9,108	10·8
1632	16,347	16·5
1633	6,377	7·9
1640	14,315	16·5

Source: J. Pilgrim, 'The Cloth Industry in Essex and Suffolk, 1558–1640' (M.A. thesis, University of London, 1938), p. 198. The total for 1628 and those in brackets for 1620 and 1622 were derived from the port books by the present author.

Statistics of the Cloth Trade

Table 12. *Destinations of Suffolk shortcloths dressed exported from London by Englishmen*

	1606	1620	1622	1628	1632	1640
Eastland	6,885	2,297	3,247	1,562	2,142	4,391
Levant and Italy	2,276	5,558	3,624	661	?	?
Germany	424	1,068	675	488	33	nil
Russia	2,103	1,111	1,079	1,667	2,084	1,367
Spain and Dominions	1,015	633	238	nil	?	?
Barbary	1,112	153	284	450	?	?
France	583	155	24	nil	?	?
Calais and Dunkirk	49	84	37	nil	112	9
Amsterdam	?	72	107	91	?	?
United Provinces	60	72	28	86	28	72
Miscellaneous	?	109	53	17	?	?
Unknown	—	114	515	67	?	?
TOTAL	(14,507)	11,494	9,910	5,089	16,347	14,315

Table 13. *The export of Spanish cloths from London by Englishmen to northern Europe*[1] *(reduced to notional terms)*[2]

	1628		1632		1640	
	Amount	%	Amount	%	Amount	%
United Provinces	2,659	79·5	4,153	65·1	6,048	44·7
Germany	603	18·0	1,389	21·8	3,954	29·3
Flanders and Dunkirk	nil	—	748	11·7	3,496	25·9
Eastland	84	2·5	80	1·3	19	0·1
Russia	nil	—	6	0·1	nil	—
Total, northern Europe	3,346		6,376		13,517	
Percentage of exports to northern Europe	3·3%		9·1%		21·5%	

[1] These figures exclude slight amounts going to Scandinavia.
[2] In 1628 Spanish cloths varied greatly in length and weight—although the latter was normally tied to the length. In 1632 the cloths were broadly divided into two groups. There were those 18 yards long and weighing 30 lb., and those of miscellaneous length and weight. In 1640 all cloths were 22 yards in length and weighed 44 lb. Cloths were converted in the port books (and are here) on a measure of their length as proportionable to the 24 yards of a notional shortcloth.

APPENDIX B

MSS. OF THE CONTROVERSY ON EXCHANGES AND THE BALANCE OF TRADE, 1622–1623

The events leading up to the controversy, whose significance has already been appraised,[1] are described in S.P.D. Chas. I, 14/18 (undated).[2] This memorandum is endorsed 'Sir Ralph Maddison's paper given unto the commissioners', and entitled 'To show it was an act of state that procured the rise of the exchange in King James his time'. Its contents are as follows:

Mr. William Anis procured a letter of state to divers persons whereof myself was one. This said Anis was agitating in the said business before Martinmas the 19th of King James; which long delay after my coming to town also caused me to address myself to the king, and to obtain the king's directions to the Lord Mandeville, Sir Robert Cotton and others to make remonstrance to the king of the business of exchange, with the ancient use, modern abuse, and their conceived remedy to be delivered with all convenient speed before Easter holidays. It was delivered to the king the 1^0 of May, 1622; from Martinmas to May this business was in public agitation, after which it was referred again to other merchants with replication unto them, and after November, 1622 committed to the commission of trade, after which Burlamachi about the year 1623 came into the commission of trade, and then affirmed the exchange was amended, being come to thirty-four, presently upon that Mr. Palmer made his report, which was anno 1623. This commission ended with King James his life.

The MSS. which resulted from the controversy, and which still survive, are listed below:

Add. MSS. 34324, fols. 153–4 (1 May 1622).
The authors of this tract were Sir Robert Cotton, Sir Ralph Maddison, John Williams, William Sanderson and Gerard Malynes. (See Malynes's *The Centre of the Circle*, p. 76.) The burden of its argument is that of Malynes's prolific writings: that the exchange is undervalued relative to the intrinsic values of currencies, with a consequent outflow of specie, and that an official par should be enforced. It was referred by Mandeville to another group, whose report is in:

[1] Above, pp. 186–9.
[2] See also G. Malynes, *The Centre of the Circle of Commerce* (1623), p. 76; S.P.D. Chas. I (Addenda), 528/84 (undated). The latter is partly based on Maddison's paper quoted above.

Exchanges and the Balance of Trade, 1622–1623

Add. MSS. 34324, fols. 155–7 (31 May 1622).
The authors were Robert Bell, Thomas Mun, George Kendrick, Henry Wood, Thomas Jennings and John Skinner. This is a detailed answer to the first document; it argues that the exchange is by no means greatly 'undervalued', that to raise it would produce harmful repercussions, that it is determined naturally by normal commercial trends, and that the balance of trade is the only real determinant of treasure flows. Its argument was obviously much influenced by Mun.

Add. MSS. 34324, fols. 159–62 (no date; but it almost certainly derives from June, 1622).
This is an answer, by the original group, to fols. 155–7; it treats the points made therein in some detail and reasserts Malynes's theories. It seems likely that the main author was in fact Malynes—for the defence of the par as a practical policy, on fol. 161, finds an almost exact parallel in his book, *The Maintenance of Free Trade*, pp. 91–2.

Add. MSS. 34324, fols. 163–5 (20 December 1622 is most probably the date at which the copy was made—presumably for consideration by the trade commission. The originals probably dated from the summer). This is really two memoranda:

(i) '*Reasons to prove the abuse of exchange of monies by bills to be the efficient cause of the overbalancing of foreign commodities in price*' (fols. 163–4). Although there is no explicit indication of the author it was obviously Malynes: the connexion of the undervaluation with the 'overbalance', and the claim that the latter is caused by 'the prices of commodities, and not the quantity only', are identical with his views in print; while, in fact, the lengthy opening analysis of the way in which the undervaluation shifts the terms of trade (and hence the 'overbalance') is in almost exactly the same words as a similar section in *The Maintenance of Free Trade* (pp. 22–5).

(ii) '*The difference between the Adventurers and the remonstrance made unto the king*' (fol. 165). This section, presumably also by Malynes, is another summary of the points at issue between the rival reports of May 1622; it is an attack on the concept of the balance of trade as propagated by Mun. There is a copy of this summary in Hargrave MSS. 321, pp. 127–9.

Add. MSS. 34324, fol. 167 (12 April 1623).
'*Considerations concerning the overbalancing of trade*', by Malynes. This also attacks Mun's views, on the grounds that the undervalued exchange is the main causally important factor in the 'overbalance'.

Add. MSS. 34324, fol. 175 (6 May 1623).
'*The answer to the paper of Mr. Mould, Malynes and the rest*', by Mun. This is a point-by-point answer to fol. 167 and an attack on Malynes's

views, reaffirming Mun's own concept of the primacy of the balance of trade over all other factors.

Add. MSS. 34324, fol. 169 (12 April 1623).
'The true cause of the undervaluation of our monies in exchange by bills with foreign countries and the effect which it worketh', by Mun. In a series of logical steps Mun here demonstrates that it is the balance of trade which produces the particular level of exchange rates and the flows of bullion; while all the money entering into exchange transactions derives ultimately from trade. In all essentials we have here the argument of Chapter XII of *England's Treasure by Foreign Trade* which integrates the exchange rates into an economic 'model' of the balance of trade. The MS. also ends with a passage on 'mere exchangers' which, with the exception of one word, is an exact rendering of the relevant section in Chapter XIII (p. 43) of the book.

Add. MSS. 34324, fols. 171-2 (12 April 1623), by Mun.
This is a report submitted by Mun which rejects an enhancement of coinage as a means to stop the outflow of treasure, and which summarizes in detail Mun's arguments against the validity of Malynes's views and the feasibility of putting them into administrative operation. Once again, the thread of the argument and some of the more important wording find exact parallels in the book published in 1664.[1]

Add. MSS. 34324, fol. 173 (12 April 1623).
A short paper by Sir Ralph Maddison which criticizes Mun's view, that all money in international trade proceeds from commodities, by adducing items which might not be included in a commodity-balance.

Add. MSS. 34324, fols. 177-8 (6 May 1623).
'The order and means how to balance our foreign trade', by Mun. This is a technical memorandum by Mun on the difficulties and ways of compiling a balance; the lessons to be learned from it; and the general policy which he advocates for rendering it as favourable as possible without harmful repercussions. There is a close correspondence with much of the material in Chapters III (on the increase of exports and decrease of imports) and XX ('The order and means whereby we may draw up the balance of our foreign trade, which is the rule of our treasure') of *England's Treasure by Foreign Trade*.

[1] See Supple, 'Thomas Mun and the Commercial Crisis', 92-3.

APPENDIX C

CONTEMPORARY SOURCES CONSULTED

Any book such as the present one must lean heavily on an established body of secondary literature. The standard titles are sufficiently well known not to need repetition here; in any case, the foregoing pages contain footnote references where facts or theories were largely drawn from historical works. The contemporary sources cited will also be familiar enough to the student of the subject; but it may be well to provide some check-list of them—if only to emphasize the author's sins of omission. Sources not cited, or hardly used, in this study are omitted from the listing. As with quotations and references in the body of this work, spelling has been modernized.

MANUSCRIPTS

In the Public Record Office

Chancery Masters' Exhibits (C. 107/20).
Depositions in the Court of Exchequer (E. 134/5 Chas. I/Easter 1).
London Port Books: 1620, 1622, 1628, 1632, 1640 (series E. 190).
Privy Council Registers: 1627–1648 (series P.C. 2).
State Papers Domestic: Elizabeth (1598–1603), James I, Charles I, Interregnum.

In the British Museum

Additional Manuscripts (principally volumes 10113, 14027, 34324).
Cotton Manuscripts (principally Galba, E. I; Otho, E. X [Malynes, *A Treatise of Tripartite Exchange*]; Titus, B. V.).
Hargrave Manuscripts (principally volume 321).
Harleian Manuscripts (principally volume 2244).
Lansdowne Manuscripts (principally volumes 150, 152, 160, 162, 768 [Sanderson, *A Treatise on the Exchange*]).
Stowe Manuscripts (principally volume 354).

In the Record Office of the Corporation of London

Journals of the Common Council: 1598–1649.
Repertories of the Court of Aldermen: 1626–1649.

In the Cambridge University Library

William Sanderson, 'A Treatise of State Merchant' (MS. Gg. v. 18, fols. 224–60).

In the Library of the Inner Temple

MS. 538. 19.

Appendix C

PRINTED SOURCES

Collections

The Acts and Ordinances of the Eastland Company, ed. M. Sellers (1906).
Acts of the Privy Council of England: 1598–1604, 1613–27.
A Bibliography of Royal Proclamations of the Tudor and Stuart Sovereigns, 1485–1714, ed. R. Steele (2 volumes, 1910).
Calendar of State Papers Domestic: 1598–1649.
Calendar of State Papers Venetian: 1600–43.
Calendar of Wynn Papers (1926, National Library of Wales).
The Commons Debates, 1621, ed. W. Notestein, F. H. Relf and H. Simpson (7 volumes, New Haven, 1935).
Debates on monetary affairs in 1626, in J. R. McCulloch, *Old and Scarce Tracts on Money* (1933).
English Economic History: Select Documents, ed. A. E. Bland, P. A. Brown and R. H. Tawney (1914).
English History from Essex Sources, 1550–1750, ed. A. C. Edwards (1953).
The First Letter Book of the East India Company, 1600–1619, ed. Sir George Birdwood (1893).
Foedera, conventiones, literae, & cujuscumque gen. Acta Publica, inter Reges Angliae & alios, ab a. 1101 ad nostra usque tempora, ed. Thomas Rymer (20 volumes, 1704–32).
Guide to the Essex Records Office, Part 1, Essex County Council (1946).
Historical Collections, ed. John Rushworth (4 volumes, 1659–1701).
Historical Manuscripts Commission, Reports: Sackville, Various.
House of Commons Debates in 1625, ed. S. R. Gardiner (1873).
Journals of the House of Commons (1803–).
Journals of the House of Lords (n.d.).
Letters from George, Lord Carew to Sir Thomas Roe, ed. John Maclean (1860).
Remembrancia, ed. W. H. and H. C. Overall (1878).
Report of the commission investigating the cloth trade (1640, in *English Historical Review*, LVII [1942]).
Statutes of the Realm (1810–22).
Tudor Economic Documents, ed. R. H. Tawney and Eileen Power (3 volumes, 1924).

Pamphlets

Anonymous, *Cambium regis: or, The office of His Majesty's exchange royal. Declaring and justifying His Majesty's right; and the convenience thereof* (1628).
———, *A caution to keep money* (1642) in British Museum: E. 146 (21).

Anonymous, *A discourse consisting of motives for the enlargement and freedom of trade. Especially that of cloth, and other woollen manufactures. Engrossed at present contrary to the law of nature, the law of nations, and the laws of this kingdom by a company of private men who style themselves Merchant Adventurers* (1st Part 1642, no more published).

——, *A Discourse of the Common Weal of This Realm of England,* ed. E. Lamond (1549; reprinted 1893).

——, A memorandum prepared for the royal commission on the exchanges (1564, in R. H. Tawney and Eileen Power, *Tudor Economic Documents* [1924], III, 346–59).

B[rowne], J., *The merchants' avizo. Very necessary for their sons and servants, when they first send them beyond the seas, as to Spain and Portugal, or other countries* (1589; 1607 edition).

B[attie], J., *The merchant's remonstrance. Wherein is set forth the inevitable miseries which may suddenly befall this kingdom by want of trade, and decay of manufactures* (1645).

Cholmeley, William, *The request and suite of a true-hearted Englishman* (1553, in Tawney and Power, III, 130–48).

Cotton, Sir Robert, *The manner and means* (1609 or 1611, in *Cottoni posthuma: divers choice pieces of that renowned antiquary Sir Robert Cotton* [1651]).

——, *A speech . . . before . . . the Privy Council . . . touching the alteration of the coin* (1626, in McCulloch, *Old and Scarce Tracts on Money*).

Culpepper, Sir Thomas, *A tract against usury, presented to the High Court of Parliament* (1621, reprinted as appendix in Sir Josiah Child, *Brief observations concerning trade, and the interest of money* [1688]).

D'Ewes, Symonds, *College Life in the Time of James the First* (1851).

Eburne, Richard, *Plain pathway to plantations* (1624).

Gentleman, Tobias, *England's way to win wealth, and to employ ships and mariners: or, A plain description what great profit, it will bring unto the commonwealth of England, by the erecting, building, and adventuring of busses, to sea, a fishing* (1614).

Goffe, William, *How to advance the trade of the nation and employ the poor* (1641, in *Harleian Miscellany* [1808–13], IV, 385–8).

Grimstone, Sir Harbottle, *Mr. Grimstone, his Speech in Parliament: on . . . the 19th of January, upon the preferring of the Essex Petition, A.D. 1642* (1642).

Harris, Joseph, *An Essay upon Money and Coins,* Part I (1756, in McCulloch, *Old and Scarce Tracts on Money*).

Johnson, Thomas, *A plea for free-men's liberties; or, The monopoly of the Eastland merchants anatomized by divers arguments (which will also serve to set for the unjustness of the Merchant-Adventurers' monopoly)* (1646).

Appendix C

Kayll [Keale], Robert, *The trade's increase* (1615).

Maddison, Sir Ralph, *Great Britain's remembrancer, looking in and out. Tending to the increase of the monies of the commonwealth* (1640; 1655 edition).

Malynes, Gerard (de), *The Centre of the Circle of Commerce. Or, a refutation of a Treatise entitled The Circle of Commerce, or the Balance of Trade, lately published by E[dward] M[isselden]* (1623).

——, *Consuetudo, vel, Lex mercatoria, or, The ancient law merchant. Divided into three parts: according to the essential parts of traffic* (1622; 1636 edition).

——, *England's View in the unmasking of two Paradoxes; With a replication unto the answer of Master J. Bodin* (1603).

——, *The maintenance of free trade, according to the three essential parts of traffic, namely, commodities, monies, and exchange of monies, by bills of exchanges for other countries, or, An answer to a treatise of free trade . . . [by Edward Misselden] lately published* (1622).

——, *Saint George for England, allegorically described* (1601).

——, *A Treatise of the canker of England's commonwealth. Divided into three parts: Wherein the Author imitating the rule of good Physicians, First, declareth the disease. Secondarily, sheweth the efficient cause thereof. Lastly, a remedy for the same* (1601/2).

[——, in MS. 'A treatise of tripartite exchange' (1610, in Cotton MSS. Otho E. x).]

May, John, *A declaration of the estate of clothing now used within this realm of England . . . With an apology for the aulnager, showing the necessary use of his office* (1613).

Milles, Thomas, *The Reply, Or Second Apology* (1604; largely a reprint of a treatise on exchanges written in 1564–5).

Misselden, Edward, *The circle of commerce. Or, The balance of trade, in defence of free trade: opposed to Malynes's little fish and his great whale, and poised against them in the scale. Wherein also, exchanges in general are considered: and therein the whole trade of this kingdom with foreign countries, is digested into a balance of trade, for the benefit of the public* (1623).

——, *Free trade. Or, the means to make trade flourish. Wherein, the causes of the decay of trade in this kingdom, are discovered: and the remedies also to remove the same are represented* (1622).

Mun, Thomas, *A discourse of trade, from England unto the East Indies: answering to divers objections which are usually made against the same* (1621, in J. R. McCulloch, *Early English Tracts on Commerce* [reprinted for the Economic History Society, 1952]).

——, *England's treasure by foreign trade. Or, The balance of our foreign trade is the rule of our treasure* (1644, reprinted for the Economic History Society, 1933).

Parker, Henry, *Of a free trade. A discourse seriously recommending to our nation the wonderful benefits of trade, especially of a rightly governed, and ordered trade* (1648).

Ramsden, John, *The causes of the general decay of trade and scarcity of money in the town of Kingston-upon-Hull, as laid before the Privy Council* (1622; in G. Hadley, *A History of Kingston-upon-Hull* [1788], pp. 113 ff.).

Roberts, Lewes, *The merchant's map of commerce: wherein the universal manner and matter of trade, is compendiously handled. The standard and current coins of sundry princes, observed. The real and imaginary coins of accounts and exchanges, expressed. The natural and artificial commodities of all countries for transportation declared. The weights and measures of all eminent cities and towns of traffic, collected and reduced one into another, and all to the meredian of commerce practised in the famous city of London* (1638).

——, *The treasure of traffic. Or, A discourse of foreign trade. Wherein is shewed the benefit and commodity arising to a commonwealth or kingdom, by the skilful merchant, and by a well-ordered commerce and regular traffic* (1641, in McCulloch, *Early English Tracts*).

Robinson, Henry, *Brief considerations, concerning the advancement of trade and navigation, humbly tendered unto all ingenious patriots; purposely to incite them to endeavour the felicity of this nation, by contributing their assistance towards the enlargement of trade, and navigation; as the most sure foundation* (1649).

——, *Certain proposals in order to the people's freedom and accommodation in some particulars. With the advancement of trade and navigation of this commonwealth in general* (1652).

——, *England's safety, in trade's increase. Most humbly presented to the High Court of Parliament* (1641).

Roe, Sir Thomas, *Sir Thomas Roe his speech in Parliament: wherein he sheweth the cause of the decay of coin and trade in this land, especially of merchant's trade. And also propoundeth a way to the House, how they may be increased* (1641).

Rozer, Edmund, *Reasons showing that the desires of the Clothiers and Woollen Manufacturers of England expressed long since in their petition to the Parliament (against the engrossing and transporting of wool and fuller's earth) will not be prejudicial to the grower* (1648).

[Sanderson, William, 'A treatise of state merchant and merchandizing state, consisting of commerce, trade and traffic, upheld by the king's royal exchanger's office' (1629, MS. in Cambridge University Library MS. Gg. v. 18, fols. 224–60).]

[——, 'A treatise on the exchange' (n.d., MS. in Lans. MSS. 768).]

Vaughan, Rice, *A discourse of coin and coinage: the first invention, use, matter, forms, proportions and differences, ancient and modern: with the advantages and disadvantages of the rise or fall thereof, in our own or neighbouring nations: and the reasons* (1675, in McCulloch, *Old and Scarce Tracts on Money*).

Violet, Thomas, *An humble declaration to the right honourable the Lords and Commons in Parliament assembled, touching the transportation of gold and silver, and other abuses practised upon coins and bullion of this realm* (1643).

Wheeler, John, *A treatise of commerce. Wherein are shewed the commodities arising by a well ordered and ruled trade, such as that of the Society of Merchant Adventurers is proved to be: written principally for the better information of those who doubt of the necessariness of the said society in the state of the realm of England* (1601; ed. G. B. Hotchkiss, New York, 1931).

Yonge, Walter, *The Diary of Walter Yonge, Esq.* (1848).

INDEX

Ability of Stuart administrators, 252–3
Adamczyk, W., 77
Africa
  trade with, 7, 20, 135, 161–2, 197, 224
  See also Barbary
Agriculture, 4, 14, 16–17
  See also Farmers; Grains; Harvests
Alefounder, Robert, 103
Aliens
  manufacture new draperies, 159
  exporting coin, 180, 187
  exporting textiles, 24, 28n.
  and money market, 94, 126–7, 129
  and trade balance, 180, 183
America
  trade with, 7, 20, 135, 161–2, 197, 224
  and treasure supply, 139, 163, 165, 203
Amsterdam
  cloth at, 143
  exchange with, 96n.
  financial agents at, 208n.
  merchants, 115
  trade at, 91, 122
Anis, William, 268
Antwerp
  bills on, 125, 126, 164n.
  cloth sales at, 210
  financial agents at, 208n.
Apprenticeship
  enforcement, 27, 235, 246
  excess, 123–4
  guide to, 29n.
  in new draperies, 155–6
  pauper, 109
  restricts mobility, 28
  See also Statute of Artificers
Armaments encouragement, 226
Ashe, James, 131, 151
Ashe, John, 151n.
Ashton, R., 125n.
Asia
  carrying trade, 224
  trade with, 7, 20, 135, 161–2, 197, 224
  See also East Indies
Aubrey, John, 151n.
Austria, price lag in, 79

Bacon, Francis, 181–2
Balance of trade (payments)
  and bullion flows, 164, 176, 187, 211–20, 225–6
  considered, 31, 67n., 93–4, 96, 181–3, 187–9, 211–19, 228

Balance of trade (payments) (*cont.*)
  and currency manipulation, 75, 89ff., 220, 249
  favourable, 31n., 182n.
  unfavourable, 54–5, 58, 66, 81, 89–96, 102, 168, 172, 175–6, 179, 182, 185–6, 188, 190, 193, 198, 201, 203–4, 207, 212–9, 229
  unfavourable with Baltic, 84–5, 86n.
Baltic, *see* Eastland
Ban, *see* Prohibition
Bankruptcy
  as indicator of crisis, 10
  of clothiers, 11
  of farmer, 55
  of merchants, 49n., 56, 174
  through tight credit, 174
Barbary, textile exports to, 24, 103, 152
Barbour, V., 19n., 83n., 85n.
Barley, *see* Grains
Barnstaple, distress in, 57n.
Barter
  in Eastland, 84n.
  of cloth in depression, 90
Bartholomew Fair, during plague, 26, 99, 101
Bath, distress in, 57n.
B[attie], J., 137n., 139n.
Bays, *see* New draperies
Bedford, poor relief in, 118
Bell, Robert, 187n., 269
Beresford, M. W., 227n.
Berkshire
  petition from, 130
  textile depression, 100, 115–17, 129–30
  textile industry, 5
Beverley, poor relief in, 118
Bills of debt
  in grain trade, 18–19
  transferable, 91, 174
Bills of exchange
  on Antwerp, 125, 126, 164n.
  in Baltic, 84–5
  cost of, 94
  as credit instruments, 40–1, 94–5, 203
  to finance imports, 80
  plans for control, 180, 188
  profit on, 214
  as transfer instruments, 184
  See also exchange
Bimetallic system
  maladjustment of, 14, 31, 164–81, 184–5, 190, 193, 198–9, 207
  and bullion and monetary flows, 94–5, 102, 193–4, 200, 212

Bimetallic system (*cont.*)
  See also Bullion; Money; Gold coins;
    Silver coins
Birdwood, Sir G., 26n.
Bishops' War
  First, 125
  Second, 128
Black Country, 4
Blackwell Hall
  opened to all, 239
  purchases at, 46–7, 65, 114
  textiles in, 29, 150, 159
  unsold textiles at, 48
Bland, A. E., 30n., 42n., 145n., 222n.
Board of Trade, precursor, 67, 233
Bocking, 103, 107, 122–3
Book of Orders, 117, 245
Bowden, P. J., 142n., 149n., 157n.
Braintree, 103, 107, 123
Brandenburg, Dukes of, mints of, 76
Brewers, 11
Bribery, 35, 49, 52, 60, 243, 248
Bricks, Cracow prices, 79
Bridgwater
  distress in, 57n.
  report on depression, 55n.
Bristol
  Company of Merchants, 29
  decay of trade, 104
  Fair closed to Londoners, 99
  investment at peace, 29
  merchants, petition, 99
  report on depression, 55n.
Broadcloth, 5
  See also Old draperies; Textiles
Brown, P. A., 30n., 42n., 145n., 222n.
B[rowne], J[ohn], 29n.
Bullion
  ban on export, 179, 181, 187, 192, 228
  export, 89, 102, 163, 176–8, 183, 186, 189,
    193, 198–9, 200, 202–3, 205–7, 209, 212,
    214–5, 221
  fear of loss, 201, 202, 206, 212, 217–8,
    220–1, 250
  flows, 164ff., 179, 181, 188, 192–3, 201,
    206–7, 211, 215, 249–50, 252
  free trade recommended, 216n., 224
  from America, 139, 163, 203
  imports, 83–4, 250
  to Baltic, 83, 89
  plans for control of dealings, 179–81, 184,
    190–2, 194
  See also Gold; Silver
Bullionist policy, 194
Burlamachi, Philip, 189, 268
Burghley, Lord, 7, 224n., 235
Butter, high prices, 110

Caesar, Sir Julius, 45n., 47n.
Calicoes, re-exports, 161

Cambridgeshire, wages reduced, 111
Capital
  circulation encouraged, 240
  circulating, 9
  efflux from cloth trade, 52–3
  English at Leghorn, 161
  excessive in textile industry, 27
  fixed, 7–9, 144
  flows and bullion flows, 164, 250
  flow into industry encouraged, 248–9
  foreign in England, 94
  frozen in textile stocks, 47, 56–7, 65, 100,
    238
  frozen in wine imports, 107–8
  idle, 55, 223, 224n.
  imports and exports, 218
  importance of liquid, 13, 40–1, 47, 218, 249
  in peaceful uses, 29
  loan, shortage of, 174
  market, 4, 37
  mobility, 9–13
  of Merchant Adventurers, 37
  of projectors in Cockayne plan, 38–9, 46–9
  plan to provide, 48, 237
  seeks outlet, 30
  supply and companies, 243–4
  turnover: in trade, 13, 30, 47, 51, 80, 83,
    237, 241; in finishing, 98; in textile in-
    dustry, 158
Carders, unemployed, 56
Carew, George, Lord, 45n.
Carleton, Sir Dudley, 39
Carrying trade
  of England, 20, 160–1, 224
  of Holland, 18
Cash
  importance of, 13, 163, 177, 192
  rôle in textile exports, 40–1
  sale for, difficult, 120, 130
  use for grain import, 18–19
  use in Eastland trade, 83–7, 89
  use in French trade, 11
  See also Coin; Currency; Gold coins;
    Money; Silver coins
Central Europe, decline in market for cloth,
  136
Chamberlain, John, 39, 42, 48
Chapman, Thomas, 70n.
Charles I
  accession, 101
  and customs, 108, 114
  financial needs, 125–8, 253
  reign, 223, 229
Cheese, high prices, 110
Chester, report on depression, 55n.
Chichester, distress in, 57n.
Child, Josiah, 176, 177n.
Cholmeley, William, 210
Christensen, A. E., 18n., 83n.
Cinque Ports, attack Merchant Adventurers,
  68

Index

Cipolla, C. M., 154n., 157n., 159n., 160n.
Civil War, 12, 39, 131, 148, 153, 198, 221, 223n., 224
  economic disturbance on eve of, 124–31
Cloth, *see* New draperies; Old draperies; Textiles
Cloth Acts, of 1550's, 28, 235, 253
Clothiers
  as exporters, 70, 88, 238
  attack companies, 62–3, 242
  evidence on depression, 54, 57n., 66
  frozen assets, 65, 122–3, 130 (*see* unsold stocks)
  manufacturing coloured cloths, 40–1
  manufacturing stammells, 149
  manufacturing white cloths, 40–1
  ordered to maintain employment, 15, 239–40
  ordered to share burden of slump, 65, 240
  plan, to curb Wiltshire industrial development, 26
  prosecuted for payment of low wages, 27
  protection against creditors, 65, 240
  protest at ban on coastal trade in fuller's earth, 141
  protest at ban on trade to Elbe and Ems, 24
  protest at debasement, 127
  unsold stocks, 11–12, 39–40, 43, 47, 53–4, 56, 65, 69, 100, 107, 111, 116, 120–1, 130–1, 144, 238–9, 241
  wool supplies, 46n.
  See also specific counties and towns
Clothworkers
  complaints, 40, 49, 150
  London Company, move to enforce finishing, 34
  poverty and emigration, 57
  protest at ban on trade to Elbe and Ems, 24–5
Coal, production, 4
Coarse cloth
  industry depressed, 53–4
  market for, 54
Coastal trade, 4
Cockayne, Alderman
  disliked, 48
  insincerity, 35–6
  loses money, 49n.
  plans for finishing, 33–4
  wealth, 51n.
  See also Cockayne Project; Projectors
Cockayne Project
  as cause of textile stagnation, 33, 46, 50, 60, 64, 138–9
  causes of failure, 37–8, 48–9
  collapse of, 48–9, 52, 252
  commercial prosperity before, 28–9
  course of trade under, 39–59
  effects of, 50–1, 81
  in general, 32–51, 228, 231n., 237, 239, 241n., 247–8

Cockayne Project (*cont.*)
  issues involved in plan, 33–9, 247–8
  lessons of, 49–51, 248
  See also Cockayne Projectors; Dyed and dressed cloth
Cockayne Projectors
  activities, 42
  arguments used, 38, 44
  attack Merchant Adventurers, 34n., 40n.
  capital, 38–42, 46–50
  charter, 39, 41, 42n.
  complaints, 43–4, 46, 59
  contract, 42–3
  difficulties, 37, 39–50
  duplicity of, 36
  formation, 35
  motives and control of trade, 35–7, 45, 50–1, 247–8
  open membership to Merchant Adventurers, 37
  ousted, 48–9
  personnel, 36
  plans, 34
  power, 39
  quotas for exports, 47–8, 238
  request right to export finished cloth to other areas, 37
  respite for, 42
  See also Cockayne Project
Coggeshall, 107, 122, 123
Coin
  anxiety over loss, 31, 177
  ban on export, 179, 181, 187, 189, 194, 231, 250
  clipped, 167–8, 173, 191, 209
  export, 90, 96, 163, 169, 176–8, 180, 186–90, 193–4, 201–2, 204, 207–9, 218
  in Eastland trade, 83, 85–7
  plans to control dealings, 190–2, 250
  transportation costs, 95, 209
  use to finance imports, 80
  valuations, 178, 180, 189, 220
  See also Currency; Mint; Money; Gold coins; Silver coins
Coining, *see* Mint
Coke, Sir Edward, 6n.
Colchester, 122n., 123n., 159
Coleman, D. C., 11n., 18n., 225n., 226n., 228n., 229n.
Colonial trade, 161n., 162
Coloured cloths
  depression in Berkshire industry, 115–117
  production, 5, 120, 149–52
  project for finishing, 34
  sales fall, 150
  Tare applied to, 115
  trade in: 121; freed, 70–1, 241
Combers
  in Essex, 12
  wages, 111

Index

Commerce, general significance of, 1, 3, 9–14, 19–20, 64, and *passim*
Commissions
  for poor law, 118, 233, 245
  for textiles, 124, 143, 145–6, 231, 233
  for trade, 61n., 67, 70–1, 93, 96, 99, 105, 188–9, 206, 212, 233
  See also Committees
Committees
  of Privy Council, 53, 66
  on crisis in 1622, 57, 59–61, 63, 66–7, 69, 87, 92–3, 124, 187–8, 213, 233
  on Eastland trade, 7
  on exchanges, 186–8, 204, 205, 207, 211, 213n., 232
  on monetary affairs, 52, 165–6, 169–71, 179–80, 182–5, 206n., 232
  See also Commissions
Common Council, 158–9
Commons, *see* Parliament
Companies, *see* Regulated companies; Trading companies; Eastland traders; Levant Company; Merchant Adventurers; East India Company
Comparative costs, doctrine, 35
Competition, *see* Economic thought; Textiles
Constantinople, 160n., 161
Copper, in debased coin, 127
Cordage, manufacture encouraged, 223
Corporations
  for regulation of textiles, 145, 147, 156, 231
  for industrial expansion, 248–9
Costs
  attempts to keep down, 245
  in new draperies, 155–8
  labour, 122, 145, 155–6, 157
  pressure on, 143–7, 246–7
  rigidity, 46, 80–1, 144, 148, 153, 177
  See also Labour; Wages
Cottington Treaty, 125, 164, 167
Cotton, Sir Robert, 170, 186, 190, 268
Cotton wool
  English trade in, 161
  from West Indies, 223
Court, W. H. B., 5
Court of Aldermen, 118
Coventry, Thomas, 67n.
Cracow
  currency manipulation at, 77
  silver prices at, 78–9
Cranfield, Lionel, 25n., 31n., 44, 138, 140, 143, 182, 185
Credit
  and bills of exchange, 94–5
  and export prices, 203
  dealings, increase, 52
  effect of currency manipulations on, 79, 170
  importance in textile market, 40–1
  instruments, negotiable, 13

Credit (*cont.*)
  primitive, 8, 13
  structure, harmed, 126–9, 131
  tightness, 55, 174–5, 198, 200
  use in France, 11
  See also Money market
Credit-worthiness
  need for, 40–1
  Cockayne Projectors lack, 50
Creighton, C., 25n., 99n., 101n.
Crisis
  and economic thought, 197–221, 228
  and faulty manufacture of textiles, 143–5, 147
  and government economic policy, ch. 10, *passim*
  and harvests, 2, 14–19
  and monetary instability, ch. 8 *passim*
  causes of: Cockayne Project, 39–51; Crown's financial needs, 125–8; currency, 2, 14, 58–9, 61, 72–96, 98, 163, 171, 249; disputes, 112–13; harvests, 2, 14–19; plague, 25–6, 99–102, 163; politics and war, 2, 102–19, 128–31, 163
  effect on clothiers, 11–12
  effect on labour, 12–13
  effect on merchants, 10–11
  in general, 1–2, 7, 19–20
  nature of, 8–14
  of 1550's, 226n.
  after 1586, 23
  of 1590's, 30
  of 1603, 25–6, 99
  of 1616, 43–51
  of early 1620's: 52–8, 150, 159, 171, 174–6, 178, 185, 188, 198ff.; contemporary opinion on, 58–64, 175, 199, ch. 9 *passim*; cause of, 73–81; government attitude, 64–72
  of 1625, 99–102, 190
  of 1629, 102–10, 118
  of 1630–1, 110–12, 116–19
  of 1636–7, 122–3
  of 1640–2, 125–31
Cromwell, Oliver, 135
Culpepper, Thomas, 54n., 60n., 139n., 141n.
Cumberland, Earl of, 25n., 34, 35, 37n., 42n., 52, 97n.
Cunningham, W., 99n.
Currency
  effects of manipulation, 73–5, 78–81, 89ff., 95, 170–1, 173, 184–5, 215, 219–20, 222, 236
  instabilities, 2, 14, 58, 60–1, 83
  manipulations abroad, 9, 14, 53, 58, 63n., 73, 76–8, 82, 96, 159, 163, 168–9, 171–4, 184–5, 198–200, 212, 215–16, 218
  manipulation, considered in England, 127–8, 167, 179, 181–2, 189, 218n., 236, 250
  nature of, 13–14
  shortage, 14, 56

Index

Currency (*cont.*)
  stabilized, 96–7
  supply of, 8, 13–14
  systems, 73–4, 76–9
  See also Coin; Debasement; Enhancement; Gold coins; Money; Silver coins
Customs
  amounts, 1599–1603 and 1611–16, 32n.
  anticipated gain from Cockayne Project, 35
  collection facilitated by companies, 243
  farmers, 125
  Great Farm, as basis for estimate of exports, 28
  increase, 99
  loss, feared, 171
  officers, consulted on depression, 66
  on textiles, 43, 63n., 70, 152
  on wine, 106
  pretermitted, 60–1
  refusal to pay, 107–8, 113–15

Danzig
  cloth sales at, 83
  currency manipulations at, 76–7
  exports to, 84
  imports from, 86
  market for grain at, 29
  silver prices at, 79
  See also Eastland
Davies, Margaret Gay, 5n., 11n., 23n., 26n., 28n., 71n., 246n., 247
Davis, R., 161n., 162n.
Dawes, Abraham, 67n.
Debasement
  Great, 75
  ease of, 73
  effects of, 73–4, 75ff., 200
  in Europe, 14, 61, 168–9, 199
  planned, in England, 102, 127–8, 169–70, 189–90, 192
  opposition to, 190
  See also Enhancement; Currency manipulation
Dekker, Thomas, on 1603 plague, 26
Delft
  cloth to, 112–13
  as mart, 121
  as staple, 91, 115
  interlopers join Merchant Adventurers at, 122n.
Demand for imports, elasticity, 214–15, 217
Depression, *see* Crisis; New draperies; Old draperies; Textiles
de Roover R., 96n., 179n., 180n., 200n., 204n., 210n., 216n.
D'Ewes, Symonds, 178
Devon
  insolvent clothiers in, 240
  public order in, 57
  textile industry in, 5, 149, 151, 155

Digges, Sir Dudley, 68, 69
Disorder
  among textile workers, 38, 56–7, 66, 101, 104, 109, 234, 244
  in general, 6–7, 15
  government aim to prevent, 64, 227, 229–30, 234–5, 239, 244–7, 251
  See also Government economic policy
Distress, *see* Poverty
Diversification of the economy, 20, 72, 124, 135–6, 148–62, 197–8, 221–4, 235–6, 247–9, 251
Dorset
  petition from, 130
  public order in, 57
  textile industry in, 5
Dozens
  production, 5
  trade in freed, 70–1, 241
Drapers of London
  complain of faulty manufacture, 59
  consulted on depression, 66
  on new draperies, 154
Dunkirk
  privateers of, 104–5, 110, 116
  Spanish cloths to, 150n.
  See also Privateers
Dyed and dressed cloth
  ability of English industry to manufacture, 38
  banned in Holland, 40, 42–5
  contracts to export, 41–3
  difficulties for exports, 43
  encouragement to export, 42
  exports, 36, 39, 42–3, 45, 87n., 99, 248
  failure to export, 41
  low quality of, 59
  organization of industry, 5, 147
  unsold stocks of, 47
  value added to exports by, 33
  See also Cockayne Project
Dyers
  complain, 40, 49
  consulted on slump, 66
Dyestuffs, 7, 35

East Anglia
  textile industry: 4–6, 12, 155; depression in, 58, 102–12, 124, 159, 238, 243; unemployment in, 108
  trade to France, 108
  wages in, 11, 246
  emigration from, 128n.
  poor relief in, 118, 245
  See also relevant counties
Eastern Europe
  cloth market: 7, 153; breaks down, 20, 76ff., 98, 136
  cheap textiles in, 139–40
  manufacture of textiles in, 138

19

Eastern Europe (*cont.*)
  wool of, 141
  exports to, fall, 75–6
  currency in: 61; manipulations of, 75ff., 168–9
  See also Eastland; Northern Europe; Poland
East India
  Company: formation, 25; defence of, 185, 212; dispute with Dutch, 112; investment in by Merchant Adventurers, 37; and coinage plans, 185; unable to muster a quorum, 26
  trade: receives capital, 53; considered, 67n.; developments in, 161; needs specie, 85, 86n.; and export of specie, 185, 194, 212; encouragement to, 223–4; re-exports from, 223
  See also Asia
Eastland
  trade to: 81–9; difficulties in, 41n., 104; depressed, 54, 80–9; returns in, 61; nature of, 85n.–86n.; importance, 88; considered, 67n.; needs specie, 85, 85n.–86n.; threat to throw open, 88–9
  textile exports to, 24, 53, 75–6, 88–9, 102–3, 150
  Dutch competition in, 83–9
  exchanges in, 84–6
  prices and currency in, 80
  imports from: 7, 81, 83, 86; of grain, 18, 88–9; confined to English or native ships, 68, 87–8, 238, 243
  money market in, 84
  manufacture of textiles in, 32, 80
  wool supplies in, 32
  See also Eastern Europe; Northern Europe; Poland
Eastland merchants (Company)
  in projected Spanish Company, 30n.
  and Cockayne Project, 45
  exports of, 82
  capital of, 41n.
  import privileges confirmed, 68, 87–8, 238, 243
  trade depressed, 81–9
  complain, 81–3
  pressure on, 68, 70, 238
  suffer by bankruptcy, 49n.
  prosecute Suffolk clothiers, 103n.
  need convoy against privateers, 104
Eburne, Richard, 74n.
Economic change
  long-term, 19–20, 149–62, 221–4
  See also Diversification; New draperies
Economic policy, *see* Government economic policy
Economic thought
  in general, 1, ch. 9 *passim*
  in government policy, ch. 10, *passim*
  and crisis, 197–221, 228

Economic thought (*cont.*)
  in relation to competition and diversification, 20, 71–2, 124, 135, 147–9, 152, 162, 197–8, 211, 215, 221–4, 242, 247–9, 251
  See also Government economic policy; Mercantilism; specific authors
Edwards, A. C., 104n., 124n.
Elbe, trade to banned, 24
Elbing
  exports to, 76n., 84
  cloth sales at, 83
  bankruptcy at, 49n.
  imports from, 86
  See also Eastland; Poland
Elizabeth
  reign, 23, 25, 135, 139
  coining under, 173n., 183
  government of, 236
Elsas, M. J., 77n., 97n.
Elton, G. R., 144n.
Embargo, *see* Prohibitions
Emden
  residence of Merchant Adventurers at, 25, 115–16
Emigration, of textile workers, 128n.
Ems, trade to banned, 24
Enclosures
  effects of on wool, 142–3, 157
  Acts for, 252
Enhancement
  ease of, 73
  in Europe, 14, 168–9, 186, 193, 199, 201, 206, 219; effects of, 73ff., 89–90, 200, 203, 206
  in eastern Europe, 87
  in Poland, 82, 86
  in Germany, 79, 82
  in Holland, 79, 92
  of gold, 166–71, 181 (*see* Gold coins)
  of silver, 166ff. (*see* Silver coins)
  plans for, 52, 169–71, 192–4
  arguments against, 170–1, 212
  See also Currency manipulations; Gold coins; Silver coins
Entrepôt trade
  in grain, 18
  at Leghorn, 160
  in England, 161–2
  encouraged, 224
  See also Diversification of economy; Economic thought
Essex
  textile depression in, 57, 103–12, 122–4, 130
  unsold stocks in, 121–2, 123n.
  unemployment in, 111, 114
  poor relief in, 108–10, 118
  J.P.s and textile depression, 104, 106, 111, 246
  overproduction in, 107, 123–4, 159
  faulty manufacture in, 145

Index

Essex (cont.)
  wages in, 111, 246
  new draperies in, 5, 102, 155–6 (see textile depression in)
  coloured cloth manufacture in, 34
  clothiers, 12, 54, 70, 107–8, 130
Europe
  manufacture of cloth in, 9, 20
  currency, 9, 14
  See also Textiles; Currency; Central Europe; Eastern Europe; Northern Europe; Southern Europe
Exchange and exchange rates
  contemporary views of determination, 94–5, 179, 186–9, 201ff.
  controversy on, 95–6, 186–9, 204–7, 211, 233, Appendix B
  problems of, 163, 186–9
  effects of currency manipulation on, 74–5, 78, 81, 170, 200, 219
  fall, 66, 95, 126, 186–9
  below par, 94–6, 168, 201ff., 222n.
  fluctuations, 209, 218
  rise, 63, 78, 85, 96, 189, 208–9
  effects of increasing, 214–15
  and export of money, 94, 164, 222n.
  and terms of trade, 202ff., 222
  in Baltic, 84–6, 87n.
  with Holland, 96n.
  plans for control, 179–80, 186–9, 194, 202, 204–6, 208, 222n., 228, 250
  See also Bills of exchange
Exeter
  depression in, 57, 101, 130
  report on depression, 55n.
  merchants of: investment in colonies and Iberian trade, 29; capital turnover of, 11; privileges of Company of, 31n.

Factors
  in Iberian trade, guide for, 29n.
  in Germany, 138, 140, 143
Factory system, 8
Falendysz cloth, price of, 78
Famine
  danger of, 88, 252
  See also Grains; Harvests
Far East, see Asia; East Indies
Farmers
  clothiers become, 11
  effects of harvest fluctuations on, 17
  become manufacturers of new draperies, 156
  See also Agriculture; Grains; Harvests
Fashion, effect on new draperies, 153–6
Faulty manufacture of textiles, 43, 46, 58–60, 66, 115, 123–4, 140, 148, 155–6, 231
  government attempts to control, 67, 120, 144–7, 231, 235, 246–7
  as possible cause of depression, 143–6

Feavearyear, A. E., 125n., 126n., 166n., 167n., 184n.
Fells, export of, 60, 141
Feltmakers, use Spanish wool, 149
Finch, Heneage, 67n.
Finished cloth, see Dyed and dressed cloth
Fish, export allowed, 106
Fisher, F. J., 2n., 3n., 4n., 15n., 18n., 23n., 26n., 28n., 29n., 30n., 44n., 71n., 74n., 75n., 136n., 144n., 147n., 153n., 157n., 159n., 161n., 162n., 210n., 224n., 226n., 235n., 236n., 248n., 249n.
Fishing
  Dutch specialize in, 83
  hit by privateers, 104
  market for in Mediterranean, 161
  encouraged, 223–4, 248–9
Flax
  imports of, 7
  processing of, by poor, 118
  growth encouraged, 223–4
Flanders
  market opened, 29
  as site for staple, 44, 116
  duties on cloth at, 60–1
  trade with: hit by privateers, 104; stopped, 105, 116–17
  Spanish wool in, 141
  Spanish cloth exported to, 149
  See also Antwerp; Dunkirk
Flemish shillings, 74–5
Forced loan, 126–8
Foreigners, see Aliens
Forest of Dean, 4
Fortrey, Samuel, 223n.
France
  trade to: depressed, 54; hit by privateers, 104; difficulties of, 107, 110; from East Anglia, 108; effect of 1606 treaty on, 153; re-exports in, 161
  textile exports to, 24
  market for new draperies in, 104, 152–3
  bill for free trade to, 31, 231
  imports from: 7; of silks, 90–1; of linens, 92; of wine, 106
  money exported to, 90
  money imported from, 91
  mint ratio raised in, 168
  gold enhanced in, 192
  effect of English harvest on, 19n.
  textile manufacture in, 11, 32, 138–9
  textiles in Mediterranean, 154, 160
  supplies of wool in, 38
  Spanish wool to, 141–2
  ships, insurance of in Mediterranean, 161
  war with, 104–6, 153
  peace with, 106–8, 110
  English merchants trading to: pressure on, 106–8; difficulties of, 106–7; consulted, 45, 122, 238; overconfidence of, 107; capital of, 114

Frankfort
  currency manipulations in, 77
  fairs, 91
Free trade
  1604 campaign, 30–1, 231, 237
  in 1620's, 68–71
  discussed, 240–4
Freshford, 151n.
Friis, A., 24n., 25n., 29n., 30n., 33n., 34n., 35n., 36, 37n., 38n., 40n., 42n., 43n., 44n., 45n., 46n., 47n., 48n., 49n., 51n., 54n., 82n.
Fruit
  imports of, 7
  trade in, 161
Fuller's earth
  export, 60, 141
  export banned, 38, 141
  coastal trade banned, 141
Funerals, wearing cloth at, 48
Furniss, E. S., 223n.
Fustians, imports of, 7, 91–2

Gardiner, S. R., 99n., 113n., 114n., 125n., 127n., 128n.
Genoese merchants and bullion trade, 125–6
Gentry, consulted, 66
Germany
  imports from: 7; Levant goods, 62; cheap linens, 91–2
  imports of silver and money from, 91, 166
  textile exports to, 24, 33, 36, 41–2, 44, 53, 56, 60, 75–6, 97–8, 103, 128, 136, 140, 150
  market contracts, 102, 121, 136, 138, 223
  market for new draperies, 153n.
  trade to: depressed, 54, 58; confined to staple towns, 115; protected by convoy, 104; hit by privateers, 104; controlled by Merchant Adventurers, 23; controlled by Cockayne Projectors, 34; by Merchant Adventurers, 121–2; liberalized, 68–71, 231
  manufacture of textiles in, 32, 138–9, 140n., 141
  wool supplies, 38, 97
  Spanish wool in, 141–2
  wars in, 59, 61
  re-exports to, 161
  currency manipulation in, 76–9, 82, 169
  staple in, 91
  See also Northern Europe
German historical economists, 226
Gig mills, 120, 146, 247
Gild
  regulations: in England, 155; in Italy, 154, 160
  system, 248–9
Glass, manufacture, 4

Gloucestershire
  occupations in, 16–17
  textile industry in, 5, 16, 34, 149
  textile depression in, 43–4, 55, 100, 116, 120, 129, 137
  unemployment in, 120
  rioting and public order in, 56–7
  clothiers complain, 43, 54, 100, 116
  unsold stocks of textiles, 47, 100, 116
  faulty manufacture in, 46n., 59
  See also Western counties
Godalming, unemployment in, 116
Goffe, William, 124, 148n., 221, 224
Gold (coins)
  importance, 171
  velocity of circulation of, 173
  valuations of, 165–7, 181, 249
  enhancement, 166–9, 171, 180–1, 193
  coining, 166, 173n., 183
  export of, 31, 92, 165–7, 169, 180–1, 190, 192, 220
  exporters prosecuted, 184, 192
  import of, 167–8, 172–3, 182, 218–19
  See also Coins; Currency; Money; Bullion; Silver coins
Goldsmiths
  and trade in coins, 180–1, 190–2, 212
  attempts to control, 180–1, 190–2
  Company, plans for enhancement, 185
  and silver, 164
  and monetary situation, 126
Gold Standard, 215
Gore, R., 32n., 141
Gould, J. D., 59n., 60n., 86n., 139n., 166n., 167n., 168n., 184n., 185n., 189n., 190n., 197n., 210n., 212n., 218n., 219n., 250n.
Government
  and Cockayne Project, 34–5, 37, 41–2, 47–9
  and crises, 59, 64–72, ch. 10 *passim*
  and Eastland trade, 88–9
  and unemployment, 108
  and poor law, 108
  and grain trade, 111
  and wages, 111, 145
  and quality of textiles, 121, 144–7, 155
  and monetary system, 167, 171, 178–94
  See also Government economic policy; Parliament; Privy Council
Government economic policy
  nature of, 64, 71–2, 225–6
  influence of economic environment on, 226ff.
  aims of, 226–7
  and desire for stability, 10, 227, 229–30, 233–5, 244–7, 251
  characteristics of, 227–30, 252–3
  and crises, 227–30, 233–53
  formulation of, 230–3
  towards unemployment and poor relief, 33, 72, 234–5, 244, 251

Index 285

Government economic policy (*cont.*)
  towards diversification, 235–6
  pressure on merchants to buy, 236–9
  pressure on clothiers to maintain production, 239–40
  towards company organization, 240–4
  towards supply of grains, 245
  towards wages, 245–6
  towards expansion, 247–9
  towards currency, 178–94, 249–50
  and Cockayne Project, 247–8, 252
  and economic thought, 229
  efficacy of, 230, 236, 250–3
  See also Government; Privy Council
Grains
  prices of, 15–16, 31, 55–7, 87–8, 101n., 110–11, 116–19, 198
  imports: 7, 31, 87, 93, 190; effects of, on economic fluctuations, 15, 18–19
  exports: banned, 101, 111; recommended, 181
  trade in, with Eastland, 29, 88–9
  nature of demand for, 15–16, 55
  stocks of, 16n.
  variations in types consumed, 18
  government controls use of, 31n., 101, 111, 117–18, 245, 252
  See also Harvests
Gras, N. S. B., 19n.
Gregory, T. E., 223n.
Grimstone, Mr., 12n., 123n., 130
Groschen, 74, 76–7, 85

Habakkuk, H. J., 141n.
Haberdashery
  depression in, 48
  use of Spanish wool in, 149
Hadley, G., 55n., 60n., 81n., 82n., 87n.
Halifax, 158
Hall, B., 82n.
Hamburg
  exports to, 36, 42, 75–6, 97
  as residence of Merchant Adventurers, 25, 91
  cloth fleet bound for, 105
  interlopers at, 25
  bankruptcy at, 49n.
  currency manipulation in, 77
  reichsdaller at, 77, 97
Hampshire
  textile depression in, 116, 129
  petition from, 130
  public order in, 57
  kersies of, export, 160
Harris, Joseph, 176, 177n.
Harvests
  bad, 7, 23n., 31, 55, 57, 101, 110–11
  good, 55
  fluctuations in, 2, 8
  demand for labour during, 12, 100

Harvests (*cont.*)
  and economic fluctuations, 14–19, 88–9, 110–11, 118, 245
  and scarcity of money, 174
  See also Grains
Hayes, Edward, 3
Heath, Robert, 67n.
Heaton, Herbert, 225n., 227n., 228n., 230n.
Heckscher, E. F., 85n., 86n., 221n., 223n., 225n., 226, 227n., 228, 229, 230n., 235n.
Hemp
  imports of, 7
  processing of, by poor, 118
  growth encouraged, 223–4
Henry III, 180
Herefordshire
  textile prosperity in, 34
  wool production falls, 149
Herring trade, 157, 161
Hertfordshire, unemployment in, 111, 118
Hinton, R. W. K., 250n.
Holland
  trade to: controlled by Merchant Adventurers, 23; controlled by Cockayne Projectors, 34; depressed, 54; liberalized, 68–71, 231; protected by convoy, 104; hit by privateers, 104; insecurity of, 112–13; difficulties of, 115–17, 121; stopped, 116–17, 121; by Merchant Adventurers, 121–2
  duties on English cloth, 60–1
  textile exports to, 24, 33, 36, 41, 44–5, 50, 55–6, 75–6, 97–8, 119, 128, 136, 140, 150
  stocks of English cloth in, 34n., 40
  ban on English finished textiles, 40, 42–5
  market in: 44; contracts, 121, 136, 138, 223; for new draperies, 153n.
  Tare on cloth, 59, 112, 115, 118–19, 121
  re-exports to, 161
  imports from: 7; of Levant goods, 62; of linens, 92
  staple town in, 24, 91, 115, 121
  commercial rivalry with England, 20, 29, 46, 83, 85–9, 243
  economic pressure on, 44–5, 248
  shipping: advantages of, 83, 86–7; insurance rates in Mediterranean, 161
  carrying trade of, 83
  manufacture of textiles in, 32, 46, 137–9, 141–2
  finishing industry in, 33, 36, 50, 92, 98
  Spanish wool to, 141–2
  cloth of, in Mediterranean, 154, 160
  merchants of: in grain trade, 18–19; and customs controversy, 113; export bullion and coin from England, 191
  trade with Baltic: 84–7; use of specie in, 85–7
  immigrants from, for linen industry, 223–4
  low rate of interest in, 174n.
  truce with Spain, 29

286 Index

Holland (*cont.*)
  currency of: manipulations, 76, 78–9, 92, 169; importance of silver in, 173n.; ratio raised, 166, 168; silver valuation in, 168; price lag in, 78
  price flexibility in, 170
  silver exported to, 168, 219
  exchange with, 96n.
Holland, Earl of, 191
Hoszowski, S., 77–8
House of Commons, *see* Parliament
Hull
  Eastland Company of, 104
  report on depression, 55n.
  difficulties in trade to Baltic, 79–80
  trade hit by privateers, 104
Hungary
  war in, 29
  manufacture of textiles in, 140

Imports
  in general, 7
  prices of, 80
  growth, 81, 90–3
  effect of currency manipulations on, 90–3, 220
  hostility to, 92–3
  paid for with gold, 166
  See also Balance of trade; Returns; specific commodities and areas
Impositions on cloth, 58–9, 60–1, 63n., 66, 70, 81, 148, 161
  by Merchant Adventurers, 49, 60–1, 63–4, 68–70
Inflation
  accompanying currency manipulation, 74–5, 170–1, 181, 190, 193, 199–200
  fear of, 171, 190, 193, 212
  advantages of, 200
  differential, 139, 203
Innkeepers, 11–12
Innovation
  hindrance to, 144
  extensive, 153
Informers, 71n.
Interlopers
  in Germany, 24–5
  trade of, 24, 25n., 115
  pressure on, 24, 25n., 52, 63n., 69, 121–2
  attack companies, 62, 242
  trade in new draperies open to, 69
  opinion on slump, 54
  join Merchant Adventurers, 122
Internal trade, 2–4
Interregnum, 205
Ipswich
  merchants: turnover of capital, 11; complain, 86; on currency manipulation, 169

Ipswich (*cont.*)
  report on depression, 55n.
  distress in, 57n.
  exports to Eastland 282
  trade hit by privateers, 104
Irish war, 130
Iron, manufacture, 4
Italy
  textile exports to, 24, 103, 160n.
  imports from: 7, 80; of silks, 90–1
  effects of bad English harvest on, 19n.
  manufacture of textiles: grows, 32, 138; declines, 154–5, 159–60
  Spanish wool to, 141–2
  market for new draperies, 152
  silks of, exported by English to Constantinople, 161
  products of, traded by English in Mediterranean, 161
  bankers in, 213
  merchants trading to, and Cockayne Project, 36

Jacobus, 183
James I
  reign, 25, 28–9, 31, 229
  and Cockayne Project, 35, 40, 42, 50, 231n., 248, 253
  plans to provide capital, 48, 237n.
  payments to, 49, 52, 60
  and currency, 52, 183–5, 190
  and exchanges, 186, 188, 204
  and recovery, 99
James, M., 131n.
Jennings, Thomas, 187n., 269
Johnson, Thomas, 222n.
Judges, A. V., 225n.
Justices of the Peace
  of clothing counties, 244
  of East Anglia, 104, 106, 109, 111, 123, 246
  of western counties, 53, 101, 244
  and wages, 27, 111, 246
  and employment, 56, 65, 112
  and grain supplies, 101, 112, 117–18
  and depression, 104, 106, 111, 123
  and poor law, 64, 109, 244
  and faulty manufacture, 146–7

Kendrick, George, 187n., 269
Kent
  textile industry, 5, 34n.
  new draperies in, 155
  unemployment in, 111, 118
  textile depression in, 129
  fuller's earth from, 141
  clothiers of, give evidence to Commons, 54

Kersies
 production, 5, 158
 export: 121, 160; freed, 70–1, 241; decline, 140
 faulty, 140
 Tare applied to, 115
Keynes, J. M., 215
King's Exchanger, Office of, 180, 184, 190–2, 204
King's Merchant Adventurers, *see* Cockayne Projectors
Kipper-und-Wipper-zeit, 76, 97

Labour
 costs: 111; in coarse cloth industry, 140; in new draperies, 155–7; in Italy, 157, 160
 supply: reduced by harvest, 100; excessive in textiles, 27, 123
 mobility of, 12–13, 155–6, 235
 See also Costs
Laissez faire, 226, 230
Lamonde, E., 210n.
Lancashire, textile industry, 5, 155
Leadenhall market, new draperies in, 159
Leate, Nicholas, 87n.
Leghorn, 160, 161
Leonard, E. M., 15n., 31n., 117n., 118n., 226n.
Letters of marque, against France, 106
Levant
 textile exports to, 24, 103, 160
 demand for English textiles in, 154
 imports from, 62, 223
 difficulties in trade to, 25n.
 sea route to, opened, 29
 Company: privileges sustained, 62; scattered by plague, 101; convoy for, 104; growth in importance of, 160
 merchants trading to: in projected Spanish Company, 30n.; and Cockayne Project, 36; consulted, 45
 See also Mediterranean; Turkey
Leyden, costs of manufacture at, 33
Licences
 for unfinished exports, 52
 See also Earl of Cumberland
Licence money, controversy over, 116
Lincolnshire, fuller's earth carried to, 141
Linen
 imports of, 7, 91–3, 96, 214
 European prices of, 79
 manufacture encouraged, 223–4
Lipson, E., 12n., 65n.
Lively, Samuel, 145–6
Locke, John, 223n.
Lombardy, economy collapses, 154
London
 population, 2
 economic importance, 3–4, 128

London (*cont.*)
 exports from, *see* Textile exports
 control of textile exports: 23, 99–102, 128; attacked, 62
 textiles come to, for export, 26, 38–40, 48, 68, 150
 plague in, 25–6, 99–102
 crisis and dislocation in, 26, 58, 100–2, 128–31
 unemployed in, 57
 merchants of: mobility of assets, 10–11; leave during plague, 26; in projected Spanish Company, 30
 See also East India Company; Eastland Merchants; Levant Company; Merchant Adventurers; Merchants
Low Countries, *see* Holland
Lower Rhenish Circle, mints of, 76
Lublin, currency manipulation at, 77
Lwów
 currency manipulation at, 77
 silver prices at, 78
Lynn, report on depression, 55n.

McCulloch, J. R., 90n., 102n., 169n., 170n., 172n., 190n., 218n., 219n.
Maclean, John, 45n., 49n., 50n.
Maddison, Sir Ralph, 18n., 19n., 84, 168n., 171n., 173n., 186, 192n., 198n., 208n., 268
 theories of, 205, 208, 217n., 220–1
Madrid, 125
Malynes, G., 26n., 27, 37n., 53n., 60n., 61n., 74n., 78, 84n., 85n., 90n., 92n., 93n., 94n., 95n., 96n., 141n., 153n., 160n., 166, 168n., 171n., 172n., 173, 174, 175, 179, 186, 187, 188, Appendix B
 theories of, 95–6, 186–9, 197–8, 201–17, 220–2
Mandeville, Lord, 268
Mann, J. De L., 155n.
Market ratio, 164–9
Market spinners, 120, 146–7, 247
Martin, Sir Richard, 167
Mart towns
 regulated by Merchant Adventurers, 24
 trade confined to, 25, 69, 115
 in Hamburg and Middelburg, 42
 change in considered, in Holland, 44–5, 121
 as entrepôts, 91
Maryland, tobacco imports from, 162
Matthews, R. C. O., 16n., 17n.
May, J., 143n., 155, 156n., 159
Mediterranean
 market for textiles in, 20, 102, 104, 153 160
 imports from, 7
 textile exports to, decline, 103, 138

Mediterranean (*cont.*)
  trade to: 161; hit by privateers, 105; expanded by peace, 153
  English carrying trade in, 160–1, 224
  shipping insurance in, 161
  See also Levant; Southern Europe; Turkey
Medley cloths, *see* Spanish cloths
Mendenhall, T. C., 17n., 54n.
Mercantilism
  nature of, 64, 194, chapters 9 and 10, *passim*
  and treasure, 177, 194, 250
  development of, 188–9, ch. 9, *passim*
  traditional view of, 225–30
  See also Government economic policy; Economic thought; specific writers
Merchant Adventurers
  control trade to Germany and Holland, 23, 62
  control textile trade from London, 24–5, 241
  mart towns of, 24–5, 36, 91
  trade of: policy and organization, 23–5; liberalized, 68–71, 121–2, 231–2, 241; needs convoy protection, 104; in convoy, 114, 239; handicapped, 112–13, 120–1
  secure export licence, 25n., 34–5
  textile exports: 23–4, 33–4, 47, 52–3, 55, 97, 99, 136–7, 140, 150, 152n.; impositions on, 49, 60–1, 63–4, 68–70
  complain: of foreign manufacture, 138; of wool export, 141; of faulty textiles, 59, 145; of stop of Mint, 126
  prosperity, 28–9, 32
  stint increased, 29
  decline, 136–7
  attacked, 30, 62–4, 68–71, 148, 237, 241–2
  defended, 136–7
  charter suspended, 34, 37
  privileges renewed, 49, 52, 71, 121–2, 124–5, 241
  controversy with Dutch, 112–13, 115, 239
  during Cockayne Project, 36–42, 47, 50, 239, 243–4
  use of cash, 41
  pressure on, to buy textiles, 65–6, 69, 238–9
  wealth, 46–7, 51, 69–71, 108, 113, 119
  hold stocks, 46–7, 113–15, 119
  opinion on depression, 53, 60–1, 63n.
  imports: 61–2; of silks, 90–1; of specie, 90, 166
  and textile industry: new draperies, 69; of Berkshire, 115–16; of Essex, 122–3
  in projected Spanish Company, 30n.
  investment of, in East India Company and capital market, 37
  scattered by plague, 100
  refuse to give up London staple, 100–1
  refuse to pay customs, 113–15
  oppose currency manipulation, 170n.

Merchant Adventurers (*cont.*)
  See also Regulated companies; Trading companies
Merchants
  importance of, 13
  mobility of, 9–11
  pressure on, in depression, 65, 237–9, 243
  consulted, 66, 81
  and currency manipulation, 75, 78–81
  turn to importing, 90
  use of exchange, 94–5
  refuse to pay customs, 108
  and terms of trade, 203, 209
  protest: at stop of Mint, 126–7; at currency manipulation, 127–8, 170–1, 181, 184, 190; at plan for King's Exchanger, 191–2; at poor quality of textiles, 143–6, 246
  and monetary flows, 165, 168, 219
  See also Outport merchants; London merchants; specific companies and areas
Metals
  imports of, 3, 7
  encouraged, 224
Middelburg
  mart town, 24, 44–5, 91
  textile exports to, 36, 42
  trade to, 44
  unsold stocks of textiles at, 44
Middlemen, 4, 11
  in wool, 46n., 66–7, 71n., 158, 247
  in grains, 245
Middlesex
  unemployment: and high food prices in, 111; relief, 118
Millard, A. M., 31n., 88n., 92n.
Milton, report on depression, 55n.
Mint
  prices abroad, 14
  in Europe, 76
  output and activity, 125, 164, 166–7, 172, 173n., 179, 181–5, 189, 191, 193, 219n.
  delay in issues of (stop of), 125–6
  prices: and bullion flows, 164–5, 184, 231, 250; plans to raise, 169; raised, 166–7
  ratio, 164–9, 181, 183, 190, 192–3, 199, 219
  coins diverted from, 180–1
  officials: plans for manipulation, 183, 190, 192–3; and King's Exchanger, 191
  See also Coins; Currency; Gold coins; Money; Silver coins
Misselden, E., 6n., 7n., 41, 58n., 59n., 60n., 61n., 63n., 75n., 78n., 79n., 91, 93, 93n., 96n., 139n., 147n., 168n., 169, 170n., 172n., 174, 175, 182n., 188, 208n.
  theories of, 93, 197, 199–201, 205–7, 212, 215n., 216, 219n., 220–1
Mixed fabrics, 5
Mohair, trade in, 161
Moir, E., 151n.
Money
  supply of, 8

Money (*cont.*)
  shortage of: 52–4, 58, 66, 67n., 92, 127, 129, 131, 164ff., 174–8, 182, 186–8, 193–4, 198ff., 249; and crisis of 1620's, 175–8
  fear of shortage, 93–4, 178–94, 198ff., 249–50
  imaginary or ghost: 73–5; and the exchanges, 74–5
  export of, 95, 175, 199, 206, 212, 214, 218, 219
  instability, ch. 8, *passim*
  See also Bullion; Coins; Currency; Gold coins; Silver coins
Money market
  restricted: in plague, 26, 101; by political climate, 129, 131
  influx of capital to, 53
  in Baltic, weak, 84
  and bills of exchange, 94–5
  effect of stop of Mint, 126–7
  See also Credit
Monopolies, 227
Moravia, price lag in, 29
Morrell, Walter, 156
Mould, Mr., 269
Mun, Thomas, 67n., 78n., 85, 91n., 93, 93n., 94, 95n., 96n., 148n., 160, 168, 171n., 173n., 176, 177n., 185, 187, 188, 192n., 208n., Appendix B
  theories of, 93, 96, 186–9, 197, 204, 207–8, 211–22, 242n.

Naval stores
  from Baltic, 88
  encouragement to, 226
Navigation
  aid to, 67n.
  laws, 88, 162, 243, 253
Netherlands, *see* Holland
Newbury, coloured cloths of, 115–16
Newcastle
  report on depression, 55n.
  colliers suffer from privateers, 104
New draperies
  manufacture of: 5, 45, 46n., 102, 155–9; free from regulation, 155–7; cost advantages, 155–8, 160; flexibility of, 155–7; encouraged, 248–9; ease of entry into, 155–6, 158; faulty, 143, 146
  development of, 20, 46, 52, 152–62, 224–5
  markets for, 20, 102, 104–5, 122, 152–4, 159–61
  wool supplies, 45–6, 142, 157–9
  unsold stocks of, 57
  trade in: of outports, 69; free to all, 70–1, 241
  export of, 153, 159; controlled by Merchant Adventurers, 121–2
  competition in Mediterranean with Italian textiles, 154–5, 157, 159–60

New draperies (*cont.*)
  depression: in 103–12; in East Anglia, 238; in Essex, 122–4, 130; in Exeter, 130
  suffer: through war, 102–8, 110; through privateers, 105
  overproduction in Essex, 107, 123–4, 159
  prosperity of, 99
  and fashion, 151, 153–6
Newfoundland
  fish from, to Mediterranean, 161
Niermeyer, J. F., 33n.
Nobility
  occupational mobility among, 10
  conspicuous consumption of, 23
  plans to provide capital, 48, 237n.
Norfolk, 5
  new draperies in, 102
  dairy produce, 110
  wages reduced, 111
Northampton, distress in, 57n.
Northamptonshire, public order in, 57
North of England
  unemployment and food scarcity in, 15
  depression in, 58
  success of poor law in, 118
Northern cloth, price falls, 54n.
Northern Europe
  market for textiles: declines, 20, 76ff., 136–7; importance of, 135, 153; aided by Dutch trade, 29
  textile exports to: 150; pay for imports, 91
  manufacture of fustians and linens in, 91
  currency manipulations in, 75ff., 168
  See also Eastern Europe; Europe; Germany
Northern kersies
  sales to Hungary, affected by war, 61
Norwich
  population of, 2
  poverty and famine in, 111
Nuremburg
  interlopers at, 24
  fairs at, 91

Oils, imports of, 7
Old draperies
  manufacture of: 5, 7; in Suffolk, 103; rigid structure of, 81
  stagnation of, 97, 136–49, 151, 153, 155, 224
  depressed, 112–19, 124–5
  markets lost, 223
  ease of convoying, 105
  suffer through refusal to pay customs, 113–15
  quality of, 112
  See also Textiles
Order, *see* Disorder
Outport merchants
  hostility to London companies, 4, 30–1, 62, 241–2

Outport merchants (*cont.*)
  plea for free trade, 237
  capital turnover, need rapid, 10–11, 241
  in projected Spanish Company, 30
  opinion on slump, 61
  ability to sell cheaply, 68
  freedom to export coloured cloths, 121, 241
  represented in Parliament, 68, 71, 231n.
  See also Outports
Outports
  of South-West, investment in colonies and Iberian trade, 29
  capital of, seeks outlet, 30
  opinion on crisis, 54–5, 66
  in depression, 55, 58
  protest: at taxes, 57; at faulty manufacture, 59; at company regulation, 62, 68
  freedom to export: new draperies, 69; coloured cloths, 70–1
  suffer from privateers, 102, 104–5
  and monetary problems, 175, 186
  See also Outport merchants
Overconfidence at French peace, 107–8
Overpopulation, theories of, 23
Oxfordshire
  textile manufacture in: 5, 55; prosperity of, 34; depression of, 55–6; stagnation of, 137
  public order in, 57
  See also Western counties

Palatinate, taxes for, 57
Palmer, Mr., 268
Paper money, 13
Paris, financial agent at, 208n.
Parker, Henry, 13n., 137n., 138n., 141n.
Parliament
  and textile depression, 54, 58–9, 62–3, 66, 68–72, 122–4, 130
  and textile industry, 27, 150
  and liberalization of trade, 30–1, 68–71, 121–2, 231–2, 241
  economic interests in, 71
  and trade: in grain, 87; to Eastland, 87n.; balance, 93
  adjourned in plague, 99
  and refusal to pay customs, 108, 113
  recall: 128; feared by Privy Council, 244
  and monetary problems, 54, 174, 185, 191–2
  and formulation of economic policy, 230–2
Parry, Thomas, 181–2
Patents, 227, 232
Paul, George, 67n.
Pawning of cloth, 11, 56, 121
Peace
  aids commerce, 29
  frees capital, 29–30
  with France, 106–8, 110

Pelc, J., 76n., 77n., 79
Pepper, forced loan on, 126–7
Perpetuanoes, *see* New draperies
Perry, R., 149n.
Personal government, social welfare under, 110, 118–19, 244–5
Pilgrim, J., 110n., 155n., 159n.
Pindar, Paul, 67n.
Plague
  of late sixteenth century, 23
  of 1603, 25–6, 99
  of 1625, 26, 99–102
  cause of crises, 25–6, 99–102, 163, 190
Plains, 5
Plymouth
  investment in colonies and Iberian trade, 29
  report on depression, 55n.
  manufacture of new draperies in, 155
Poland
  textile sales encouraged in, 29
  currency manipulation in, 76–80, 82, 169
  silver prices in, 78–9
  monetary confusion in, 87
  See also Eastern Europe; Eastland
Poole
  report on depression, 55n.
  distress in, 57n.
Poor Law
  Elizabethan, origins of, 6, 23, 244
  problem of, 15
  enforcement of: 57, 117–19, 124, 231–2, 234, 237, 244–5, 249, 252; in Essex, 108–10, 118; in Norwich, 111; in Hampshire, 116
  development of, 226n.
  efficacy of, 64, 252
  See also Poverty
Population
  of England, 2
  of London, 2
  of Norwich, 2
  of Gloucestershire, 5–6
Portugal
  effect of bad English harvest on, 19n.
  market re-opens, 29
  plans for company, rejected by Parliament, 30–1, 231
  re-exports to, 161
Postan, M. M., 14n.
Posthumus, N. W., 84n., 165n., 173n.
Potash
  imports of: 7; from Baltic, 88
Potticary, Christopher, 117
Poundage, *see* Customs
Poverty
  in depression, 54–6, 130, 198, 235, 245
  in textile areas: 64, 103–4, 224; of Gloucestershire, 56–7, 116; of Norwich, 111; of Essex, 111; of Godalming, 116; of Somerset, 116; of Berkshire, 117

Index

Poverty (*cont.*)
  in London, 118
  in Gloucestershire outside textile areas, 56–7
  and labour costs, 140
  and scarcity of money, 174
  See also Poor Law
Prices
  inflexibility of, 13, 74, 170, 177–8
  rise: 12; lags behind currency depreciation, 78, 165, 171, 200, 215n.
  effect of manipulation on, 74–5, 219
  long-term movement of, 139
  pressure on, 176–7, 200
  of exports, 203, 207, 216–17
  See also Inflation; Silver prices; Textiles; Wool
Privateers
  elimination aids commerce, 29
  depredations, 102, 110
  See also Dunkirk privateers
Privy Council
  and textile industry, 5, 115–16, 144, 146, 152, 240
  and textile depression, 43–4, 47–9, 53–5, 57, 64–72, 100–1, 104, 106–10, 116–19, 236ff.
  and Cockayne Project, 35, 37–40, 42–5, 47–9, 243
  pressure on merchants to buy, 65–6, 106–8, 122–3, 232, 237–40, 243–4
  pressure on clothiers to employ, 65–6, 239–40
  and wool trade, 46n.
  and capital provision, 48, 237n.
  and trade: to Levant, 62; to Eastland, 88; balance of, 93, 182; Merchant Adventurers' control of, 68–71, 121–2, 124–5, 232, 238–9
  solicits local opinion, 66
  and mart towns, 24, 91n., 121
  and the exchanges, 95–6, 186
  and plague, 99–100
  and poor law, 108–10, 117–19
  and wages, 111
  and Tare controversy, 112, 115, 118
  and refusal to pay customs, 113–14
  and grain prices, 117–18
  and monetary problems, 167, 173n., 181–6, 189, 191, 231
  and currency manipulation, 170, 183–4, 190
  power of, 251–2
  and formulation of economic policy, 230–3
  See also Government; Government economic policy
Proclamation
  on export of unfinished textiles, 34–5
  on Merchant Adventurers' trade, 69, 122, 124–5

Proclamation (*cont.*)
  on poor law, 109, 124
  on quality of textiles, 120, 146
  on wages, 122
  on Eastland trade, 88–9
  on coins, 167, 181, 184, 187, 191
  on exchanges, 186–7, 206, 208
Profit
  margin, 63
  effects of currency manipulation on, 219
Prohibitions, 9, 243
  of finished textiles in Holland, 40, 42–4
  of trade to Elbe and Ems, 24
  of trade to Spain and Flanders, 105
  of new draperies in Spain, 105
  of imports in French ships, 106
  during war, 108
  See also Stoppages
Propensity to consume, 16–18
Provincial ports, *see* Outports
Public order, *see* Disorder
Purchasing power, variations in, 8
Pym, John, 130

Quality of textiles, *see* Faulty manufacture
Quarter crowns, 91
Quotas, allotted to merchants to buy up textiles, 47, 48, 56n., 65–6, 69, 107, 238, 244

Raleigh, Sir Walter, 19n.
Ramsay, G. D., 124n., 138n., 142n., 143n., 145n., 146n., 149n., 151n., 152n.
Rate of interest
  in England: 94n.; increase, 174
  in Holland, 174n.
Reading
  textiles of, 34n., 115–16
  See also Berkshire
Reals of eight, imports of, 91, 187
Recovery
  from depression, 58, 96–9, 103, 118–19
  of exports to northern Europe, 76
Re-exports, 161–2, 223–4
Regulated companies
  attack on, 30–1
  defence of, 242
  arguments against, based on competition, 148, 222, 242
  controversy over, 237, 240–4
  functions, 242–3
  See also Eastland Company; Merchant Adventurers; Trading companies
Regulation of textile standards
  absence, 152, 155–7
  See also Faulty manufacture
Reichsdaller
  enhanced, 79
  silver content at Hamburg, 77, 97
  imports of, 90, 91

Index

Rents
  fear of loss, during currency manipulation, 170
  to be paid at intrinsic values, 200
Restoration, 223
Returns
  by merchants, 11, 40–1
  absence of, 59, 61–2, 63n.
  considered, 67n.
  during currency manipulations, 80
  difficulties: from Baltic, 82, 86–8; in specie or by exchange, 84–5, 90
  Dutch competition in, 83
  profits on, 89–91, 93
  in silver, 168
  at high prices, 203, 209
  for silver exports, 219
  from Levant, 223
  See also Imports
Reyce, R., 158n.
Ricardo, D., 74
Richardson, William, 67n.
Richmond, poor relief at, 118
Rider, 183
Rioting, see Disorder
Roberts, Lewes, 19n., 85n., 86n., 138n., 141n., 160n., 174n., 221, 224
Robinson, Henry, 19n., 94n., 95n., 124, 128n., 129, 130n., 137, 138n., 139n., 142, 208n., 209n., 211n., 221–3
Roe, Sir Thomas, 3–4, 45n., 124, 128n., 129n., 137, 138n., 139n., 152, 192n., 221, 223–4
Rogers, J. Thorold, 31n., 57n., 101n., 110n.
Roman Catholics, 130
Rostow, W. W., 15
Rotterdam, as mart town, 121
Royal Exchanger, see King's Exchanger
Ruding, R., 173n., 180n., 181n., 182n., 184n., 186n., 187n., 191n., 192n.
Rushworth, J., 127n., 128n., 129n., 130n.
Russell, William, 87n.
Russia
  trade to: depressed, 54; hit by privateers, 104
  market for Spanish cloths, 102–3, 150
  goods from, exported to Mediterranean by English, 161
  English merchants trading to: and Cockayne Project, 36; consulted, 45
Rye
  prices at Danzig, 79
  See also Grains

St. James's Fair, postponed in plague, 126
Salisbury, Earl of, 156
Salt
  manufacture: 4; encouraged, 223, 248–9
Saltpetre, imported from Baltic, 88

Sanderson, William, 1, 19n., 139n., 169n., 186, 188, 204–5, 268
Sandwich, report on depression, 55n.
Sandys, E., 30, 222
Saxon dynasty, mints of, 76
Say-dyed cloth, 152n.
Says, see New draperies
Schumpeter, Joseph A., 216n.
Scott, W. R., 23n., 29n., 30n., 32n., 126n.
Scottish merchants, 86n.
Seignorage, 169, 183, 184
Sellers, M., 88n., 89n.
Serges, 130
Serra, Antonio, 216n.
Severn, 57
Shakespeare, William, 234
Shaw, W. A., 76n., 77n., 167n., 168n., 190n., 192n.
Shipbuilding, 7
Ship Money, 127
Shipping, encouragement to, 226, 243
Shoes, prices at Danzig, 79
Shrewsbury Drapers, 54n.
Silesia
  mints in, 76
  price lag in, 79
  textile manufacture in, 137, 140
Silk
  import of, 7, 90–1, 93
  raw, English trade in, 161
Silver coins (and bullion)
  export of, 31, 53, 92, 102, 167–78, 181–2, 184–5, 192–4, 199–200, 209, 219–20
  inflow of, 166–7, 183, 218
  plans for enhancement, 52, 169–71, 181–5, 190, 192–3, 199–200
  manipulation of, 73–5, 166
  valuations of, 164–71, 249
  plans for debasement of, 102, 127–8, 169–70, 183, 189–90
  arguments against enhancement of, 170–1, 181, 183–5, 193, 199–200
  scarcity of, 167–8, 173, 178, 182–3, 193
  importance of, 171–3, 219–20
  and exchanges, 74–5
  flow of, 139, 164–5
  from America, 163, 165, 203
  coining of, 125, 164, 166–7, 168n., 173n., 183, 189
  from Spain to Flanders, 125
  returns in, 168
  velocity of circulation of, 173
  stopped at Mint, 125–6
  See also Bullion; Coins; Currency; Gold Coins; Mint; Money
Silver prices
  fall: through currency manipulation, 73–5, 85, 89, 171, 198; in Poland, 78–9, 82, 86; in northern and eastern Europe, 76–81
  effect of, on exports, 81

Silver prices (*contd.*)
  rise: 97; in Poland, 89
  lag, 91
  stabilized, 96
Skinner, John, 187n., 269
Slump, *see* Crisis
Smith, Adam, 15n., 140, 177, 213, 225, 230, 250
Smith, Sir Thomas, 87n.
Smuggling of wool and fuller's earth, 141
Soap, manufacture encouraged, 248-9
Solicitor-General, report of, 99
Somers, J., 130n., 131n.
Somerset
  textile industry in: 5, 34, 55, 100; prosperity of, 34; depression in, 44, 55, 116, 129; stagnation of, 137
  manufacture of Spanish cloths in, 149, 151
  clothiers: 131; evidence before Commons, 54; lack sale, 100
  rioting and public order in, 57
  See also Western counties
Sound Toll Accounts, 84
Southampton
  report on depression, 55n.
  merchants of, on currency, 90
South-east England, 17
Southern England
  textile industry in, 5, 155
  poor law in, 118
  See also specific counties
Southern Europe
  market for textiles, 7-8, 102, 122, 153-5
  goods of, 91
  trade to, unstable, 103
  Spanish cloths exported to, 150
  English merchants trading to, 119
Spain
  market in: opened to outports, 27; for new draperies, 104-5, 123n., 152-3; insecurity in, 105
  textile exports to, 103, 210
  ban on new draperies in, 105
  imports from: 7; of silks, 91; of money, 91, 181
  trade to: depressed, 54, 110; anxiety over, 92; harmed by privateers, 104, 110; banned, 105
  English merchants trading to, 110, 122
  plan for Company rejected, 30-1, 231
  war with, 23, 101-2, 104-5, 107, 110, 153
  treaty, with: 29, 153; Cottington, 164
  threat by, to Denmark, 102
  economic pressure from, 110
  manufacture of textiles in, 32, 138
  wool supplies from, 32, 38, 141-2, 149, 151
  effect of poor English harvest on, 19n.
  silver from, to Flanders, 125, 164n.
  currency of, in Mediterranean, 161
  enriched by enhancement, 170
  See also Mediterranean; Southern Europe

Spanish cloths
  production of: 5; rise of, 149-52
  counterfeiting of, 152n.
  trade in, 121
  exports of, 149-50
  quality of, 151
Specie, *see* Coin; Currency; Money
Specie points, 84-5, 95, 201, 205, 208-9, 222n.
Spence, R. T., 42n., 97n.
Speyer, currency manipulation in, 77
Spices, import of, 7
Spinners
  in Wiltshire, 55
  unemployed, 56
  wages, 122; around Sudbury, 111
Spinners
  distressed, 245
  See also Market spinners
Stability, *see* Disorder; Government economic policy
Stade
  as mart town, 25, 91
  shortage of liquid funds at, 166
Stafford, L., 67n.
Stammell cloths, 5, 149
Standard of living
  low, 2, 144, 234, 246
  effect of harvests on, 14-15, 17
Staplers
  on slump, 61
  attack companies, 62
  attack Merchant Adventurers, 237
  trade opened to, 68
  permission to join Merchant Adventurers, 121-2
Staple towns, *see* Mart towns
Starch, manufacture encouraged, 248-9
Statistics
  of textile exports
  See New draperies; Textiles; Appendix A
Statute of Artificers
  intent of, 27-8, 235, 245
  prosecutions on, 26
  in new draperies, 155-6
Statutes of Employment, 179-81, 182n., 183, 199, 212, 215, 250
Statute of Monopolies, 71n.
Steele, R., 26n., 31n., 34n., 48n., 62n., 67n., 68n., 88n., 99n., 101n., 105n., 106n., 121n., 130n., 131n., 141n., 166n., 167n., 180n., 181n., 184n., 187n., 190n., 191n., 192n.
Stiles, Thomas, 87n.
Stocks of textiles
  unsold: 30, 43, 46-8, 55, 57, 100; in hands of clothiers, 11, 43, 54-6, 65, 69-70, 100, 107, 111-12, 116, 121-2, 123n., 130-1, 238-9, 241; in hands of merchants, 11, 43-4, 47, 113-14, 117, 119, 238
Stone, L., 23n., 30n.

294   Index

'Stop' of the Mint, 125-6
Stoppage of trade
  with Holland, through commercial controversy, 112, 116-19, 121
  with Flanders, 116-17
  See also Prohibitions
Stourbridge Fair
  closed, 26, 99
  opened, 101
Stafford, Earl of, 135
Straits, production of, 5
Stretching of cloths, 145-6
Stroudwater, 149
Stuart Court, impecunious, 227
Suckling, John, 67n.
Sudbury, wages around, 111
Suffolk
  textile industry in: 5, 34n., 156; depressed, 55-6, 82, 102-3, 112, 129-30, 156; wages in reduced, 111
  distress in, 20, 55, 57n., 82
  clothiers: to Commons, 54; attack companies, 63; and textile export, 70, 103n., 238; insolvent, 240
  lack of sales, 103, 121
  dairy produce, 110
  fuller's earth, transported to, 141
Suffolk shortcloths
  exports: 103; decline, 39n., 41n., 42, 55; to Baltic, 82
  production, 102
  markets for, 102-3
  stagnation, 103
Sugar
  imports of, 7
  re-exports of, 161
Supple, B. E., 10n., 55n., 96n., 145n., 212n., 270n.
Surrey
  unemployment in: and high food prices, 111; relief of, 118
  clothiers, hold unsold stocks, 239
Sutton, Richard, 67n.

Tare, 59, 112-13, 115, 118-19, 121
Taunton, distress in, 57n.
Tawney, R. H., 30n., 42n., 145n., 180n., 222n.; and A. J. Tawney, 3n., 5n., 16n., 17n.
Technology, 2, 143
Terms of trade
  unfavourable: 59, 93, 186, 202ff.,; fear of, 127
  altered by currency manipulations, 75, 86, 89, 170
  attitude towards, 148, 202ff.
  and regulated companies, 242-3
Textiles
  industry: 5-7, 46; importance of, 2; concentration of, 6; structure and organization of, 8, 11-12, 143-4, 146, 148, 158;

Textiles (contd.)
  prosperity in, 28-9, 31, 34-5, 99, 119; weakness of, 59-60, 64, 73, 81, 119, 128; stagnation of, 33, 46, 50-1, 119-20, 124, 136-48; effect of political events on, 128-31; desire to restrain development of, 6-7, 71-2, 224n., 234-7; in Wiltshire, 26-7; affected by harvest, 100; factor mobility (ease of entry) in, 7, 11-13, 27-8, 123-4, 155-6, 158, 245; employment in, Gloucestershire, 5-6
  production of: 8; estimate, 16n.; declines, 42, 129, 135-6
  prices of: 45, 80; too high, 31-2, 46, 80-1; fall, 40, 43, 54, 60, 63; low, 56; raised, 79; rise, 97; relative, 139; pressure on, 143-4
  cost of: relative, 139; high, 140, 210; see also Costs; Rigidity
  need for liquid capital, 40-1, 47
  new types developed, 120, 136, 149-60
  effect of Cockayne Project on, 33, 38, 43, 46, 50
  manufacture abroad, 31-2, 38, 42-3, 45-6, 50, 52, 58, 60, 63n., 64, 66, 81, 137-43, 149, 153, 210-11, 222, 236
  competition in Europe, 20, 46, 54, 60, 68, 78-9, 138-41, 143
  demand, for nature of, 204, 210-11, 215-17
  market for: domestic, 8, 59, 62, 66-7; proclamation to expand, 48, 68; and harvests, 14-19, 111; estimate of, 16n.; effect of monetary scarcity on, 176; lack of effective demand in, 200; European: 43, 62; decline in, 20, 80-1, 120, 135-48, 200; increases, 153-4; aided by peace, 29; importance of, 2, 9; dislocation in, 43; destroyed by currency manipulation, 79-81
  exports of: 6, 19-20, 23-4, 26, 28, 31, 39, 42, 44-5, 52-3, 55-6, 75-6, 88-9, 97, 99, 101-2, 112-13, 119-20, 128, 136-7, 190, Appendix A; role of credit in, 40-1; through London, 99, 102; impositions on, 49; effects of currency manipulations on, 79-81
  manufacturing areas: complain at taxes, 57; protests of, 43; asked for opinion, 66
  stocks of: abroad, 34n., 40, 98; see also Stocks of textiles
  English advantages, 139
  Statute for, 150n.; see also Cloth Acts
  See also Crisis; Dyed and dressed cloth; New draperies; Old draperies; Unemployment; Unfinished cloth; specific counties
Thirty Years War
  and currency manipulations, 4, 58, 61, 76
  as cause of depression, 61
  as stimulus to foreign manufacture, 140
  See also War

Thompson, J. W., 41n.
Timber, 3, 7, 224
Tobacco
  imports: 7, 162; criticized, 92-3
  re-exports, 161
Token money, unimportance of, 13, 178, 182
Tomaszewski, E., 77, 78, 79
Towerson, William, 100
Trading companies
  on crisis, 54
  attacked, 59, 62-4
  as cause of depression, 66
  considered, 67n.
  control relaxed, 68-71, 88
  dissolution considered, 113-14
  consulted on silver, 185-6
  See also Regulated companies; specific companies
Treasure, see Bullion; Gold coins; Silver coins
Trinity House, protests at ban on trade to Elbe and Ems, 24-5
Tunnage, see Customs
Turkey
  wool supplies of, 38
  new draperies in, 159-60
  as cloth market, 223
  See also Levant; Mediterranean
Turner, William, 67n.
Tuscany, 224
Tyne, 4

Underemployment, 13, 27, 177
Unemployment
  in textiles, 6, 12, 23, 43, 53, 56-8, 64, 101, 103-4, 106, 108-9, 112, 114, 116, 119, 199, 234-5, 238
  as criterion of depression, 2
  coincidence with bad harvest, 15, 110-11, 116-19
  spiral of, 55
  stocks of raw materials for, 109
  provision of work for, 118
  threat of, 120, 223
  and deflationary pressure, 177
  measures against, 231-2, 234ff.
Unfinished cloths
  production of: 5, 120, 137; stagnation of, 137, 147
  exports: 33, 35-6, 39, 42-3, 50, 55, 98-9, 137, 140, 150; licence for, 25n., 34-5, 52, see also Cumberland; banned, 34-5; needs liquid capital, 40-1; controlled by Merchant Adventurers, 121; confined to London, 43; hindrances to, 45-9; Cockayne Projectors plan to control, 36-7
  market for, in Europe, 33
  weavers of, 149
  manufacture in Holland, 138

Unfinished cloths (contd.)
  quality of, 145-6
  See also Dyed and dressed cloths; Old draperies; Textiles
United Provinces, see Holland
Unrest, see Disorder
Unwin, G., 24n.

Vaughan, Rice, 90n., 168n., 171n., 172n., 173n., 208n., 209n.
  theories of, 219-21
Velocity of circulation
  increases, 74
  of gold and silver, 173
  falls, 178
Venice
  textile manufacture in, 137-8
  trade of, in textiles, 159-60
Viner, Jacob, 177n., 216n., 223n.
Vintners' Company, ordered to buy up wine, 107
Violet, T., 85n., 192n.
Virginia, tobacco from, 162

Wadsworth, A. P., 155n.
Wages
  pressure on, in textiles, 10, 57, 111, 122, 145, 245-6
  government support of, 27, 55, 111, 122, 228, 231, 235, 244-6
  low in textiles, 124, 144, 224
  unskilled, in Cracow, 79
  See also Costs; Labour
Wales, 5
War
  on continent: 9; effects of, 59, 61, 64, 79, 81, 98, 136n., 140; see also Thirty Years War
  with Spain, 23, 101-2, 104-5, 107-8
  with France, 105-6, 108
  prevalence of, 227
  as cause of depression, 63n., 66, 163
  cessation brings prosperity, 29
Warsaw, currency manipulation in, 77
Warwick, Earl of, 109
Weald, 4
Wear, 4
Weavers
  in Essex, 12, 123
  in Wiltshire: 55; plan to curb textiles, 26
  around Sudbury, 111
  unemployed, 56
  distressed, 245
  unapprenticed, 246
Webb, Benedict, 151n.
Wedgewood, C. V., 76n.
Wells, distress in, 57n.
Westcombe, 151

Western counties
  textile industry in: 4–6, 12, 33; depressed, 20, 43–4, 50–1, 58, 116–19, 120, 124–5, 137; organization of, 158, 247; stimulated, 99; protected by merchants, 114; tensions in, 120, 146–7, 152
  unemployment in, 238
  destitution in, 55
  rioting in, 66
  quality of cloth in, 145–7, 247
  clothiers of, 151–2
  J.P.s and poor law, 244
  success of poor law enforcement, 118
  use of grain regulated in, 101
  abundance of land in, 17
West Indies, cotton from, 223
West Riding, textile industry of, 5–6, 158
Wheat, *see* Grains
Wheeler, J., 24n., 25, 91n., 239n., 242n.
Willan, T. S., 4
Williams, John, 186, 268
Wilson, C. H., 83n., 85n., 225n., 226n., 229n.
Wilson, Thomas, 180n., 189n.
Wiltshire
  textile industry of: 5, 55, 147, 149, 157; pressure on, 26–7; plan to curb development of, 26–7; prosperity of, 34; depression of, 43–5, 53, 57, 100, 116–17, 120–1, 129; stagnation of, 137
  clothiers in: prosecuted, 27; complain of lack of market, 100, 121
  unemployment in, 53, 57
  spinners and weavers in, 55
  rioting in, 56–7
  cloths of, unsold at London, 61, 100
  J.P.s of, and yarn trade, 147
  House of Correction, 56
  See also Western counties
Wine
  imports of, 93, 106–7
  customs on, 108
Wither, Anthony, 145–6
Wolstenholme, John, 87n., 182
Wood, Henry, 187n., 269

Wool,
  production of, 6, 149
  prices of: high, 31–2, 45–6, 247; efforts to raise, 71n.; rise, 99; low, 53, 60, 67n., 80; fall, 129
  supplies of: 38, 45, 210; in Europe, 31–2, 42, 141–3, 211; from Spain, 141–2, 149, 151; in new draperies, 45–6, 157–9
  export of: 45–6, 58, 60, 67n., 141–2; banned, 38, 42, 46, 68, 141, 236
  shortage of, in Germany, 97
  quality falls, 142–3, 151, 157
  in Spanish cloths, 149
  carded and combed, 154
  middlemen (broggers) in: and trade, 46n., 66, 71n., 158, 247; acts concerning repealed, 71n., 247
  growers: to share burden of slump, 65, 240; attack companies, 62
Worcester, distress in, 57n.
Worcestershire
  textile industry in: 55; prosperity of, 34; depression in, 43–4, 55, 129; stagnation, of, 137
  clothiers, appear before Commons, 54
  See also Western counties
Worsted industry, 5, 142

Yarmouth
  report on depression, 55n.
  fishing and trade hit by privateers, 104
  manufacture of new draperies in, 155
  fish to Mediterranean, 161
Yarn
  imports of, 7
  export banned, 38
  organization of production of, 120, 146–7, 158
Yeomanry, economic gains in sixteenth century, 23
Yonge, Walter, 56n., 57n., 66n., 175
Yorkshire
  textile industry, 4
  clothiers complain, 130–1
  fuller's earth carried to, 141

Date Due

MAR 9 '66			
DEC 20 '67			
JAN 31 '68			
~~MAY 17 1982~~			
DEC 07 '94			

PRINTED IN U.S.A.